In Plain Sight:
Scenes from Aridly Abundant Landscapes

La Biennale di Venezia

18. Mostra Internazionale di Architettura

Partecipazioni Nazionali

In Plain Sight: SCENES FROM ARIDLY ABUNDANT LANDSCAPES

Edited By Faysal Tabbarah *and* Meitha Almazrooei

الجناح الوطني لدولة الإمارات
بينالي البندقية

National Pavilion UAE
La Biennale di Venezia

Co-Publisher

KAPH
ART BOOKS FROM THE MIDDLE EAST

Commissioned By

مؤسسة سلامة بنت حمدان آل نهيان
SALAMA BINT HAMDAN
AL NAHYAN FOUNDATION

Supported by

وزارة الثقافة والشباب
MINISTRY OF CULTURE & YOUTH

Contents #

Faysal Tabbarah
Curator's Note

[*01*]

القحط. إنه القحط.. مرة أخرى!
وفي مواسم القحط تتغير الحياة والأشياء، وحتى البشر يتغيرون

“*Drought*. It’s *drought*, again!
When drought seasons come, things begin to change. Life and objects change. Humans change too, and no more so than in their moods”†

There is a narrow and fertile strip of land on the northeastern edge of the Arabian Peninsula, no more than 20 to 30 kilometers
[*02*] wide and 280 kilometers long.† This "continuous fertile strip of garden: palms, fig trees, man-
[*03*] goes, mulberry trees, and pomegranates"† is nestled between Al Hajar Mountains, an impenetrable mountain range of striking red, muted yellow, and dark brown hues that is dotted with its fair share of green to the west, and the blue waters of the Gulf of Oman to the east.

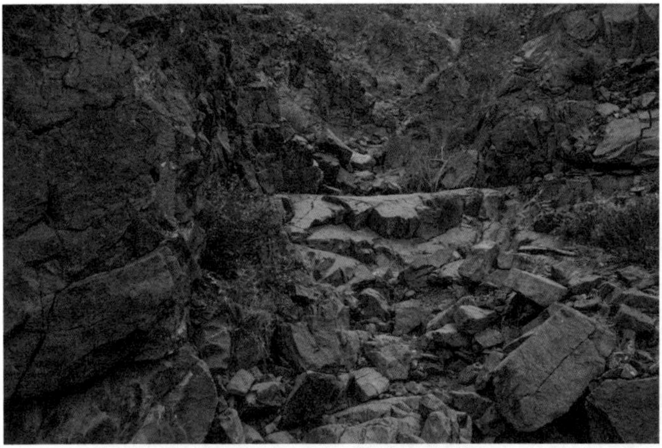

fig. (001) A walking trail along Wadi Abadilah. Photo by author.

Historical travel within this landscape was not limited to Arab travelers, and the observations of those from the West mirrored those that Al Maqdisi had recorded. In the early 1500s, Duarte Barbosa, a Portuguese writer and officer stationed in India, who also happened to be Ferdinand Magellan's brother-in-law, arrived on the fertile coastal strip. Specifically, Barbosa arrived to Khor Fakkan on the east coast of the present-day United Arab Emirates (UAE) and noted that
[*04*] the village was surrounded by "gardens and farms aplenty."† Much like others who came here before him and after, it seems that Barbosa was surprised to see that this area was productive and abundant. Unfortunately, this was short-lived, since after Barbosa's trip, Aphonso de Albuquerque, the infamous Portuguese Governor of India (1509–1515) sacked Khor Fakkan along with other key port towns along
[*05*] the fertile coastal plains of the Gulf of Oman and the Arabian Sea.†

01

Abdelrahman Munif. *Endings*, (Interlink Books, 1998).

02

John Craven Wilkinson, *Water and Tribal Settlement in South-East Arabia: A Study of the Aflaj of Oman* (Oxford: Oxford University Press, 1977), 12.

03

S. M. Zwemer, "Three Journeys in Northern Oman," *The Geographical Journal* Vol. 19 No. 1 (January 1902): 54-64.

04

Duarte Barbosa, *The Book of Duarte Barbosa Vol. 1*, trans. Mansel Longworth Dames (London: Bedford Press, 1918), 73.

05

National Library and Archives "Portuguese Era," last accessed Januaary 30, 2021, https://nla.ae/en/historical-periods

06
Zwemer, "Three Journeys," 54.

07-09
Zwemer, "Three Journeys," 56.

Between May 1900 and May 1901, Samuel Marinus Zwemer, an American missionary nicknamed the Apostle to Islam, made three key journeys within and across the present-day UAE. In one journey made predominantly on camelback, Zwemer travels eastward from Abu Dhabi to Muscat, crossing through Al Hajar, a mountain range that separates the relatively flat desert plateau of Arabia from the fertile coastal plains on the Gulf of Oman. Speaking of the Gulf, Zwemer muses that it "was for centuries past an island, with the sea on one side and the desert on the other."† [06]

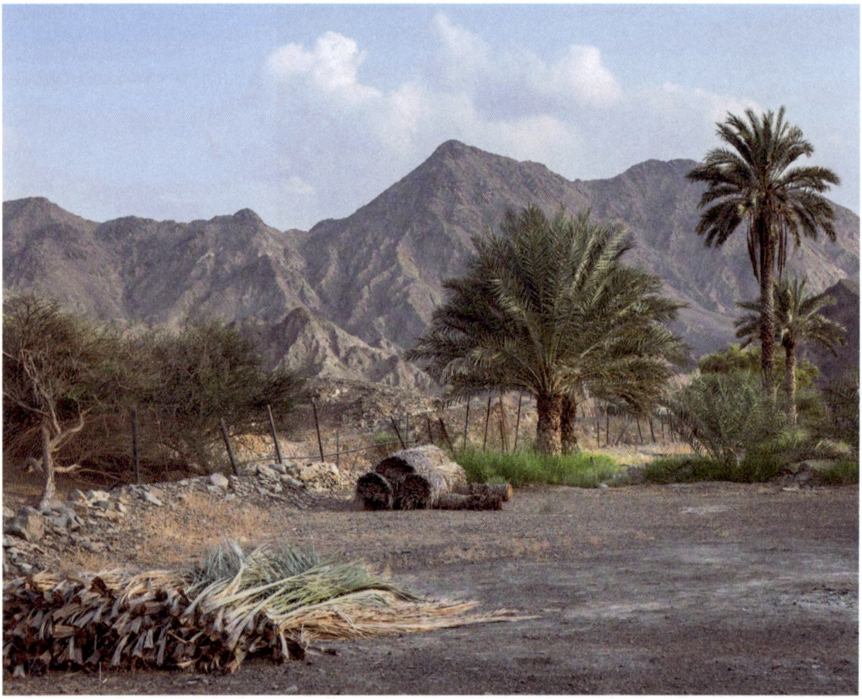

fig. (002) An agricultural plain within Al Hajar. Photo by Reem Falaknaz.

Arriving in Abu Dhabi from Bahrain by boat, Zwemer and his companion are welcomed by its ruler with "huge dishes piled with rice, steeped in gravy, and crowned with several pounds of prime roast mutton, the whole surrounded with dates bread-loaves on a large mat, and washed down with perfumed water."† Then, while traveling [07]
further north, he writes that the coast between Abu Dhabi and Dubai

[08] "is desert, and so flat that a hill 220 feet high is called Jebel Ali (high mountain),"† while in Sharjah "Young date-plantations are a sign of the progress of civilization, and commerce is
[09] crowding the nomad spirit out."†

From Sharjah, Zwemer heads towards the coast with occasional rests "at noon under
[10] some scraggy acacia."† He describes the landscape at the beginning of this leg of the journey as a "bare desert of white sand without pastur-
[11] age."† On the second day, as he approaches Al Hajar, he passes "villages and cultivated
[12] fields... good pasture and plenty of water."†

10-16

Zwemer, "Three Journeys," 58.

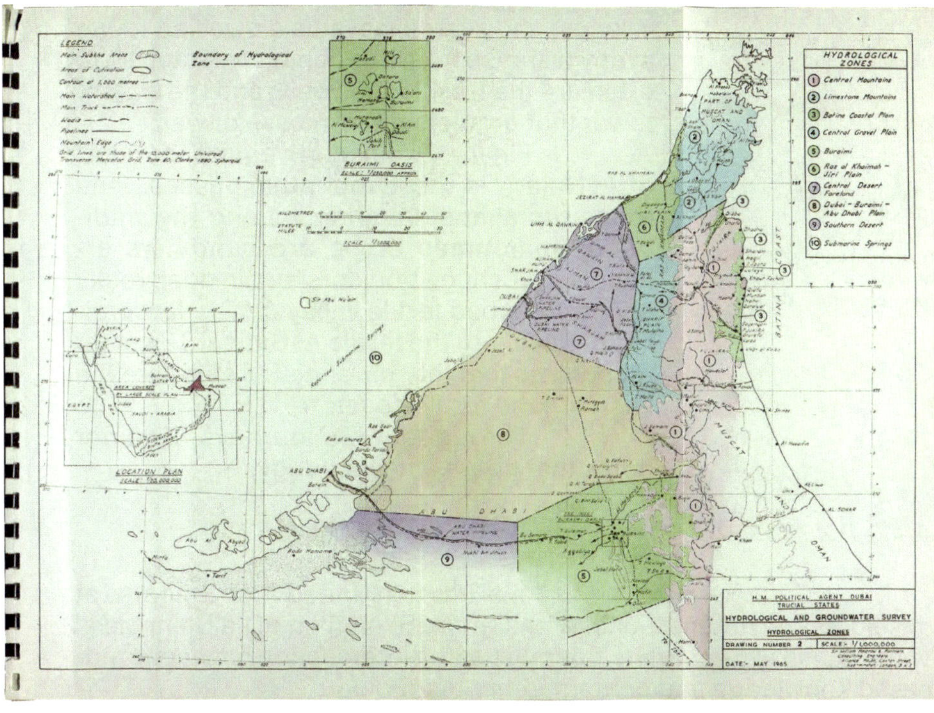

fig. (003) Hydrological and Ground Water Survey, 1965.

On this route, Zwemer also comes across "an oasis where water burst from a big spring, and trees and flowers grew in luxury... surprised to
[13] find a considerable population of shepherds and goatherds"† despite
[14] the fact that the landscape "appears arid and sterile."† This surprise is odd because in the same paragraph, he writes that "vegetation is
[15] fairly abundant."†

Of the shepherds' dwellings, Zwemer
describes them as "constructed of boul-
ders or rocks; the tent is rarely seen... and is
rather characteristic of North Arabia than of
the south."† Elsewhere in the region, he has [16]
described villages as "a cluster of stone-built
huts around a larger mosque or sheikh's house,
narrow paths between the cultivated terraces,
and a background of palms overtopped by fine
mango."† Remnants of these villages and ter- [17]
raced farms are still visible today as far north
as Ras Al Khaimah. Of the socio-spatial condi-
tions at the time, he also suggests that "in the
fertile valleys the population always centers in
villages, and scarcely ever is a dwelling found
at any distance from this common center. Here
often are the fresh-water wells and the watch-
tower that protects them in case of war."† [18]

Finally, Zwemer arrives into the heart
of Al Hajar; "In these mountain passes... the
roads run almost invariably along the wadi-
beds; sometimes these are sandy water-
courses with huge boulders, again deep rocky
ravines or broad fertile valleys."† On descend- [19]
ing Al Hajar into the fertile Al Batinah, Zwemer
recognizes that the "perennial streams are the
secret of the fertile coast."† [20]

Throughout his journeys, Zwemer
notes that he was "never hungry."† [21]

17-19

Zwemer, "Three Journeys," 63.

20

Zwemer, "Three Journeys," 59.

21

Zwemer, "Three Journeys," 56.

22

2010-2022: UN Decade for Desert and Fight Against Desertification. UN. https://www.un.org/en/events/desertification_decade/whynow.shtml

23

Joseph Phelan, "How Dubai is pushing back its encroaching deserts" (2022), *BBC*, https://www.bbc.com/future/article/20220125-how-dubai-is-pushing-back-its-encroaching-deserts

Aridly Abundant in Venice

Conceived for the National Pavilion United Arab Emirates at the eighteenth International Architecture Exhibition of La Biennale di Venezia, *Aridly Abundant*, operates at the intersection between land-based knowledge and contemporary technology.

The project tackles the relationship between architecture and aridity by asking: what architectural conditions can emerge when we reimagine arid environments as spaces of abundance? At a time of increasing climate change, aridity is fast becoming a future condition for many parts of the world. Thus, the project aims to uncover ongoing arid land-based practices to rethink mainstream construction that foreground questions of aridity within architectural production and discourse.

Arid and semi-arid environments make up approximately
[22] 32%† of the earth's surface. For the Arabian Peninsula, aridity is a
part of our past and will be a condition for our urban futures, where
67% of land is considered arid, and 32% is hyper-arid. In the UAE,
[23] 80%† of land is a desert encompassing semi-arid, arid, and hyper-arid environments. Contemporary built environments render aridity and its conditions, such as food and water scarcity, invisible, alienating people from the food and water systems that support them. Today, the Prevalence of Undernourishment index (PoU, or the world's population below minimum level of dietary energy consumption) increased from 8.4% to 9.9% (i.e., approximately 800 million people) between 2019 and 2020, making the United Nations' Sustainable Development Goal (SDG) 2: Zero Hunger in 2030, even more difficult.

Thus, *Aridly Abundant* takes the production of architecture in the UAE's arid environment as a case study, while continuously looking, or traveling, across other aridities. Specifically, the project explores the potential for abundance within the UAE's Al Hajar which encompasses a desert plateau, wadis, and coastal plains. In so doing, *Aridly Abundant* aims to reveal the latent abundance within arid environments and to provoke a future built *in*, *with*, and *for* aridity.

Thinking through building *in* aridity brings to the foreground the challenges associated with constructing sustainable built environments. Exploring building *with* aridity refers to integrating material found within arid environments and contemporary technology. Building *for* aridity implies imagining built environments that mitigate the precarity of their contexts. All of these ideas work together to forage for abundance and provoke alternative positive futures.

To highlight this, the project transforms the National Pavilion UAE into a space that provokes alternative architectural conditions where arid landscapes are reimagined as spaces of abundance through a display of existing and imagined building tactics. In doing so, the project also attempts to raise awareness, shift perceptions, and reveal alternative imaginaries of abundance within aridity.

Constructing Aridity

To challenge conceptions of arid environments as spaces of scarcity and precarity, *Aridly Abundant* investigates aridity as a historical and future condition of life to advocate for architectural production that is rooted in its own material, cultural, and historical context. To do so, it is important to understand the dynamics that have driven particular ideas around aridity.

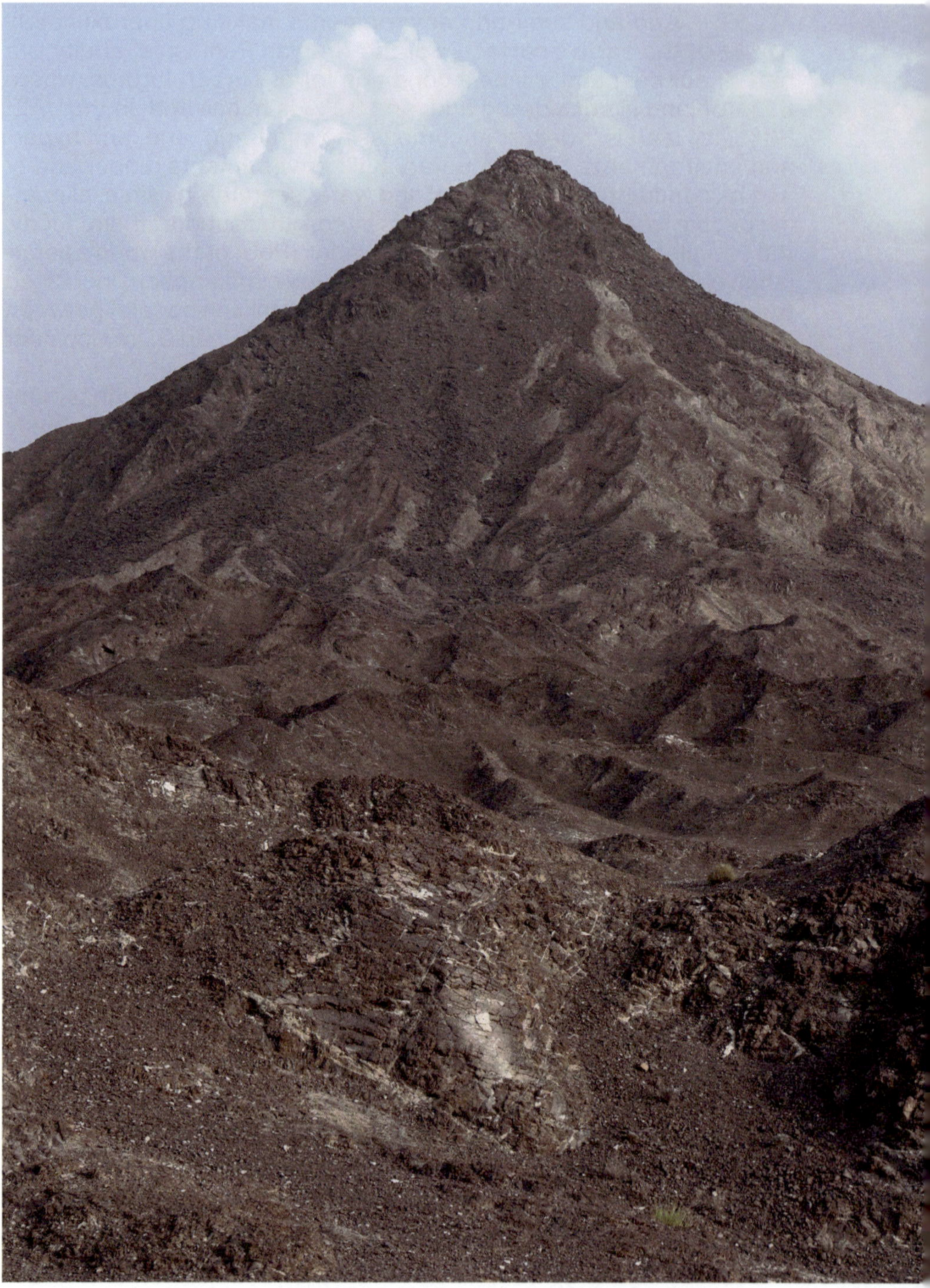

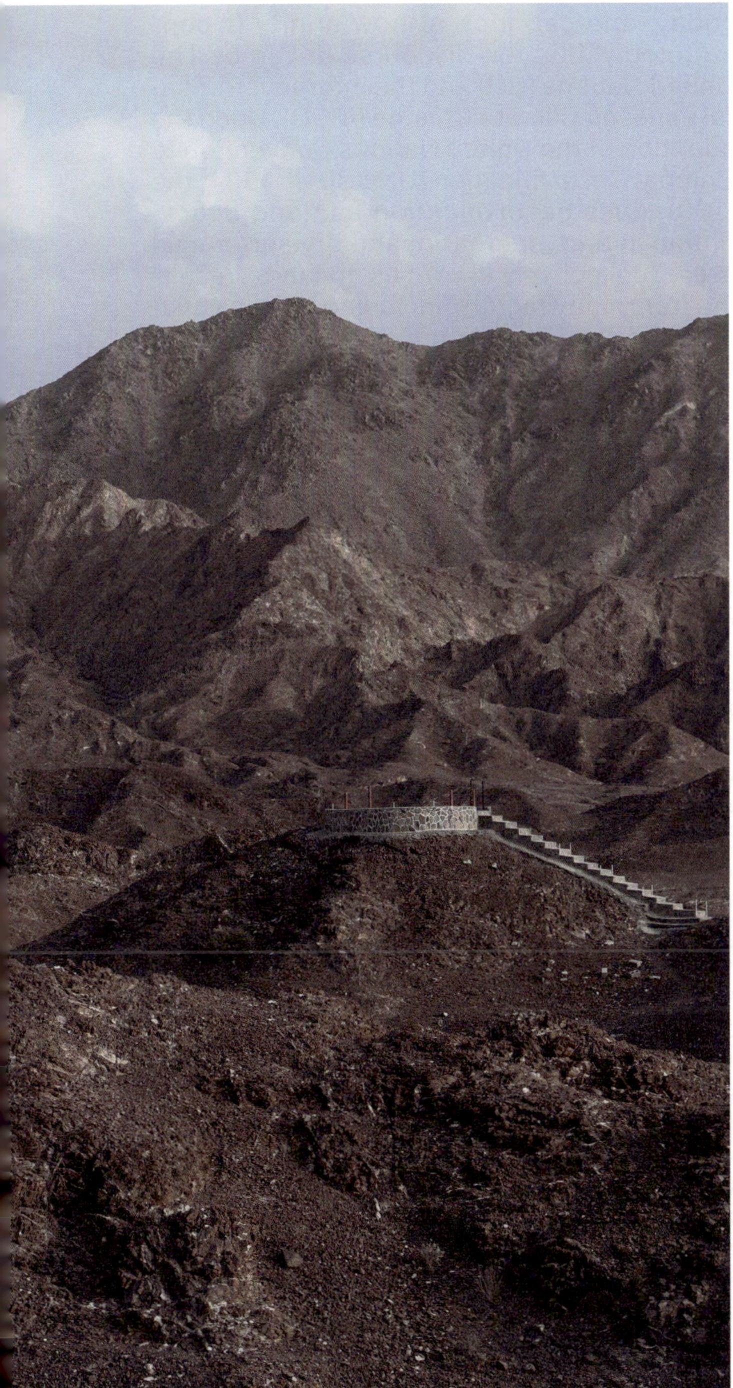

fig. (004) A view across Al Hajar Mountains with a relatively recent water well in the distance. Photo by Reem Falaknaz.

24, 25

"Chapter 3: Desertification," *IPCC*, Accessed March 28, 2021, https://www.ipcc.ch/srccl/chapter/chapter-3/

26

"Land Use, Land Use Change and Forestry (LULUCF)," Department of Environmental Science Aarhus University, Accessed March 28, 2021, https://envs.au.dk/en/research-areas/air-pollution-emissions-and-effects/air-emissions/reporting-sectors/land-use-land-use-change-and-forestry-lulucf/

27

Fromentin, Eugene. *Un Eté dans le Sahara*. Ebook. https://www.gutenberg.org/files/37914/37914-h/37914-h.htm

Today, one can look at how aridity is constructed within the discourse driven by The United Nations (UN) and the Intergovernmental Panel on Climate Change (IPCC). Upon the adoption of the United Nations Convention to Combat Desertification (UNCCD) in 1994, the UN defines desertification as "land degradation in arid, semi-arid, and dry sub-humid areas, collectively known as drylands, resulting from many factors, including human activities and climatic variations."† With regards to [24] the human causes of desertification, the IPCC suggests that these include "expansion of croplands, unsustainable land management practices and increased pressure on land from population and income growth."† What is also [25] extremely relevant within the UN's framework is its taxonomy of land use into six types: forest, cropland, grassland, wetland, settlement, and other-land.† Nowhere do we see [26] a recognition of the complexity of deserts or drylands, be they arid, semi-arid or anything else on the spectrum; we are to assume that the complexity of these lands can be defined within the category of other-land, rendering them invisible and unproductive.

This kind of language and attitude towards aridity has historical roots, especially within the cultural sphere. In 1869, French painter and writer Eugene Fromentin finished *Le Pays de la Soif* (The Land of Thirst). A fairly large painting at 143 centimeters wide and 103 centimeters high, thrusting the contemplator into a desert expanse, it depicts six men, sparsely covered with white fabric robes, at the edge of death in a desert landscape. As the painting's title suggests, the men are dying from thirst. The title comes from the last words of a travel memoir, *Un Eté dans le Sahara* (A Summer in the Sahara), that Fromentin published in 1856 which documents a trip he took across the Algerian Sahara in 1853. The scene interprets and reimagines a story that he recounts in the final pages of the same memoir; while in the Sahara, he was told that a caravan setting off at a similar time of the year had been "surprised by the desert wind,"† leading to the [27] death of eight travelers and a number of animals. One of the key works that are often said to have influenced Fromentin is Théodore Géricault's painting *The Raft of the Medusa* (1819), which depicts a shipwreck scene on the Mauritanian coast. While in Géricault's painting, it is the vicious waters of the Atlantic that are made to be the villain, here, it is the vastness of the desert, painted in a monochromatic set of browns, showing an endless landscape and false mirages.

28-30

Linda Nochlin, *The Politics of Vision: Essays on Nineteenth-Century Art and Society* (New York: Harper & Row, 1989).

Fromentin's work perfectly fits Linda Nochlin's analysis of French Oriental paintings. In her seminal essay, "The Imaginary Orient," Nochlin argues that the concept of absence is instrumental in analyzing and understanding Orientalist paintings. Describing this through Jean-Leon Gerome's *The Snake Charmer*, the painting that Edward Said puts on the cover of the first edition of *Orientalism*, Nochlin reveals the conscious mechanisms that were at play at the time of these paintings. In her analysis, Nochlin's points to the absence of history, the observer, the artist's agency, and finally, the absence of scenes of work, or more accurately, the prolif-
[28] eration of idleness.†

All four elements are absent in Fromentin's painting, but I want to highlight what Nochlin describes as the absence of history, which makes it difficult to contextualize and situate these kinds of paintings. They purposely depict the Orient as unchanging and unmoving, stuck in some vague bygone era. In the case of Fromentin's painting, there are no clues as to whether the scene is from the early 1850s, given the story he heard that was the inspiration for the painting, or from some unknown time much earlier. The only marker could have been found through the clothing, and with the choices he made, it is rather difficult to ascertain. In the case of this painting, I would also add there is the absence of a more immediate time, as gleaned by the absence of shadows. Fromentin paints shadows so short in length that they barely appear, portraying a sense of an unchangeable, static desert time where it is perpetually dry due to the high noon sun.

Fromentin's relationship with the Sahara had not always been as myopic as represented in the painting. In the earlier pages of the travel memoir, he is much more nuanced; it is as though Fromentin, as a writer, sees the landscape differently. For example, on crossing a Roman bridge to El Kantara, a village 150 kilometers southwest of Costantine and at the most northern edge of the Sahara, he writes that:

"you fall, by a rapid slope, on a charming village, watered by a deep
[29] stream and lost in a forest of 25,000 palm trees. You are in the Sahara."†

Fromentin goes further, recounting a story heard among the French, asking rhetorically:

> "Is it true that the first military column which, in 1844, crossed this famous bridge, stopped with a sudden movement of admiration, and that the music began to play with enthusiasm? I only know about this what I have been told; but that evening, the sight I had before my eyes would have made me believe in this tradition." † [30]

Fromentin's work exists along a continuum of narratives around arid landscapes. In 1837, the French Ministry of War began its plans for what would later become a 39-volume publication titled *Commission D'exploration Scientifique D'Algerie* (*The Scientific Commission for the Exploration of Algeria*), which conducted its research between 1840 and 1842. These documents create the foundation for an Orientalist narrative that paints the desert as a once extremely lush landscape when it was occupied by the Romans, but has since disintegrated by the indigenous population through a combination of overgrazing, burning, and inability to care for the productive landscape. † [31]

Rewriting this narrative as one of lost abundance, Diana K. Davis' foundational work on environmental Orientalism in North Africa highlights a key statement from the *Scientific Commission*, in which it is stated that "this land, once the object of intensive cultivation, was neither deforested nor depopulated as today... it was the abundant granary of Rome." † Even the architecture surveys found in the [32]
Scientific Commission focus heavily on the roman ruins, rendering them amidst a lush forest landscape.

Narratives and false science around desertification are linked to a long-standing forest imaginary that consistently had explicit military undertones; † simply put, timber had long [33]
been the primary source of fuel as well as raw material for military shipbuilding. One of the earliest references to deforestation emerged in the fourth-century BCE in the work of one of Aristotle's students, the early ecologist Theophrastus of Eresus. In his *De Causis Plantarum (On the Causes of Plants)*, Theophrastus writes about the relationship between deforestation, drainage, and freezing, stating that "now that the water has been drained away and prevented

31, 32

Diana K. Davis, "Desert 'Wastes' of the Maghreb: Desertification Narratives in French Colonial Environmental history of North Africa," *Cultural Geography* 11 (2004): 359-387.

33

Richard H. Grove, *Green Imperialism: Colonial Expansion, Tropical Island Edens and the Origins of Environmentalism, 1600-1860* (Cambridge: Cambridge University Press, 2003).

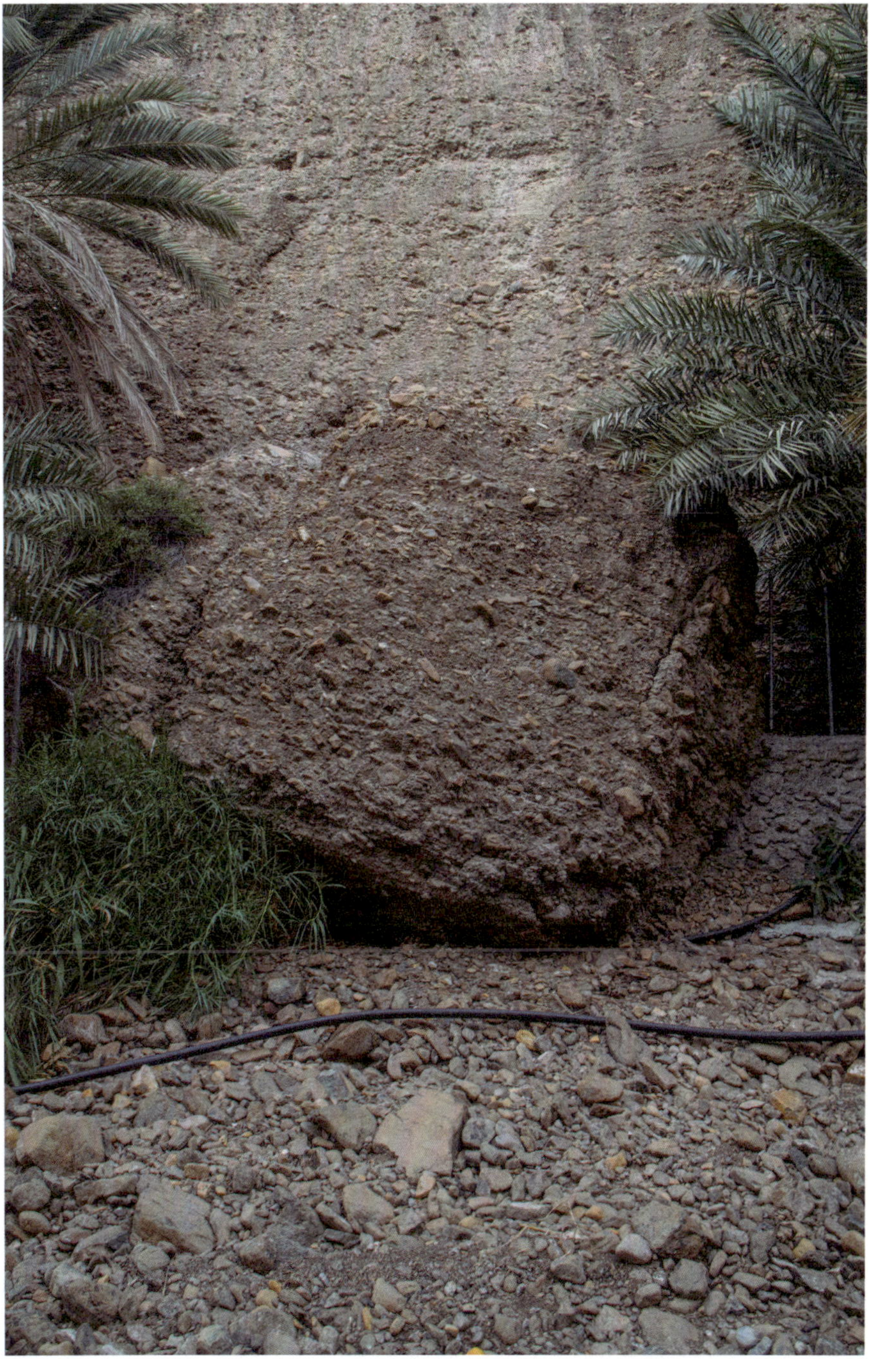

fig. (005) A fallen rock in Wadi Abadilah. Photo by author.

34

Donald J. Hughes, "Theophrastus as Ecologist," *Environmental Review* Vol. 9, No. 4, (Winter 1985): 296-306.

35

Grove, *Green Imperialism*, 27.

36, 37

Yves Charbit and Arundhati Virmani, "The Political Failure of an Economic Theory: Physiocracy" *Population* Vol. 57, No. 6 (Nov- Dec 2002): 855-883.

38

Davis, "Desert," 360.

from collecting, the country has become colder and freezing more common."† Perhaps it is not a coincidence that Theophrastus worked at a time when Alexander's increasing military expansion resulted in the transfer and movement of seeds and plants across vast territories. [34]

Another set of key events that enabled anti-desert narratives to flourish occurred in the Venetian Empire in the 1450s. A combination of forces including increasing timber trade with the Muslim world, a significant demand of timber for military shipbuilding locally, as well as the downstream silting up of a lagoon forced the Venetian Council of Ten to respond to the acute externalities of deforestation, resulting in policies aimed at curbing deforestation and reforestation. Unfortunately for Venice, these policies did not work as intended, resulting in an existential crisis for the Venetian Empire which subsequently opened the door for French, British, and Dutch expansion into the Mediterranean and the Indian Ocean.† [35]

The emerging European environmentalist movement was bolstered by a foundational event that occurred in France. In 1758, François Quesnay published the *Tableau Économique* (*Economic Table)* in which he began to describe physiocracy, an economic system that privileges agricultural land and agricultural production as "exclusive"† forces in the economy. In the *Tableau Economique,* Quesnay divides the population into three classes: the productive class (those working in agriculture and other extractive practices); the proprietary class (landowners); and the sterile class (including all that do not directly engage with agricultural production such as crafts folk and merchants).† This economic system lies in stark contrast with mercantilism that is built on trade surplus which the French, English, and Dutch East India Companies had been founded upon and continued to engage with at the time of this development. Despite its short shelf life, by centering agriculture, physiocracy enabled cultural shifts in the relationships between the natural environment and economics which continue today. [36] [37]

Finally,in 1927, French officer Louis Lavauden coined the term desertification, proclaiming it "purely artificial... caused uniquely by human action."† [38]

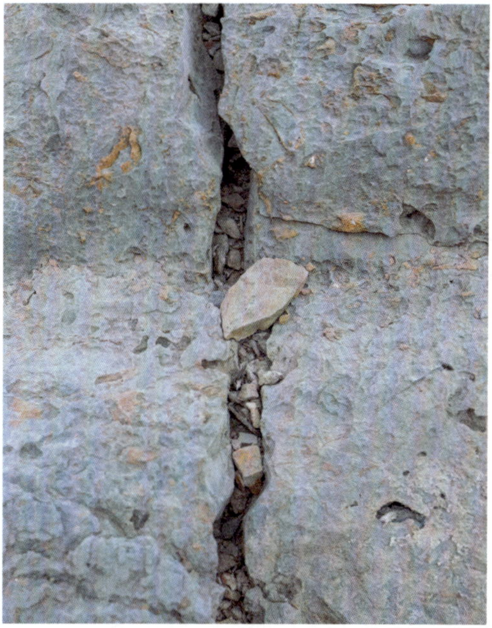

fig. (006) When seen up close, the materialities within Al Hajar express a wide range of visual characteristics. Photo by Reem Falaknaz.

Foregrounding Aridity, Honestly

I began this introduction with the first words from novelist Abdelrahman Munif's novel, *Endings* (1977). In it, Munif tells the story of a village transforming from a period of relative comfort and complacency to one of severe drought, with the promise of the construction of a dam at the center of a dream of modernization and development, moving the town away from the desert.

Not long after, in 1988, *The New Yorker* published John Updike's review of Munif's best-known novel, *Cities of Salt*, the first of five volumes collectively known by the same name. First published in Arabic in 1984, *Cities of Salt* builds on the themes explored earlier in *Endings* and in most of his work. This happens through the voice of its omnipresent narrator and through a protagonist who disappears into the desert, unpacking the possible tensions between modernization and land-based practices.

Translated into English by Peter Theroux, *Cities of Salt* makes Updike extremely uncomfortable, despite the conceptual overlaps between both authors' work. Updike is well known for his *Rabbit* series, itself a pentalogy (i.e., a work in five volumes), which is deeply connected to post-war transformations in America. Perhaps most importantly for us, Updike's work is centered in the physical environment, a fictional town in Pennsylvania. While acknowledging the initial value of the "dramatizing the impact of American oil discovery and
[39] development"† in the Gulf, his discomfort with the tone and style of the novel emerges when he writes that:

"It is unfortunate... His voice is that of a campfire explainer; his characters are rarely fixed in our minds by a face or a manner or a developed motivation; no central figure develops enough reality to
[40] attract our sympathetic interest."†

About halfway into the novel, the supposed protagonist, Miteb Al Hathal, a patriarch defeated from what he considers to be the irreversible and rather unfortunate tides of modernization, walks into the desert and never comes back. The novel continues and a series of other pseudo-central figures come and go. Where Updike was looking for a protagonist, in the image of his Harry "Rabbit" Angstrom from his own pentalogy, a central figure for the reader to sympathize with for the duration of the story, Munif, writing in Arabic, it must be noted, centers the desert landscape and through it, the attitudes and practices that it enables.

While Munif narrates the desert's transformation, and by extension, its inhabitants, Libyan novelist Ibrahim Al Koni resists a false constructed imaginary of deserts by describing it as "not really a place... a transcendental place... a shadow of a place... the desert has everything."† [41]

Elliot Colla, a prolific translator of Al Koni, writes that:

> Al Koni's novels take place in a desert world that is, despite its desolation, surprisingly rich in the sense that everywhere there are living beings struggling to live... Thus, Al Koni's novels paradoxically suggest that only here... does life emerge in its richest sense." For Al Koni, "the question of the desert is first and foremost an existential question. Actually, the desert is not just a desert. It is a symbol of human existence.† [42]

39, 40

John Updike, "Review of 'Abd al-Rahman Munif's Cities of Salt," (The New Yorker, October 17, 1988).

41-43

"Ibrahim Al Koni Interview: In the Desert" interviewed by Anders Hastrup Lousiana Channel April 22, 2014, https://www.youtube.com/watch?v=K8sMbKQ-HEE

Where Fromentin's painting assumes time is at an eternal standstill, where it is perpetually a summer noon sun, Al Koni conceives of time in his novels as a metaphysical and unseen condition. In Al Koni's work, if a desert is not a place, then a linear understanding of time is also challenged. "The desert is the only place where we can visit death and return home safely."† [43]

The first of Al Koni's works to be translated into English is the relatively short novel *The Bleeding of the Stone.* The novel centers around the *waddan*, a mythical wild sheep known for its meat, and its relationship with Asouf, a young goat herder who is the only one who knows its exact location, and their struggle against hunters seeking the waddan

and who are responsible for the near complete disappearance of gazelles in the desert. In the opening pages of the book, "Asouf plunged his arms into the sands of the wadi to begin
[44] his ablutions."† In seeking to cleanse himself in the sand, Asouf's intimate relationship with the desert challenges its constructed imaginary as a space of desolate despair.

44

Ibrahim Al Koni, *The Bleeding of the Stone*, (Interlink Books, 1990).

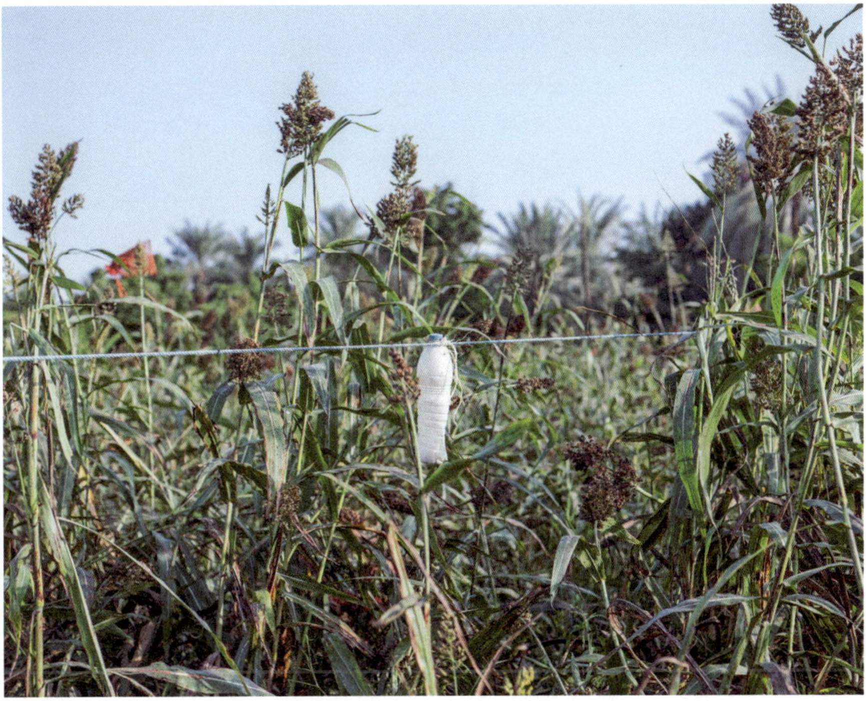

fig. (007) Agricultural tactics within Al Hajar hint at subtle relationships between natural and synthetic materials. Photo by Reem Falaknaz.

In building worlds and giving voice to characters that explicitly exhibit the entanglements between communities, individuals, and landscapes, Munif, Al Koni, and others such as Tayeb Salih, capture the elusive, bring into light subtle and nuanced conditions, and eradicate misconceptions. In that spirit, *Aridly Abundant* attempts to amplify the ways in which a sustainable built environment might emerge if we look closely at what is in plain sight.

Faysal Tabbarah
Editors' Notes

01

Rawafid: Interview with Abdelrahman Munif.

02

One of the field notes is written by Samar Halloum.

In a televised interview, author and journalist Ahmed Ali Alzain suggests to Abdelrahman Munif, the venerable author of *Cities of Salt* and other sagas, that he lived a life passing through places, in a state of ongoing transience, rarely settling down in one place to search for permanence. Generously acknowledging this interpretation, and after describing his relationship to a number of Arab cities, Munif takes a rather slow second to ponder and proceeds to tell Alzain that "we are all Bedouins," and then points to his collar and says "even if we wear ties, we will
[01] remain Bedouins."†

While it seems rather obvious that I should jump in and complicate the word Bedouin, explaining all the ways in which this adjective paints a diverse group of people with a rather large brushstroke, I won't. In reading Munif, I have come to understand that by using the term Bedouin, he refers to those who read the landscapes they pass through, settle in, and receive what the landscapes provide. This describes individuals and communities that weave together historical knowledge and foresight.

Sparked by this provocation from Munif, this book was conceived as a collection of travels through aridity. Meitha Almazrooei, my co-editor, and I, asked contributors to think about the relationship between travel, travel writing, and the built environment. What coalesced was a diverse set of positions and attitudes towards travel writing that ranged from documenting journeys through historical texts and images in search of lost relationships with aridity and the practices it engenders, to authors who physically traveled to contemporary arid spaces in search of nuance and abundance, and essays that explore the blurry and conceptual edges of aridity.

Alongside the travel-based contributions, the book presents a series of field notes, ostensibly framed as research findings. In the field notes, I attempt to narrate the places, materials, and tactics that I encoun-
[02] tered on numerous trips myself.† Supporting these field notes is a series of photographic catalogs that depict the range of tactics used in constructing Al Hajar's built environment that I have witnessed in my fieldwork. Traveling with me and at times separately, Reem Falaknaz narrates her own experiences in Al Hajar Mountains through a series of photographs that are also contained within the publication.

On a voyage to center aridity across time, space, and ideas, the book attempts to recast the genre of travel and expedition literature, challenging the ways in which arid environments have historically been depicted through broad generalizations. While the accompanying exhibition reimagines arid landscapes as spaces of abundance, provoking alternative architectural conditions through a display of existing and imagined building tactics, the textual and visual format of a travel book is an opportunity for a slower and more contemplative form of immersion, challenging perceptual and conceptual assumptions.

Meitha Almazrooei

Editors' Notes

Accompanying the National Pavilion United Arab Emirates exhibition in the 18th International Architecture Exhibition – La Biennale di Venezia, the publication *In Plain Sight* contains twelve essays commissioned for their diverse perspectives. The writers responded to provocations around the visual and material representation of the United Arab Emirates landscape, a conceptual framework by curator Faysal Tabbarah for the exhibition *Aridly Abundant*.

The responses came back in various genres, which elaborated on aspects of the initial brief. The publication opens with Omar Abdel-Ghaffar's and Ahmad Makia's essays that center the narrative of historical protagonists and their notations on traveling through the Arabian Peninsula. Building on Makia's inquisitions on time, Alia Al-Sabi shares her findings on Najm Suhail, a seasonal calendar used by farmers and seafarers (among others) that leaves room for miscalculations and lost time.

Dalal Musaed Alsayer delves into the archive and looks at representations of the environment across different media. She examines what is foregrounded in the frame and how the images are perceived historically while questioning their current place in the archive. Meanwhile, Aziza Chaouni narrates her initial encounter with the Sahara, an experience that cemented her architectural practice.

It is difficult to parse through fiction and reality, but Mohamed M. Elnagar is conscious of that when he narrates history through the eyes of a single rock. Continuing in the spirit of materials, Wesam Al Asali illuminates the multitude of ways stones are used in housing, holding on to historical construction methods. He intertwines the history of dome construction, the laborious steps involved, and embodied material knowledge seen across geographies from Aleppo to Fujairah. Keen in his observations, Kevin Mitchell shares his notes on wall construction methods around Al Hajar Mountains.

Meanwhile, Samar Halloum travels with migratory birds and follows their points of rest, flight, and discomfort triggered by human manipulation of the environment. On an eye-opening road trip, Ibrahim Nehme provides a glimpse of his first-hand encounters with smells, conversations, and solicited clairvoyance. Rand Abdul Jabbar's visit to Wadi Wurayah is consolidated in a poem that politicizes the geological features of the valley. The book ends with Deepak Unnikrishnan's fable, which discloses the tender relationship between a grandmother and her granddaughter residing alongside a mountain range.

Through these essays, *In Plain Sight* searches for the terms and visuals to read and interpret life and its surrounding landscape in the UAE.

Salama bint Hamdan Al Nahyan Foundation
Foreword

Commissioner of the National Pavilion
United Arab Emirates – La Biennale di Venezia

We live surrounded by the stories we tell each other. Some of them are our stories and some of them are handed down to us from others, such as past generations, friends, and society. The 18th International Architecture Exhibition – La Biennale di Venezia is a platform for storytelling. Its theme has been a provocation from curator Lesley Lokko: to consider the African continent as a protagonist of the future, to think about Africa as a laboratory. This is an exciting opportunity to tell new stories, to imagine, and reimagine the way we look at things. The purpose of the National Pavilion United Arab Emirates is to tell untold stories about our country, our nation, what we are thinking and what we are doing.

When we hear stories about our region, it is predominantly about the desert. We are often told that there is scarcity: scarcity of life and scarcity of food. However, the UAE has mountains, lakes, and islands as well as a desert. In each landscape, as curator Faysal Tabbarah demonstrates, there are opportunities for abundance. Throughout the country, people have responded to their surroundings and available materials with creativity and innovation, building exciting structures and homes. Faysal Tabbarah was selected as the curator of the National Pavilion UAE because of the rigorous research in his thesis. It aimed to make us look again at our varied landscapes through the lens of abundance and to reimagine this notion of abundance, not as a luxury, but as a world of possibilities. He does this by looking at history and the way that people made sense of the materials around them to create shelter, food, and beauty. Tabbarah challenges us to be more thoughtful and to reimagine our world while playing with the notion that aridity does not mean a lack, rather he proposes that we should view it as abundant, letting a world of new opportunities open up.

By telling a different story, it allows us to change the way we look at things – very much in line with the aspirations of Lesley Lokko – and tell ourselves some new stories, stories of hope, abundance, and possibilities.

Generative research methods take time and effort – physical, intellectual, and financial – to explore new ideas, examine old ones, and give form to these thoughts so that we can test them and respond to them. The exhibition is always the work of many people, both in front and behind the scenes. It would not be possible without the creativity, generosity, and enthusiasm of everyone involved, too many to name. To all those people that have supported our ability to bring new ideas to discuss at the National Pavilion UAE, we thank you for your continued support. To all of those who come, engage, and participate in the dialogue around the exhibition, we need you and we need your voices, to challenge, to support, to amplify and to act. We thank you.

As the proud commissioner of the National Pavilion UAE, along with our partners at the Ministry of Culture and Youth, we are committed to creative practices of inquiry, prototyping and storytelling through art, culture and heritage. We are delighted to bring you the *Aridly Abundant* exhibition and its publication.

UAE Ministry of Culture and Youth
Foreword

His Excellency Sheikh Salem bin Khalid Al Qassimi,
UAE Minister of Culture and Youth

In the past several editions of La Biennale di Venezia, the National Pavilion United Arab Emirates has been successful at challenging the status quo and highlighting some of the most pertinent subjects being discussed today. Innovative concepts, forward-thinking topics, and impeccable presentations have been hallmarks of the UAE's contributions. These themes continue in this year's exhibition on sustainable futures, as well.

At the 18th International Architecture Exhibition – La Biennale di Venezia in 2023, the National Pavilion UAE explores the precarious territory between adversity and opportunity. The theme *Aridly Abundant* unmasks the most striking quality of our terrain – aridity – and places it at the forefront of the built environment.

Often aridity denotes scarcity, but through the exhibition, we discover how aridity can be associated with abundance. Curator Faysal Tabbarah very deftly puts the narrative together to let the viewer experience the abundance that aridity brings in its wake. The exhibition leads us through a surreal experience, touching on the deepest trenches of human imagination and urges us to rethink and reimagine our relationship with our surroundings.

As the UAE celebrates 2023, the Year of Sustainability, we see it as a time of introspection, taking note of where we stand in terms of our responsibility towards our planet and future courses of action. In this way, *Aridly Abundant* is a timely theme that takes a deep dive into the possibility of adapting to and re-configuring elements of arid landscapes to create a more sustainable future with minimal impact on the environment.

In our lives, we often hark back to traditional knowledge to navigate the most critical issues in the present day. Taking this idea, the National Pavilion UAE has encouraged highlighting age-old practices in its work. In the current exhibition, examples of this include earthen materials and land-based practices which are presented as viable construction materials and methods that have a lower carbon footprint and greater impact.

I commend the commissioner, Salama bint Hamdan Al Nahyan Foundation, for such an outstanding and thought-provoking exhibition backed by relevant research. As with past exhibitions, this year's brilliant contribution delivers a narrative that tackles the myriad of possibilities for the future.

Curator's Acknowledgments

Aridly Abundant could not have happened without the work of a near-infinite amount of individuals and institutions.

My gratitude goes to the Salama bint Hamdan Al Nahyan Foundation and the Ministry of Culture and Youth (MCY) United Arab Emirates for trusting me to tell previously untold stories and to my home institution, the American University of Sharjah.

I am personally thankful for: Kevin Mitchell, whose mentorship and banter are equally invaluable. Meitha Almazrooei, who jumped on board as my co-editor over the briefest of coffee conversations - and perhaps more importantly for the space she gives me and my long-windedness. Reem Falaknaz for telling the stories I was unable to. Samar Halloum, the lead researcher on this project, who made it happen seconds after joining. The project's team: Basel Al Taher, Dina Hirzallah, Rana Salah, and Sara Alchaar, whose enthusiasm and ingenuity allowed me to keep asking questions I would not have answered alone. Aya Shaker for the gift of bits and bites. The team at National Pavilion UAE: Laila Binbrek for her kindness and calmness, Farah El-Rafei for keeping the wheels turning, as well as Rawan Al Ramahi, Jay Yambao, Anita Buscaino, Dana Al Sadek, and Emanuela Semiani. The team behind 40Mustaqel: Nada Hesham, Mina Maurice, Shahd El Sabbagh, and Hussein Salem for translating ideas into a visual identity. Omar Darwish for his assistance when called upon. The team behind Tosetto: Silvia, Michel, and Bako, for visits to Italian quarries and making the exhibition a reality. Ammar Kalo for coffee breaks and bouncing thoughts. Nada Taryam for the space to work on other things. Dina Al Khatib for the constant presence of her critical eye. Immense gratitude to friends and colleagues: Abeer Seikaly, Dalal Musaed Alsayer, Gregory Watson, Haitham Issam, Hala Al Ani, Ibrahim Ibrahim, Jonathan Foote, Mira Almazrooei, Nadia Christidi, Talal Al Ansari, Talin Hazbar, Tulip Hazbar, Riem Ibrahim, and Dean Varkki Pallathucheril for their time, insights, and care.

Finally, to Zaina, for the many, many sacrifices.

Editors' Acknowledgments

We would like to acknowledge the work of friends, colleagues, and scholars who have informed the content of this book, be it an involvement that was direct or from a distance.

The long conversations with the contributors in this book diverged us from our initial conceptual framework and geographic boundaries and brought us to the multitude of lenses published in this volume - be it poetic, historical, personal, or methodical. Ahmad Makia, Alia Al-Sabi, Aziza Chaouni, Dalal Musaed Alsayer, Deepak Unnikrishnan, Ibrahim Nehme, Kevin Mitchell, Mohamed M. Elnagar, Omar Abdel-Ghaffar, Rand Abdul Jabbar, and Wesam Al Asali, thank you.

Nour Salamé at Kaph Books, for her breadth of knowledge and for guiding us through the production process. Zeina Assaf, for her singular insight and careful reading of all the text in the book. Ban Kattan, for translating the book to our mother tongue with seeming ease and humor. Manal Khader, for lending us a hand with the translation. Deema Alghunaim, for the translation of Rand Abduljabbar's poetry. Mohamad Hamdan for editing the Arabic version of this book.

Reem Falaknaz for bringing the book to life with her lens. The team behind 40Mustaqel: Nada Hesham, Mina Maurice, and Shahd El Sabbagh for their unmatched effort in experimenting with how the content can live on the page.

Reem Falaknaz

Prologue

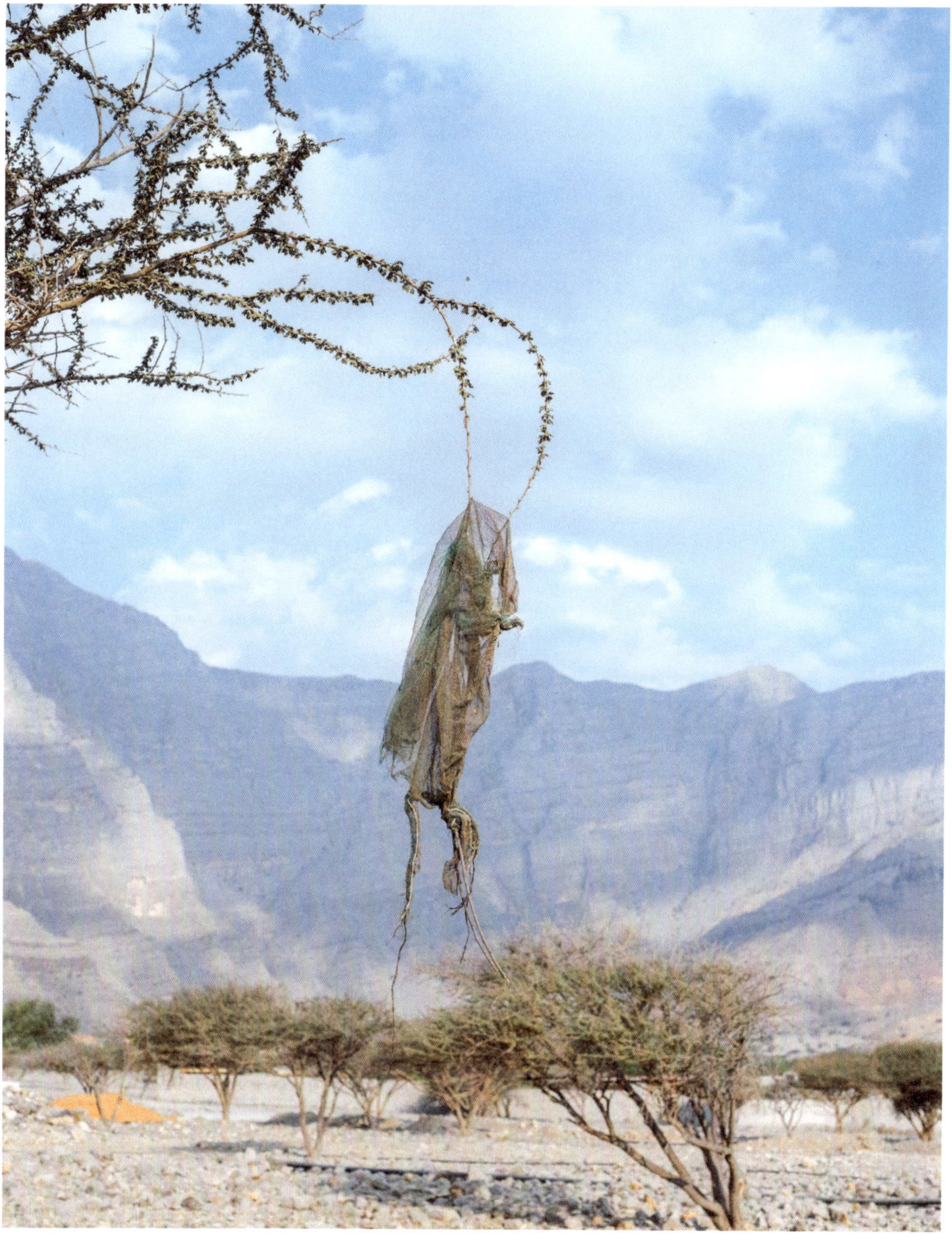

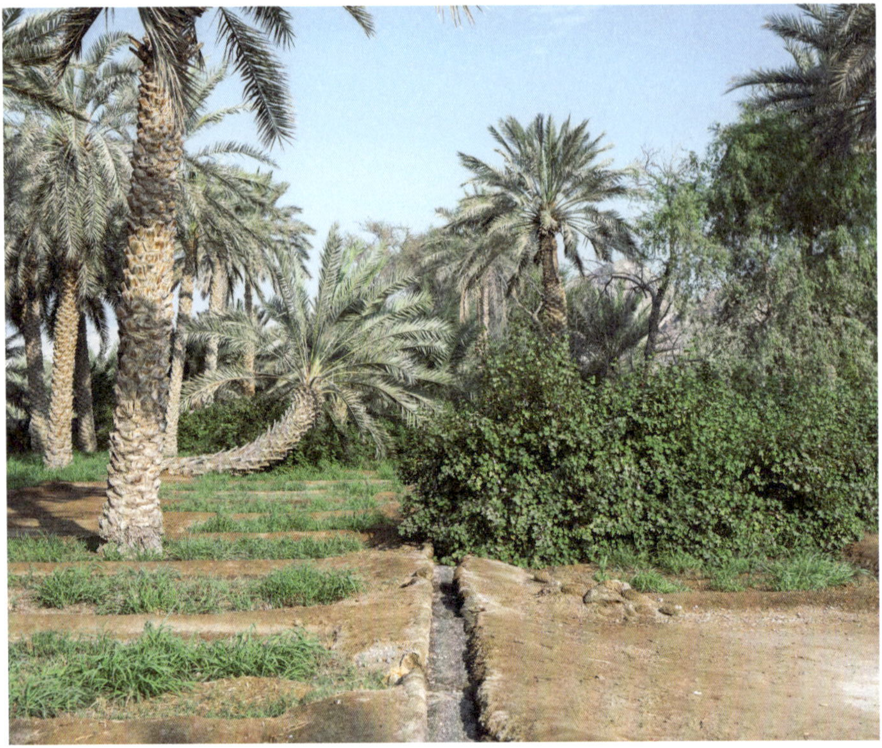

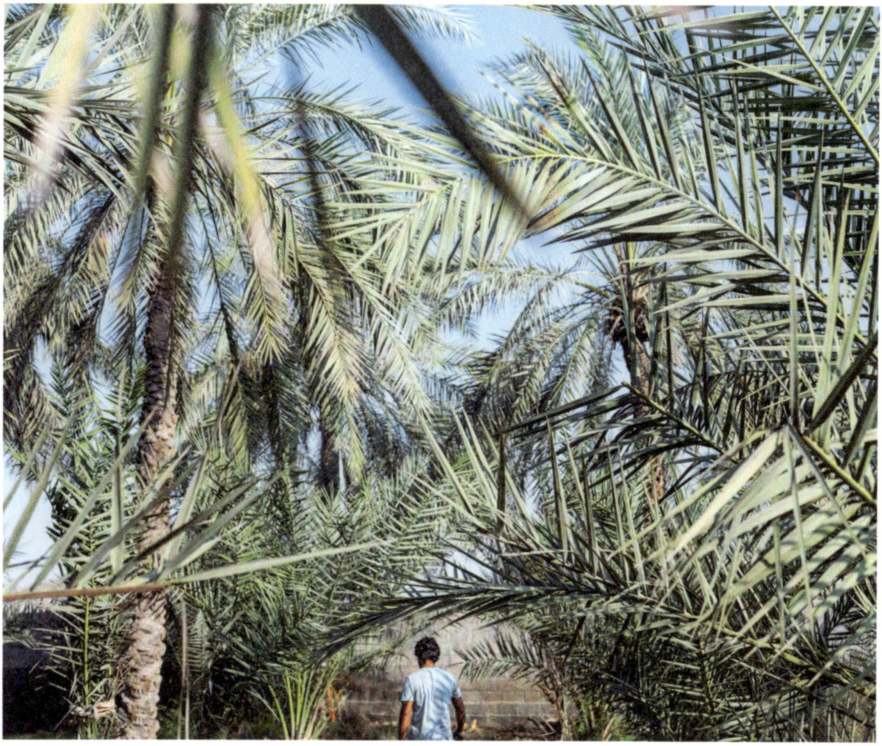

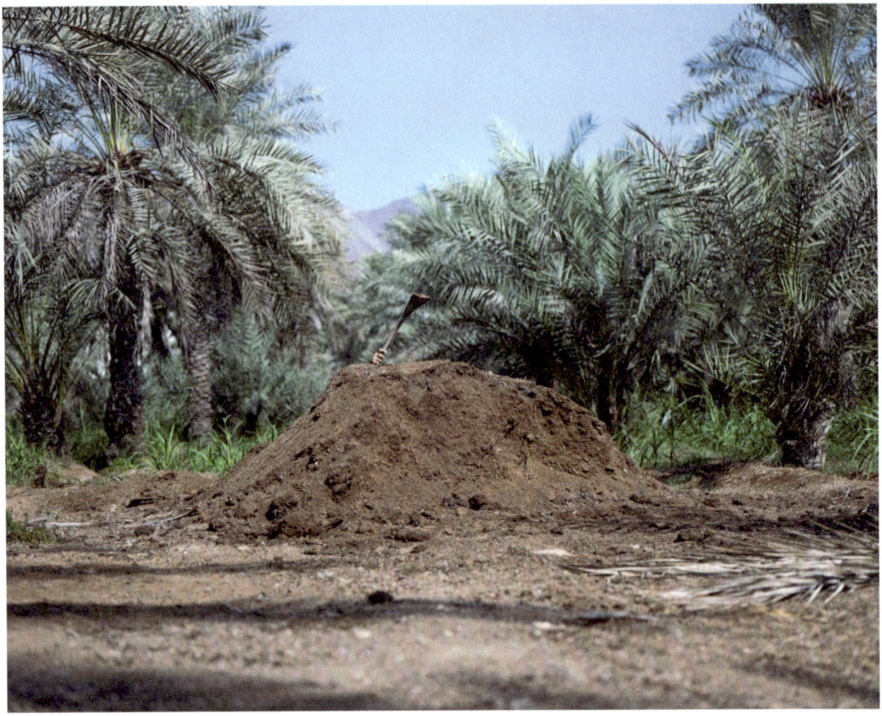

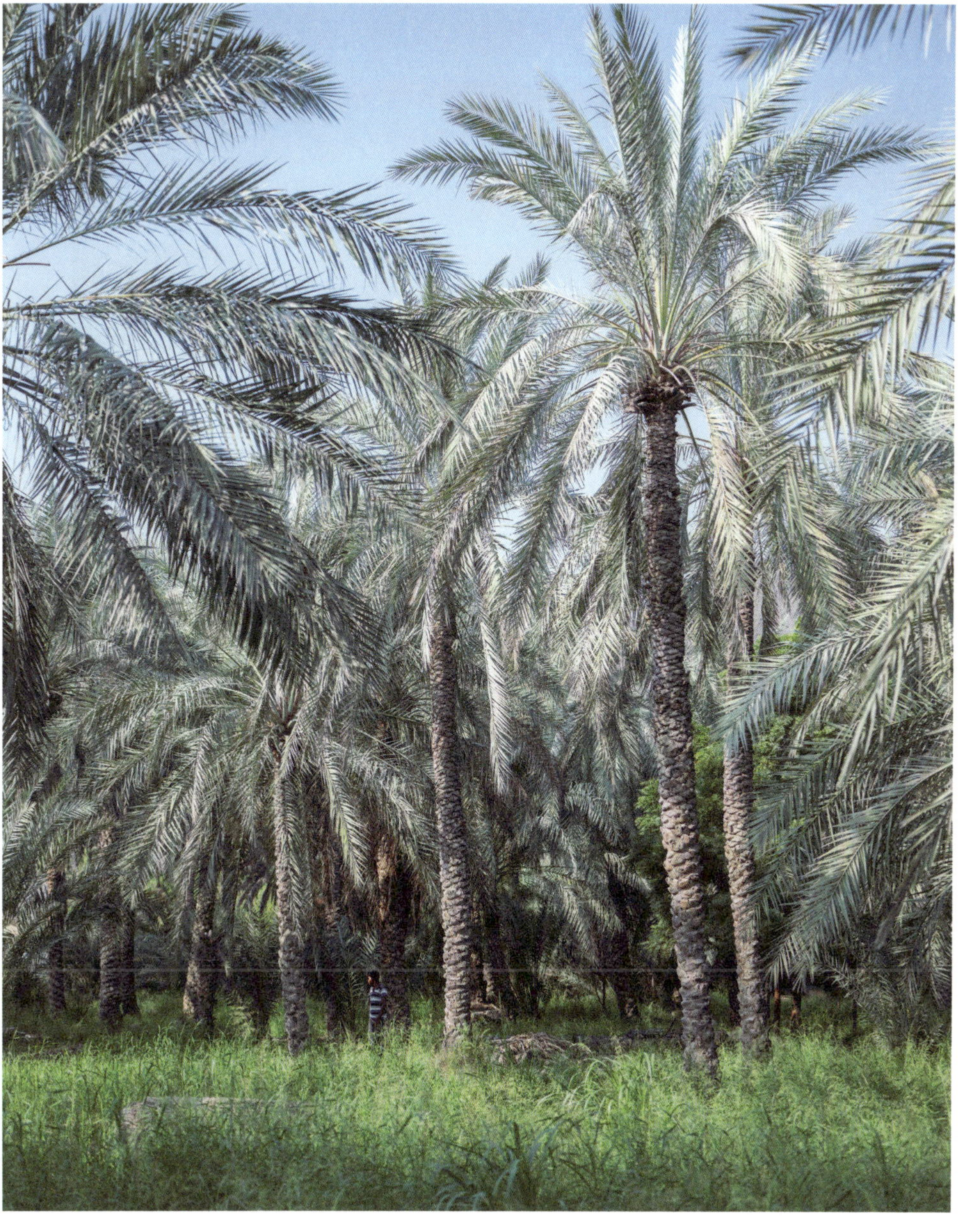

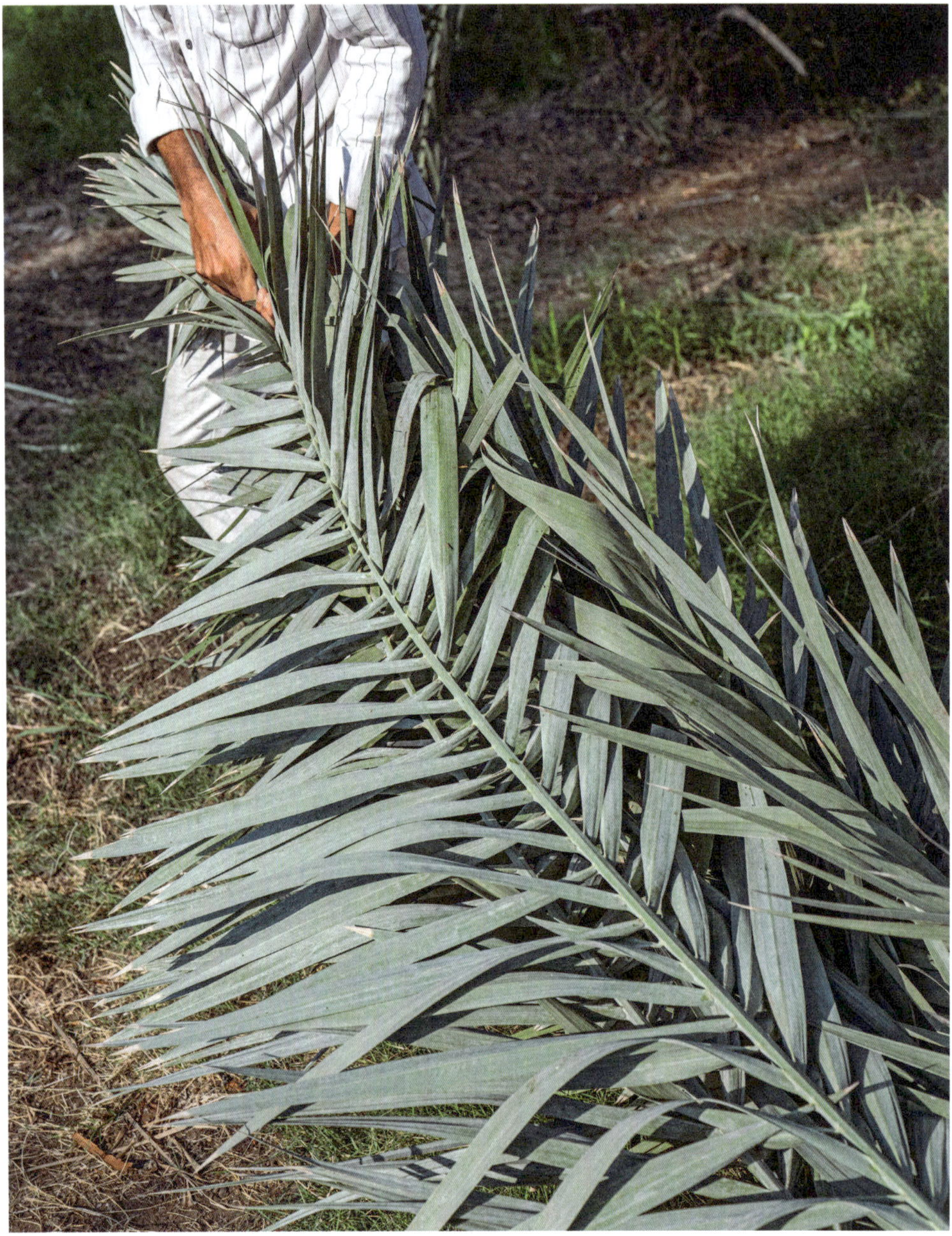

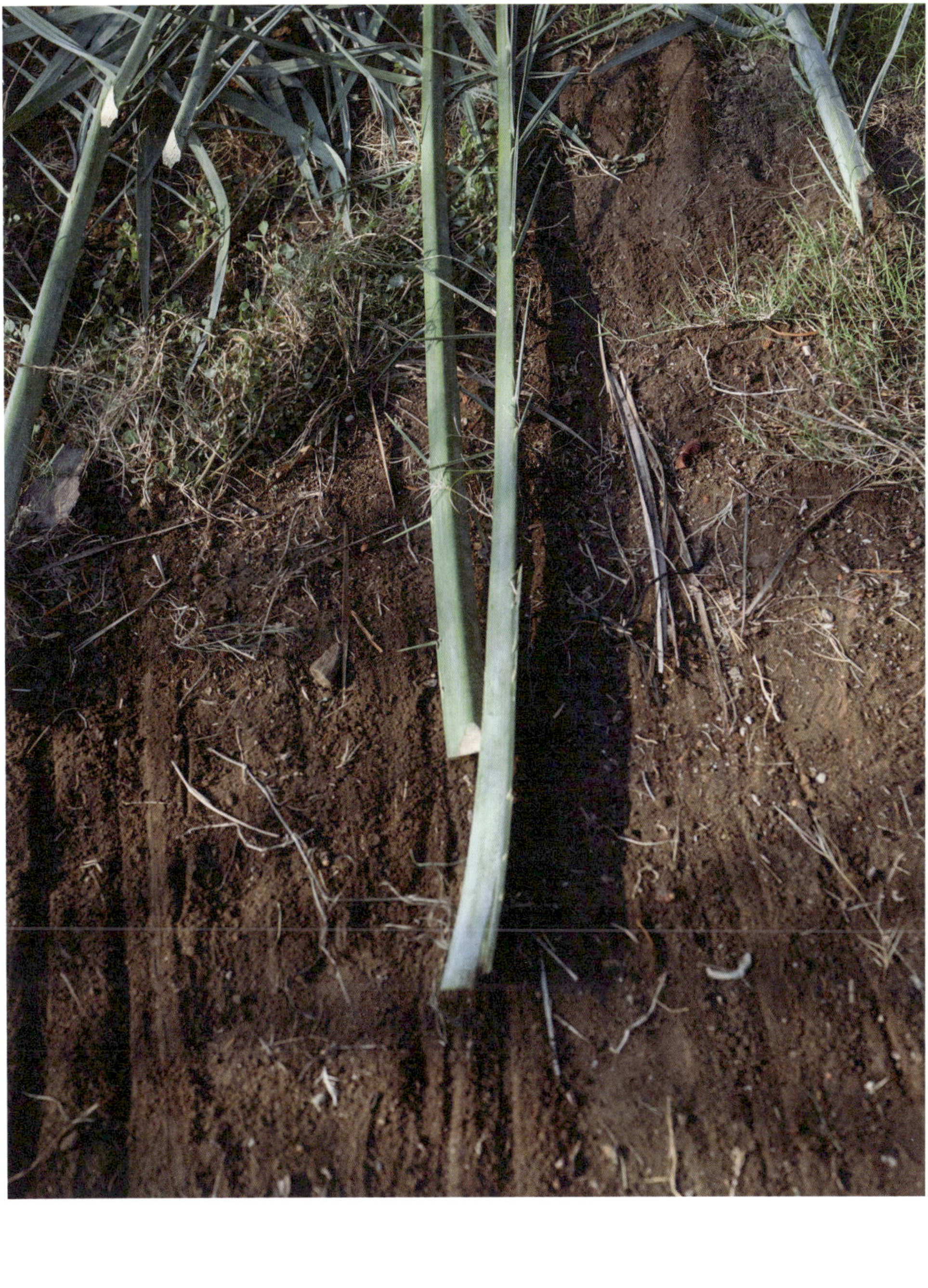

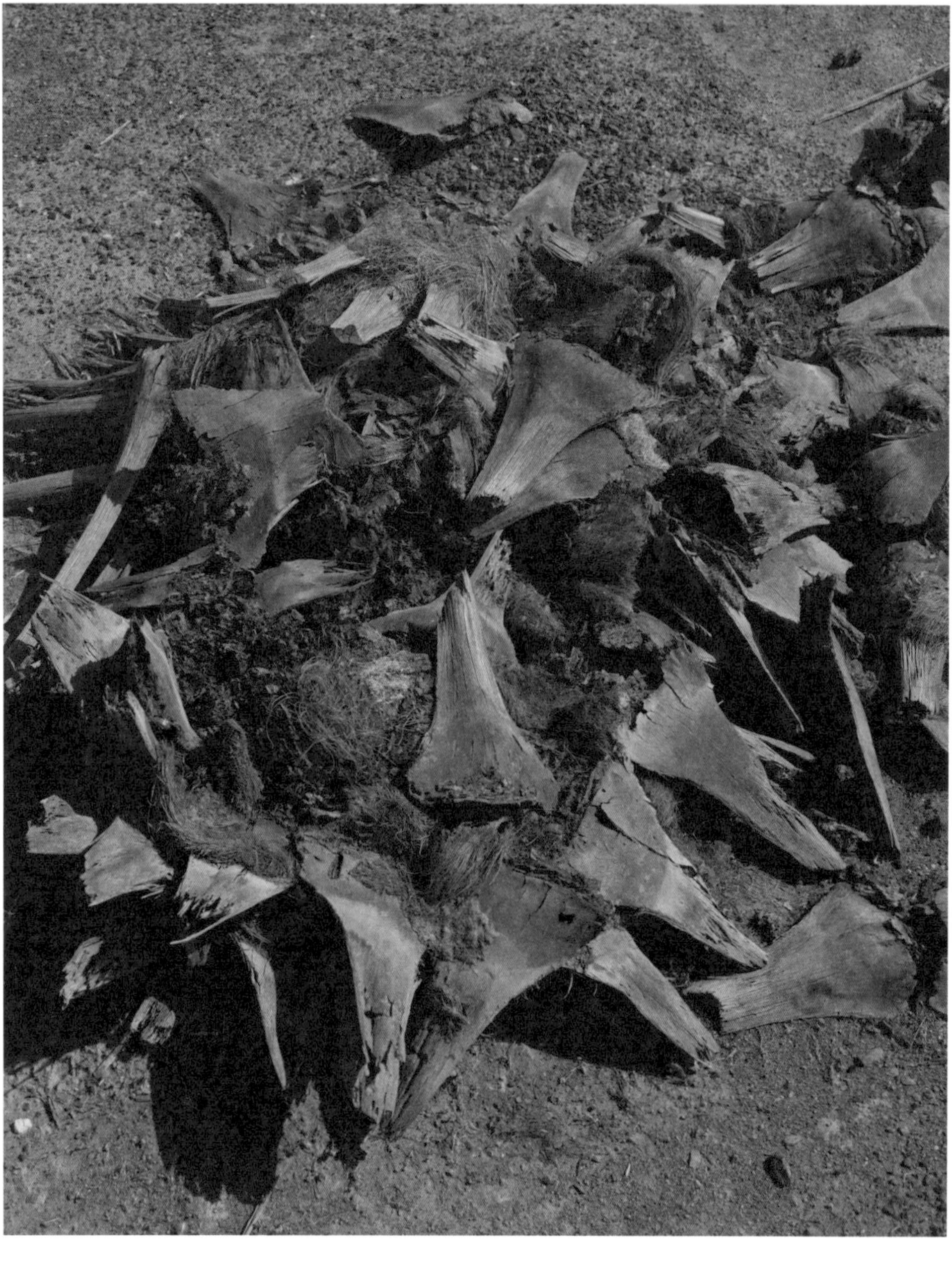

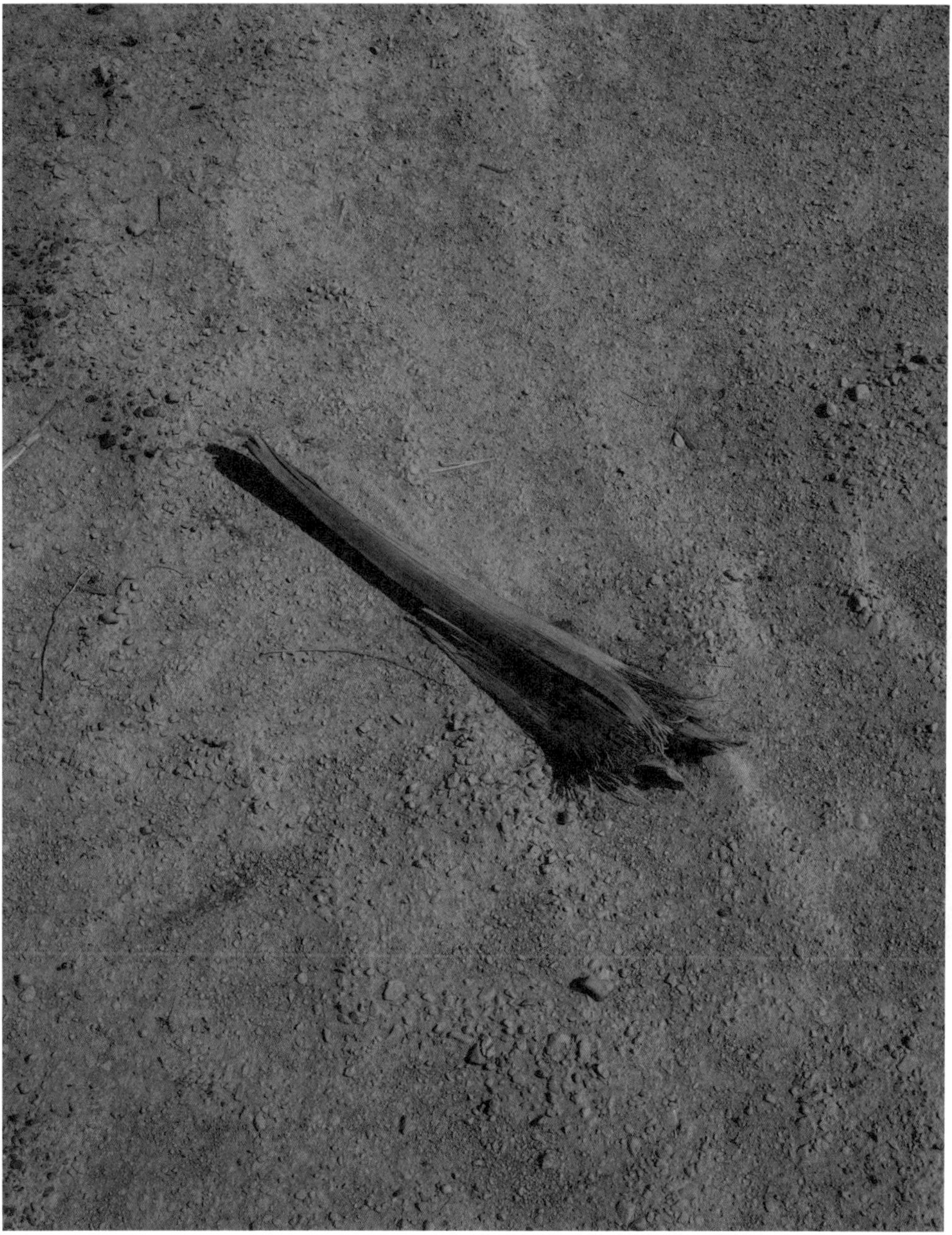

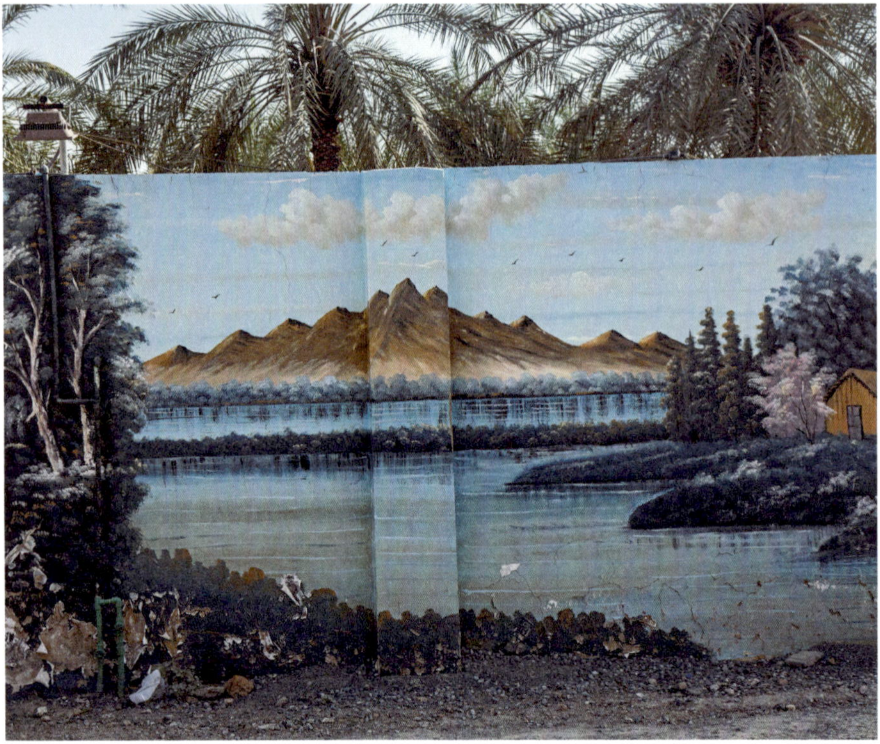

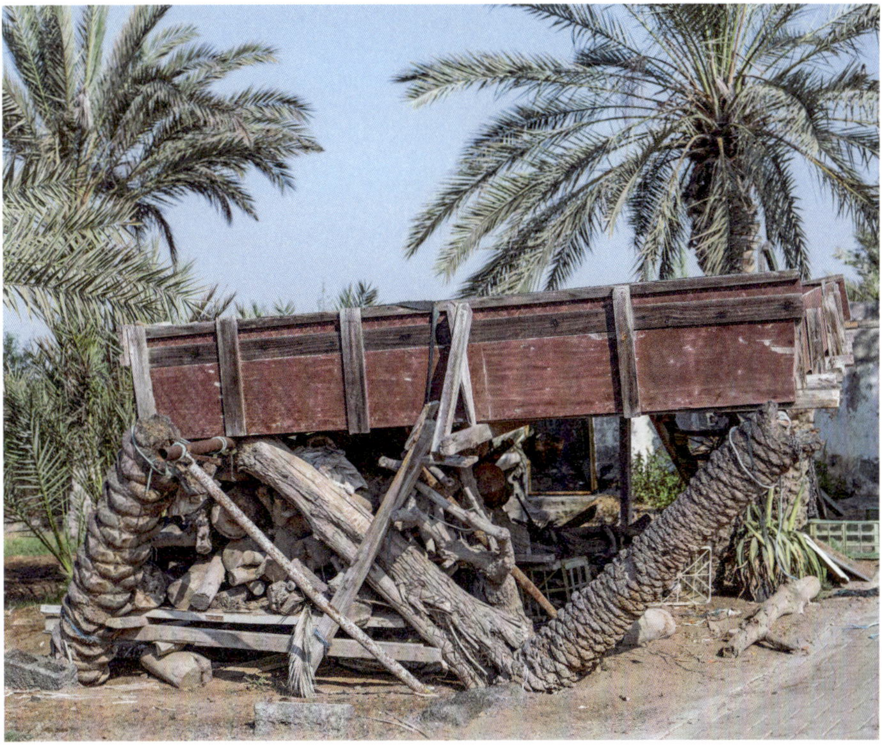

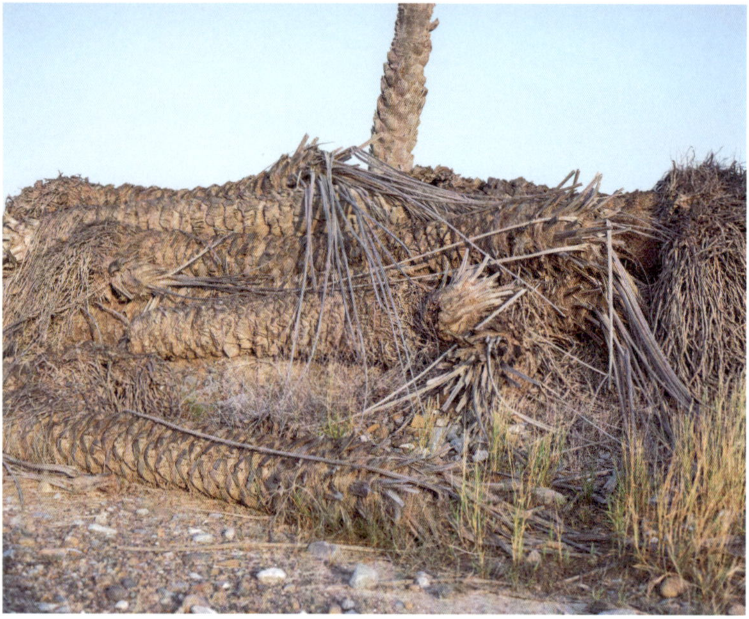

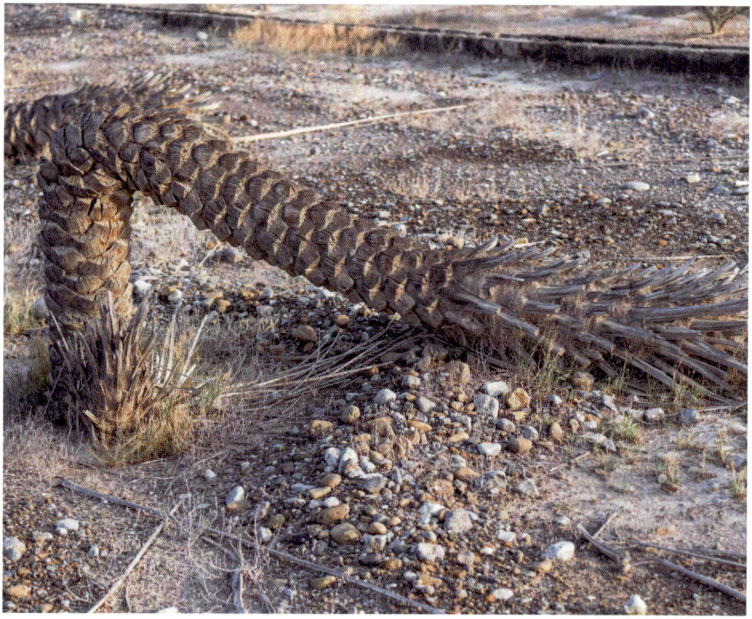

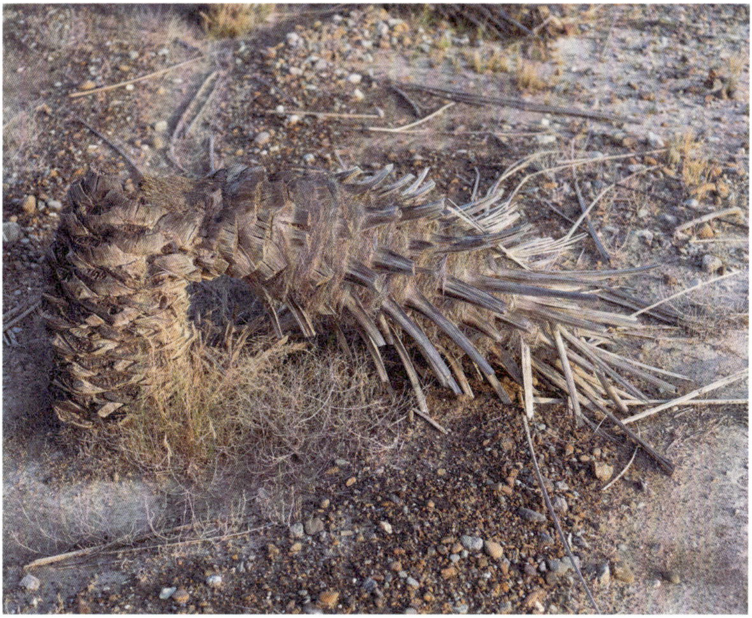

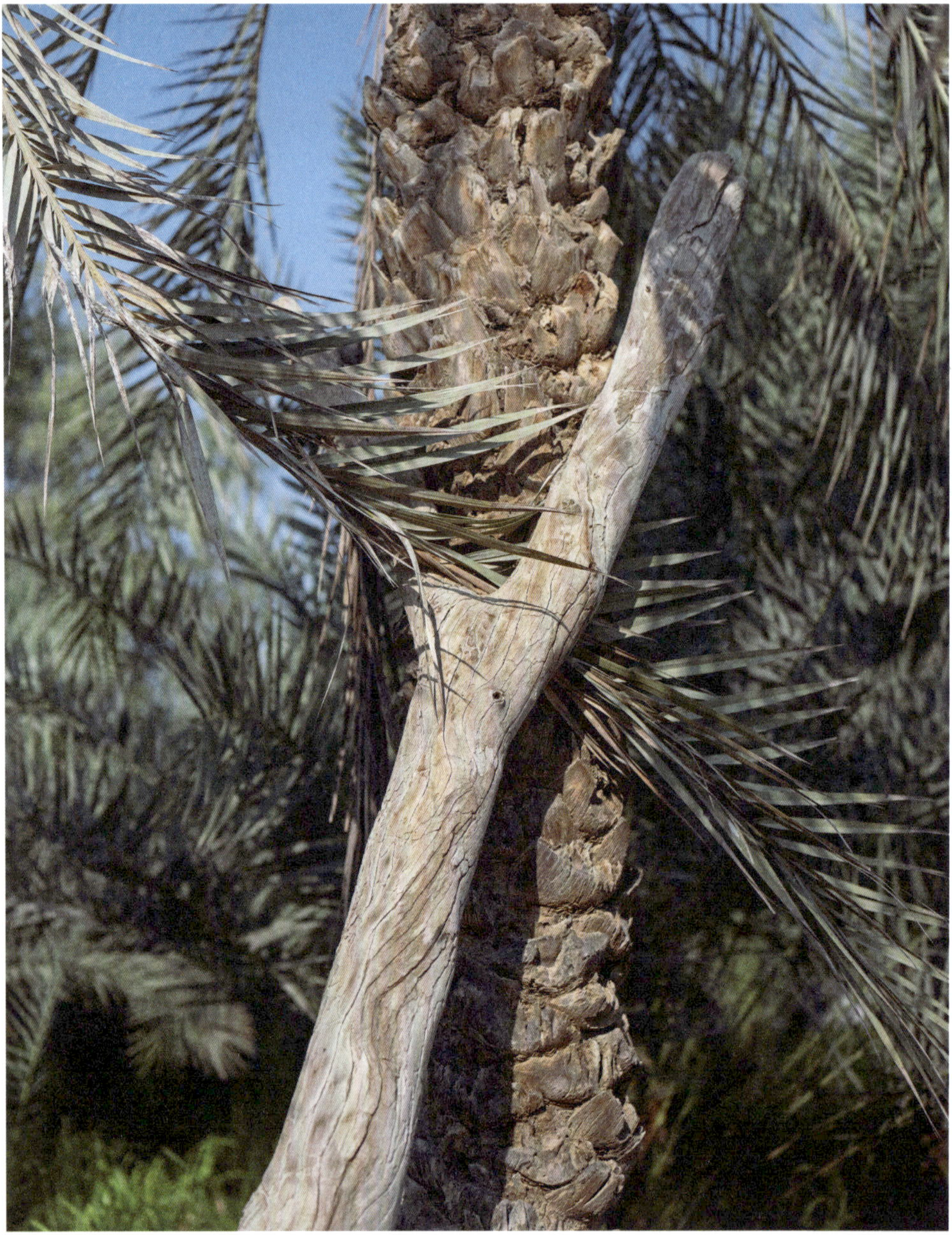

Omar Abdel-Ghaffar

The Quenching Potential of Difficult Poetry

مـا تَنْقُصِ الأَيَّـامُ وَالدَّهْـرُ يَنْفَدِ»

[01] “I consider time a tr

and that which every day dimin

01

Ṭarafah ibn al-'Abd (543-569 CE).

«أَرى العُـمْرَ كَنْزًا ناقِصًا كُلَّ لَيْـلَةٍ

sure decreasing every night;

es will soon be lost forever.”

The canonical pre-Islamic *Mu'allaqāt* (Hanging Poems) are not as unfamiliar as they seem. What makes these poems difficult is that the Arabic language many of us speak today has lost its ability to describe arid space. In this loss, we, ourselves, risk living a more desiccated life. Many of us have lost the ability to see the teaming life – and emotion – that filled the Arabian Desert and gave birth to one of the great literary traditions of the world. Although the distance between us increases over time as the sensory experience of the desert becomes less familiar, understanding the poems' cultural, geographic, and temporal context allows us to see how we share many of the same experiences with people from centuries ago, in spite of the unfamiliar words that obscure this fact. Reaching out and attempting to grasp the poet's extended hand – manifested, after all, in words – will not only change our understanding of the desert but will change our understanding of ourselves. Rather than overlook the unfamiliar, or see how we can best exploit it for meaning, we should struggle with the art, cultivating a shared experience across time and space.

The Hanging Poems are a group of allegedly pre-Islamic poems that have been celebrated for centuries among Arab litterateurs from West Africa to Central Asia. The seven poems derive their name from the notion that they were "hung" on the Kaaba – so exquisite did their contemporaries find them. They are believed to have been composed from the sixth to the seventh centuries. These seven canonical poems were first compiled by Ḥammād al-Rāwiya (c.694–773 CE), a Kufan scholar. Much ink has been spilled over the past century about the authenticity and origins of these poems, but we can relegate these concerns to the historians. Here, we will indulge in the beauty of the images and the intensity of the emotions, feeling rest assured that these poems are around a millennium and a half years old, give or take a few years. Through their words, the poems transport us to a distant time, but also to a distinct kind of space: the desert as seen by poets from late antiquity, abundant with life and emotion.

The desert of our poets is expansive and defies many of our own impulses to pin down and tie. They described the desert because it brought their vast and scattered community together through a set of shared images and emotions. Many of these men and women were nomads; they traveled from coast to coast on the Arabian Peninsula, recounting tales, finding love, and trading goods along the way. They often describe the desolation of seeing their beloved one leave, an inevitable consequence of nomadic life. But they also managed, through their travels and travails, to create a literary tradition that would be relatable to people throughout the

Arabian Peninsula – and the world. Our own Ṭarafah, whose words I chose to open this essay with, spent most of his life between modern-day Iraq and Oman. Yet, his poem came to be hung on the Kaaba, on the other side of the Arabian Peninsula, and to touch us, wherever we are in the world today.

The desert has always been an evocative, emotional space. This, to the modern eye, seems like an oxymoron. As a result, when we encounter the poets of this period, their lines trouble us. They trouble us not because the emotions are unfamiliar to us, but because we feel intimidated by their evocation of bizarre-sounding plants and objects. Many of the words are unfamiliar to the modern reader and form a barrier that hinders the flow of emotion. The words are ancient and unfamiliar, but not unfamiliar because they are ancient. Rather, they are unfamiliar because they describe a landscape that seems to us distant and indescribable. Modern Arabic, including its local dialects, is studded with words older than we can imagine. But these are familiar ancient words. In the Hanging Poems, the barriers arise from how words have fallen out of use, not from the amount of time that has passed. This unfamiliarity gives us pause.

Pausing at the Ruins

As we have modernized, many of us have developed robust lexicons to describe the technological innovations around us, and laid to waste language's lexicon of nature. But as we occupy an increasingly accelerating world, we are in greater need than ever before to reconstitute our relationship to ancient words. Reconstituting our relationship with ancient words means, more than anything, pausing. It means stopping at the word and practicing humility and empathy before it: savoring the word, sitting with it, and acquainting ourselves with it. In this era of scrolling and speed reading, unfamiliar words in the Hanging Poems invite us to read slowly – so slowly that one might say, read meditatively. Reconstituting our relationship with these words then is a constant exercise in pausing generously. It's a skill that we develop between the stanzas of these poems, and carry with us in the world – allowing us to be better readers, critics, friends, and neighbors. When we neglect this skill, we consign ourselves to the petty, the small, and the limited. We bar ourselves from the exuberance of genuine engagement with the words and therefore, the emotions of others. We risk leading a dry, sterile life that is, above all else, profoundly lonely. In light of these consequences, what the Hanging Poems ask of us is minor: they ask us to simply pause and familiarize ourselves with the words.

02

All the poems in this essay were translated by the author with consultation of W. A. Clouston, *Arabian Poetry for English Readers* (London: Darf Publishers, 1986). The Arabic texts are from al-Zawzanī, Ḥusayn ibn Aḥmad, *Sharḥ al-Mu'allaqāt al-sab'* (Damascus: Al-Maktabah al-Umawīyah, 1963).

Pausing is a central theme in the Hanging Poems. Most of the seven poems open with the poet pausing before ruins in the desert, remembering a lost love. The poet encounters these ruins and describes them in minute detail, reflecting on how bygone love can create space for new life. Usually, the poet happens upon ruins inhabited by people long gone. New life has taken root, and the poets relish in their descriptions of melancholy and change. They paint a picture of the desert that is constantly changing; tribes leave their abodes and make way for new flora and fauna. The ruins parallel the poet's lost love, which then creates the space for pausing and reflecting. The pausing elicits a deep emotional reaction from the poet, oftentimes requiring the intervention of his friends to calm him down. The intense emotions that we see later on in the poem arguably arise from that initial pause. I hope that we can mirror that motif of pausing by pausing ourselves before the poems, to gaze at the desert, and allow ourselves to feel what these poets must have felt. We may not see the same ruins that they saw, but the experiences they describe certainly echo ours. Take, for example, Labīd's (550-661 CE) reflection when he encountered the ruins:

دمنٌ تَجَرَّمَ بعدَ عهْدِ أنيسِهَا ◦ حِجَجٌ خَلَوْنَ حَلالُهَا وحَرَامُهَا

رزقَتْ مرابيعَ النُّجومِ وصابَهَا ◦ ودقُ الرَّواعدِ جوْدُهَا فرهامُها

منْ كلِّ سَارِيَةٍ وغادٍ مُدْجِنٍ ◦ وعشيَّةٍ متجاوبٍ إرْزامُهَا

فَعَلا فُروعُ الأَيْهُقَانِ وَأطْفَلَتْ ◦ بالجلهتينِ ظباؤهَا ونعامُها

والعينُ ساكِنةٌ على أطْلائِها ◦ عُوذاً تأجَّلُ بالفضاءِ بِهامُه

01. *Epochs have passed since these ruins were last inhabited, years of profane and sacred months.*

02. *They were blessed with rains that accompany spring's constellations, thundering clouds have pounded raindrops and sprinkled others*

03. *Every rain cloud offered it some rain: those that rain at night (sāriya), those that darken the sky (mudjan), and those evening clouds whose thunder answers one another's calls.*

04. *So the wild arugula has grown, and on both sides of the valley the gazelles and ostriches beget their young,*

05. *The wild cows, wide-eyed new mothers, stand still above their young, while their monthling fawns begin to form herds in the desert... †*

[02]

Labīd's sensitivity to the environment and his reflection on his own condition allow him to see something uplifting: that lost love can make way for new beginnings, that new life can inhabit the very spaces where life once was. The pausing allows him to collect his feelings and to reflect on certain realities that are found in nature and in our own emotional experiences. He contrasts the hard, abandoned ruins with the tender mothers, but the means by which these new herds are developing, is the rain. Labīd freely refers to the clouds according to their shape, their time, and even their sound. The words he uses for these clouds are unfamiliar to many of us today, but they allow us to reflect on the seemingly miraculous experience of overcoming lost love.

03

Antarah ibn Shaddad al-Absi was a poet and knight, famous for his adventures in search of honor and to prove himself worthy of his lover Abla. His poetry records many of his exploits, but he has become the stuff of legend and fairytale as well.

The unfamiliar words are important not because they're practical or useful – but precisely because they are not. They are important because they force us to pause and contemplate. The words force us to slowly parse out the most intimate emotions of men and women from 1400 years ago. This gives us two incredible opportunities: one, to see what they saw. To enter that mysterious
[03] garden with Antarah (525-608 CE),† to lie on the ground with him, probably on our bellies, and to watch in complete stillness as the cricket hums his song. More miraculously, the second opportunity of pausing allows us to viscerally feel what they felt. To get the sense of the delight that Antarah felt as he approached Abla, or to romp across the desert with Ṭarafah and his friends, or to weep over the ruins with Imur' al-Qays.

An unfamiliar word in the Hanging Poem can become the doorway to a deeply familiar feeling. This connection points to the importance of art, and of the word-as-art; that miraculous way in which a word can transport us to new images and imaginations. The Hanging Poems, with their unfamiliar words, give us even more of a chance to connect the word to the landscape to the emotion. This chance is generated from how slowly we must read these poems, how we must labor after each word, struggling to understand and then conjure the image. In that process, that pause, we are given a rare opportunity to pull from our own emotional repository in order to make sense of the words. The sights might be as foreign as the words, but the potential for familiar feelings broadens the longer we pause.

In pausing with these unfamiliar words, we develop two skills. First, we see the marvelous in the mundane. The next time you lean in for a kiss, or go to a concert with some friends (Ṭarafah describes his friends as stars in the night sky, luminous in their musical ecstasy), or bemoan a heartbreak (Imru' al-Qays wept so hard that his sword hilt became wet), or cook for people you love (he slaughtered his best camel to impress his lover's friends), you can rest assured that you are tapping into that wonderful experience of being human. It allows us to make sure the mundane does not become trivial; our everyday interactions and emotions become opportunities to pause, contemplate, and reconnect. And this connection becomes the second gift that the Hanging Poems will give us, if we are patient enough to learn the words of the desert. They allow us to recognize in our daily activities the universal experience of humanity. The tradition – common in many old cultures (and modern ones) of referring to poetry (and to films, stand-up comedies, and plays) – is an opportunity to contextualize our daily life within a larger arc of human experience. In doing so, we're able to cultivate a sense of empathy. We begin to understand that grizzly emotion when Antarah tells us he misses Abla so much that he wants to kiss the swords that cut his flesh, because they shimmered like her smile. And from there, it's only natural to be able to empathize and feel the emotions of our neighbors, colleagues, and perhaps, if we read carefully enough and allow ourselves to feel authentically enough, even our enemies.

The poems give us another important insight; that being authentically personal is the only way to achieve true literary effect. The words of these poets have been memorized, sung, written, and commented upon, for over a millennium and a half. They moisten eyes that have never seen the deserts of the Arabian Peninsula or the various shrubs described. And yet these poets never sought to transcend their immediate clan groups. They sought to be true to themselves and their emotions, to express their experiences frankly and clearly. And for that reason, they still have meaning to us, even if this meaning is clouded behind unfamiliar words. With a bit of effort we can, in fact, feel what they felt. In this world where we may feel forced to choose between parochial identity politics and a flattening globalization, these poets show us that bravely laying out our own emotions is the only way we can invite others to share a moment with us. However, we must offer others the generosity we hope future generations will offer our own: personal but deeply sincere literature. After all, the Arabic word for banquet (*ma'daba*) is derived from *adab,* the Arabic word for literature. Perhaps those ancient Arabs knew that the real banquet, spanning millennia and crossing oceans, offering comfort, respite, and inspiration, could be nothing but a good piece of adab. What I will try to do in the next few paragraphs is to help you settle into your spot at this banquet and to introduce you to a few words that might be strangers today, but that I hope will soon become old friends. These friends, like all good friends, allow us to make sense of the emotions and experiences that we feel and to connect to our everyday encounters (with people, plants, or clouds) within the larger human experience. This ability to connect is, ultimately, our most pressing need as humans today, because it breaks down the callousness that arises from estrangement and alienation.

Ṭarafah's Trees

Our unfamiliarity with desert plants sets up a barrier between us and these poems, but also creates the generative opportunity for pause. Take, for example, some of the most pristine lines of Ṭarafah that swaggering poet:

أَلاَ أَيُّها اللائِمِي أَشهَدُ الوَغى ◊ وَأَنْ أَنْهَل اللَّذَّاتِ هَلْ أَنْتَ مُخْلِدِي
فإِنْ كُنْتَ لاَ تَسْطِيْعُ دَفْعَ مَنِيَّتِي ◊ فَدَعْنِي أُبَادِرُهَا بِمَا مَلَكَتْ يَدِي
وَلَوْلاَ ثَلاثُ هُنَّ مِنْ عَيْشَةِ الفَتَى ◊ وَجَدِّكَ لَمْ أَحْفِلْ مَتَى قَامَ عُوَّدِي
فَمِنْهُنَّ سَبْقِي العَاذِلاتِ بِشَرْبَةٍ ◊ كُمَيْتٍ مَتَى مَا تُعْلَ بِالمَاءِ تُزْبِدِ
وَكَرِّي إِذَا نَادَى المُضَافُ مُجَنَّباً ◊ كَسِيدِ الغَضَا نَبَّهْتَهُ المُتَوَرِّدِ
وتَقْصِيرُ يَوْمِ الدَّجْنِ والدَّجْنُ مُعْجِبٌ ◊ بِبَهْكَنَةٍ تَحْتَ الخِبَاءِ المُعَمَّدِ
كَأَنَّ البُرِيْنَ والدَّمَالِيْجَ عُلِّقَتْ ◊ عَلَى عُشَرٍ أَوْ خِرْوَعٍ لَمْ يُخَضَّدِ

01. *You, who censures me for immersing myself in brawls and pleasures, can you guarantee me immortality for frugality?*

02. *If you cannot to block death's blow to me, then allow me, before it comes, to enjoy the pleasures I still have.*

03. *If not for three pleasures that youth affords, I swear by your own prosperity, I would not care how soon my friends visited my deathbed:*

04. *One, to rise before the censurers awake, and to drink golden wine, sparkling and frothing when cut with water.*

05. *Another, my rush to the aid of a distressed friend, encircled by foes, who calls out to me. I am then as fearsome and determined as a wolf among the ghaḍā trees, startled by the sound of steps, running to quench his thirst at the brook.*

06. *Thirdly, to spend a dark, cloudy day flirting with a beautiful woman of good taste under a tent supported by pillars,—*

07. *A woman whose bracelets and rings seem strung on the stems of ʿushar shrub, or of ricinus, not stripped of their soft leaves.*

Ṭarafah's emotions are relatable, almost modern in their nature: life is for living, and none should stand in one's way. How wonderfully universal are his images; good drink, helping a friend, and pleasant flirtation – these are what make life sufferable. The details he includes are also remarkable: is there not something particularly romantic and cozy (even to us today) about a cloudy day? Or something deeply fulfilling about helping a friend in need? And yet, Ṭarafah's poetry is also brimming with words unfamiliar to our ears. First among them is the word he uses to describe certain women: *bahkana*, meaning a woman who is beautiful and pleasant in conversation and spirit. Abandoned in today's world, the word seems to open the floodgates for new, unfamiliar words. Although in another instance, his references to trees build a distance between us and him – the *ghaḍā*, the *'ushār*, the ricinus. The unfamiliar words cool our ability to feel the emotions he expresses, even though these are emotions we might have felt at a certain point. While glancing at the dictionary or the footnote, the passion seems to fade and a distance grows between us and Ṭarafah.

But this unfamiliarity must not necessarily create distance. The difficulty of these texts lies in the question of what should the modern reader do about the unfamiliarity of the desert's sensory experience, about the anthology of shrubs that Ṭarafah confronts us with. I suppose a reader could do one of two things; either search for them and consider them, or just pass over them completely. What we lose from passing over these words is not enough to lose the spirit of the line. It will take a bit of humility and much care, but I wager that someone could ignore the names and still sense the poetry. However, once we see the fullness of the 'ushar's leaves, or the delicateness of the ricinus leaf, the words build still another dimension. Our slow reading and pausing gives us new insights into what Ṭarafah may have experienced. We realize that he uses the leaves to portray emotions; fullness, wholesomeness, delicateness, elegance, and grace. We move from imagining his cozy conversation on a cloudy day to experiencing it viscerally with him. Ṭarafah's clouds may echo Labīd's – they are omens of blessings to come – but they certainly paint an image to which many of us today relate. He gives us the chance to compare it with an experience of our own, using images that we may have never known existed. The pausing isn't just about reaching for the dictionary: Ṭarafah challenges us to start seeing the poetry in the everyday shrubs that surround us.

On the relationship between love and plants, we must return to Antarah, perhaps one of the most well-known of the pre-Islamic poets. His story is particularly compelling; the son of a black enslaved woman, he struggles to prove himself to his clan and to be worthy of his free-born lover. His lover, Abla, was clearly a woman of exquisite beauty, and Antarah loved her dearly. Yet, his love for her is braided into his love for the landscape of the Arabian Peninsula. Let's examine just one passage:

إذْ تَسْتَبيكَ بِذِي غُرُوبٍ وَاضِحٍ ◊ عَذْبٍ مُقبَّلُهُ لِذيذِ المَطْعمِ
وكَأَنَّ فَأْرَةَ تاجِرٍ بِقَسيمَةٍ ◊ سَبَقتْ عَوارِضَها إليْكَ مِنَ الفَمِ
أوْ رَوْضَةً أُنُفاً تَضَمَّنَ نَبْتَها ◊ غَيْثٌ قليلُ الدِّمْنِ لَيْسَ بِمُعْلَمِ
جادَتْ عَلَيْهِ كُلُّ بِكرٍ حُرَّةٍ ◊ فَتَرَكْنَ كُلَّ قَرارَةٍ كالدِّرهَمِ
سَحًّا وتَسْكاباً فَكُلَّ عَشِيَّةٍ ◊ يَجْري عَلَيْها الماءُ لَمْ يَتَصَرَّمِ
وَخَلا الذُّبابَ بِها فَلَيْسَ بِبارِحٍ ◊ غَرِداً كَفِعْلِ الشَّارِبِ المُتَرَنِّمِ
هَزِجاً يَحُكُّ ذِراعَهُ بِذِراعِهِ ◊ قَدْحَ المَكَبِّ على الزِّنادِ الأَجْذَمِ

01. *She captivates you with a mouth of bright white teeth, a sweet place for kissing, delicious to the taste.*

02. *She gazes with the two eyes of a tender but mature gazelle, unparalleled in beauty. Moving towards her mouth is like approaching a merchant's musk bag in a case of perfume.*

03. *Her mouth is a small garden, with bright herbage guaranteed by rain. Unsoiled, untrodden.*

04. *Watered by the first showers of the rain cloud, leaving behind a shimmering puddle like a silver dirham*

05. *Flowing and pouring; water flows through it every evening, and is never cut off from it.*

06. *The cricket alone enjoys the garden, and did not cease humming like a jolly drunkard;*

07. *Humming, he rubs one foreleg against the other, like a crippled man bent on the flint stone and striking it.*

In his obsession, Antarah seems to be moving freely between Abla and nature. His delight at kissing her evokes in him the image of a beautiful garden, not vice versa. The precision and care that the poet must have taken to observe a cricket and report back to us shows not only his meticulous eye, but the interconnectedness of experience. The melancholy cricket transitions us, in the poem, to the sadness that Antarah felt about being away from his beloved – he too, was a crippled man desperately struggling for a spark of light.

The feelings; excitement, delight, a sense of being immensely lucky, and yet profoundly unlucky, are all clear, legible emotions. Nonetheless, the intensity of the emotion, the giddiness of it all, is unfortunately lost to the modern reader. After all, your average speaker of modern Arabic today cannot parse out the specific terminology that Antarah uses to describe the regular rain patterns that keep this garden green, or the words he uses to describe the water, *saḥḥ* and *tiskāb,* which appear redundant at first. The repetition of two words that mean the same thing is oftentimes seen as a hallmark of pre-modern poetry. However, if we pause, we can try to understand what Antarah is trying to tell us. The garden is lush because its waters flow appropriately, neither a victim of torrential rain or desiccation. Sometimes the water flows, and sometimes it seems poured into the garden directly by a miraculous hand. The idea of a mysterious garden is familiar, but we have lost the sensitivity to language that connects us to Antarah's description. The miraculousness of Abla's lips; inviting, fresh, beautiful, offering solace and coolness, is not difficult to relate to. However, it may be difficult to discern from the language because so few of us have experienced entering a well-watered garden after days of desert travel. The unfamiliarity of the words, like the terms Antarah uses to describe the flint (*zinād*), might have us just skip over the passage. But pausing long enough to understand gives us the wonderful opportunity to see how this legendary warrior was enough of a romantic to relate to a tiny cricket in a garden.

The desert was not all romance and love, and the flora and fauna of the desert did not only evoke love in the poets but other noble attributes as well. Imru' al-Qays (c. 501–544 CE), who had his fair share of romance, describes to us the difficulty of passing nights without his lover:

تَسَلَّتْ عَمَايَاتُ الرِّجَالِ عَنْ الصِّبَا ◊ وَلَيْسَ فُؤَادِي عَنْ هَوَاكِ بِمُنْسَلِ
أَلاَ رُبَّ خَصْمٍ فِيْكِ أَلْوَى رَدَدْتُهُ ◊ نَصِيْحٍ عَلَى تَعذَالِهِ غَيْرِ مُؤْتَلِ
وَلَيْلٍ كَمَوْجِ البَحْرِ أَرْخَى سُدُوْلَهُ ◊ عَلَيَّ بِأَنْوَاعِ الهُمُوْمِ لِيَبْتَلِي
فَقُلْتُ لَهُ لَمَّا تَمَطَّى بِصُلْبِهِ ◊ وَأَرْدَفَ أَعْجَازًا وَنَاءَ بِكَلْكَلِ
أَلاَ أَيُّهَا اللَّيْلُ الطَّوِيْلُ أَلاَ انْجَلِي ◊ بِصُبْحٍ، وَمَا الإِصْبَاحُ مِنِكَ بِأَمْثَلِ
فَيَا لَكَ مَنْ لَيْلٍ كَأَنَّ نُجُومَهُ ◊ بِكُلِّ مُغَارِ الفَتْلِ شُدَّتْ بِيَذْبُلِ
كَأَنَّ الثُّرَيَّا عُلِّقَتْ فِي مَصَامِهَا ◊ بِأَمْرَاسِ كَتَّانٍ إِلَى صُمِّ جَنْدَلِ
وَوَادٍ كَجَوْفِ العَيرِ قَفْرٍ قَطَعْتُهُ ◊ بِهِ الذِّئْبُ يَعْوِي كَالخَلِيعِ المُعَيَّلِ
فَقُلْتُ لَهُ لَمَّا عَوَى إِنَّ شَأْنَنَا ◊ قَلِيلُ الغِنَى إِنْ كُنْتَ لَمَّا تَمَوَّلِ
كِلانَا إِذَا مَا نَالَ شَيْئًا أَفَاتَهُ ◊ وَمَنْ يَحْتَرِثْ حَرْثِي وَحَرْثَكَ يُهْزَلِ

01. *Men abandon their follies with youth, but my heart does not cease to love you.*

02. *Many jealous counselors have warned me of the disaster of your love, but I turned away from all of them.*

03. *Many a night has lowered its curtains around me while in agony, It engulfed me like a sea wave, to inflict me with anguish.*

04. *I said to the night, as his huge bulk plodded over me, His breast, his loins, his rear weighed on me and then passed into the distance,*

05. *"Oh long night, dawn will come, but will be no brighter without my beloved.*

06. *How strange you are, with stars hanging as by ropes of hemp to a solid rock."*

07. *At other times, I have filled the leather water-bag of my people and entered the desert,*

08. *And trod its empty wastes while the wolf howled like a gambler whose family starves.*

09. *I said to the wolf, "You gather as little wealth, as little prosperity as I.*

10. *What either of us gains he gives away. So do we both remain emaciated."*

04

Al-Ṭā'ī, Ḥabīb ibn Aws, *Dīwān Abī Tammām*, (Cairo: Muḥammad Alī Ṣubeih Printers, 1942) 216-217.

05

Friedrich Nietzsche, *The Dawn: Thoughts on the Prejudices of Morality*. Preface (to the Second Edition, 1887).

The melancholy tone of the poetry is almost unbearable. The lovesick insomniac, disembodied, watching the night pass, bitter even at the brightness of the stars, is as timeless as any literary figure. Yet, Imru' al-Qays still confronts us with the desert; the desert still is a space teaming with life for him. The wolf – at once feared and admired by the shepherd-nomad – is Imru' al-Qays' companion, to which our poet relates. Imru' al-Qays too is a howling wolf who despite his suffering is still generous. The desert in its aridity then is an opportunity to express the virtues that the poets found grand and noble: generosity, caring for kin, and bravery. These virtues are recorded and passed down in poetry. After all, Abū Tammām (c. 807–845 CE), the compiler of the first anthology of Arabic poetry, wrote that "Were it not for the virtues set out by poetry, those seeking greatness would never know whence to achieve noble traits." † These virtues were expressed not only [04]
in the desert, but through the desert.
The ability to relate, whether to the wolf or to the cricket, seems to be an important exercise to our poets. The fauna of the desert is deeply familiar to them, and through pausing, the poets are able to build beautiful connections between nature and the human experience. Our task is far simpler; we just need to pause long enough to build a connection with these poets. They will take us on their journey through the desert, and expand our ability to empathize and relate. As the great litterateur Ṭaha Ḥussein wrote in many op-eds throughout the 1920s, these poems shouldn't inspire us to write about the past or the desert. Rather, they should inspire us to gaze at the world with a more contemplative, discerning, and loving eye.

Cultivating Habits of Pausing

Before becoming a philosopher, Friedrich Nietzche was a philologist, a "lover of words," as Greek etymology tells us. At a time when modernity was just beginning to industrialize, he offered a great reason for pausing before words: "For philology is that venerable art which demands of its votaries one thing above all: to go aside, to take time, to become still, to become slow – it is a goldsmith's art and connoisseurship of the word which has nothing but delicate, cautious work to do and achieves nothing if it does not achieve it Lento." † Today, [05] this ability to pause and to savor, to truly love the word, is a radical personal and social act. In an era where we rush (or scroll) through life, and dismiss the unfamiliar – or more tragically, declare an identitarian inability to understand it – the Hanging Poems give us the opportunity to pause and reorient ourselves. At first blush, this appears to be an exercise in reading, and it is, initially. But it has the potential to form us into more thoughtful, caring people.

Ultimately, our profound need today for literature, in general, and for the Hanging Poems, in particular, is not didactic or educational in the narrow sense of the term. Instead, they force us to pause, they remind us that what truly matters to us today and to humans since time immemorial has been one and the same: love, friendship, contemplation, and kindness. Whether the unfamiliar words in the Hanging Poems stick in our minds is of very little consequence. What really matters is that we reach out and make the effort to understand. The generative aspect of pausing before words is not lexical, but ethical.

I began this piece by pointing to how in Arabic, the word for literature and the word for banquet share a lexical root. The original, ancient association was probably based on ideas of generosity and sharing. But perhaps we can generate a new association for our modern times: that of pausing. Perhaps what banquets and literature have in common is that both are an invitation for us to pause, put everything down, and indulge. Not everything will be familiar whether in literature or on the table, but that makes things only more exciting. We meet new people, try new things, and savor new words, only to recognize just how much we have in common. And through the conversation, the timidity, the concentration, the occasional glance at a dictionary, and the pause, we create the opportunity for a more tender world to be born.

Acknowledgments

I would like to thank Tim Barbera and Majid Dohan, who read and commented on early drafts of this essay. The guidance of Faysal Tabbarah and Meitha Almazrooei has been invaluable. This paper is to a large part inspired by *Wednesday Chats*, a series of op-eds on literary criticism published by the Egyptian intellectual Taha Hussein in the early 1920s. His vision for a generative aesthetic relationship with the past has been deeply formative.

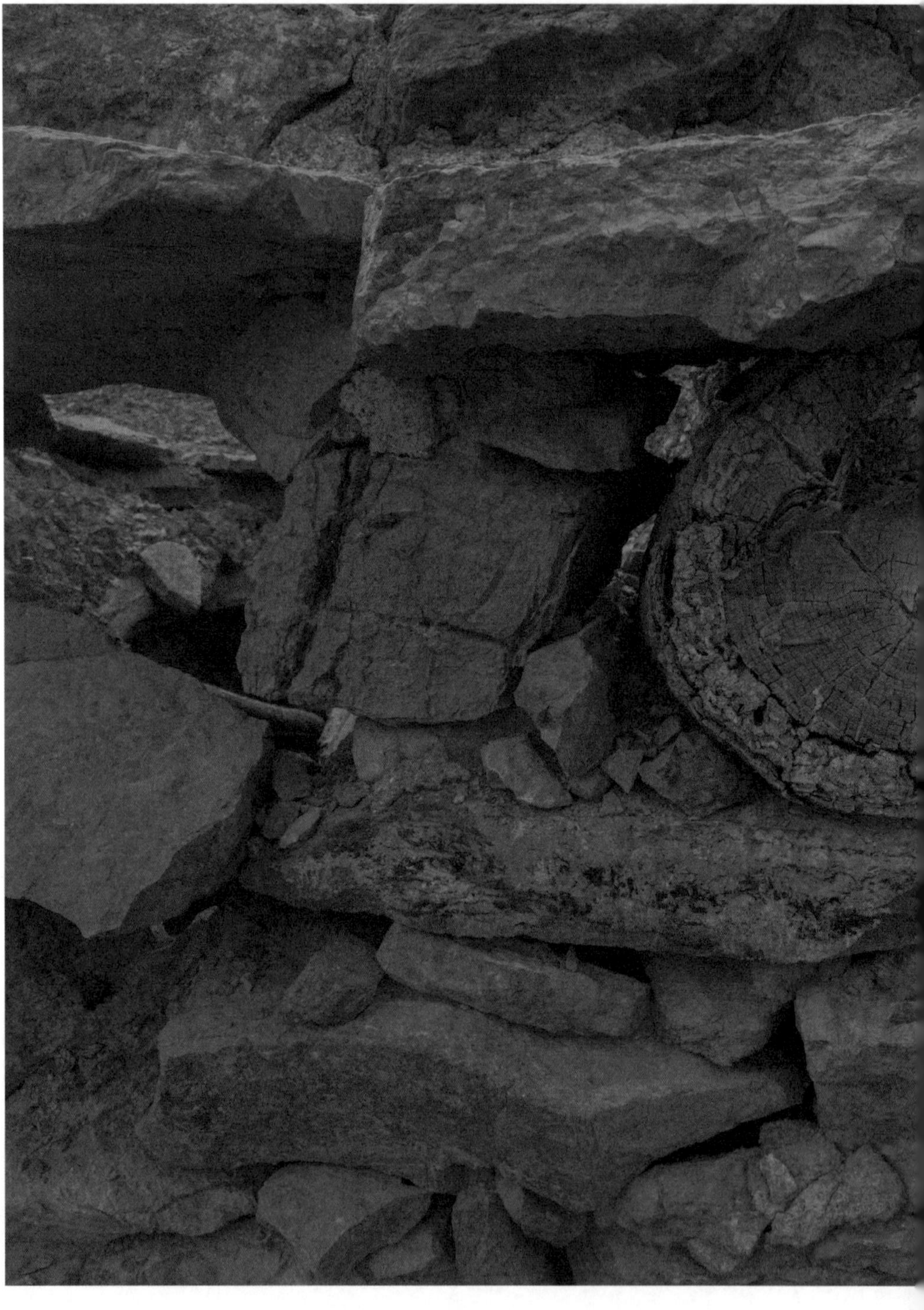

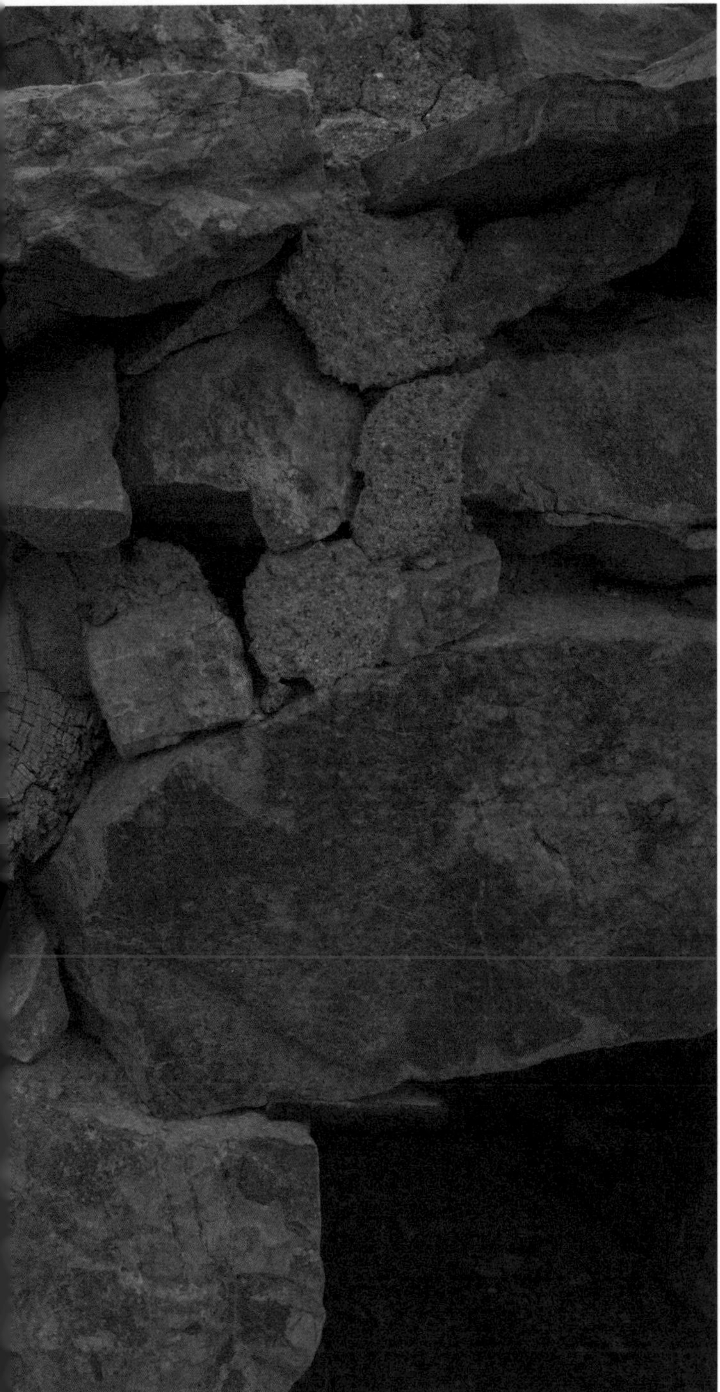

A detail of timber beams in a stone house. Photo by Faysal Tabbarah.

Ahmad Makia

Wanderlust, Phantom Eyes, Pierced Realities: Time-Traveling in Shibh Al Jazira Al Arabiya

The nexus of vision and travel was paramount for the birth of monotheistic culture
[01] and philosophy in *Shibh Al Jazira Al Arabiya.* † Some of the earliest forms of social contact and cultural connectivity were propelled by human movement, exploration, and nomadism across the environmental landscapes of the region. The persistent threat of dehydration and starvation encouraged inhabitants to travel through the landscapes in search of pockets of wilderness and microclimates, such as oases, mangroves, plantations, and wadis. Many people stumbled on and discovered pockets that have come to constitute the region's historic areas of human settlement rather than the more recent port and oil cities.

01

Shibh Al Jazira Al Arabiya is the Arabic term for the Arabian Peninsula.

The performative act of walking, journeying, and exploring natural surroundings contributed to the particularities of spiritual culture in Shibh Al Jazira Al Arabiya, namely its own self-generated version of monotheism. Derived from the navigation and roaming of the uniform and indistinguishable desert topography came philosophies on how this land effectively mirrors the mind and provides a leap towards an unseen world, perhaps akin to similar contemporary imaginations of voids, simulacra, and hyperreality. Bearing in mind as well that sand is a shifting, migratory, and microscopic environmental matter which doesn't absorb human trails or paths, as the forest or jungle landscape. Rather than conceiving Shibh Al Jazira Al Arabiya as a literal desert, which is arid, sandy, and lifeless, it was augmented to become a portal and mediation of an otherworldly universe. In it lies a matrix, beyond the sensed and visible, leading its pursuer to a state of heightened consciousness and euphoria. From this environment, visions came of the molecular, atomic, geometric, and the unknown which can be sensed within the literal, material world.

Sensing the unseen through the traversing of the desert might have also been enhanced by phenomena such as mirages. This optical illusion, in which the brain thinks it sees water, caused desert travelers to feel like they are hallucinating, since a mirage is witnessed yet has no shape, form, or color. Additionally, auditory hallucinations are known to be more common while traveling deep in the desert, given that its interiors have no geographic barriers or other competing noises. Across several indigenous spiritual cultures, the desert is said to transmit a sound which is whole, robust, and absolutely still. This landscape is conceived as a mystical plane that channels non-subjective phantom voices by using human bodies as a vessel. Rather than dissonance between the body and its surroundings, the act of crossing and traveling across Shibh Al Jazira Al Arabiya enabled feelings of oneness and immersion with the immaterial and non-superficial world. In the region, these travels and experiences contributed to the unified, monotheistic belief system of Islam.

The navigation of deserts also functioned as a simultaneous mapping between the surface of the land and the constellation of the sky, revealing to travelers the interconnections between the elements of shared environments and spaces. The region's early cultural references emphasized how collectivity is found in the human and the singular; how oneness is found in expressions of multiplicity and pluralism. Therefore, intellectual and spiritual cultures of early monotheism in the region encouraged missionaries to convert polytheistic tribes and communities with divergent belief practices to come together under the moniker of collectivity and fraternity in expressions and rituals of oneness.

As a cultural and visual starting point, much of the region's culture is transformed to imagine the world which is unseen through the phantasmagoria of the non-figurative, innovating depictions of entropy, infinity, and the cosmic. Unlike the scenic profusion of Hindu, Buddhist, and Christian religions with landscape and human representation, Islam proposed aniconism, a visual and aesthetic culture culled from the figuration of immediate space and lived sensation.

The evolution of monotheistic culture in Shibh Al Jazira Al Arabiya further emphasized the role of the "unseen" and the non-subjective, as opposed to its predecessors. Ushered in with the growth of Islam in the region, locally-generated knowledge questioned the function of the eye and its attendant role in human perception, supplanting it with interpretive phantom and wandering-like qualities. Since the material world is superficial and does not fully comprehend immateriality, vision should always be enhanced, contextualized, and "phantom-ized." What the eye perceives is not rational or evident but a canvas for over-representational and hyper-stitious images, where superstitions can become lived realities. Hence, the "evil eye" motif affirms that a wandering or desiring eye can bring malice and misfortune to not only the one being eyed, but the owner of the eye as well. Vision, in essence, is an impression of the world outside what is perceived as concrete and material.

Thoughts, dreams, and desires can transform into reality, as eyes are potent neurological transmitters, which power the imagination, encouraging manifestations. Given human bias and desire, the eye distorts a context to challenge a believer in understanding distinctions and polarities of the interior and exterior. The emergent and hybrid spaces between them are where both faith and oneness with God are found. It is in this space where faith is practiced, where one time-travels outside of the present, outside of the material world which surrounds them, and enters a world where one can access infinite wisdom and strength.

The philosophical role of what lies outside the eye in the spiritual culture of Shibh Al Jazira Al Arabiya became more technical and explanatory during the Abbasid era. Ibn al-Haytham, a well-regarded innovator, polymath, and author of *The Book of Optics*, explained that vision is a process in which light bounces from an object to the eye and thereby, creates what humans sense or interpret as vision. Ibn al-Haytham was the first to point out that vision occurs in the brain rather than at the surface of the eye and emphasized how imagination and subjectivity play a critical role in the formation of images. At the time of his theory on optics and human perception, the Islamic Empire was flourishing. Its commercial and spiritual links grew across Asia and Africa bridging new encounters with other peoples, and new thinking emerged about what is universal and how humans manifest across the world through the powers of vision and ideation. What had been previously uncharted about the landscape further amplified thinking and reasoning around human vision through performances of travel and navigation.

Less commonly known about Ibn al-Haytham is his invention of the camera obscura (darkened chamber), also known as the pinhole camera. With this invention, he presented an allegorical, yet material manifestation, of the world which lies outside the human and what they see. Building on existing ontologies from Shibh Al Jazira Al Arabiya, the pinhole architecture of the camera obscura represents an inverse of a received image. By creating a darkened chamber with a small pinhole, an optical phenomenon happens where the pinhole projects the outside into the chamber but as a reversed image. A widely used philosophical metaphor for human perception and the creation of images, Ibn al-Haytham's discovery upturned existing ideas about how light, rather than being human-centered, in fact, comes from external sources to illuminate the objects and affects of the world. This light effect not only revolutionized a technical shift, but enabled practices and thought that made it possible to look and imagine, in a different way, narrative-izing the transposed image.

A few centuries after Ibn al-Haytham, the process of transposition became embodied, where travel and wander, especially in regions like Shibh Al Jazira Al Arabiya, became disruptive to the status quo. This was especially true in Europe at the twilight of the Industrial Revolution and Age of Enlightenment. Increased narratives of a pending "clash of civilizations," – given unprecedented

02

Ian Almond, *History of Islam in German Thought* (New York: Routledge, 2010), 31.

03

Brycchan Carey, *British Abolitionism and the Rhetoric of Sensibility* (New York: Palgrave Macmillan, 2005). Also see examples by Roger Casement and Anne Mellor.

internationalization and industrialization via European colonial expansion as well as growing monopolization and centralization of power in Europe after the medieval period - called for a new dialogical relationship with other cultures. Owing to the setup of the binary of East vs West, or Orient vs Occident, belief systems and cultural particularities were interrogated and represented to create distinctions between shifting power dynamics. A convenient example is perhaps Emmanuel Kant's *On a Newly Raised Noble Tone of Philosophy* (1798) in which he declares that "The Arab, or Mongol, nurtures contempt for the town-dweller, and deems himself noble in comparison with him, as wandering about in the desert with one's horses and sheep is more entertainment than work."† Behind Kant's description of the Arab [02]
or Mongol wandering without working is his opposing Protestant postulate of hard work. These distinctions are profound in how self-created images of the democratic and industrial West versus the unproductive and unsettled East were envisioned, through the setup of opposing polarities in human experience and social development.

The distinctive element of the European traveler, as echoed by Kant, was that it conceived its ethos as "sensible" and philanthropic rather than frivolous and aimless as performed by the Arab or Mongol. At the time, it was common in Europe and Britain to travel to the colonies not as "colonizer," but so as to study the relationship between the colonizer and colonized, and develop a space of empathy and reflection about these dynamics, especially as the slavery abolition movement had gripped the American continent. Expeditious traveling contributed to the birth of humanism and universalism in their modern interpretations, and new cultures around human rights. Here sensibility began to justify and inspire European travel. Rather than looting and extracting resources, these travels were to learn from the other, safeguard their memories and heritage, learn their customs and languages, and apologize for their slavery. Their "European" authored work was that of a spectator and observer, reinforcing an idealized image of the knowledge-based European laborer.† [03]

However, these histories of binary "civilization clashes" of spirit and intellect, are not uniform. Rather, some thinkers found the properties of Arabian-inspired immaterialism and wanderlust to be of use, especially as a critique of Protestant ethics and rational or categorical practices of a colonial West. The French Revolution, an alleged hallmark of Western advance, finds its early inspirations in literature like *Lettres Persanes (Persian Letters)* penned by Montesquieu. A major cultural figure of Bourbon nobility, Montesquieu posed as the voice of two Persian emissaries living on the grounds of Versailles in France and observing the inhabitants' behaviors. The book was a fictional epistolary exchange by the emissaries to their hometown of Isfahan, in which they offered staged impressions and critical readings of French society. Through Montesquieu's method of phantom authorship – reinforced by the publishing of *Persian Letters* via the fictional house of Pierre Marteau – the book was banned for what the monarchy considered to be its anti-French attitude. Yet, the novel was extremely successful and popular with multiple editions published during this time.

What the publication of the book revealed, especially with its successful reception, is that there existed a public desire to displace the instituted and material character – imagined by figures such as Kant – and look to the "other" for judgment and analysis on its own condition. Especially important to note is that the author, by taking on the contemplative character of a Persian wanderer and observer, did not simply support caricatures of a perceived Oriental culture but harked back to the self-enclosed culture and its articulations of identity. The characters were perceived to have access and vision to knowledge unknown to others, mainly those of inherited French subjectivity.

Moreover, these cultures of critique through phantom authorship did not only deconstruct idealized images of Europeans, they also provided new spaces for other social binaries, such as gender. After the tragic loss of her family at the age of 20, Isabelle Eberhardt (1877–1904) moved to Algeria and traveled extensively across the territories, documenting them in her journals. A Swiss explorer, intellectual, feminist, and polymath, she even transformed herself and took on a new identity as Si Mohammed Saadi of the Qadriyya order in Algeria, a Sufi monastery reserved for men only. Eberhardt's conversion was an exception given her impressive knowledge of the faith and renouncement of accessible institutional subjectivity. Rather than settling in Europe, she opted for a nomadic existence in the deserts of Algeria as a living manifestation of her anti-colonial attitude towards French rule in North Africa and empathy with the oppression of the Tuareg people. Her conversion revealed a contempt for the status quo and privileged the monotheistic, Arabian-landscape-inspired lifestyle.

04

Amin Maalouf, *The Crusades Through Arab Eyes* (London: Saqi Books, 2006).

Another example is Virginia Woolf's seminal *Orlando* (1928). The novel projects the euphoria of travel, escapism, and transformation of the eponymous character by narrating situations, experiences, and encounters in the Islamic world. When the main character Orlando visits Constantinople, the city is described as a mystical place that is covered in mist, echoing the effects of mirages that blur the seen/concrete and hidden/intangible. Woolf selects Constantinople as a critical place where Orlando's new and manifesting identities begin to unravel which deliberately reveals how her own native English is perceived as inimical to the emergence of subjectivity.

Eberhardt, Woolf, and Montesquieu are all major figures of the Western art canon, especially as contributors to the linear progress of its human rights-based frameworks and cultures of emancipation. However, figures like them, and other Arabian and Oriental crossing figures, such as Gertrude Bell and Wilfred Thesiger, are coming under scrutiny today given contemporary practices of decolonization and cultural recovery. Centered around examples such as the Saidian discourse of Orientalism, popular cultural practices today support the deconstruction of major Euro and Anglo-centric culture which adopts non-Western and Eastern spirituality, as identity or artifact. Some claim that this knowledge is a result of how the imperial West remakes culture in its own vision to support practices of possession and extraction, while reiterating its superiority through a binary logic of othering.

However, time-traveling and cultural adoption aren't exclusive to Western colonialism and expansionism. *The Crusades Through Arab Eyes* (1983) by Amin Maalouf, an intellectual and "native" to the region, adopts a vision of the Arabs during the Crusades, as an outsider or phantom author.† Attempting to not rewrite history but transpose it, [04]
his methodology of "Arab Eyes" does not conflict with Woolf's own literary methods, in which critical thinking is proposed through the adoption of what lies outside the status quo. Major figures of Islamic modernism, such as Jamal al-Din al-Afghani and Muhammad Abdo,

looked to enhance and refine their faith as well as subjectivity by adoptive practices and cultural mutations. Their version of modernization acknowledged the need for emulating the technological, scientific, and legal achievements of the West as a means to resist colonial exploitation. Rather than only contextualizing themselves as inferior and subjects of Orientalism, they sought to integrate a dynamic and modern understanding of enlightened "European-made" philosophies with their own social codes, visions, and understanding.

05

Malcolm X with Alex Hayley, *The Autobiography of Malcolm X* (New York: Grove Press, 1965), 388-389.

Time-traveling through Islamic Arabia, as it were, provides new visions, cultural effects, and critical questioning of what lies beneath the "material surface." Exemplifying this confluence and diffusion of polarities is Malcolm X. A major figure in Black America's civil rights movement, he traveled to Egypt, Lebanon, Saudi Arabia, Nigeria, Ghana, Morocco, and Algeria in 1974. His time in the region, especially in Makkah, had a profound impact on his political thinking and career. While en route, he converted to Islam and renamed himself Hajj Malik Al Shabazz, claiming to have found a new sense of completeness and unification in the human figure. He also found a new departure from what he had been preaching in the United States: rallying for Black separatism and demonization of the white race. Prior to his time in Shibh Al Jazira Al Arabiya, he understood them to be "the earth's most explosive and pernicious evil is racism, the inability of God's creatures to live as One." It was during his pilgrimage from Jeddah to Makkah, he discovered "... [people] were hugging and embracing. They were of all complexions, the whole atmosphere was of warmth and friendliness. The feeling hit me that there really wasn't any color problem here. The effect was as though I
[05] had just stepped out of a prison."†

Fast-forward to the Cultural War era in the early 1990s and neoliberal globalism after modernity and postcolonialism, the navigation of the region's landscapes was once again a prime field site for the rise of new philosophies. In 1990, Jean Baudrillard published three essays in France's *Le Monde*, to describe a new turn in global visual culture as mediated images from the Kuwait invasion started to populate the world through constant live-streaming. Being the literal ground on which early thoughts on media domination, landscape militarization, and mediated surveillance emerged, Baudrillard questioned the tactics of staging troops and frontlines as a means

06

Jean Baudrillard, *The Gulf War Did Not Take Place* (Australia: Power Publications, 1995).

to record and transmit images of unknown landscapes. His critique is that the staging of war and the literal experience of it, have come to dissolve into one another. Published later as *The Gulf War Did Not Take Place* (1991), he questioned the superficiality of images and the mediation of real-time, outside time, or of what's true and what's imagined, similarly echoing and reiterating what early pioneers and wanderers of Shibh Al Jazira Al Arabiya's environs relayed back to their communities.† [06]
In the discussion of the power of the image, the constant sensing and monitoring of the region's landscapes enabled a new discourse on what's become a dominant trend in the role of the hyper-visual, simulation, and speculative in image-making.

When exploring the history of human-landscape engagements in Shibh Al Jazira Al Arabiya, the practitioners mirror its philosophy: hybrid and in-between, cognizant of the limitations and superficiality of their surroundings, yet finding access and foresight into "bigger truths" through experiencing and wandering the landscapes of Shibh Al Jazira Al Arabiya. Together the constellation of trends and movements proposed here oppose conceptions of time-traveling as a technology that allows a human to migrate and experience time, not as fact or evidence, or an exact representation of how things were, or are, or can be. Rather, it is to question what's present and inherited, and what's beyond the surface as a portal to another spiritual world. From deep pasts to present realities, the behavior and attitudes towards the region's landscape have played a significant role in this experience of an outside non-place, where expressions of polarity and binary are rendered moot.

Many of the concepts shared here from traveler and wanderer to superficiality of the image and desert mirage are all associated with the contemporary built world of today's post-oil Arabian Gulf and Peninsula region. Instead, this constellation proposes adventure, ambiguity, and amorphousness as critical practices in the development of global intellect and critical thought.

Alia Al-Sabi

An Ode to Suhail

Not too long ago on a ferry ride going to Rockaway Beach in Queens with a view of the Manhattan skyline, a Colombian friend remarked on what it was like to grow up in Bogotá, where the Monserrate Mountain dominates the cityscape at an altitude of about 3,000 meters above sea level. She said that being in the constant proximity of such a towering natural landmark was humbling in ways New Yorkers would probably never understand, not with the island's buildings crowding the sky like giant rods protruding from the base of a mega construction site. I thought about this as I gazed upon Al Hajar Mountains on a hillside in Ras Al Khaimah one breezy afternoon in December 2022. As a long-term resident of Sharjah, where the sea gently beckons as it stretches out into the wide horizon, I wondered what it must be like to live amidst a rocky terrain that lines your vision everywhere you turn. I sat in silence to take in the sounds: the low hum of buzzing flies, faint sounds of construction in the distance, the scribble of my pen jotting down notes, and the wind. Far was the hustle and bustle of the streets in the cities less than a two hour drive from where I sat. Mountain lore is rife with stories of contemplation, divine in nature or otherwise, and I found myself in a quiet moment of sheer presence thinking about the state of suspension that sitting on a hillside can evoke. A little bit of ground at an altitude above ground. Between land and sky is an invitation to confront the inherent magnitude of the landscape that surrounds us, and how it inhabits our subconscious mind even as we think of it as a space that we, primarily, inhabit.

What started as an open foray into the agricultural lands and the mountains of the eastern region with fellow researchers along a predesignated route marked on google maps, led me down a rabbit hole of research that was sporadic and aimless at first. I looked for material on agricultural trends and forecasts in the region, and the threats and challenges facing farmers due to climate change. And this is how I learned about Al Duroor Calendar, an ancient calendar in the Arabian Peninsula used mainly by farmers, seafarers, and desert dwellers to navigate time, space, and the changing seasons, which is still updated annually today. The origins of this calendar are unclear. It is said that the Arab navigator Ahmad ibn Majid allegedly referred to it as far
[01] back as 500 years ago†

01

An Aramco article mentions Ahmad ibn Majid's usage of the Persian Yazdegerd Calendar, which doesn't quite correspond to the timeline.

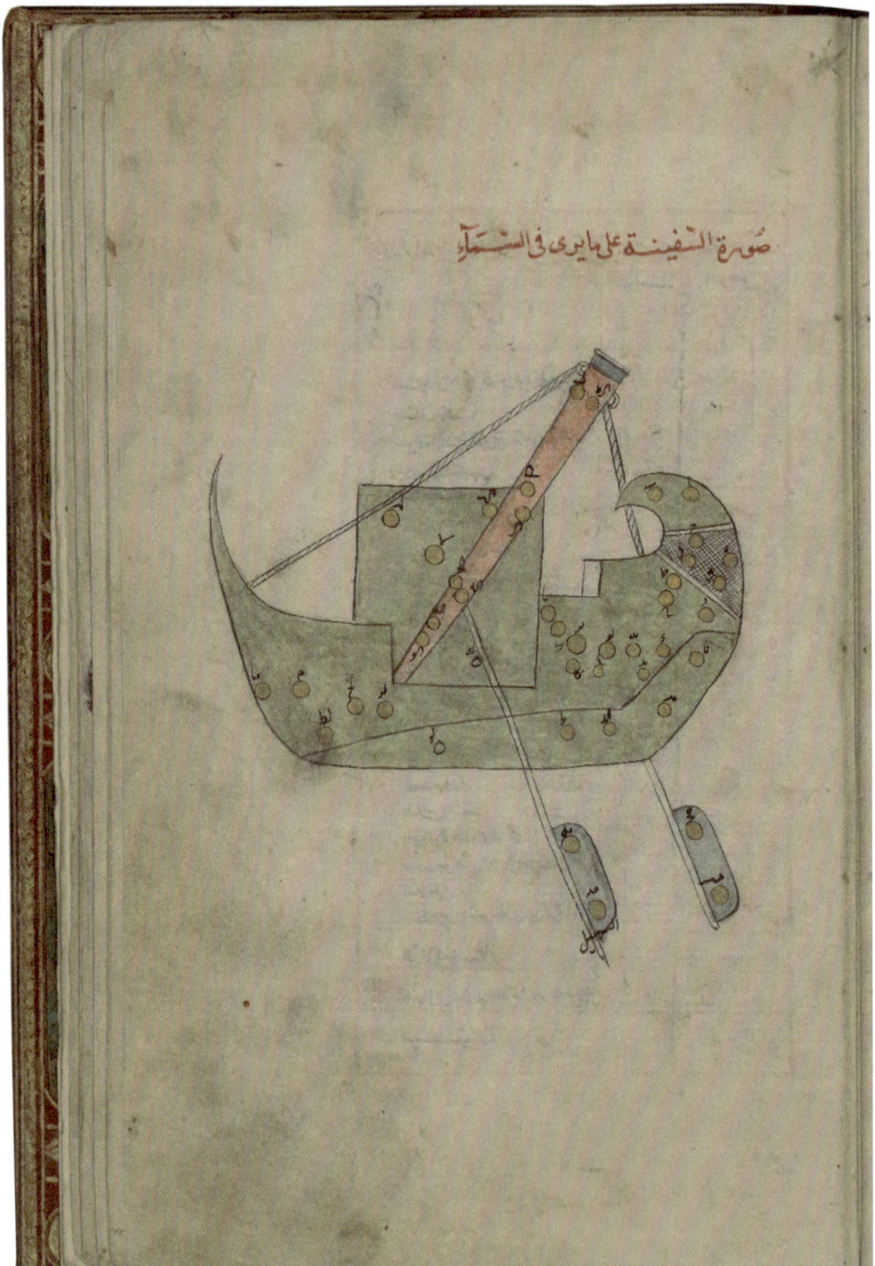
صورة السفينة على ما يرى في السماء

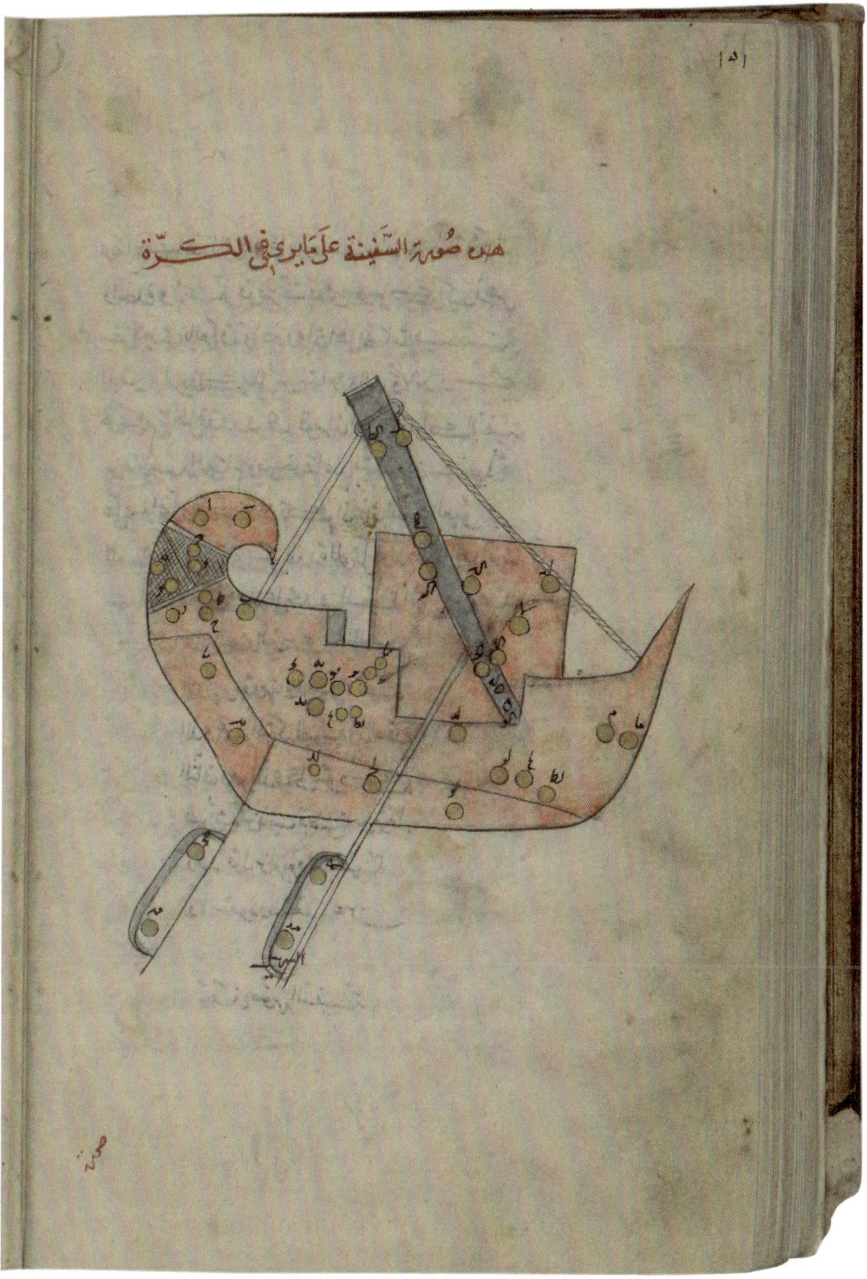

fig. (001) 13th-century Islamic manuscript illustration from *Suwar Al-kawakib* (1417) of the constellation of Argo Navis, showing Suheil at the tip of the oar. The constellation is shown as mirror images to show it both as it appears on a celestial globe, and as it appears in the night sky. This work was originally created around 964CE by the tenth-century Persian Islamic astronomer 'Abd al-Rahman al-Sufi. Courtesy of Bibliothèque nationale de France.

Still today, every year, in the last two weeks of August, a group of Emiratis will scope the night sky for the Suhail star, also known as Canopus, whose first sighting just before the break of dawn will signal the beginning of Al Duroor, or what they call the Suhaili Year.

The Suhaili Year is a 365-day calendar divided into four sections representing four seasons. The first 100 days are the autumn period called *al asfari* (الأصفري), or when the leaves turn yellow, followed by 100 days of winter, then 100 days of spring-summer (the period between April and June of a moderate summer), and finally, 60 days of extreme summer known as *al qaith* (القيظ). The last five days are known as *al masareeq* (المساريق), or the stolen days, which are meant to account for unpredictable or turbulent weather. To break it down further, each group of 100 days on the calendar consists of 10 sets of 10 days, with each set of 10 called *al dur*, the singular form of *al duroor*. There's more to this calendar than this blunt account of its temporal cycle and relevance for navigation and agriculture before the advent of technology. Its significance in Emirati lore and even the language of the elders is what compelled me to dig further. Account after account of Al Duroor Calendar referenced the multitude of ways in which the star, Suhail, occupies a large space in pre-modern Arabic poetry and literature, and the various mountain, desert, and sea cultures in the region for millennia.

سورة النّحل ١٦

وَبِالنَّجْمِ هُمْ يَهْتَدُونَ...

"and by the star[s] they [man] will be guided..." † [02]

For the Arabs, Suhail was like a celestial companion guiding matters of their night and day. The second-brightest star† in the sky [03] after Sirius (الشِّعْرَىٰ, mentioned in the Quran 54:49), Suhail is about 310 light-years away from Earth and is invisible from most northern locations, never rising above the horizon for observers north of the latitude 37° 18' N. For those in the southern hemisphere, however, it represents a southern pole that was used for navigation and predicting changes in the weather for centuries. The Andalusian philosopher Ibn Rushd (also known as Averroes) is said to have

02

Quran XVI.16.

03

It is worth noting that Suhail, as in the star Canopus, is not the only instance where the name Suhail appears. There are three other bright stars that share the name. Lambda Velorum, now officially named Suhail by the International Astronomical Union, was traditionally called السهيل الوزن where الوزن means "weight." The name was mentioned by the tenth-century Persian astronomer Al-Sufi, who referred to the star's rising with difficulty from the horizon. Gamma Velorum was traditionally known as السهيل المحلف or Suhail the Oath-Taker; and then Zeta Puppis was traditionally known as Suhail Hadar سهيل هدار.

traveled to Marrakesh to observe this star in 1153 CE, as it was imperceptible from Córdoba in the Iberian Peninsula. For Ibn Rushd, the different latitudes that informed various visibility points were proof of the sphericity of the Earth, an argument posited by Aristotle
[04] before him. † Almost 600 years before that, the Arabs who traveled from the Arabian Peninsula to places like Khorasan, wrote poetry lamenting the absence of Suhail in their night skies. In one instance, Malek bin Al Raib Al Tamimi, a Najdi poet (641 CE) was en route to Khorasan accompanying Saeed bin Affan, when he was bitten by a snake. Thinking he was going to die, he recited what became his most attributed elegy (بكائية مالك بن الريب التميمي), in which he yearns to behold Suhail before the departure of his soul.

وَلمَّـا تَراءَت عِنْـدَ مَـروٍ مِنيـتي   أَقُولُ لأَصْحـابِي ارْفَعُونِي لأنّني
وَخَـلَّ بِهَا جِسْمي وَحانَتْ وَفاتِيا   يَقِـرُّ بِعَيْني أَنَّ سُهَيـلٌ بَـدَا لِيـا

And when demise showed up at Marow
And seeped into my body weakening it, and death became inevitable,
I asked my companions to lift my body up
[05] *For it pleases me to see Suhail* †

In local tradition, the sighting of Suhail is a harbinger of abundance in harvest and the end of al qaith, or the hottest period of the year. Continuing in the ancestral tradition of mastering poetry and astrology, there are countless proverbial sayings that cite Suhail in relation to the changing of the seasons. Emirati legend has it that a man who wandered the land for years in search of livelihood arrived in Eastern Arabia and worked there for a while. Years later, after he had amassed a fortune and was on a final journey home, he encountered a Bedouin man who lived alone in the desert, and who sold words of wisdom in return for one camel per counsel. The traveling man bought three, one of which being: if Suhail appears, beware of the flood (إذا طلع سهيل لا تأمن السيل). Although the man didn't quite understand the meaning of this advice, he still abided by it. So, when Suhail appeared looming in the sky as he was about to rest for the night, he took shelter elsewhere before a flood washed over the wadi where he was to camp.

04

Roshdi Rashed (ed.), *Encyclopedia of the History of Arabic Science*, Vol. 1-Routledge (1996), 266; For sacred geography aficionados, another curious Suhail fact is that the Kaaba itself is astronomically aligned – the major axis of its rectangular base pointing towards the rising of Suhail along the direction of the structure's southern wall; https://articles.adsabs.harvard.edu//full/ 1995JHA...26..253K/0000257.000.html

05

"Elegy Of The Warrior - Malik Ibn Ar-Rayb - (Poetry Before His Death)" YouTube video, 1:30, posted by أهل العلم People Of Knowledge, February 23, 2017, https://www.youtube.com/watch?v=EviowPA8QU4

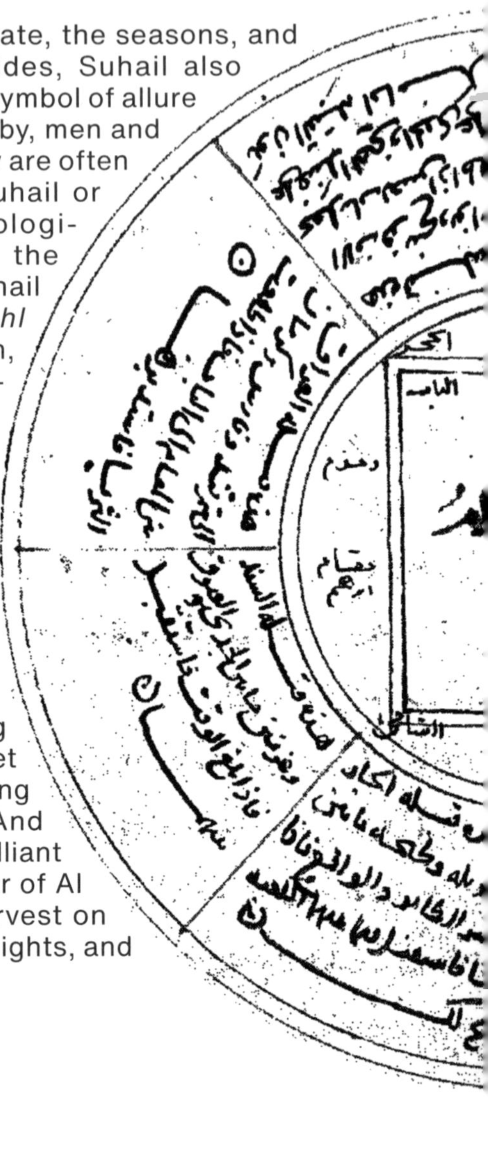

fig.(002) Scheme of the Kaaba's sacred geography found in a fifteenth-century manuscript of a geographical treatise by the medieval Arab geographer Al Maqdisi, showing the orientation of the qiblas in alignment with the rising and setting of various stars such as Suheil. Courtesy of Deutsch Staatsbibliothek, Berlin.

Beyond the climate, the seasons, and the changing tides, Suhail also appears to be a symbol of allure for Arabs, whereby, men and women of beauty are often described as Suhail or Suhaila. Etymologically speaking, the root word of Suhail in Arabic is *sahl* (سَّهْل), or the plain, easy, and spacious terrain, but also, it is the antonym of hardship or al *hazn* (الحَزْن). If I were to draw the linguistic connections between Suhail and Al Duroor, then how could we not look at the word duroor itself as a way to understand the depth of these ancestral traditions. The root word of *al duroor* (الدرور) is *durr* (دُرّ), which in Arabic means effusiveness, a big pearl, a thing of great value, a planet that spins so fast it appears still, among others in a long list of definitions. And so, with the sighting of Suhail, the brilliant star of ease and light, the Suhaili Year of Al Duroor begins, with its cycles of harvest on land and sea, softer suns and cooler nights, and abundant waters and winds.

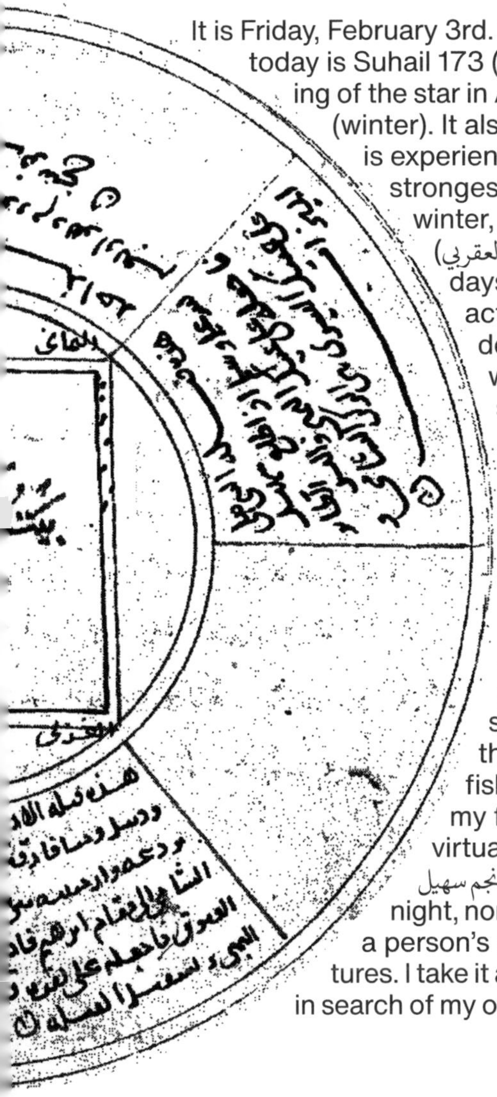

It is Friday, February 3rd. The Al Duroor app on my phone tells me today is Suhail 173 (the number of days since the first sighting of the star in August), and the third day of the 80th dur (winter). It also tells me that the United Arab Emirates is experiencing *shamal thamaneen* (شمال الثمانين), the strongest among the northern winds that blow in winter, and that we are in the *arba'een al aqrabi* (أربعين العقربي) in the calendar, which lasts for 40 days from February 1–March 12 and is characterized by heavy and extensive rainfall, despite a decrease in the intensity of cold weather. According to Al Duroor, severe storms called *al tuhf* (الطهف) and *al khub* (الخب) wind might occur, causing strong waves in the sea. And in a poetic turn, the app describes the more minute aspects of the weather, where "water runs through tree branches, and flowers begin to bloom" and announces to those who wish to know, that now is the time of *safi*, *sheri*, and *zubaidi* fish breeding, and the planting of date palm tree cuttings. There's something wonderful about tuning into the daily movements of the winds, of the fish in the water, and in the soil. Yet, perhaps my favorite discovery on this road trip turned virtual celestial escapade is this local proverb: لا بيسير بالليل، ولا بيتبع نجم سهيل, (those that won't walk at night, nor follow the star Suhail) – meant to indicate a person's reluctance to take risks or go on adventures. I take it as my own (free) counsel to walk the earth in search of my own proverbial Suhail.

Dalal Musaed Alsayer

Conspicuous: Drawing, Photograph, Map, Poem

What are photographs without context?
What happens when drawings are the only form of "*documentation?*"
What happens when mappings become the basis of "*fact?*"

I begin this essay with the three aforementioned questions, posing them to my readers and myself. I ponder them when I sit in an archive looking at representations of the Arabian Desert taken by travelers, companies, and so-called explorers; when I am writing about the desert and how these representations paved the way for Arabian knowledge and narratives to be reshaped; when I am teaching and engaging with my students about the environment; as I learn from my students how much we need to talk about architecture, environment, expertise, colonialism, histories and so much more.

In an attempt to think about these questions, I will look at three different mediums – drawing, photography, and maps – to understand how Western, historical, and visual representations of the region shaped contemporary perceptions. Using the examples that follow, I ask myself, and my readers, to sit with these representations and the subsequent questions that arise.

My interest in nineteenth and twentieth-century visual representations of the Arabian Peninsula by so-called Western explorers and companies began when I started researching British and US-operated oil towns in Kuwait, Iran, and Saudi Arabia almost a decade ago. Through looking at black and white photographs and color-coded concession maps, I became intrigued by the ways in which the images' authors
[01] attempted to make the landscape "legible" to them.† Staring at the images, I asked myself: how were they made? Who was the audience? What was there before these representations? This fascination stayed with me, and I slowly began collecting maps, drawings, photographs, and books written about the Arabian Peninsula, compiling my own archive. When I decided to use a photographic collection for one of my first essays in my doctoral studies, my advisor suggested that I read *Environmental Imaginaries of the Middle East and North Africa.* Ultimately, this book lived with me throughout the years as I read it, re-read it, and shared it, again and again. It became my guiding

01

On the idea of "legibility," see James C. Scott, *Seeing Like A State: How Certain Schemes to Improve the Human Condition Have Failed* (New Haven, CT: Yale University Press, 1998); See also: Timothy Mitchell, *Rule of Experts: Egypt, Techno-Politics, Modernity* (Berkeley, CA: University of California Press, 2002); and Ferguson, James. "Seeing Like an Oil Company: Space, Security, and Global Capital in Neoliberal Africa." *American Anthropologist* 107, no. 3 (September 2005): 377–82. https://doi.org/10.1525/aa.2005.107.3.377.

framework as I think and write about Western representations of the region, and primarily, its environment. The opening paragraph of the book reads:

> Representations of the Middle East nearly inevitably include desolate scenes of empty and parched deserts, punctuated, perhaps, with a lonely string of camels, a verdant but isolated oasis, or a beach with large dunes of golden sand, sometimes with a pyramid, an oil derrick, or a minaret in the background. [...] Inherent in this imagery is the fact that much of the Middle East and North Africa, a largely desert region, has been considered ecologically marginal since at least the late nineteenth century. More often than not, these lands have been defined as degraded by human action over many centuries.† [02]

When I read the publication for the first time, I understood that my fascination with these representations made sense, that there was something that warranted them crucial to research. However, reading it a few years later, I felt an uneasiness. How do we not talk about this? Why did it take me this long to realize that my understanding of my environment was based on constructed representations that were taken at face value and considered to be real, factual, and true? What can be seen in them? What is obscured and omitted? What does this tell us about spatial conceptions?

Embarking on this essay, I wanted to explore how the perception of the Emirati landscape and narratives were conceived from images taken by travelers. Specifically, I am interested in how different modes of travel shaped the way in which the environment was constructed. Walking on foot or atop a camel allows for a general street view and a leisurely and languid perusal of souks with so much more hidden behind closed doors of residents. Arriving from the sea evokes a scene of low-rise forts and palm groves that sparsely populate the flat desert beyond. From several kilometers high, the aerial vantage point erodes the minutia of the complex desert landscape. The use of

02

Diana K. Davis, "Imperialism, Orientalism, and the Environment in the Middle East: History, Policy, Power and Practice," in *Environmental Imaginaries of the Middle East and North Africa, Ecology and History* (Athens, Ohio: Ohio University Press, 2011), 1.

03

See Henni, Samia, ed. *Deserts Are Not Empty.* (New York, NY: Columbia Books on Architecture and the City, 2022).

04

Samuel Marinus Zwemer, who served as a missionary to Arabia between 1891 to 1905, was the first person to photograph the UAE in 1901 when he captured Qasr Al Hosn; Samuel Marinus Zwemer, "Three Journeys in Northern Oman," (1902), *The Geographical Journal*, XIX, no. 1 (1902): 54-64.; Some of Hermann Burchardt's photographs taken in the UAE are digitized as part of the Arabian Gulf Digital Archive: https://www.agda.ae/en/search/hermann%20Burchardt%20photographs; Other photographs can be seen in Hermann Burchardt, Annegret Nippa, and Peter Herbstreuth. Unterwegs am Golf: von Basra nach Maskat Photographien von Hermann Burchardt / Along the Gulf: from Basra to Muscat Photographs by Hermann Burchardt / Rihla fi al-Khalij. (Berlin: Schiler, 2006).

photographs and sketches – that render parts of Abu Dhabi and Ras al Khaimah absent from their larger social, economic, political, and environmental relationships to water, land, and the region, – lay the foundation of the contemporary environmental imaginary of the United Arab Emirates (UAE). Through these images, certain architectural elements were favored over others and specific, intangible histories were overlooked, resulting in a dominant trope and narrative based on the images' authors and their positionality. The implications of taking these early twentieth-century drawings, photographs, and maps of the UAE at face value, as "absolute truths" and without critique, has far-reaching implications from policy to practice. In believing that the desert is an isolated entity absent from its larger social, economic, and political milieu, means that there is a belief that the landscape can be easily modified with little
[03] regard to the repercussions.†

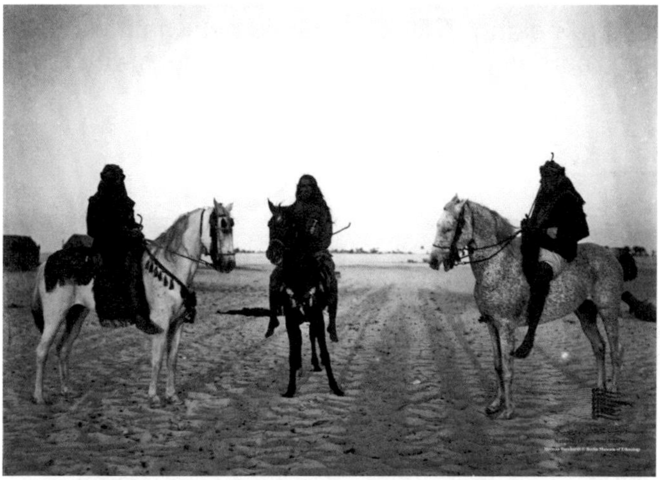

fig. (001) Burchardt, Hermann. Unknown Title (Unidentified Men Riding Horses in Abu Dhabi). February 1904. Photograph. NA.0042.00000158. Berlin Museum of Ethnology. Digitized by Arabian Gulf Digital Archive. https://www.agda.ae/en/catalogue/na/na/0042/00000158.

Land, Photography, People

The photographs that I found on the website Arabian Gulf Digital Archive (AGDA) turned out to be some of the first photos of the
[04] UAE.† They were taken sometime in February 1904 by German traveler Hermann Burchardt and are currently housed in the Ethnological
[05] Museum of Berlin.† In December 1903, and after spending a year in Yemen, Burchardt

05

Hermann Burchardt (1857-1909) was a German self-proclaimed explorer and traveler of Jewish descent. After his father died in 1887, he inherited a large sum of money which he used to travel to Africa and Asia to explore his other passion: photography. After spending two years learning Arabic, Turkish, Farsi, and rudimentary Swahili, at Berlin's Department of Oriental Languages (Seminar für Orientalische Sprachen), he embarked on his decades-long journey in 1892. He rented an apartment in Damascus, Syria, which served as his base between travels and hired Abu Ibrahim, a Syrian Arab, to serve as his guide and confidant. During the following years, he traveled to Tangier, Samarkand, Sana'a, Siwa Oasis, Basra, Kuwait, Bahrain, Hofuf, Qatar, Abu Dhabi, Dubai, Muscat, and parts of East Africa, amongst other cities. He died en route to Sana'a from Mokha when his caravan, which included the Italian vice-consul Marquis Benzoni, was ambushed and they were killed by gunmen. See Burchardt, Nippa, and Herbstreuth. *Along the Gulf.*

undertook a months-long trek starting in Basra and ending in Muscat, stopping along the way in Kūt (present-day Kuwait), Bahrain, Al-Hasa, Hofuf, Abu Dhabi, and Dubai.† Staying in Abu [06]
Dhabi and Dubai from February 4 to 22, 1904, Burchardt took a series of photographs that include Qasr Al Hosn, seasonal houses, and the famous photograph of Sheikh Zayed bin Khalifa Al Nahyan.† [07]

What I found intriguing about Burchardt's photographs was that they were all generally centered on a single object, such as an animal, building, or person. In one of his Abu Dhabi photographs, we can see three horses – two lighter ones and one black steed that was said to belong to Sheikh Zayed bin Khalifa – each carrying a man wearing dark clothes with

06

While many call Burchardt an explorer, it might be a stretch since he was only able to travel to the region because of his large inheritance from his father. Burchardt traveled solely for leisure.

07

See also James Langton, "How One Intrepid Photographer Captured the First Image of 'Zayed the Great,'" *The National News*, August 5, 2019, https://www.thenationalnews.com/arts-culture/art/how-one-intrepid-photographer-captured-the-first-image-of-zayed-the-great-1.894420.

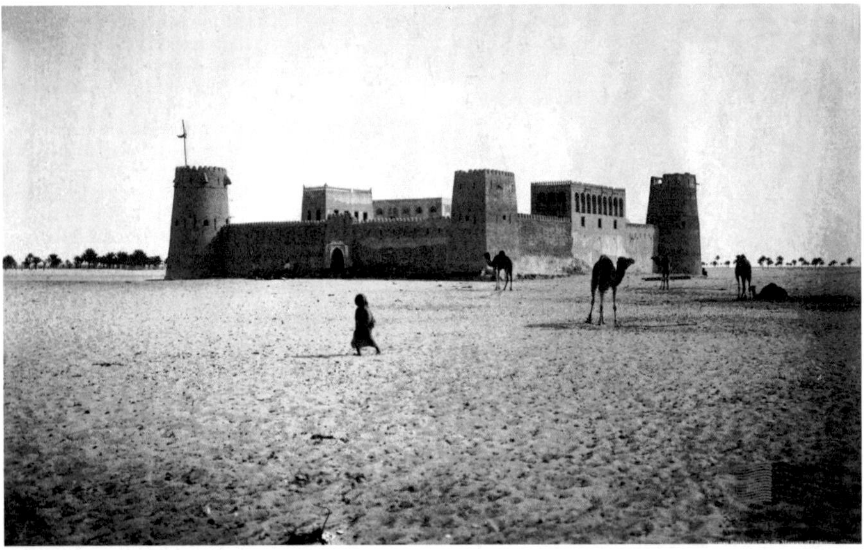

fig. (002) Burchardt, Hermann. *Unknown Title (Qasr Al Hosn, Abu Dhabi).* February 1904. Photograph. NA.0042.00000167. Berlin Museum of Ethnology, Digitized by Arabian Gulf Digital Archive. https://www.agda.ae/en/catalogue/na/na/0042/00000167.

his face concealed *fig.* (001). There are no distinct features identifying any of the men. The lighter horses, seen in profile, are on either side of the black horse who is facing the camera. A tent or a house appears in the background, but it is unclear, since the photograph is out of focus. The way that the horses are posed, frozen into an immobile stance, blurs any possibility of understanding the horses beyond their presence. The fact that the horses may have been purebred Arabian stallions was omitted in Burchardt's representations.

In another photograph, Qasr Al Hosn is Burchardt's main focus *fig.* (002). What can be seen is the original inner fort with dispersed palm groves in the background. In the foreground is a lone figure, unidentified and indistinguishable. Several wandering camels also populate the middle ground. The photograph keeps a lot of questions unanswered, such as: who is the figure? Do the camels have a function? Where is the sea and the other settlements? In the account of his trip, Burchardt did not mention anything about Qasr Al Hosn or its role as a fortress
[08] connected to maritime trade.† Through his myopic representation, Burchardt's photograph perpetuated the Orientalist gaze of desert, camel, and architecture.

08

Jayanti Maitra and "Afrā" Ḥajjī, *Qasr Al Hosn: The History of the Rulers of Abu Dhabi, 1793-1966* (Abu Dhabi, UAE: Center for Documentation and Research, 2001).

09

Hermann Burchardt, "Ost-Arabien von Basra Bis Maskat Auf Grund Eigener Reisen [East Arabia from Basra to Muscat Based on My Own Travels]," Zeitschrift Der Gesellschaft Für Erdkunde Zu Berlin 5 (1906): 305-22.

In a third photograph, we see houses made of woven mats with pitched roofs and a central beam holding up the structure, connected to two columns *fig.* (003). Men are sitting in a circle on the floor outside of the house, with a few people outside the circle, sitting or standing, alone or in pairs. Women and children are seen on the other side of the house. Similar to Burchardt's other photographs, we are left with no clear understanding of details such as: who the houses belonged to, whether they were permanent or temporary, or how many people lived in them. Burchardt did not provide information about the histories and narratives behind the houses.

Two years later, almost to the day, on February 3, 1906, Burchardt delivered an address to the Gesellschaft Für Erdkunde Zu Berlin (Berlin Geographical Soci-
[09] ety),† titled Ost-Arabian von Basra bis Maskat auf Grund eigener Reisen (East Arabia from Basra to Muscat

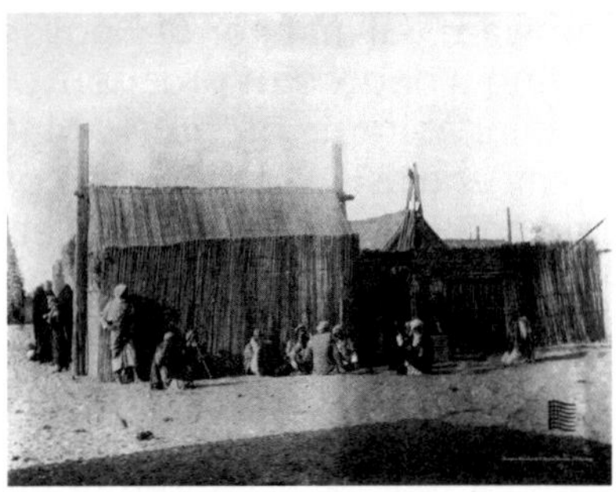

fig. (003) Burchardt, Hermann. *Unknown Title (Housing in Abu Dhabi).* February 1904. Photograph. NA.0042.00000180. Berlin Museum of Ethnology. Digitized by Arabian Gulf Digital Archive. https://www.agda.ae/en/catalogue/na/na/0042/00000180.

based on my own travels). Burchardt recounted his journey from Basra to Muscat describing encounters and sites. As I was reading the text, I could sense the Orientalist milieu that Burchardt was steeped in. Although he does describe the sheikhs' hospitalities, they are few and far between. His paragraph-long descriptions always depict the unnavigable seas, the demanding Arabs, and the untrusting questions thrown his way. Bewildered, he stated:

> After the usual *salam* and coffee and tea drinking, the questioning began. The same questions are asked everywhere. What's your name, where are you from, why are you traveling, do you get a
> salary from your government, do you hold an (public) office position? † [10]

To Burchardt, it was baffling and tiring that people did not fully trust him but would actually question his presence, even with all of his official documents. He went on to state: "No Arab believes me that I
travel for pleasure." † In the age of exploration and conquest, it seemed [11]
that traveling for pleasure was a reasonable response to his presence. It is Burchardt's positionality and his privilege that make it hard to divorce his Orientalizing gaze from these images. Although not directly part of the colonial enterprise, Burchardt's objectifying focus and his descriptions, which are vague and curt, bolstered the constructed image of the Arabian Gulf, and by extension its environs. Burchardt's descriptions of his time on the *būm* (deep-sea dhow) often follow in this manner: "It was an uncomfortable journey, the sea was high, waves often pounded the
ship, soaking everything." † With little to no attention given to anything [12]
but his comfort and reception.

In his account of Dubai, Burchardt stated that in the market, he found "many goods marked 'Made in Germany,' mostly enameled ironware. All manner of English cakes and drops were available, indi-
cating a degree of prosperity." † He remarked that, however, "(t)hey [13]
[the inhabitants of the Arabian Peninsula] have never heard of Germany and ask whether it is a province of the *Daula* (Ottoman Empire)
or whether it belongs to England." † By not allowing himself to ask how [14]
these products arrived in Dubai, Burchardt robs us of pieces of history that he had the privilege to witness and capture. Burchardt was more focused on his accommodations than on understanding complex trade routes, geopolitical allegiances of the region, socio-economic demands, and the many reasons for a German visitor to travel in the region. What would have happened if Burchardt shed his colonial garb and documented these complexities?

10, 11, 12

Burchardt, "Own Travels," 314.

13

Burchardt, "Own Travels," 317.

14

Burchardt, "Own Travels," 314.

While he captured these photographs and they served as snapshots of a city that no longer exists, what use are they without context? How much can one person learn by spending such as short time as a visitor, often not even fully welcomed? What do the photographs and the short account tell us? While I do not have any definitive answers to these questions, it is unfortunate that he did not tell us more about the Arabia of 1903.

15

While it is unclear who Lt. Crichton is, it could possibly be G.C.L. Crichton who served as the political agent in Gilgit and was appointed in Kuwait as the controller for finance in the 1950s.

Sea, Drawing, Building

While I was able to write about Burchardt's photographs without any travel, the second set of objects required that I physically visit The National Archives at Kew, London, United Kingdom. On the second floor of the archives, in the map and drawings room, is an album filled with some of the earliest drawings of Ras al Khaimah and Abu Dhabi, along with those of Oman and the Strait of Hormuz. As I sat on the large table holding the oversized album, I flipped through the pages and gazed at the small handheld images behind the mylar film. Most of them were drawn between 1809 and 1935. Then, I zoomed in on
[15] the undated watercolor and ink drawing by Lieutenant Crichton† that I had seen online *fig.* (004). Entitled *View of the Fort of Ras-ul-khima*, it depicts mountains in the background, rows of palm trees, the sheikh's fort in the middle ground, and lastly, the sea in the foreground. Framed with an ink border, the signature Lt. Crichton is located in the bottom corner, bold and clear. Ras al Khaima and Critchton are written on the image in pencil, most likely by the archivist.

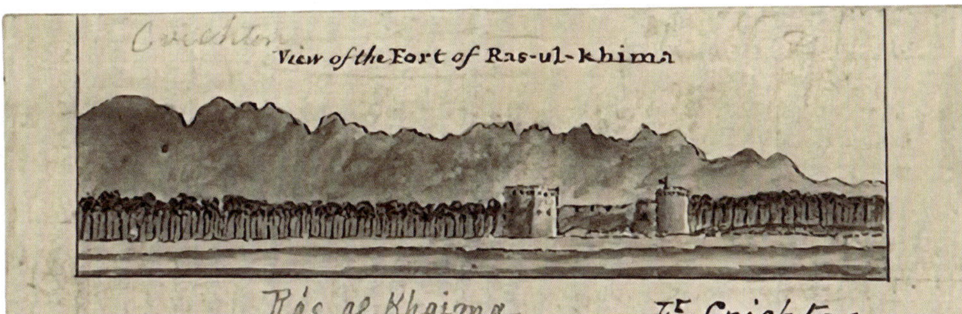

fig. (004) Crichton, Lt. *View of the Fort of Ras-Ul-Khima.* Undated. Watercolor Drawing. ADM 344/1229. The National Archives of the UK Government. https://discovery.nationalarchives.gov.uk/details/r/C11439803.

16

"H.M.S. Shoreham (1930)," Dread Nought Project, 2021, http://www.dreadnought-project.org/tfs/index.php/H.M.S._Shoreham_(1930).

17

Geoffrey Mason, "Service Histories of Royal Navy Warships in World War 2: HMS Shoreham (L 32) - Shoreham-Class Sloop," *Naval History*, 2005, https://www.naval-history.net/xGM-Chrono-18SL-HMS_Shoreham.htm.

18

The National Archives of the UK Government, "Admiralty: Hydrographic Department: Coastal and Riverine Views," *The National Archives*, 2022, https://discovery.nationalarchives.gov.uk/details/C16280.

Flipping through the album, I found a second set of drawings. The pair of ink drawings, one depicting Ras al Khaimah and the other Abu Dhabi, were drawn onboard *H.M.S. Shoreham* (1930) during its tenure in the Arabian Gulf *fig.* (005). The *H.M.S. Shoreham* was commissioned on April 21, 1933, as the British Royal Navy's new headquarters ship in the Arabian Gulf and Captain James Vandeleur Creagh was appointed its commander.† [16]
The *H.M.S. Shoreham* became central to British naval activity in the region traveling between the Red Sea, Malta, and Bombay, India until it was decommissioned in July 1946.† It was in [17]
1935, under the charge of Captain Vernon Saumarez Butler, and onboard *H.M.S. Shoreham*, that a British officer with the initials R.B. drew the pair of drawings. The first drawing depicting Ras al Khaimah included the sheikh's fort on the far left and label that said "White Tower (not white 1935)" on the far right. Between these two landmarks, he also points out that there is a "ruined tower," and a "conspicuous tree." Under the location of the sheikh's fort, written in neat text, is: "Town, without distinctive points, NE from fort." This labeling technique continues in the Abu Dhabi drawing which depicts the sheikh's fort on the far right, with "Mud and Mat Huts, some seasonal" on the left side with a "Minaret like Lt. Ho." in the middle. The drawings show nothing else except the directional information: "Fort bg 127° 1.9m" for Ras al Khaimah and "F.S. 113° 9.3 c." for Abu Dhabi.

Without any descriptions, references, or annotations along with these images, it was difficult for me to discern what these drawings were for. It seems likely, though, that this set of drawings were meant to be navigational, to create a visual representation of a place; and memorable, to create a snapshot of a foreign place to remember one's trip. When I was unable to figure out why these drawings

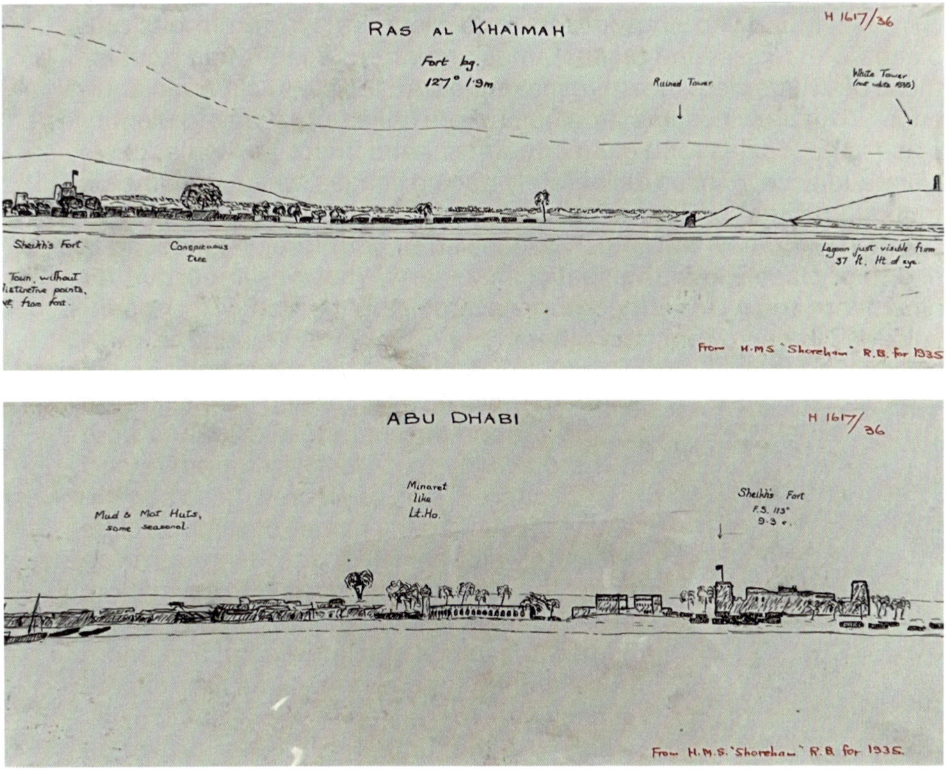

fig. (005) Top: Unknown. *Ras Al Khaimah.* Undated. Ink Drawing, ADM 344/1229. The National Archives of the UK Government. https://discovery.nationalarchives.gov.uk/details/r/C11439803.

Bottom: Unknown. *Abu Dhabi*. Undated. Ink Drawing. ADM 344/1229. The National Archives of the UK Government. https://discovery.nationalarchives.gov.uk/details/r/C11439803.

were made, I asked the archivist to help me locate the acquisitions and transfer details. This revealed that these drawings were indeed navigational. The records state that these drawings were:

> [...] from albums and sketch books of coastal and riverine views, panoramas and sections which were employed on charts to provide pictorial reference for navigators, especially approaching harbours, ports and hazards, and for the accurate visual identification of geographic locations world-wide. [...] They provide a record of geological formations, physical geography, coastal topography, shipping,
> [18] shore installations, lighthouses and other buildings.†

Much like photographs and memoirs, written in bits and pieces with misspelled place names and often unidentified "locals," these drawings were meant to make the UAE legible to a foreign audience.† The drawings in their albums were ultimately a way to identify places and locales for a distinctly British, and in this particular case, naval audience.† These deliberately framed images, which were meant to aid in navigation and to serve as place markers, offers us a way to understand how the British conceived of both foreign landscapes and their place within the spatial imaginary. What was important for nineteenth and twentieth-century naval ships? Apparently, forts, conspicuous trees, towers, and other markers of space. Wanting to know more about these drawings and the people who made them, I began exploring British naval ships and their history in the Gulf. I found out that these drawings were not the only way that the British understood the landscape. British naval crews also had the practice of painting the names of ships on cliffs to indicate which ship has passed through in an attempt to help incoming ships with navigation. The ship names painted on the landscape created new meanings and knowledge and, more often than not, ignored what was there in the first place.

At the time that these drawings were made, many of the Gulf inhabitants depended on maritime trade for their livelihoods and composed maritime songs marking their passage of time and space. The *nūkhitha*'s (ship captain) ability to navigate according to climate, season, time, and place was often ignored by the colonial enterprise in their attempts at making the region legible.† The lack of a layer of information, which shaped the region's relationship to the Arabian Gulf, demonstrates that there was no attempt on behalf of British naval officers to understand the region or fold in local knowledge. It was, after all, "to provide a record of geological formations, physical geography, coastal topography, shipping, shore installations, lighthouses, and other buildings."† But what happens when these are the only kinds of historical documentation?

19

See Scott, *Seeing Like A State.*

20

On naval ships and navigation, see Luciana de Lima Martins, "Mapping Tropical Waters: British Views and Visions of Rio de Janeiro," in *Mappings*, ed. Denis Cosgrove (Chicago, IL: University of Chicago Press, 1999), 148–68.

21

Historically speaking, each nūkhitha was known by name within the region for his experiences and navigational prowess; however, in Burchardt's accounts, the nūkhitha is melded into an abstract figure with no mention of any names or histories. Burchardt knew he was to communicate with the nūkhitha to seek safe transportation, but there is little on the importance of the profession, title, and person.

22

The National Archives of the UK Government, "Admiralty: Hydrographic Department: Coastal and Riverine Views."

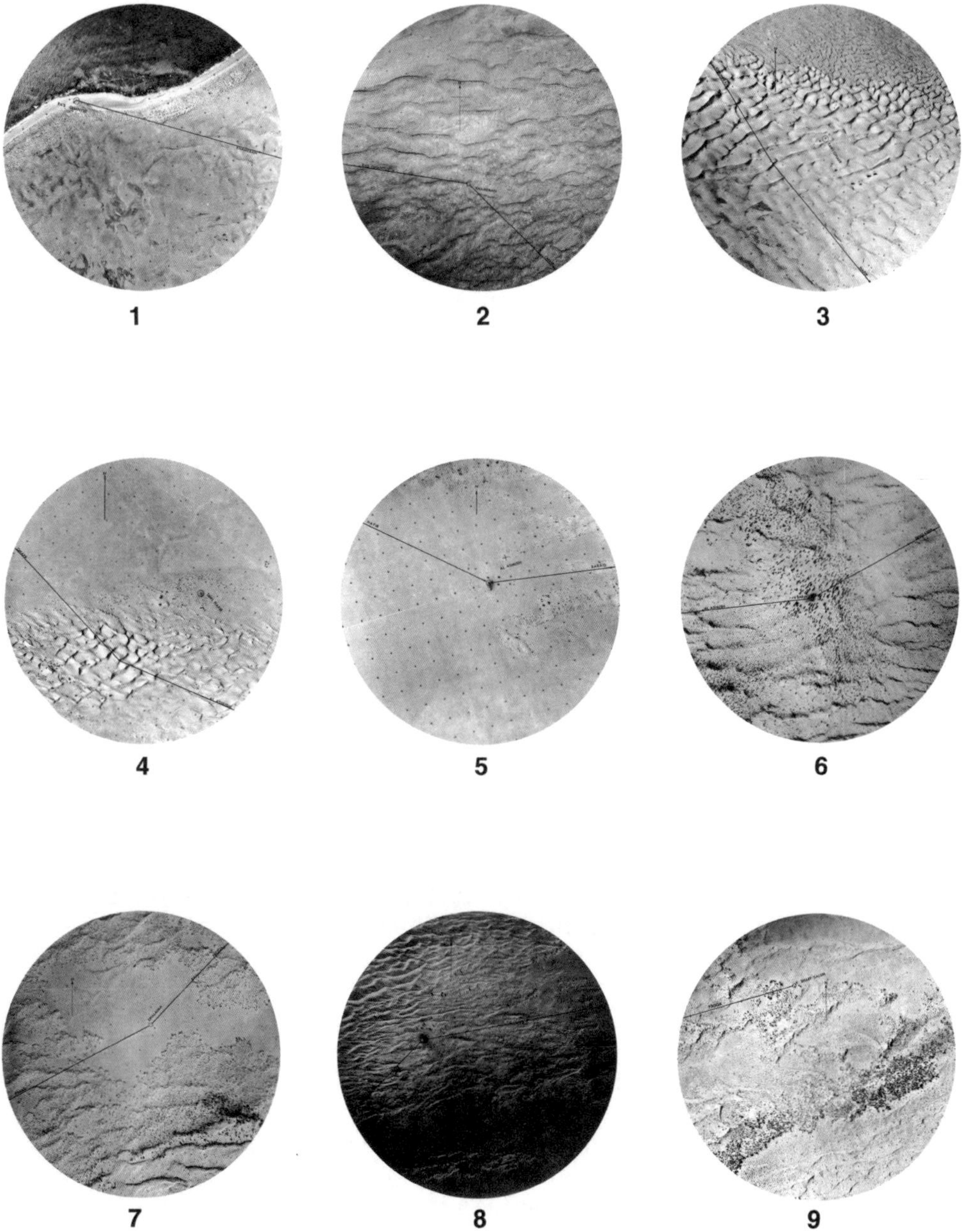

fig. (006) Aerial photography of a revised land boundary between Abu Dhabi and Dubai, February 1969, showing the turning points of the boundary and adjacent landmarks. Foreign and Commonwealth Office Library.

With Britain's long history in the Arabian Peninsula, there is an abundance of books that collate correspondences, maps, and aspirations. Wanting to know more about the British involvement in the UAE, I began reading books that "document" the country's nascent beginnings. In one particular book, I found about 30 images, mainly maps of the UAE, drawn during the late 1960s.† I was particularly interested in one page that included a series of nine aerial images, some inland and some on the coast, within circular frames *fig.* (006). The images are overlaid with a light grid with a larger plus sign marking latitudes and longitudes and a smaller plus sign for smaller increments. Each of the nine landscapes were overlaid with straight lines, some have one, while others have two. These lines delineate locations, places, and intersections. Annotated in English and absent of their larger context, the nine images illustrate the importance of making the landscape yield to universal and regimented notions of place-making. [23]

As I sat in the library looking at these images, I could almost feel the wind sweeping across the sand as if they were digital instead of analog. It was a surreal feeling to look at these images of a still desert, when I knew for a fact that it was anything but. The desert's complexity, its relationship to climate, to people, to histories, was reduced into a singular image, overlaid with a grid. The orthogonal lines within the landscape overlook the undulations of the desert, imagining the snapshot as an authentic and continually true representation of what the airplane's camera captured. Time and change, it seems, were not necessary. In the same way that the trees in both the drawings and photographs serve as the backdrop, the desert was also relegated as the background. As I looked at these images, I remembered that hidden within them are two things: scale and technology. What happens when the line shifts from imagination to reality?

The thin line that transverses the image, in reality, translates to several meters thick on the ground. The drastic shift in scale reveals the implications of this thin line. It simply is not a thin line.† [24]
Equally, the opposite shift in representation from a landscape down to the size of your hand, "allows us to see at scales impossible for the

23

Walker, Julian F., ed. *The UAE: Internal Boundaries and the Boundary with Oman.* Arabian Geopolitics 4. (Slough: Cambridge Archive Edition, 1994)

24

See. Aseel AlYaqoub, "Pipe Dreams: The Evolution of Kuwait's Territorial Carvings and Imagined Cartography.," in *Architecture of the Territory: Constructing National Narratives in the Arab World*, ed. Collective for Architecture (Beirut, Lebanon: Kaph Books, 2023), 5–17.

25

Denis E. Cosgrove, Geography and Vision: Seeing, Imagining and Representing the World, International Library of Human Geography, v. 12 (London; New York: New York: I.B. Tauris ; In the United States of America and Canada distributed by Palgrave Macmillan, 2008), 168.

naked eye to see and without moving the phys-
[25] ical body over space."† This divorce between physical body and space (and equally, time) displaces the audience. The nine images are stripped bare of their complexities, rendering them mere representations suspended in time and space. Denis Cosgrove reminds us that "(t) o understand the contents, meaning, and significance of any map requires that it be reinserted into the social, historical, and technical contexts and processes from which it emerges
[26] and upon which it acts."† This has yet to be done. We are left to fill in the gaps that the images leave behind.

The second aspect, technology, increases some of the uneasiness that I feel as I look at these images. In *Close Up at a Distance*, Laura Kurgan states that "consumers [...] will never know who has tasked a satellite to take a picture (unless they did it themselves) in order to see something close up, but
[27] from far away."† The nine images, taken some time in 1969, required novel technology, painstaking technique, and time to construct. This oscillation between "up close" and "far away," between scales and dimensions, is at the heart of the technological realities that we, the audiences, are divorced from. The suspended images are so removed from their context that they offer little more than Burchardt's photographs or Crichton's drawings. I cannot help myself from thinking that the technology that was needed to take both this photograph and Burchardt's are what shaped contemporary understanding of this environment. What I mean by this is that both photographs are a frozen frame in time, space, and distance, that were staged and carefully assembled. The authorship required to create them blurs the complex social, environmental, and physical narratives behind the glossy images. I could not discern why these representations were made but their implications are far-reaching. Since these photographs were abstractly constructed, do these nine images still exist in real, tangible space? What did they replace? What role did the making of the photographs play in what was replaced? As Cosgrove reminds us: "Of particular concern have been the various means whereby knowledge gained in [the] survey is transferred back to the place of compilation, and whereby the map itself enters recursively into circuits of knowledge that
[28] generate further mappings."†

26

Cosgrove, *Geography and Vision*, 156.

27

Laura Kurgan, *Close Up at a Distance: Mapping, Technology, and Politics* (Brooklyn, NY: Zone Books, 2013), 20.

28

Cosgrove, *Geography and Vision*, 159.

As Davis has explained, time and time again, what happens when we believe that the desert is the problem? Instead of living with the desert, the current dominating narrative is to make the sand stay still, just like in the nine images. Unmoving, yielding, and tamed. But the truth is that that has never been the case. So, what happens when mappings, become the basis of fact?

Histories, Poems, Narratives

These representations hold within them an act of erasure, inscription, omissions, and framing, where much is lost. With minimal to no explanatory texts, it is difficult for us working in archives to discern locations, subjects, and narratives. Thus, as researchers we are at the mercy of the authors' bookkeeping and (often rudimentary) knowledge of Arabic. What is missing is as important as what is present. Both the absence and presence tell us what was considered important and what was the ultimate aim of these representations. In the case of Burchardt's photographs, the experience was in itself important to him and those in Berlin. Burchardt's wealthy background allowed him to travel in the Arabian Peninsula for several years and to return to Berlin to discuss his "findings," which alludes to his personality and ambitions. His account of the region also sheds light on what was deemed necessary to document: a Westerner's experience, discomfort, and all.

Equally, the British Navy illustrations' minimal textual annotations indicate a sole focus on navigation. The size and roughly drawn nature of the illustrations also allude to their audience. They were intended to be fast, easy to transport, and quickly understood by British naval officers. Much can be gleaned from what little was drawn, written, or photographed. At the same time, knowing who the audience is unpacks the complex, inherent geopolitical, and social dynamics of these representations.

Nonetheless, I am also cognizant that these images, being the only "evidence" held in archives, tend to serve as a foundation for "truths," knowledge, and histories of places for scholars and historians. The reality is that the "truths" found in archives are often clouded with subjectivity, colonialism, and bias. This is not to say that they are useless, but rather that as researchers who hold the burden of writing histories that they are intricately tied to, we should approach them with eyes wide open. The burdens we carry on our shoulders are two-fold. For not only are we entrenched within a legacy of Western knowledge, a truth made evident by the fact that this piece was written in English, but we are also

29

Ousha bint Khalifa Al Suwaidi, "مَطّ قلبي روحي وشَقَّه", Fatat Al Arab - Ousha Bint Khalifa Al Suwaidi, The late Poet Laureate of the United Arab Emirates, 2021, https://ousha.ae/poetry-ar.html?poetry-ar-85.png&%20مَطّ قلبي%20روحي%20وشَقَّه

trying to find our voices within the dearth of "evidence." How do we navigate what we found in archives with the stories that we grew up hearing? I think one of the first steps in an all-encompassing bibliography is to systematically incorporate multiple narratives and to study not only what is documented, but critically, what is missing. We often disregard oral histories and personal accounts as hearsay instead of something we can learn from. I, too, have fallen into this fallacy of dismissing local knowledge because it was not objective enough, but is there such a thing as the absence of subjectivity? Maybe it is time to bring it all together and call for a more inclusive and expansive bibliography that includes sources that were never accounted for. For in-between the drawings and the inscriptions lay a kernel of other histories – of landscapes and fauna, of topography and forts, of narratives and representations. Ras al Khaimah and Abu Dhabi were neither invented nor discovered, they were always there. So how can we write their histories?

Here, I turn to another source, one that is intimately personal and at the same time, collectively embraced. Using words or specifically, poems, the UAE's most famed poet, Ousha bint Khalifa Al Suwaidi, known as Fatat al-Arab wrote about the Emirates, the sea, and the desert in one breath.

مُويـةٍ مِ اللِّـجْ مِـزْرَقَّه
طَبَّعْتِنِي وِالهَوَى شَـامِي

آه يـَامَنْ عـَايَنْ الدَّقَّه
فِي الخَـلَا وَارْجَـابَهْ احْيـَامِي

The water turned blue in the the heavy downpour,
and drowned me while the Shamal blows

You who has exhausted me,
[29] *and left me alone in the vastness†*

Although devoid of visual representation, Ousha's words paint a complex visual rendering of the Emirati environment. The desert and the sea are a continuum that speaks to emotions and are embedded within the psyche. In describing the northern, Levantine breeze, the listener (or reader) understands that it is at once a strong wind in the morning and a soft breeze at night. It is a wind that descends onto the Arabian Peninsula in the summer, often laden with sand that was picked up from the northwestern region. Through this, time, space, distance, temperature, and texture coalescence into a single description.

By folding in other sources, alongside the representations taken by Orientalists, we can add a more complex layer to the histories that we write. Taking historical representation at face value with little to no interrogation renders them useless. Thus, it is our job to critically examine what we find in archives and what we hear in oral histories. Our role as historians and researchers should also be that of the investigator and the analyst. It is only when we take on this critical stance, examining and pulling apart "evidence," that we begin to really conduct research. As Marc Bloch reminds us: "from the moment when we are no longer resigned to purely and simply recording the words of our witnesses, from the moment we decide to force them to speak, even against their will, cross-examination becomes more necessary than ever. Indeed, it is the prime necessity of well-conducted historical research."† [30]

This cross-examination comes in many ways. Whether it is through bringing in alternate sources and voices or through the repeated interrogation of "evidence." In the case of the images discussed here, as a repetition of what we began with, we ask ourselves:

What **are photographs without context?**

What **happens when drawings are the only form of "*documentation?*"**

What **happens when mappings become the basis of "*fact?*"**

Humbly attempting to answer these questions, I say that photographs without context allows us to glean something else. For instance, the photograph of housing shows us material histories, labor relations, and construction techniques. That is what should be taken as a point of departure, to assemble histories of vernacular construction techniques. While subjectivity and biases can often only

30

Marc Bloch, *The Historian's Craft* (Princeton, N.J.: Recording for the Blind & Dyslexic, 2007), 64.

31

See Bruno Latour, *Reassembling the Social: An Introduction to Actor-Network-Theory* (Oxford: Oxford University Press, 2005).

32

See, for example: Ricardo Camacho, Dalal Musaed Alsayer, and Sara Saragoça Soares, eds., *Pan-Arab Modernism 1968-2018: A History of Architectural Practice in the Middle East*, Print edition (Barcelona: Actar Publishers, 2021); Faysal Tabbarah, Dima Srouji, and Meitha Almazrooei, eds., *On Foraging: Food Knowledge and Environmental Imaginaries in the UAE's Landscape* (Abu Dhabi, UAE: Warehouse 421, 2021); Hamed Bukhamseen and Ali Ismail Karimi, eds., *Between East and West: A Gulf* (New York, NY: Actar Publishers, 2018); Ricardo Camacho, Sara Saragoça, and Roberto Fabbri, eds., *Modern Architecture Kuwait. Volume 2: Essays, Arguments & Interviews*, First edition, vol. 2, 2 vols. (Salenstein: Niggli, 2018); Roberto Fabbri and Sultan Sooud Al-Qassemi, eds., *Urban Modernity in the Contemporary Gulf: Obsolescence and Opportunities* (Abingdon, Oxon ; New York: Routledge, 2022); George Arbid and Philipp Oswalt, eds., *Designing Modernity: Architecture in the Arab World 1945-1973* (Berlin: Jovis, 2022); Sultan Sooud Al Qassemi and Todd Reisz, eds., *Building Sharjah* (Boston: Birkhauser, 2021), among others.

33

Bloch, *The Historian's Craft*, 43.

be understood with temporal and physical distances, what would happen if we included subjectivity? Knowing that the authors of the drawings and photographs epitomized the Oriental enterprise allow us to critically enhance, counter, and unravel found representations with other forms of documentation. Leaning into these contradictions and discrepancies shows us what knowledge was valuable and for whom. Thus, documentation becomes an active agent within the narrative of history, allowing us to pull apart preconceived notions and begin to interrogate what is "fact" and what was constructed
[31] and assembled with prejudiced Orientalism.† In recent years, scholars writing about architecture and urbanism in the Arabian Gulf have done just that.

In writing these volumes, authors have moved beyond the discursive narratives of the past and are instead embraced a multitude
[32] of voices, histories, and approaches.† Labor, time, distance, and exchange are at the center of these discussions which are unearthing sources and connections that were often overlooked or ignored in the histories that we have inherited. Taking Crichton's drawings, Burchardt's photographs, and the aerial images into a much larger, often disregarded context with multiple sources and voices allows us to "understanding
[33] [of] the living."† The context-less representations still allow us an the landscapes and practices in the Gulf, but more work needs to be done to unearth and amplify other voices and sources. While I will continue visiting archives and using found representations, I think that, similar to the Orientalists who traveled seas and lands to "discover" us, I ask you to "rediscover" with me the environment, histories, and narratives of the Arabian Peninsula.

Acknowledgments

I would like to thank the curator of the National Pavilion United Arab Emirates at the Venice Biennale, Faysal Tabbarrah, and co-editor Meitha Almazrooei for their kind invitation to contribute and their meticulous editing and insightful guidance. Aseel AlYaqoub's generous comments have made this piece clearer and stronger. James Kemp's insightful knowledge of British Naval history helped me locate some crucial photographs. Both the English and Arabic work has benefited from the insightful and generous comments of Talal Al-Rashoud. I would also like to thank the archivists at the National Archives of the United Arab Emirates, National Archives of the UK Government at Kew, and the librarians at the Middle East Library at St Antony's College, University of Oxford. I am grateful and indebted to St Antony's College, University of Oxford which granted me the time, space, and resources to write this piece while I was an academic visitor for the academic year 2022–2023.

Aziza Chaouni

Desert Unlearning

[*01*] **"You think you are making a trip, but soon it is making you – or unmaking you."†**

I recall that it all started during a hot summer night in a desert camp, by the oasis of M'hamid El Ghizlane. The still air felt unusually heavy, pushing its unforgiving, stone-like weight onto our bodies. With our toes resting on the sand, still burning from their prolonged exposure to the sun, we found some respite in our glass of sweet tea and the formidable spectacle of the starry desert sky. An unexpected breeze woke us up from our torpor, and our group started a heated discussion on the future of desert tourism in the region. It took the first rays of daylight to put an end to our discussion. The words we exchanged that night often resonate in my mind because they were the prelude to a life-changing experience.

This first night in the oasis of M'Hamid El Ghizlane was my first time in a desert, and the first stop on a six-month traveling fellowship that I was awarded after my graduation from the Harvard Graduate School of Design. My proposal envisioned a research trip throughout the Sahara Desert, crossing eight countries, with the goal to study and survey exemplary community-led and ecologically sensitive tourism projects. Until embarking on this journey which shaped the person, architect, and academic I was to become, my encounter with deserts has been mainly through oral history and literature.

My very first memory of a desert is related to stories recounted with a theatrical sense of drama by Driss Laadam, a house guard who has worked with my family in Fez since I was a year old. He was originally from a small oasis near the town of Errachidia, "the doorway to the Sahara," as he used to call it. To my astonishment, Driss had a strange habit that no one I knew possessed. For most of the year, he would leave his room to sleep on a carpet in our garden. As a child, I loved to lie on my back by his side, looking up at the sky, after dinnertime, and listening to the accounts of his life back in the oasis – a life where sweet dates fell into the palm of your hand, where the murmur of water running through the
[*02*] *seguias*† filled your ears, and where majestic palm trees and plush fruits trees offered you generous shade. I also listened with awe and fear to his desert stories, filled with the presence of an unforgiving, mysterious landscape composed of a sea of endless sand dunes, a landscape which necessitated herculean efforts from men to make it hospitable.

01

Nicolas Bouvier, *The Way of the World*, Trans. Robyn Marsack, (Eland: London, 2007) xi.

02

Traditionally constructed with clay, the seguias are water channels used to irrigate agricultural parcels inside the Moroccan oases, using gravity. To equitably share water resources, people took turns receiving water in their parcels. The quantity of water they received was proportional to their parcel size and the number of palm trees they owned. This ancestral system is still in use in many Moroccan oases, but it has been offset by the excessive pumping of the water table.

I vividly recall the chilling story of the *khettara* (hydraulic system) repair crew from Driss' village. Every year, a group of courageous men was sent north to inspect the underground channels. About 80 kilometers long, this centuries-old system was vital to oasis survival. Through gravity, the khettara crossed the desert and brought water to the oasis from the foothills of the Atlas Mountains. Armed with oil lamps and a pick ax, these men had to crawl inside underground channels to clean them from debris and repair them when needed, braving, along the way, dampness, darkness, scorpions, and snakes. One year, two of these men never returned back to Driss' oasis; a khettara collapsed and trapped them underground, burying them alive. The entire village took care of their orphaned families until all the children became adults. While growing up, these children were treated like royalty, receiving the best toys and clothing during festive seasons. The horror of this episode, which most certainly fed many of my childhood nightmares, was counterbalanced by the warmth and solidarity of the village described by Driss.

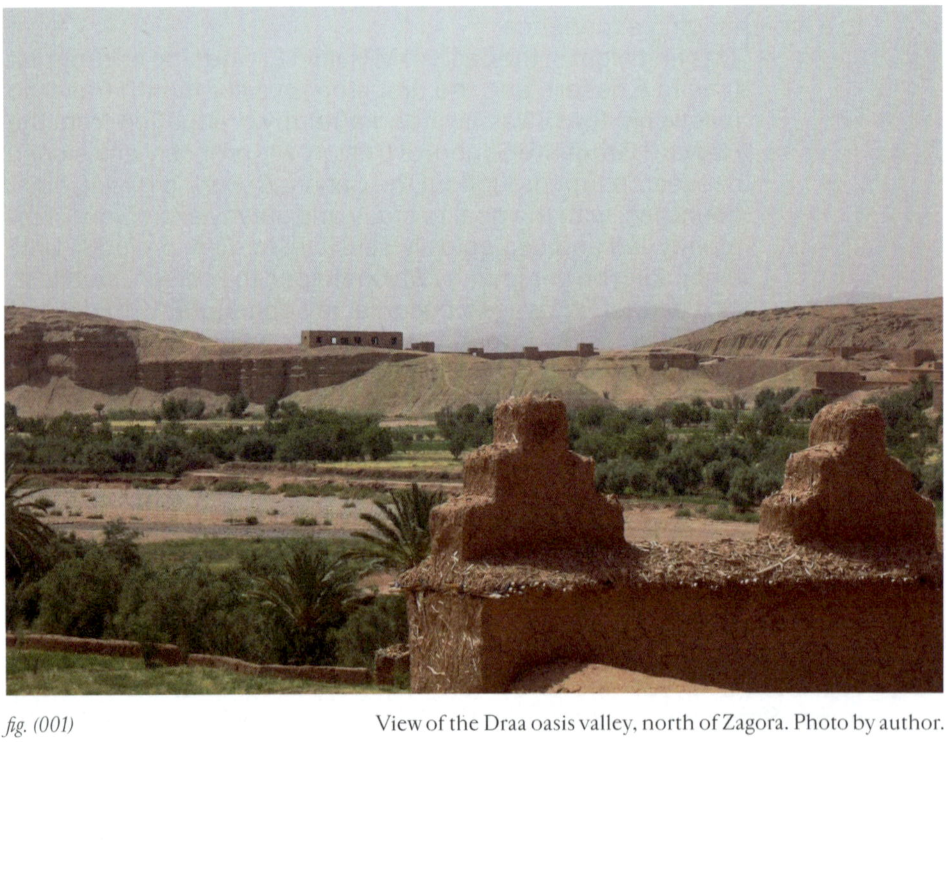

fig. (001) View of the Draa oasis valley, north of Zagora. Photo by author.

Another story that impacted me was one about Driss' grandfather and the origin of his family name. Around 1905, when Driss' grandfather was young, his village underwent a decade of severe drought. All attempts had failed to make the rain return, not even the special prayer sessions held by the holy men and clerics in the Errachidia region. The oasis started to fade, herds died, sand dunes crawled, and famine dug its claws into the village, deeper and deeper each year. The villagers who survived had only skin hanging onto their skeletons. When he came of age, Driss' grandfather refused to leave his famished village to seek work and a better life. Instead, he relentlessly started digging wells until one day when water had come gushing out. By finding the most precious of all treasures in the desert, he ensured the revival of his village. From then on, his last name was changed to "Laadem" meaning the "greatest" of them all. Since hearing this story, a glass of water never tasted the same to me. It had ten times more power than any other drink I knew. Driss shyly admitted that his generation lacked his grandfather's courage. With his cousins and friends, he left
[03] the oasis for Fez after a devastating disease, the Bayoud,† attacked all the palm trees. It robbed the villagers of their economic livelihood based on date sales, took away a key source of nourishment for them and their livestock, and stripped the oasis from the upper layer of its three-tiered canopy system, weakening its capacity to resist the advancement of
[04] sand dunes.† The damage was unfathomable. Children, women, and the elderly were left behind in the oasis, surviving on meager remittances sent by their relatives. After he finished sharing his stories, Driss often told me that his heart longed for his family and oasis, which he missed despite its decline. During these moments, when sadness broke down the pitch of his voice, I used to describe the one thing he longed the most to experience: the sea. I promised him that I would take him with me one day to see it, just as he would take me to see the Sahara. It was a deal: trading one immensity for another, the sea for the desert.

When I started primary school, a whole new desert chapter opened up before me. Indeed, my fascination for deserts, and in particular, with Driss' Sahara, blossomed from my voracious reading of novels by Jean-Marie Gustave Le Clézio, winner of the 2008 Nobel Prize in Literature. I was enamored by Le Clézio's hypnotic description of deserts and the Blue Men that inhabited them. His

03

The Bayoud, a vascular disease of date palm, caused by *Fusarium oxysporum f. sp. albedinis* is the most damaging disease of date palm in Morocco and accounts for as much as 75% of yield losses; Abdelhi Dihazi et al, "Use of Two Bacteria for Biological Control of Bayoud Disease Caused by Fusarium Oxysporum in Date Palm (Phoenix dactylifera L) Seedlings," *Plant Physiology and Biochemistry*, Vol. 55, (2012), 7-15.

04

The oasis is composed of three categories of planting: palm trees, fruit trees, and shrubs. The combination of all three creates a cool microclimate.

novel *Désert* (1980) was his most poignant and contains two intertwined stories. Its first half and end depict the massacre between 1902 to 1912 of the Tuaregs, nomadic tribes that were also called the Blue Men by French military troops during the occupation of the Sakia Al Hamra region, in Southern Morocco. Nour, a young nomad, witnesses the tragic unfolding of this war, in which the Tuaregs, led by the legendary Moulay Ahmed ben Mohammed El Fadel,† fought valiantly for [05] their freedom. I remember that the text of this first part occupied only half of each page, leaving the rest blank, as if the desert wind had blown the rest away, and as if Le Clézio wanted me to read everything slowly to fully enter the world of his novel.

The second storyline of the book takes place 50 years later. It narrates the life of Lalla, a young girl and descendant of the vanquished Blue Men. She lives in a shantytown located outside of an unnamed Moroccan city. To escape from her destitute condition, Lalla inhabits the mystical world of her ancestors, fed by visions of sand dune mazes and harrowing winds, and has encounters with Es Ser,† [06] a spirit warrior from tribe of the Blue Men. A metaphor for the desert itself, he is described as "a dream that has come from afar [...], a dream inside which she enters."† [07]

In the book, Lalla falls in love with Haratin, a mute shepherd with similar origins who can speak to the animals. They attempt to return to the desert, to no avail, and then she migrates to Marseille, where she leads an impoverished life until becoming a successful model. Despite the unexpected turn of events, she ends up returning to Morocco to give birth to Haratin's child. The powerful calling of the desert – which is not just composed of landscapes of *regs* or *ergs*,† but a boundless [08] kingdom and a spiritual resource – has proven too strong to resist.

05

Moulay Ahmed ben Mohammed El Fadel was also known as Maa al Ainain, or "water of the two springs." In *Désert*, Le Clézio wrongly translates his name as the "water of the two eyes" instead of the "water of the two springs." Spring and eye are written in the same manner in Arabic. He was a theologian, philosopher, astronomer, and founding father of the city of Smara.

06

Es Ser, in Arabic, means the secret.

07

Translated by the author; J. M. G. Le Clézio, *Désert*, Paris, Gallimard, coll. "Folio," (1980) 204.

08

Regs are a rocky desert while ergs are a sandy desert.

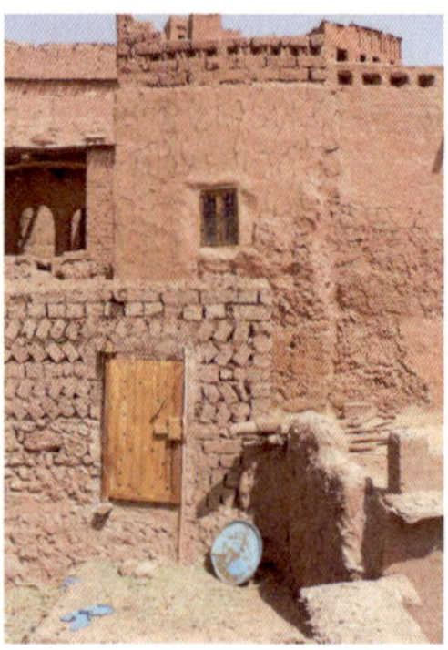

fig. (002) Old kashbah in the Zaouia village, oasis of M'hamid El Ghizlane. Photo by author.

Using a simple vocabulary and repetitive, austere prose, the desert described by Le Clézio is "a country where there is no man, no
[09] cities, nothing that stops you or troubles you," † a limitless territory out of the space-time continuum, a world that can exist without men and goes beyond men's existence. The nomads in *Désert* do not want to master and possess nature, they do not live in a "universe shrank by social conventions [...], they do not know the obsession of property, hunger for hearty pleasures, refusal of
[10] suffering and death." † Humbled by their wandering through the desert, they know that life is, in itself, a renouncement. Amid the vast arid void that surrounds them, Nour and Lalla, my younger-self alter egos in *Désert*, never seem lonely. They live in harmony with the elements around them, and hold a simple sense of happiness, that we, as city dwellers, seem to have lost. It is this happiness that Driss Laadem wanted his children and wife to experience on a daily basis. This is why he made a promise to never bring them to the city, which he saw as a source of moral and physical corruption. Every time I requested to meet his family, this is what he would tell me.

Paradoxically, despite my obsession with deserts, I had never visited the Sahara while growing up in Morocco. Its access appeared to be surrounded by an invisible barrier, constructed
[11] of myths and imaginaries imported by 'inlanders,' † who painted the Sahara as a place of doom. In the 1980s, the farthest point our family managed to reach was Marrakech, and if lucky, 50 kilometers south of it to the snowy Atlas peaks of Oukaimeden. Every time I muttered my wish to head south beyond the Atlas Mountains, I was swarmed by phrases like:

[12] "Why can't you sit still on your behind for a change" †
"There is nothing interesting for you to see there, you will only find sand"
"There are palm groves in Marrakech, why travel so far to see something similar?"
"We hear of cars and trucks falling off the road at the dangerous crossing points in the Atlas Mountains"
"You will most certainly be greeted by poisonous serpents and scorpions"

09

Translated by the author; Le Clézio, *Désert*, 204.

10

Translated by author; J.M. G. Le Clézio, *l'Inconnu sur terre*, Paris, Gallimard, coll. "le Chemin," (1978) 224.

11

In colloquial Moroccan Arabic, inlanders, or n*ass addakhil*, refer to Moroccans living beyond the Anti-Atlas range, that is beyond the beginning of the Sahara Desert.

12

Kasbahs in colloquial Moroccan Arabic refer to tall, rammed earth courtyard houses one finds along the Saharan region. A group of kasbahs forms a *ksar* which is a fortified village.

13 My late father's favorite.

14 My late grandmother's all-time favorite.

"Sand storms will swallow you alive"
"The heat will melt you and waste you away"
"Old rammed earth kasbahs† will come crashing down upon your head" [13]
"If you remain such a tomboy in search of adventure no one will want to marry you"† [14]
"You will get kidnapped"

I can fill pages with the replies I heard that left me fuming inside. I knew all too well, thanks to Driss Laadam, that all these statements were pure nonsense.

So, my postgraduate traveling fellowship was somewhat an act of revenge in disguise, the accomplishment of an unrequited love affair with the Sahara, an excuse for the journey I had always wanted to fulfill. This journey was to take me across the Sahara Desert from west to east, with the first stop in the oasis of M'hamid El Ghizlane, where a local, Halim Sbai, who had started a community-rooted tourism initiative, caught my attention.

M'hamid El Ghizlane is located at the southern tip of the famous Drâa Valley, a UNESCO biosphere composed of a 200-kilometer-long palm tree grove, which used to be an old caravan route linking Timbuktu to Moroccan imperial cities. The construction of the Mansour Eddahbi Dam upstream of the Drâa River near the town of Ouarzazate, disturbed the irrigation of the oases downstream. Due to its location at the end of the valley, the oasis of M'hamid suffered the most. Halim Sbai, a local guide, offered authentic encounters with farmers and nomads, and shared with tourists the true hardships of his oasis, which faced decreased water resources, rural exodus, and predatory forms of tourism. Together they planted tamarisk trees at the edge of the oasis to prevent sand dunes from advancing further.

Moha and Abdelkhalek, friends from the Moroccan Ministry of Tourism who knew Halim, tagged along on my first stop. I suspected that my fellowship highly concerned them: by coming with me to M'hamid, they wanted to be certain that I was indeed ready to undertake my Saharan trip through Mali, Mauritania, Tunisia, Libya and Egypt (today, I realize that such a trip would be unthinkable). Crossing the Atlas Mountain range, and driving down towards the Drâa Valley for the first time was cathartic, the poetic words of Le Clézio were humming in my mind. I was in awe of the majesty of the landscape: a continuous sea of palm tree oases, unfolding like a sinuous green snake against jagged rocky hills. A glorious sunset welcomed us in M'hamid, warming the color of the rammed earth walls of the kasbah where we sat. The day after our arrival, we visited Halim's camp and toured his oasis. While sharing a glass of hot tea after dinner, our tired feet free of shoes, we started discussing the potential of eco-tourism in the region of M'hamid, to help restore the ecosystem of the oases and support disadvantaged populations, among them landless nomads who were forced to settle down. Halim knew of a secret route east of the Drâa Valley, which would be well suited to launch such an initiative. He was so excited by this idea that he offered to show us the route the following day.

In order to avoid the unforgiving June sun, we decided to

This was the night that would set the events that follow into motion.

jump in the 4x4 the moment the first rays of light started to appear, choosing to ignore our sleepless night. We slowly moved north through the desert landscape that transformed from flat and sandy to hilly and rocky. I could not take my eyes off the tamarix and acacia trees we drove by, each stood alone like a lonesome warrior ready to defend its territory, just like the Blue Men in Le Clézio's *Désert*. Halim put on desert blues music by the Malian group Tinariwen. Electric guitar sounds blended with traditional Tuareg and African music filled the car. The music's unhurried beats seemed synchronized with the gentle undulations of the 4x4 pacing on the dirt road. Rocked by the car's sways, the music, and the repetitive nature of the landscape, I was falling into a hypnotic state, which I was fighting, not to lose a moment of the trip. At one point, Halim informed us that he had forgotten the cooler in which he had put our food, but that we should be able to find food in a nearby village. Two hours later, there was still no village in sight. The sun was now high up in the sky at 10:00 AM. We had had no breakfast as we were rushing to take off and shared a few walnuts that Abdelkhalek had luckily taken with him. After one more hour of driving, Halim decided to stop the car by an acacia tree and asked us to join him underneath it. With the back of his palm, he sponged down droplets of sweat that had gathered on his forehead, and he said with hesitation: "Listen...May god be merciful...forgetting the food and water is the least of our concerns...I forgot my GPS and it looks like we are lost...There is no phone signal in this area. We will run out of fuel in a few hours...this has never happened to me before...but I have a plan let's each climb a hill and check if we see any village or oasis, then we will reunite by the car and we will drive to the next valley and start again the same process..."

We climbed hill after hill, and the same rocky landscape repeated itself as if our minds were playing tricks on us and had reproduced the same hill with the exact stone arrangement over and over and over again. Oddly, we diligently climbed the rocky hills under the scorching heat, with no water and no food, and reported back, for hours on end. After repeating the climb six times, my muscles started to ache and my brain started to boil. I decided to rest and sit by the shade of the car, when I saw him.

First, the hill's jagged stones slowly flattened and its surface started glistening like the scales of a shiny fish. Then, he appeared. A dark man was waving at me from afar, and making large gestures with his arm, asking me to approach him. I closed my eyes and opened my heavy eyelids with difficulty. The man was still standing, waving at me. He was real! I screamed in joy, but no sound came out of my throat. For several long seconds, I gathered my strength and managed to call my friends. I cried victory: our savior was right there, ready to help us. I saw them move with unease, a worried look on their faces. I thought: were they intending to leave me here and selfishly ask the man to only save them? Were they intending to cook me up as a thank-you meal for the mysterious savior? My steaming brain was fomenting the most improbable scenarios, when Halim gently took my hand and told me: "Aziza, you are seeing a mirage. We desert people also see them sometimes. Believe me, there is no man here to save us, we are going to find our own way back." I insisted that the man was real. Undeterred, I said: "You are wrong Halim, I can see two men now waving at us further back."

It took a while for Halim to calm me down and bring me back to my senses, he walked with me towards the saviors and we both saw that they were simply piles of stones. I stood there horrified: I experienced a mirage, the desert was tricking me. I had to remain hyper-alert to not tip over into the dangerous alternative reality that I had just escaped.

> We drove to the next valley with our last drop of gas. The three men started their respective climbs, as I laid down on the bare ground, sharp rocks penetrating my back and tears flowing down my face. I thought: will I irreversibly lose my mind? What would appear before my eyes now? Le Clézio's desert spirit Es Ser came to mind, so I thought of conjuring him and asking him for help.

Suddenly, a loud scream pierced the silent, solemn atmosphere. It was Abdelkhalek. "Oasis, oasis!" he shouted. Was he also experiencing a mirage? Seeing Moha and Halim dance around him gave me some hope. I limped and joined them on the hill. Before me, lay a surreal sight: a verdant, tiny oasis nestled in the bottom of the same arid, rocky valley we encountered endlessly during the day. It was the most beautiful thing I had ever seen. I rubbed my eyes. I had to touch it, taste it, smell it, and lie in it to believe it. My eyesight had become untrustworthy. When we set foot inside it, I felt that I was literally walking into Driss Laadem's heavenly oasis: it was deliciously cool, gentle leaves caressed our bare arms and faces, sweet almonds and apricots filled our hungry stomachs, birds' songs came to our ears, and water from a well refreshed our exhausted bodies... Halim prevented us from drinking it since its hardiness could potentially harm us. The happiness we felt inside the bountiful, nurturing oasis was indescribable. We were in full communion with nature, just like Le Clézio's *Désert* heroes. I was ready to stay in this paradise forever. What else does one really need?

I started thanking out loud all the men and women that tended to the oasis. I admired their courage, knowledge, and strong will that made what is seemingly improbable, possible. I wanted to meet them and show them my appreciation for this fertile land that had saved us. I wanted to ask them to forgive us for having shamelessly eaten the fruit of their arduous labor, without asking them permission. After resting in the tiny oasis, we started our search for a living soul under a starlit desert sky, having strong hopes that a settlement must be located near cultivated land. After a few hours, we saw lights and when we approached, we found a small house. Barking dogs informed the housemaster of our arrival. A humble, short man in a green djellaba greeted us, his eyes avoiding ours. He was a shy man of few words. He confirmed that he was the owner of the oasis we passed through. He was the only person cultivating it. My admiration for him increased a thousandfold. We shared our story and asked for forgiveness. He was glad his oasis fruits and almonds were of use to us and he appreciated that we did not touch his well, since its water is way too precious during the summer. He told us that he had never encountered tourists before. He offered to host us in his home for the night and to walk us to a nearby village at dawn.

The austerity of his stone and rammed earth home, with its four rooms organized around a central courtyard, deeply touched me. Its simple, introverted architecture was in perfect harmony with its arid surroundings

Strangely, the danger and deceitfulness of the desert that I had just experienced did not deter me from it, quite the opposite. That very night, I realized that I had fallen head over "hills" for the Sahara. I was in love not with Le Clézio's or Driss Laadam's Saharas, but with a version of my very own.

At that moment, I felt ready to start my research journey.

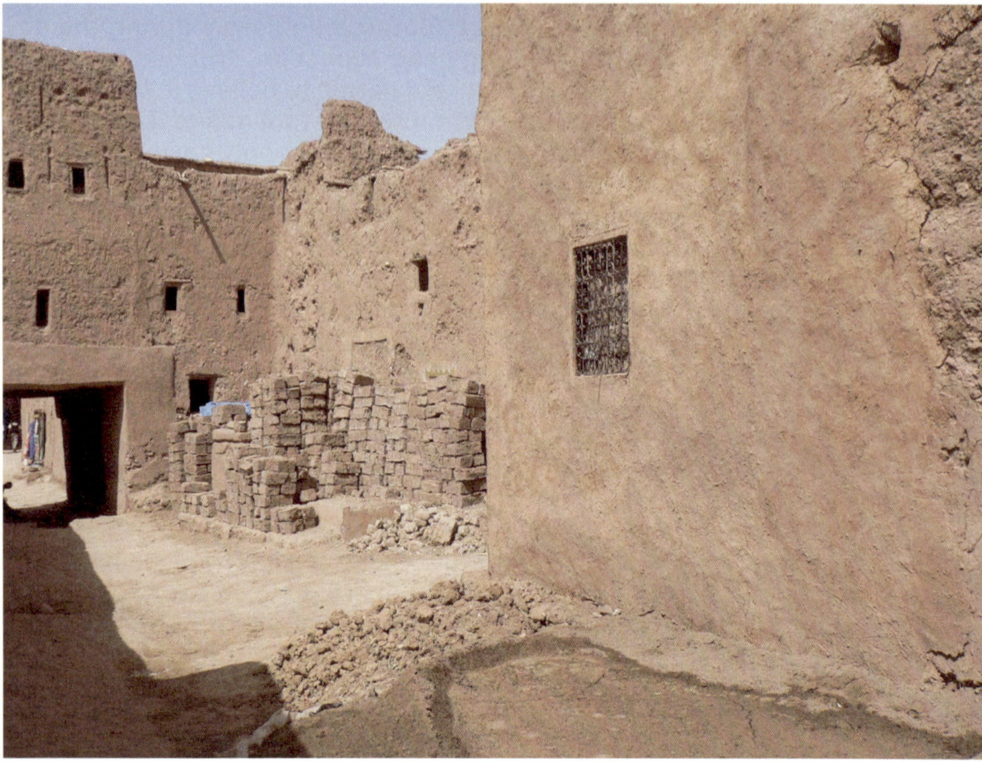

fig. (003) Mudbrick stacks in the Zaouia village, oasis of M'hamid El Ghizlane. Photo by author.

Field Notes

Faysal Tabbarah

A Note on Our Field Notes

In the following pages, you will find what the research team has come to describe as field notes. Gathered together from road trips done both individually and in groups, these notes contain many voices and were conceptualized, assembled, and written through a rather messy process, but always a collaborative one.

Why the format and tone of *a field note?*

This decision, coming in laboriously, was in response to another question that I have been consistently confronted with throughout this project: what are your research findings?

> This question, along with its near-infinite variations, I could never answer simply or concisely. After many conversations, I found myself replying to it in a different way, by recounting a collection of seemingly disparate anecdotes which required both trust and imagination from the listener. In one of which, I describe how an elderly owner of a leisure farm in the Western Al Hajar Mountains, our area of focus, told me that water-saving techniques, such as drip irrigation, do not produce strong trees. Humorously, he accompanies his statement with a full-body gesture reminiscent of a flexing bodybuilder. In other moments, especially when talking to architects, I tell them how this same farm owner says that he sleeps in his house but lives on the farm, repeating the mirroring images of sleeping and living in case it was too subtle.

When it became clear that these anecdotes must find their way into this publication, they became stories, in a flawed attempt to elevate them from the alleged fleetingness of an anecdote. Only after some time did it become rather apparent that this seemingly misfit combination of observations, interpretations, and analysis, what a trained anthropologist might call a thick description, contained the project's research findings in the form of field notes.

In addition to these field notes, this body of work included studying primary and secondary records and speaking with experts who are building future and resilient systems within arid environments, as well as owners of leisure, subsistence, and commercial farms in Al Hajar. Together, all of this research produced a wealth of information that helped us conceive of an exhibition that provokes different possibilities for alternative built-environments which reimagine arid landscapes as spaces of abundance.

Specifically, the research framework oscillated along three entangled categories: places, materials, and tactics. Here, places are defined as spaces in which agricultural thinking is expressed within the Western Al Hajar. These places highlight the interaction between people, culture, environments, local knowledge, and technology. The second category, materials, points to the range of matter, including raw, semi-processed, and fully industrialized materials that are used for construction. Lastly, tactics categorizes the ways in which individuals and groups reconfigure different materials in deliberate ways to support their everyday activities in agricultural sites. These tactics provoke an ad-hoc, multi-material, and misfit attitude towards place-making which challenges the assembly logics that are proliferating in mainstream construction.

While places, materials, and tactics can be described separately in research, in the field, they are always entangled. Layered upon these categories, is the exceptional nature of every tactic that resists falling into a pattern. Here, I have come to understand that there are particularities from each that almost never repeat from one instance to the other, making each story unique, holding a hidden wealth of knowledge, history, and culture.

Tactics of Marking

Throughout Al Hajar Mountains, stones of various sizes, from the easily hand-held to those that require some effort, are used to mark the landscape as a form of communication with others whom one would probably never meet. Along walking trails, small stones are placed methodically to identify directions, forks in the road, or property boundaries. Sometimes, small stacked stones appear to indicate that you are in the resting spot of other wanderers who have spent some time appreciating what the stones can offer. Even in the most remote areas, it is surprising to find these markers of recent human activities as they become a slow and delayed language between those who occupy and pass through these spaces.

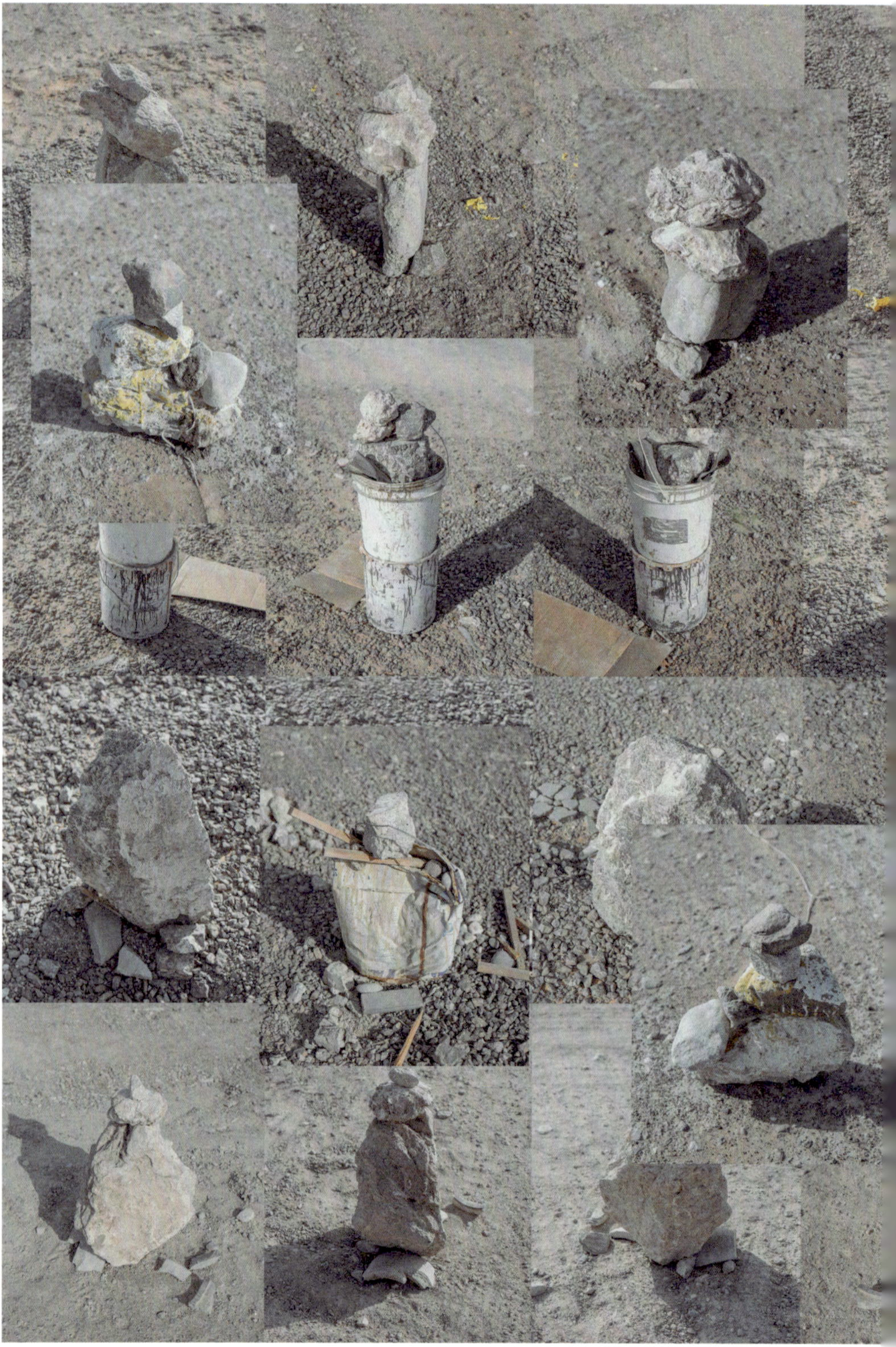

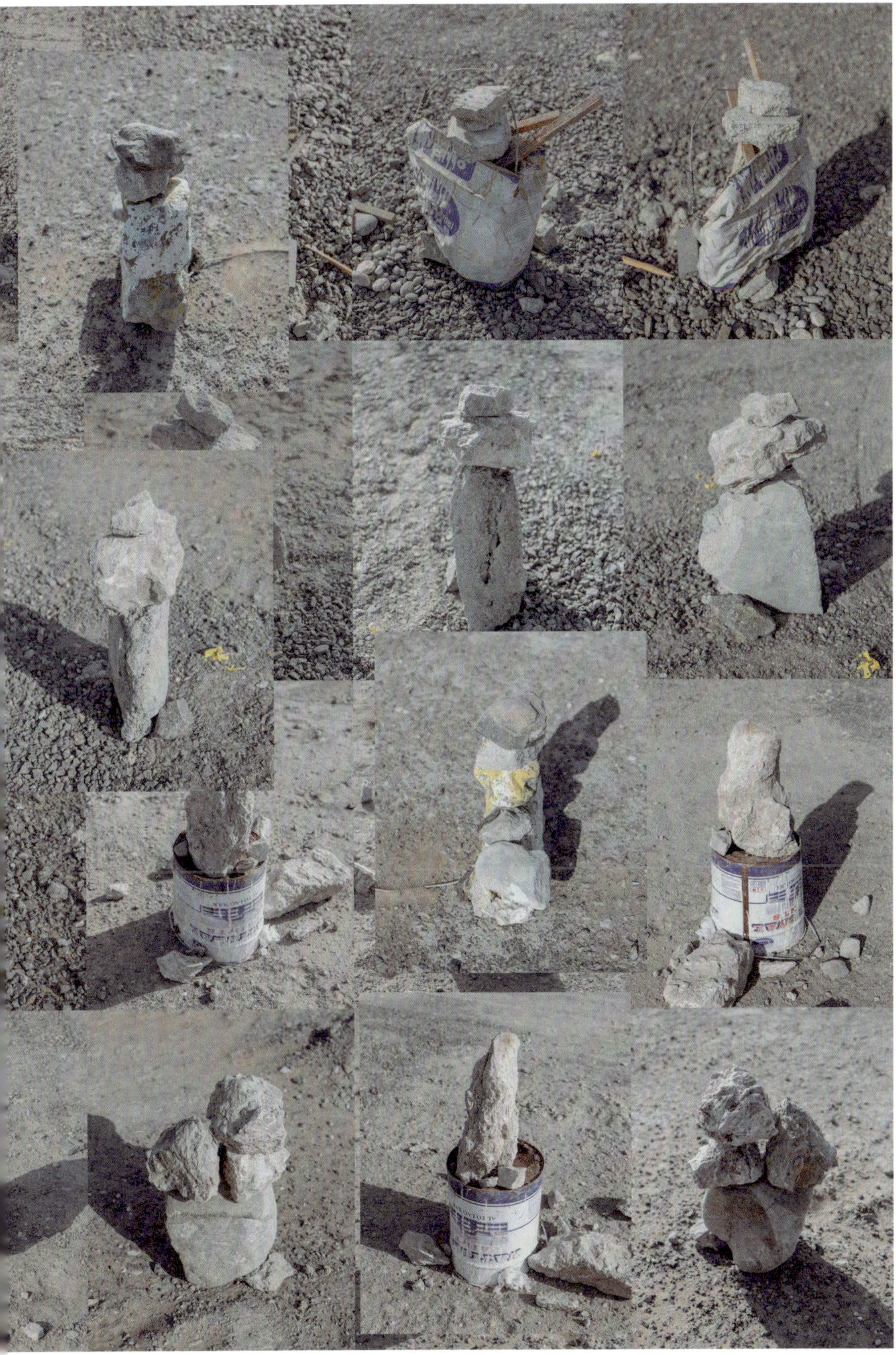

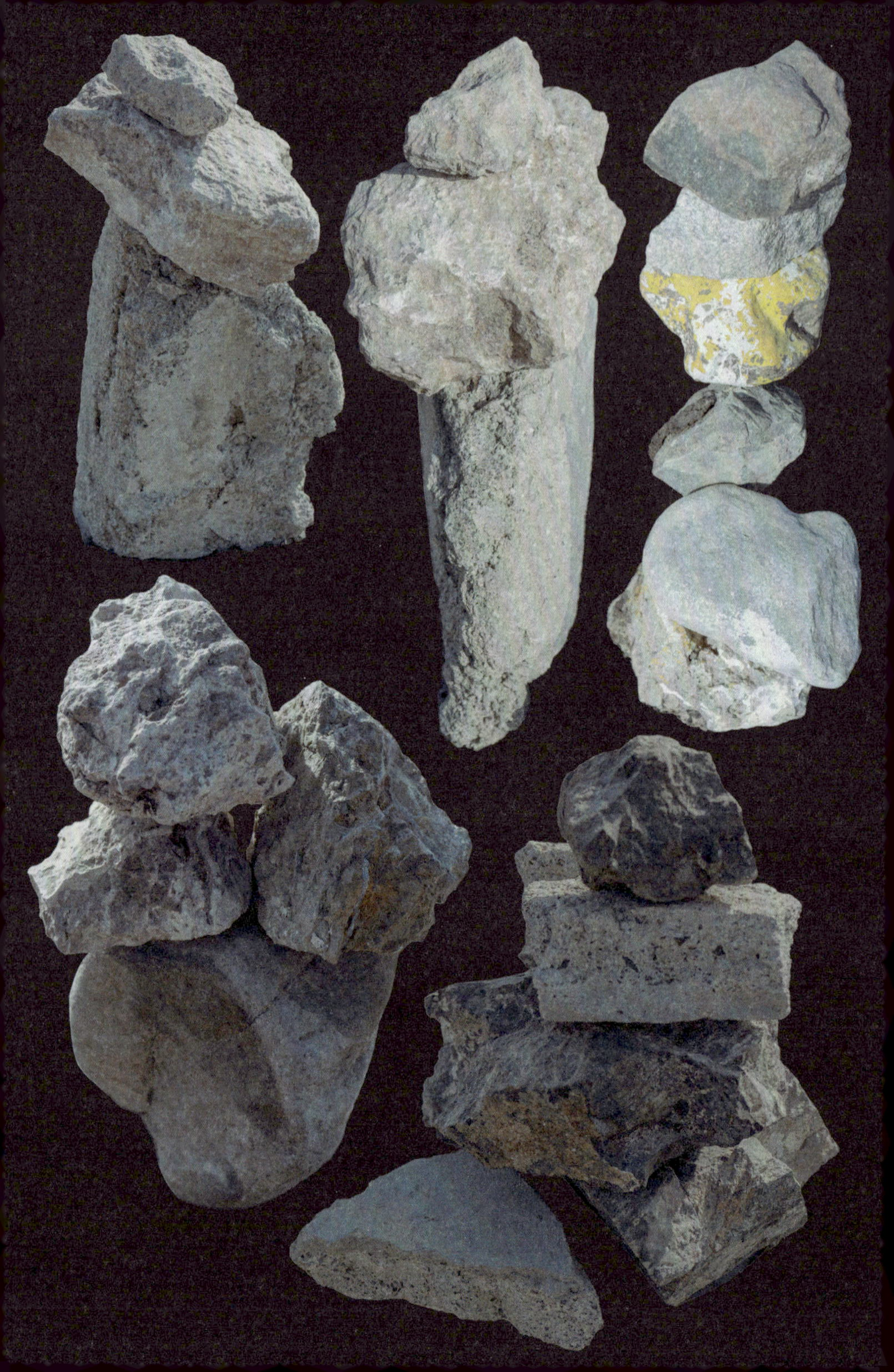

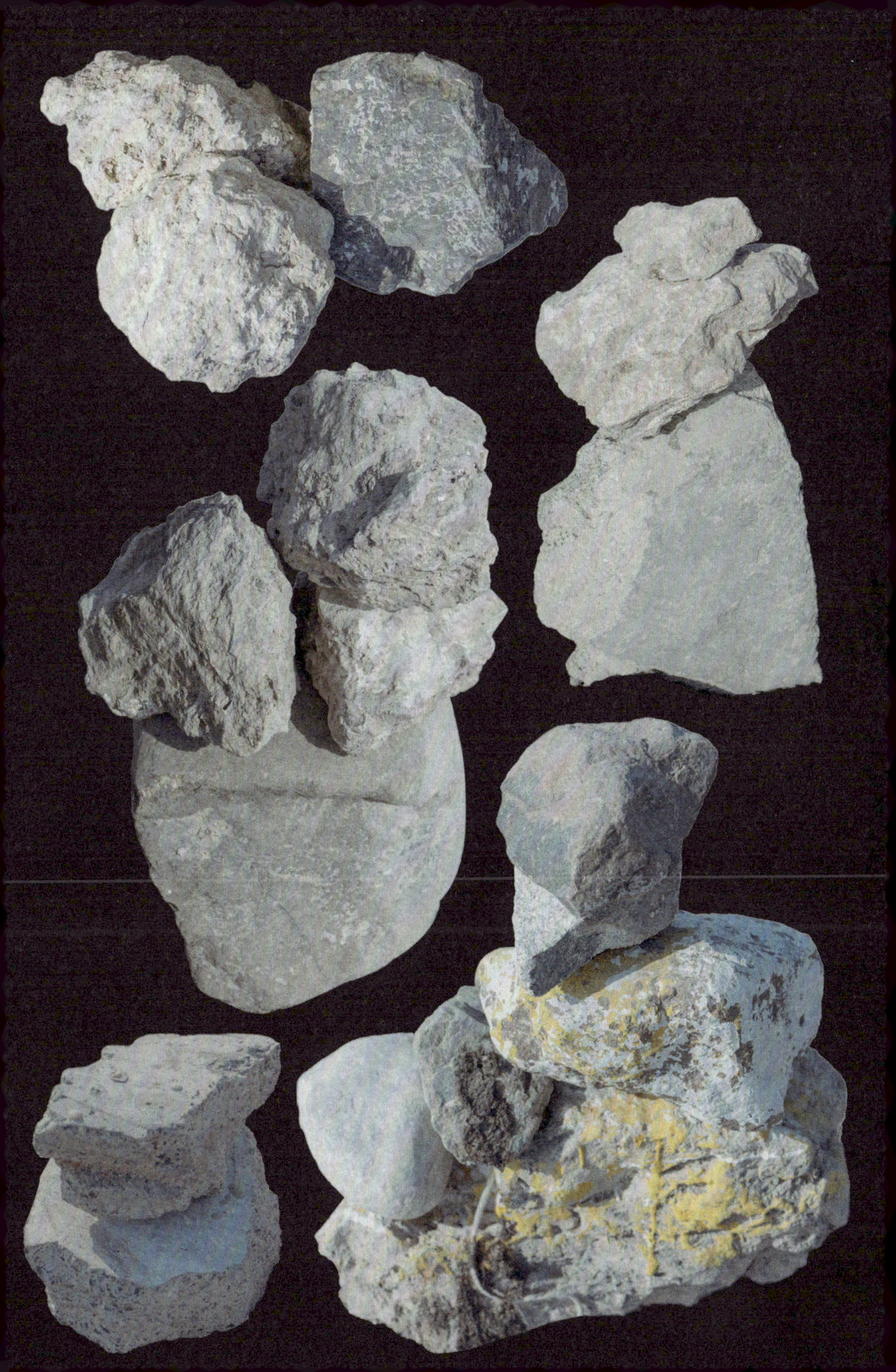

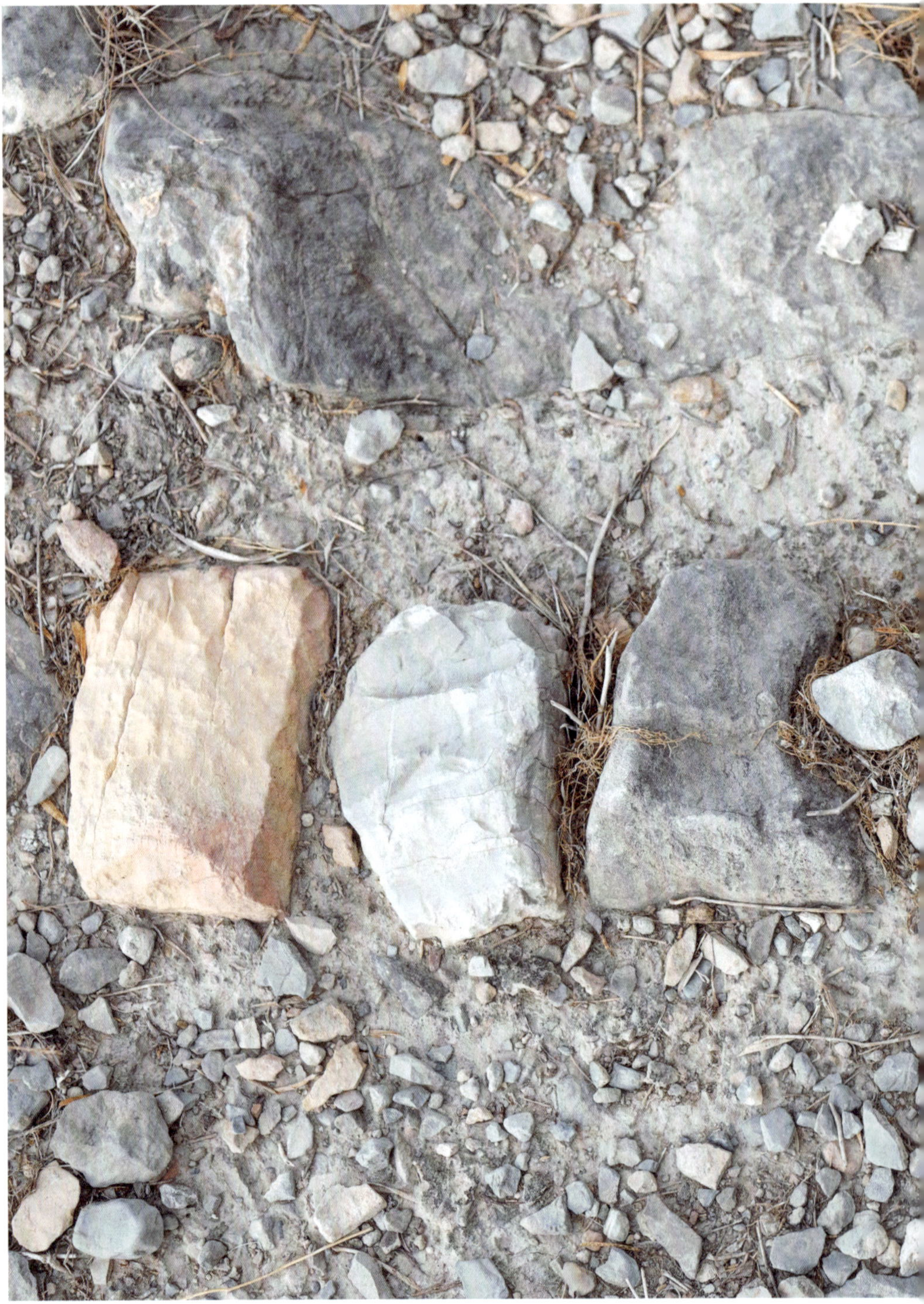

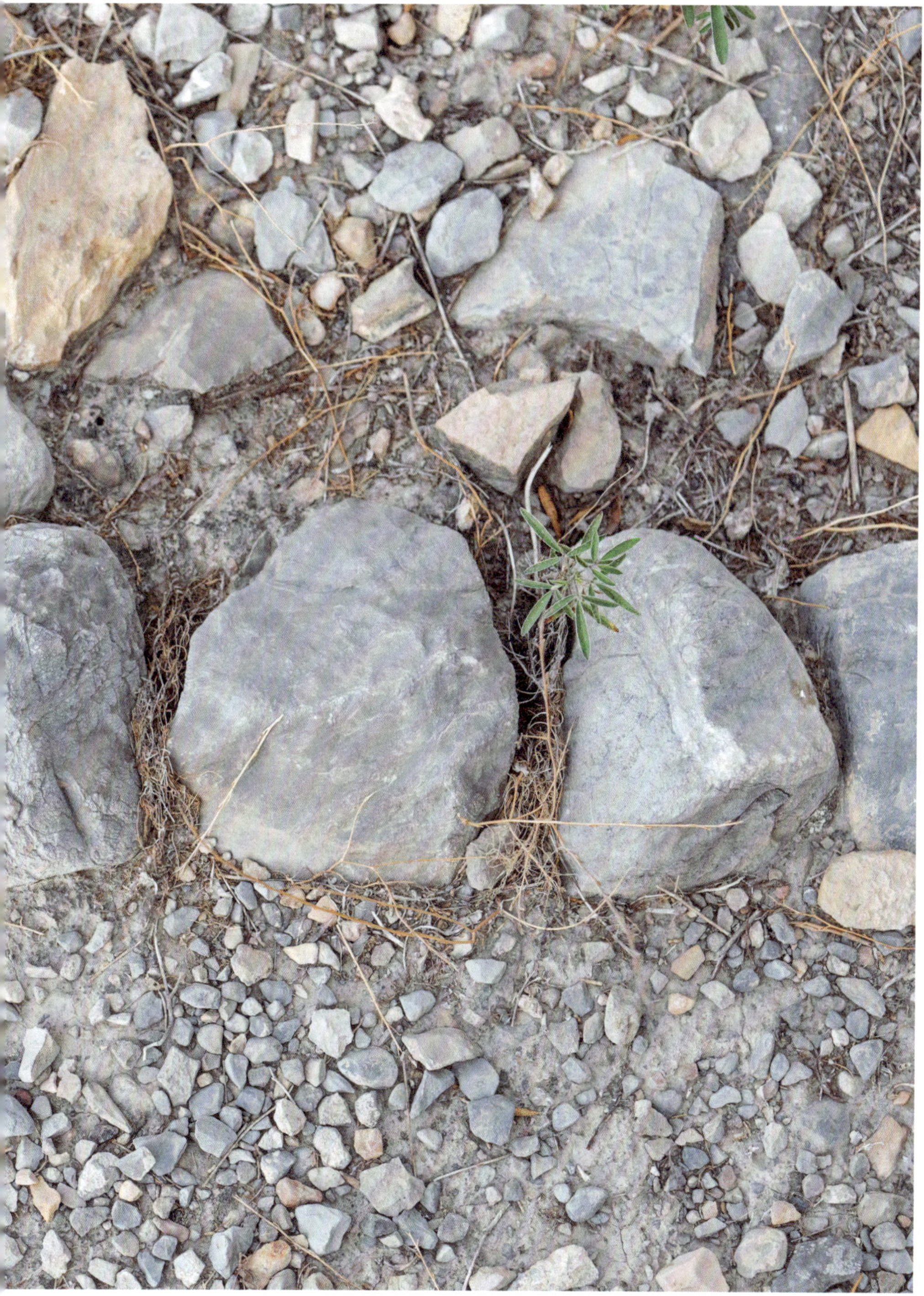

Faysal Tabbarah

A Note on an Oddly Natural History Exhibit

In 985 CE, the Arab geographer Al Maqdisi wrote *The Best Divisions in the Knowledge of the Regions* (*Aḥsan Al Taqasim Fi Maʿrifat Al Aqalim)*, in which he describes three towns within Al Hajar Mountains that are still standing in present-day Oman: Suhar on Al Batinah coast, Nazwa in the mountains, and Dhank in the western foothills. Al Maqdisi recounted that Suhar "is the gateway to China, the storehouse of the East and of Al Iraq... The open place appointed
[01] for prayer is in the midst of date palms."† In this land "there are wells of
middling water, a canal of fresh water, and an abundance of goods of
[02] all kinds."† Within the mountains, Nizwa is rich in water, with drinking
water and irrigation from flood waters, while Dhank on the eastern
foothills, much like Hafit (as far as I can tell, the same as present-day
[03] Hafit close to Al Ain) "is in the midst of palms."†

I began making a series of road trips along this complex cross-section sometime in 2018. To get to the Western Al Hajar in 2023 suggests driving eastward from one of the major urban centers, Abu Dhabi, Dubai, or Sharjah on the western coast along the Gulf. This journey also parallels the camelback trip that missionary Samuel Zwemer, and many others it seems, took in 1902 from Abu Dhabi to Muscat.

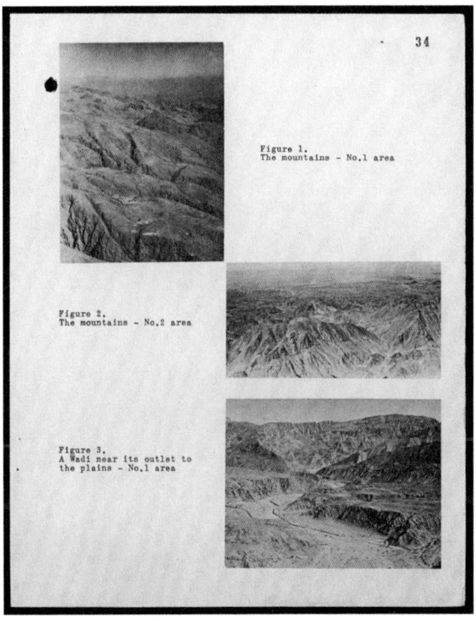

fig. (001) A series of aerial photos of Al Hajar Mountains from the early 1960s. Water Supply FO 371/163058/34. © Images reproduced by permission of The National Archives, London, England.

The 90 minutes that it takes me to drive from Downtown Dubai to the depths of Al Hajar is like driving through an oddly natural history exhibit spanning a quintessentially twenty-first century city, giving way to the near-infinitely photographed rolling sand dunes dotted with ghaf trees and shrubs. Some 60 minutes into the drive the sand dunes slowly become more solid as the gravel plains begin to take over, usually somewhere along Al Dhaid, with increasingly larger rocks appearing over time. This geological road trip cuts through urban centers, urban edges, desert, gravel plains, mountains, and coastal foothills with villages and small towns along the way. My road of choice has become the newly inaugurated Khorfakkan Road given its centrality, allowing me excursions towards the Emirate of Fujairah in the south, and Dibba Al Hisn on the Omani border towards Musandam in the north.

The historic cross-section described by Al Maqdisi parallels the conditions along the ring road and the E89 and E99 highways where one experiences Al Hajar's foothills, wadis, and its fertile east coast in relatively similar ways.

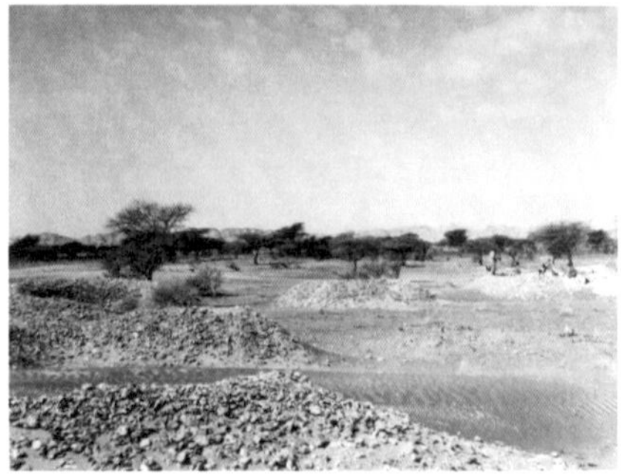

fig. (002) Al Aini Falaj with Al Hajar Mountains in the background - 1954, Julian Walker © UAE National Library and Archives.

These areas are particularly useful for studying the relationship between environmental and spatial imaginaries emerging within the arid landscapes of Al Hajar and its environs given the fairly considerable underground water reserves that it has been building up for millions of years.† This spatial imaginary is neither traditional [04]
nor does fall into the ever-so-seductive trap of neo-vernacularism. It is a tactically astute model producing spaces that are historically relevant and very much in the present, but also one that blurs agricultural production, public, and private spaces. This blurring is, in large part, a function of historical *falaj* infrastructures, which are water collection, management, and distribution systems that are deeply connected to spatial and social practices. By constructing spaces that defy clear categorization and challenge hegemonic spatial norms that separate production and domesticity, landowners and farmers in Al Hajar and its environs provoke an alternative land-based spatial imaginary.

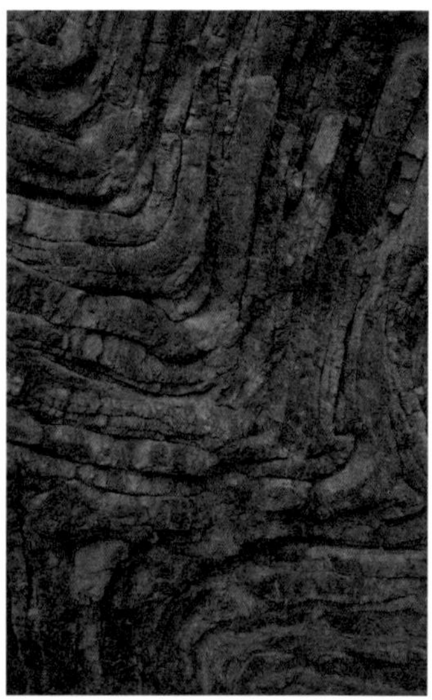

fig. (003) Complex geological formations can be seen across Al Hajar Mountains, such as this example from Wadi Kub in the interior of the mountain range. Photo by author.

My use of the concept of the imaginary has its roots in Jean-Paul Sartre's work on the imagination as a human activity that is distinctly different from observation. In *The Imaginary: A Phenomenological Psychology of the Imagination*, Sartre shows us that the imaginary is "distinct from both the structure of perception and that of conceptual thought."† Our ability to imag- [05]
ine, Sartre posits, allows us to view and
construct our worlds.† Subsequently, in [06]
Liberation Ecologies, Richard Peet and Michael Watts urge us to "recognize the emancipatory potential of the environmental imaginary and to begin to chart the ways in which natural as much as
social agency can be harnessed." † For [07]

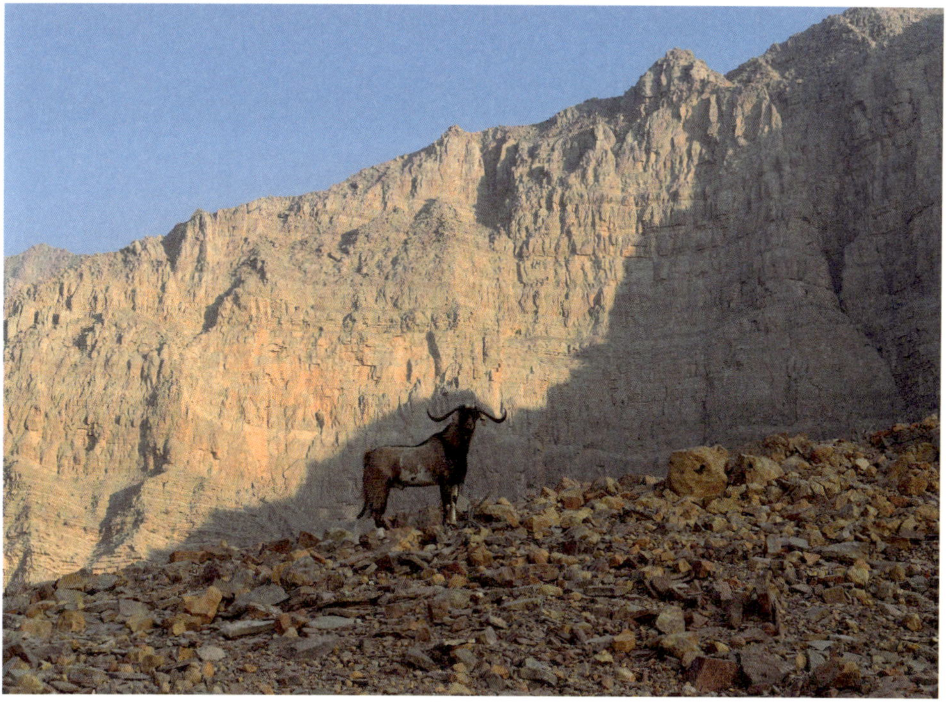

fig. (004) An Arabian Tahr, a native of Al Hajar Mountains. Photo by Samar Halloum.

Andrew Jamison, Ron Eyerman, and Jacqueline Cramer, adopting an ecological worldview means "stressing the systemic interconnection
[08] of natural and social processes."† Thus, an environmental imaginary describes how people bring their natural surroundings to bear on how they understand and shape their social, cultural, and physical worlds. These constructs deeply influence the production of space and an architectural imaginary.

A Short Environmental History of Al Hajar and Water

Located at the threshold between two main meteorological regions, the Saharo-Arabian subtropical hot desert region and the
[09] Indian Ocean's monsoon regime,† Al Hajar is more than 700 kilometers long, stretching from the Musandam Peninsula in the north at the mouth of the Strait of Hormuz to Ras Al Hadd in the south, the easternmost tip of the Arabian Peninsula.

Formed in the Late Cretaceous (a geological period between 100.5 to 66 million years ago), Al Hajar occupies areas in both the United Arab Emirates (UAE) and the Sultanate of Oman,
[10] varying in width from 50 to 150 kilometers,† while its highest peak is

3,035 meters.† [11] On its eastern foothills is Al Batinah region† [12] (roughly translated as on the inside, or within), a relatively narrow fertile stretch of coast about 20 to 30 kilometers wide and 280 kilometers long, separating Al Hajar from the Gulf of Oman's waters.† [13] Save for a few mountainous interruptions, Al Batinah spans the entire length of the UAE's eastern coast, from Dibba in the north to Kalba in the south, and is home to the Emirate of Fujairah as well as a number of key towns within the Emirate of Sharjah, such as Khor Fakkan. Al Batinah extends further south in Oman, including the historical port town of Suhar, before finally terminating in the Omani capital city, Muscat.† [14] As the fertile plain disappears in both cardinal directions, the mountains engage the Gulf waters directly and rather abruptly.† [15] Overall, the range is characterized by its sharp red and brown peaks, and is relatively continuous, making the movement of people through it strategically important. Historically, this occurred through three primary drainage routes, only one of which cuts through the UAE territory, connecting from an area close to Al Ain on the east to Suhar in Al Batinah. A contemporary road network makes movement through and around Western Al Hajar a much easier task.† [16]

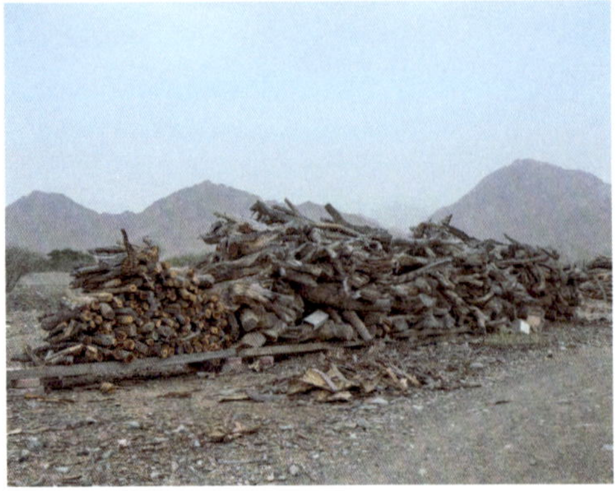

fig. (005) Collected timber can be seen across many sites in Al Hajar Mountains, challenging a narrative of an absence of wood that propagates literature around construction in the region. Photo by Reem Falaknaz.

There are four geological areas in Al Hajar, resulting in rather nuanced differences in human settlement and culture. In the north is the Dibba Zone, a narrow 10-kilometer-wide depression extending 25 kilometers inwards, separating the Musandam Peninsula from the Semail Ophiolite.† [17] The Semail Ophiolite makes up the majority of Al Hajar at approximately 600 kilometers out of the entire 700-kilometer range† [18] and is primarily composed of igneous rocks, giving the landscape its distinct darker color. Other

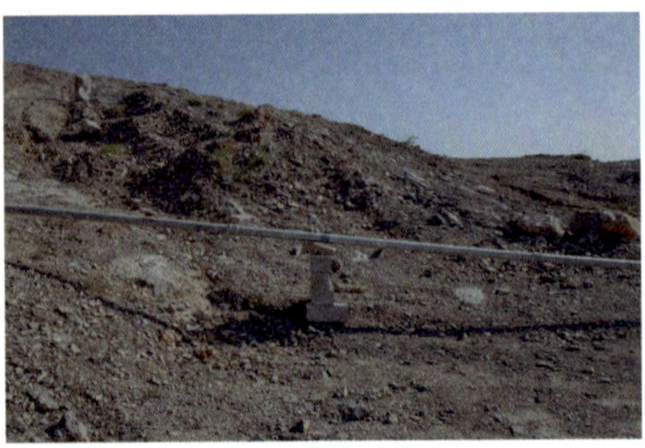

fig. (006) Contemporary water infrastructures appear along driving routes within Al Hajar Mountains. Photo by author.

[19] geological conditions include three large sedimentary massifs† that are primarily limestone and dolomite, which is where the yellowish tints begin to emerge. It is within the limestone regions that the most
[20] groundwater recharge occurs.† Finally, Al Hajar has its own wood-
[21] lands within the Omani territories.†

The historic access to water has made this area home to subsistence and commercial agriculture. Today, both activities continue, and leisure farming has also emerged. This is typically done by families that have moved to urban centers but maintain a practice of agriculture in their ancestral lands. Water build-up occurs from rainwater naturally channeling through the mountain's ridges, most of which percolates into the ground, allowing for a fertile coastal plain on the eastern foothills. Some water also flows into the edges of the sand dunes to the west, producing a fertile chain of towns around Al Ain oasis. It is here that Zwemer described villages that "are nestled in one continuous fertile strip of garden palms, fig trees, mangoes, mulberry trees, and pomegranates. On the outskirts of the gardens is a plain, green with grass and shrubs, where sheep and camel herds tell of Arab wealth. The oasis is due to a half-dozen springs of excel-
[22] lent water from the Okdat range..."†

Thus, agricultural practices exist on both the eastern and western foothills, as well as within Al Hajar's wadis. This exists in contrast to the environmental imaginary of the absence of water constructed along the coast from Abu Dhabi to Ras Al Khaimah. However, despite the relative abundance of water within Al Hajar, Colonel K.W.
[23] Merrylees, a British "professional water diviner,"† had as early as 1954 indicated that in a recently dug Khor Fakkan well "the water table had already receded below the reach of the suction which had been
[24] installed."† Today, this oscillation between absence and presence in Al Hajar emerges both in the landscape and in conversations.

Abundance: Imagined and Managed

Despite my many road trips, I am always taken by surprise when I realize that I'm driving on a highway that cuts through what was once a mountain's mass. Even here, the amateur geologist can find nuance and change, with yellower sedimentary limestone giving way to darker igneous rocks. One rare sighting is the patches of deep red stones with white veins, mainly seen around Hatta in Dubai. If you drive after a rain, shades of turquoise also emerge. Sometimes, if I choose to go to Khor Fakkan directly, I drive through four or five tunnels that are *inside* the mountains. Throughout the drive, the seemingly untouched landscape is disrupted by elements of civilization such as electrical power lines both big and small, single-story commercial enterprises, the area's version of drive-by malls, but also, importantly, elements of water. Zwemer's water wells and watch towers have given way to white plastic water tanks and PVC pipes, signaling the continuing importance of water. Another water element that appears today is the 2000-gallon water tanker truck. Where water was once hidden in the earth and ran through open or subterranean channels, its vessels are now very much visible. They sit on top of relatively small structures such as one-story concrete buildings or steel structures, or on the ground.

There are radical differences in the ways abundance was historically imagined and managed between Al Hajar and the other coastal regions of the UAE. The narrative around finding a spring in Abu Dhabi validates archival findings that speak of a contrast between the coastal desert plateau and the mountainous region and its foothills. This produces a complex and layered narrative around abundance through the lens of water that continues today. Historically, agriculture was "entirely dependent on irrigation"† and John Craven [25]
Wilkinson argues that settlement is dependent on where water is and isn't, or was and wasn't. I also experienced this in my fieldwork. Despite there being no rain-fed agriculture in the past and today,† the [26]
ways in which the landowners and farmers describe water oscillates between absence and presence. When I ask about water, most of the landowners and farmers point with pride to the water wells on their land describing its purity and low levels of salinity. However, they are also cognizant of the increasing depth of the wells when compared to the turn of the century as well as the erratic nature of rain.

Within the Western Al Hajar, there existed two types of water collection, delivery and management systems, the *falaj ghayli* (plural *Aflaj ghayliyah)* and the *falaj da'udi* (plural *aflaj da'udiyya*). In general, a falaj is a system of constructed channels, sometimes above ground and sometimes subterranean, performing as "an organization for distributing water amongst those who have rights to it."† [27]
The falaj ghayli refers to an open-air system channeling surface water from a wadi or a spring, for instance, while a falaj da'udi refers to channels collecting water from a subterranean source such as an aquifer, or a mother well, and includes subterranean channels that eventually emerge above ground.† In my fieldwork, [28]
I have noticed that contemporary farmers

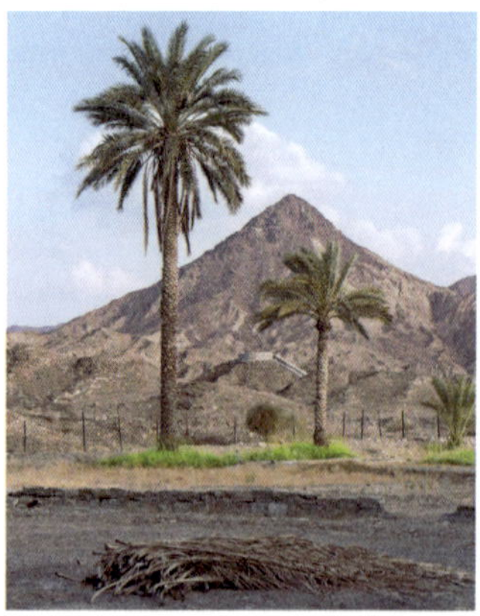

fig. (007) A farm and a water well within Al Hajar Mountains. Photo by Reem Falaknaz.

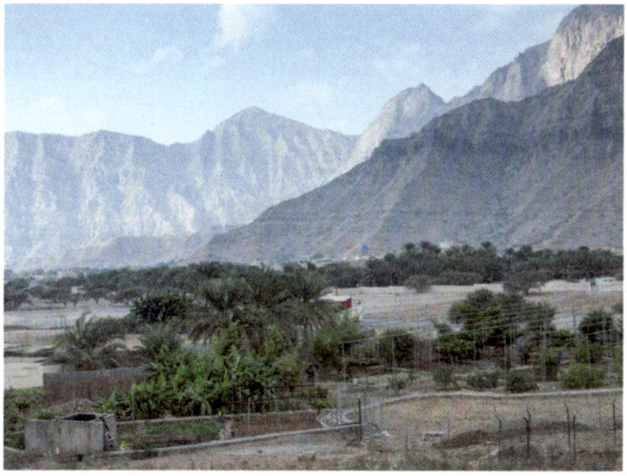

fig. (008) Complex networks or agricultural spaces and domestic neighborhoods at the foothills of Al Hajar Mountains. Photo by Reem Falaknaz.

and landowners use the word falaj to describe both open and subterranean channels. Coincidentally, Wilkinson has made a similar observation in his 1977 book *Water and Tribal Settlement in South-East Arabia: A Study of the*
[29] *Aflaj of Oman.*†

Historically, the ghayl and the da'udi were used primarily within the mountains themselves, while Al Batinah relied primarily on
[30] wells located closer to the irrigable land.† In the case of a falaj, it is important to understand the relationship between its layout and the social conditions it creates, especially as towns were usually adjacent to the irrigable land. At times township and agriculture were too blurred to tell one from the other, blurring production, public, and private spaces. In general, regardless of whether an open or subterranean system was used, one of the first points of contact between the community and water happens at the *shari'a*, the place where access is open for all. This is usually some distance before the channels reach the town or the irrigable land, but once at that point, the
[31] divisions distinguish between domestic and agricultural use.†

When coming into the irrigation zone, the falaj bifurcates to individual farms, and once again to water individual basins. This makes sense given the primary method of irrigation was flood irrigation for about 10 palms per basin. Here, we arrive at the important juncture of water shareholding. Simply put, the principle used for fair distribution is a circular system where the water from the main falaj is accessed by each farm for a specific period of time (e.g., each plot receives water for a full day), after which the next plot in line receives water for the same amount of time. At the end of the loop, the first plot receives water again. This can be divided by days or by hours in the day. Measuring time used to happen by either the movement of the sun or by a mechanical system, sometimes as simple as a bowl with a hole in the bottom that collects water over time, a mechanism used in most places with a falaj system such as North Africa. Given the complexities of delivering equal amounts of water, due to issues of flow, land size, slopes, and other physical constraints, the typical
[32] number of users is around eight.†

While much of the historical physical infrastructures of the falaj have been abandoned, the communal practices driven by them have been reshaped. In the current closed loop of wells feeding single farms, new social conditions have emerged, resulting in their own spatial constructions. Specifically, we find three recurring spatial characteristics: first, the agricultural space is imagined, designed, and inhabited as a generative extension to domesticity, not hidden, and not relegated to food production or sensorial aesthetics, despite also being both of these things. In the blurring between private and public space, this spatial imaginary and the practices it enables actively resist capitalist forms of spatial organization. Second, these spaces exhibit an adaptive attitude towards topography. While this is the case more in the mountainous interior, these farms are a far cry from the contemporary farm that is characterized by an aesthetic of flatness that is born out of values such as efficiency and maximizing commercial value. Finally, the relationship between environmental and spatial imaginaries in Al Hajar produces a temporal and adaptive space, one that silently rejects rigid spatial organizational strategies, even if they are purported to be flexible, such as in the case of the so-called open plan promised by the concrete frame. All of these are spaces of temporal and performative interactions. What I mean by this is that the inhabitants of these spaces react temporally to the relationship between the space and time of day or season.

Thus, uncovering and describing the entanglement of spatial production and environmental imaginaries within a continuously transforming agricultural space has the potential to reshape the discourse in the urban centers towards land-based, counter-hegemonic and more climate resilient spaces at a time of extreme climate crisis.

01, 02, 03

Al Muqaddasi, *The Best Divisions for Knowledge of the Regions*, translated by Basil Anthony Collins, reviewed by Muhammad Hamid Al Tai. (Reading: Center for Muslim Contribution to Civilization – Garnet Publishing LTD: 1994) 86.

04

Walid Yasin Al Takriti, *Archeology of the Falaj: A Field Study of the Ancient Irrigation Systems of the United Arab Emirates* (Abu Dhabi: Department of Historic Environment, Abu Dhabi Culture & Heritage, 2011), 30.

05

Jean-Paul Sartre, and Arlette Elkaim-Sartre, *The Imaginary: A Phenomenological Psychology of the Imagination.* (Abingdon: Routledge, 2004). XIII.

06

Sartre and Elkaim-Sartre, *The Imaginary*.

07

M. Watts and R. Peet, *Liberation Ecologies* (London: Routledge, 2004), 15.

08

Andrew Jamison, Ron Eyerman, and Jacqueline Cramer. *The Making of the New Environmental Consciousness: A Comparative Study of Environmental Movements in Sweden, Denmark and the Netherlands* (Edinburgh: Edinburgh University Press, 1990), XI.

09

John Craven Wilkinson, *Water and Tribal Settlement in South-East Arabia: A Study of the Aflaj of Oman* (Oxford Research Studies in Geography: 1977) 38.

10

Wilkinson, *Water and Tribal Settlement,* 59-66.Edinburgh University Press, 1990), XI.

11

Wilkinson, *Water and Tribal Settlement,* 12.

12

Al Takriti, *Archeology of the Falaj,* 30.

13, 14

Wilkinson, *Water and Tribal Settlement,* 12.

15

Mike Searle, *Geology of the Mountains of Oman, Eastern Arabia* (Springer Nature Switzerland AG, 2019): 27.

16

Wilkinson, *Water and Tribal Settlement,* 12.

17

An ophiolite is a geological term used to describe a part of the ocean's crust that has been exposed above sea level; Fidelity Lancaster and William Lancaster, *Honour in Contentment: Life Before Oil in Ras Al-Khaimah (UAE) and Some Neighbouring Regions* (Gottingen, Germany: De Gruyter, Inc., 2011), 191.

18

Searle, *Geology of the Mountains of Oman,* 167.

19

A massif is used to describe the primary mass of an individual mountain, as opposed to the whole range.

20, 21

Wilkinson, *Water and Tribal Settlement,* 12,49.

22

S. M. Zwemer, "Three Journeys in Northern Oman", *The Geographical Journal* Vol. 19 No. 1 (January 1902): 62.

23

Hessa Al Romaithi, "A Vain Hunt for Water", *The National,* (December 28, 2008), https://www.thenationalnews.com/uae/a-vain-hunt-for-water-1.589945.

24

Penelope Tuson, *Records of the Emirates 1820-1958,* (London: Archive Editions, 1990), 714.

25, 26, 27

Wilkinson, *Water and Tribal Settlement,* 28,74.

28

Fidelity and Lancaster, *Honour in Contentment,* 191; The authors use the words *falay ghyali and falay da'udi.* In most parts of the UAE, the Arabic equivalent to the letter J is pronounced as a Y. As such, *falay* is a colloquial pronunciation of the word falaj, derived from the three-letter root *flj*, meaning to cut or to divide). Other researchers such as J.C. Wilkinson make a different distinction, referring to a *falaj ghayli* as a *ghayl falaj* and a *falaj da'udi* as a *qanat* (roughly translates to channel).

29

Wilkinson, *Water and Tribal Settlement,*1; However, Wilkinson does make a distinction between a falaj or qanat system as ones that exist across a wider territory feeding multiple farms, and wells that serve a more localized territory.

30

Wilkinson, *Water and Tribal Settlement,* 83.

31

Ibid., 97-98; I have provided a very short description as this has been covered at length and in great detail in other sources, such as in the Wilkinson book referenced here.

32

Ibid., 102; Wilkinson has identified this principle as *dawran/dawaran* (roughly translated as circular movement).

Tactics of Blurring

Throughout Al Hajar Mountains' agricultural pockets, various synthetic fabrics, in subtle shades of greens and beiges, are used to protect plant material. In becoming an integral part of the agricultural landscape, these fabrics extend, blur, and challenge readings of the color green within Al Hajar. Consequently, blurring produces a built environment that oscillates between conceptions of indoor and outdoor space by stretching the gradient between the two extremes. Sometimes, green or beige-colored fabric is absent, and rolls of translucent grey plastic sheets are used instead.

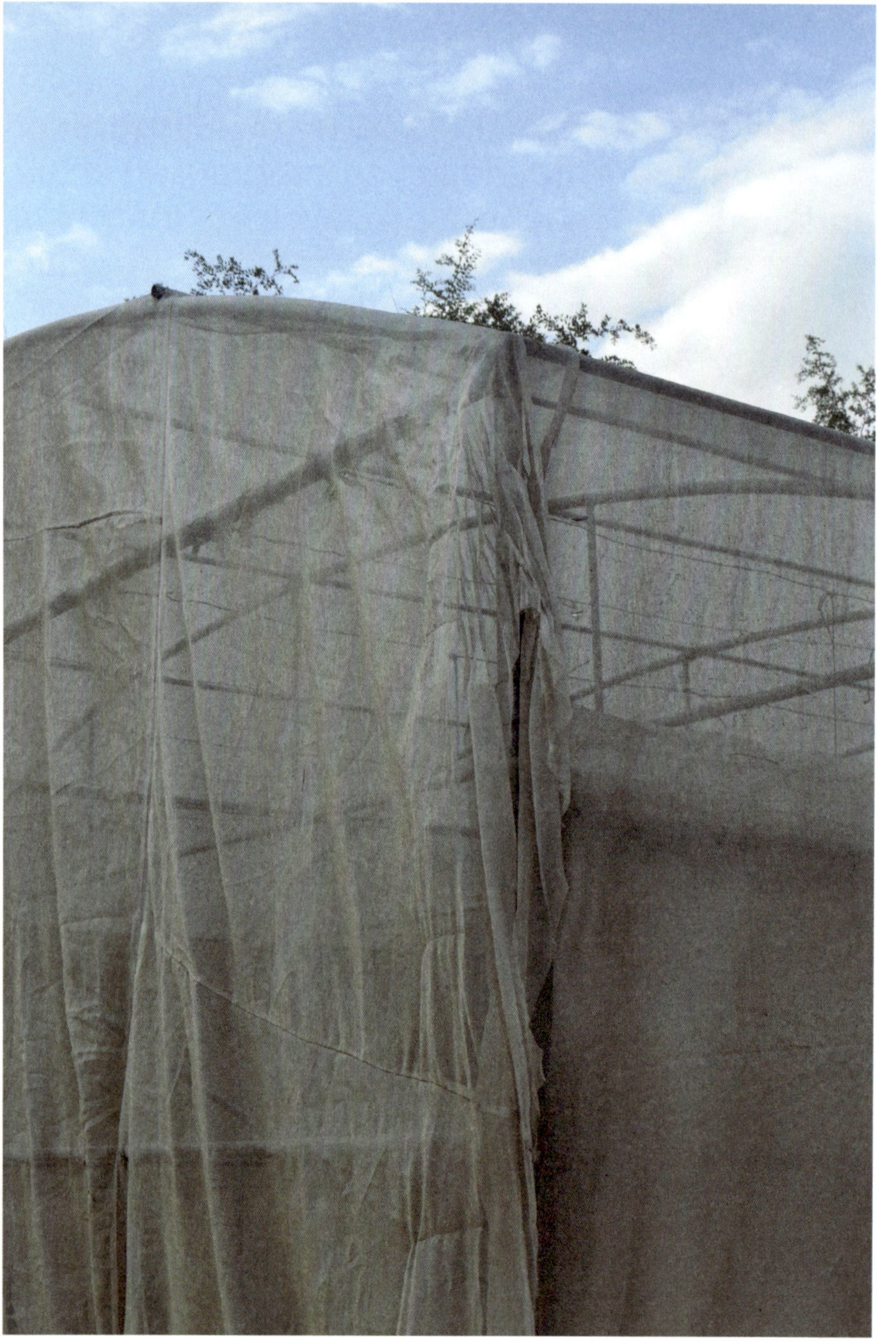

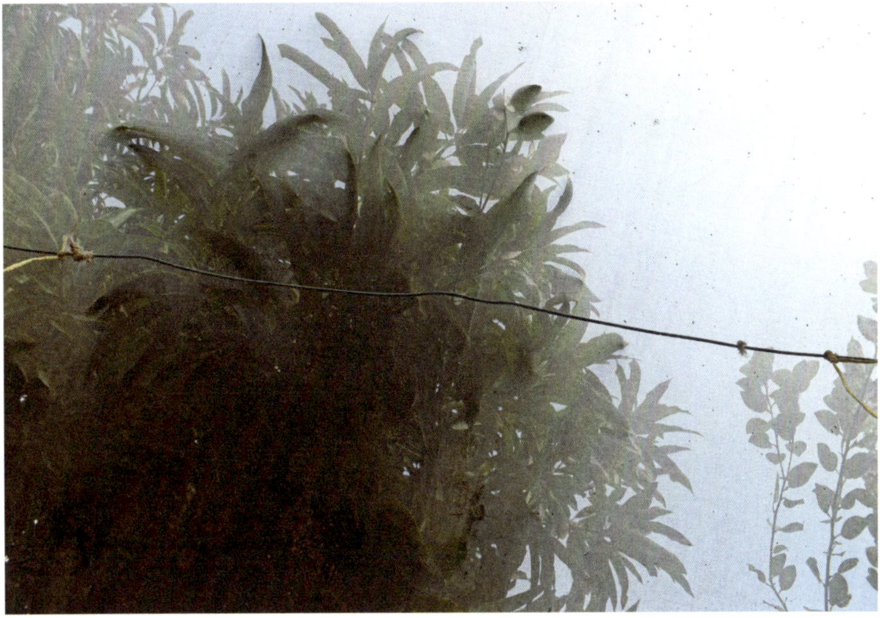

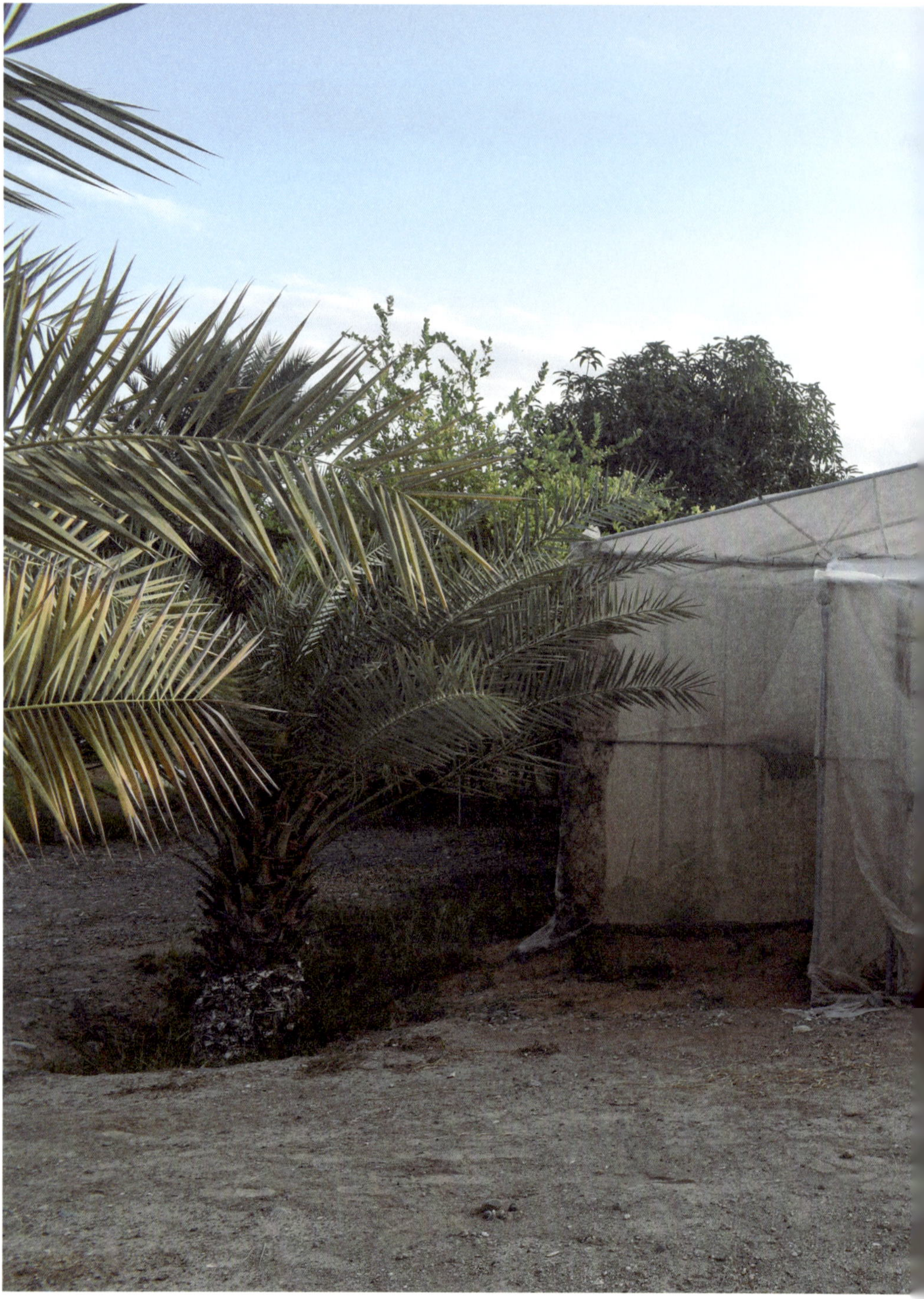

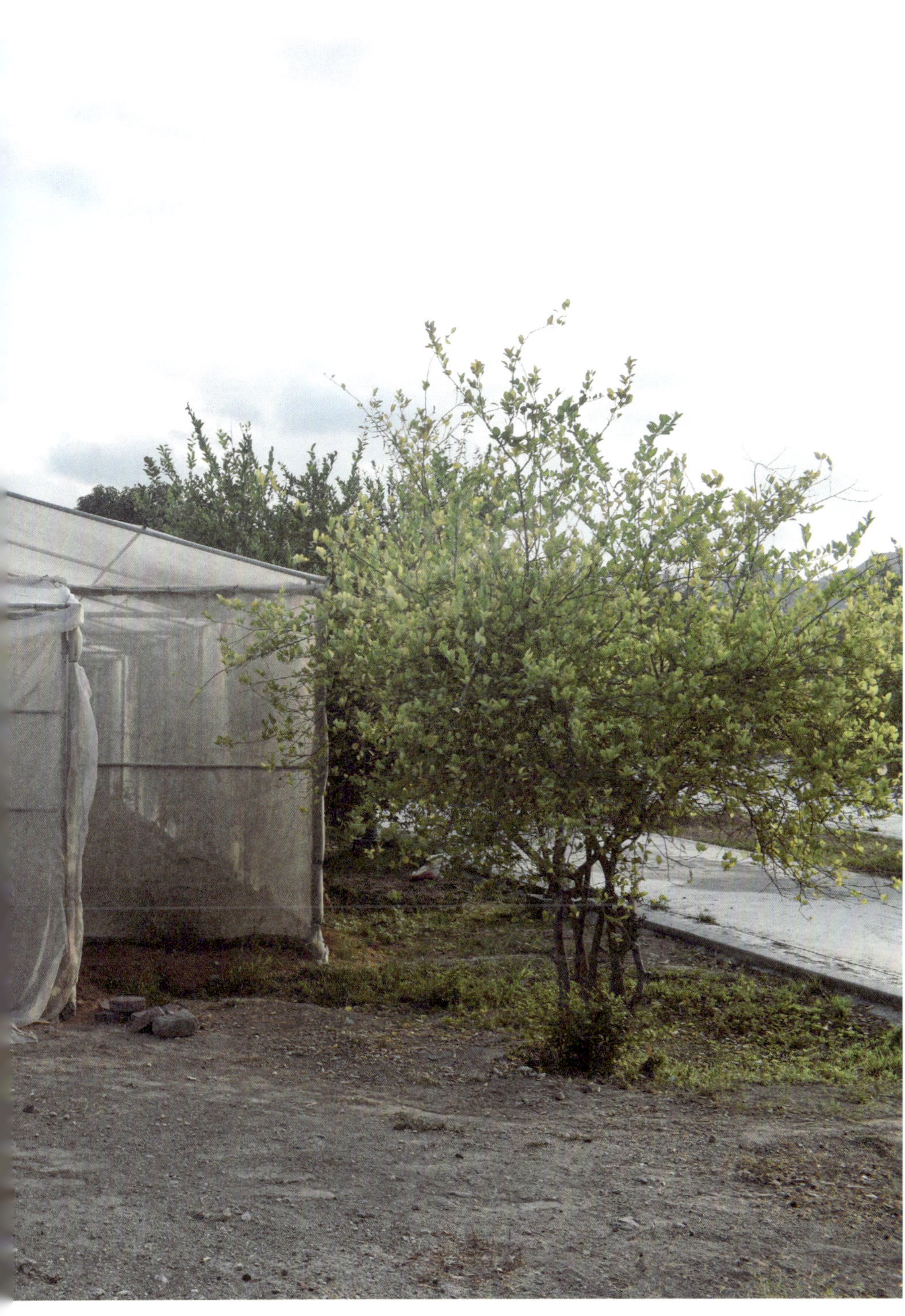

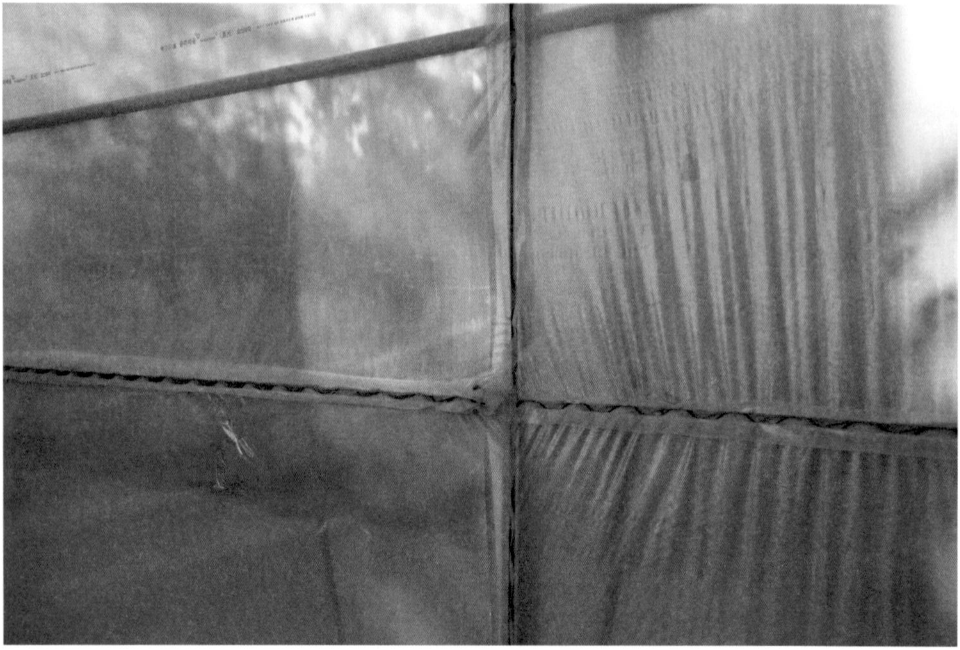

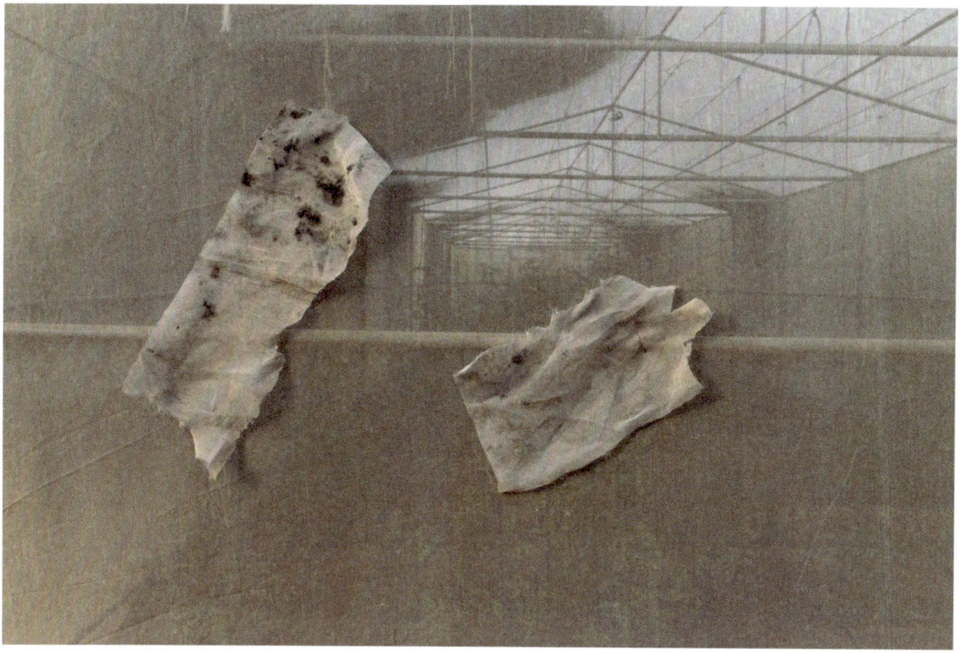

Tactics of Stacking

Stacking is an extreme and often more permanent form of marking. Within Al Hajar Mountains, the most typical type of stacking is the dry stacked stone, but other types have long existed, such as air-dried brick and mortar. Dry stacked stone, usually sourced from the area in which the structure is erected, undergoes almost no shaping. It results in non-linear patterns, emerging where wedge-shaped stones line up next to spheres, cubes, and a whole array of other shapes. Today, concrete masonry units (CMU) seem to have replaced most stone stacking tactics. Where the CMU comes from is sometimes hard to determine, but it must be noted that cement manufacturing is a significant industry in Al Hajar. However, historical continuities have not been entirely disrupted, as CMU is sometimes stacked much like stone, and when it fails to produce the same porosities that stones produce, such as when it is needed for air circulation, it is altered with strategically placed holes that seem to expand over time as a result of the saline environment.

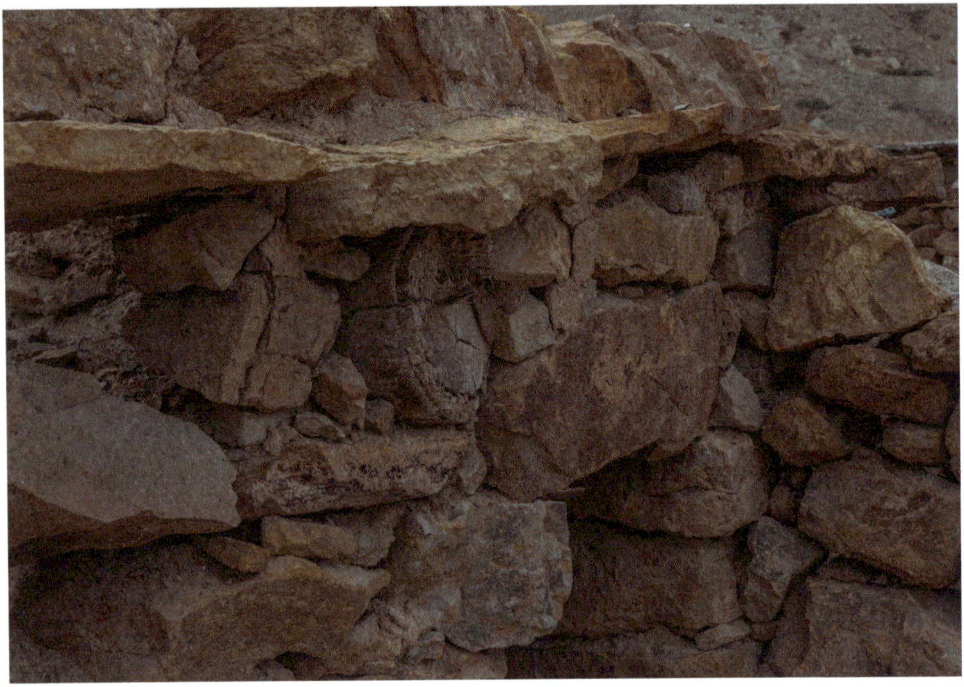

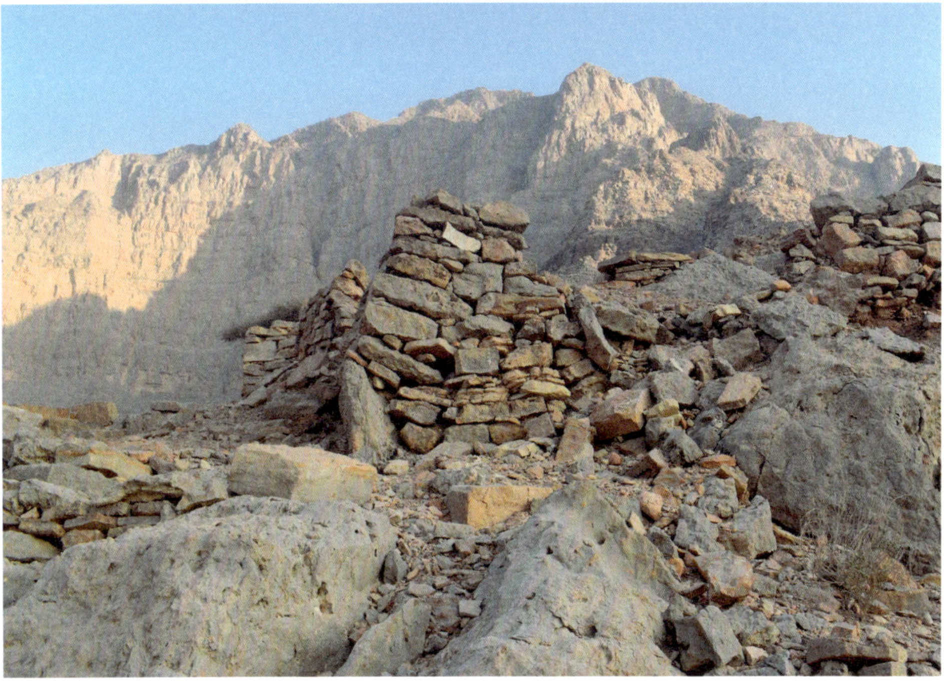

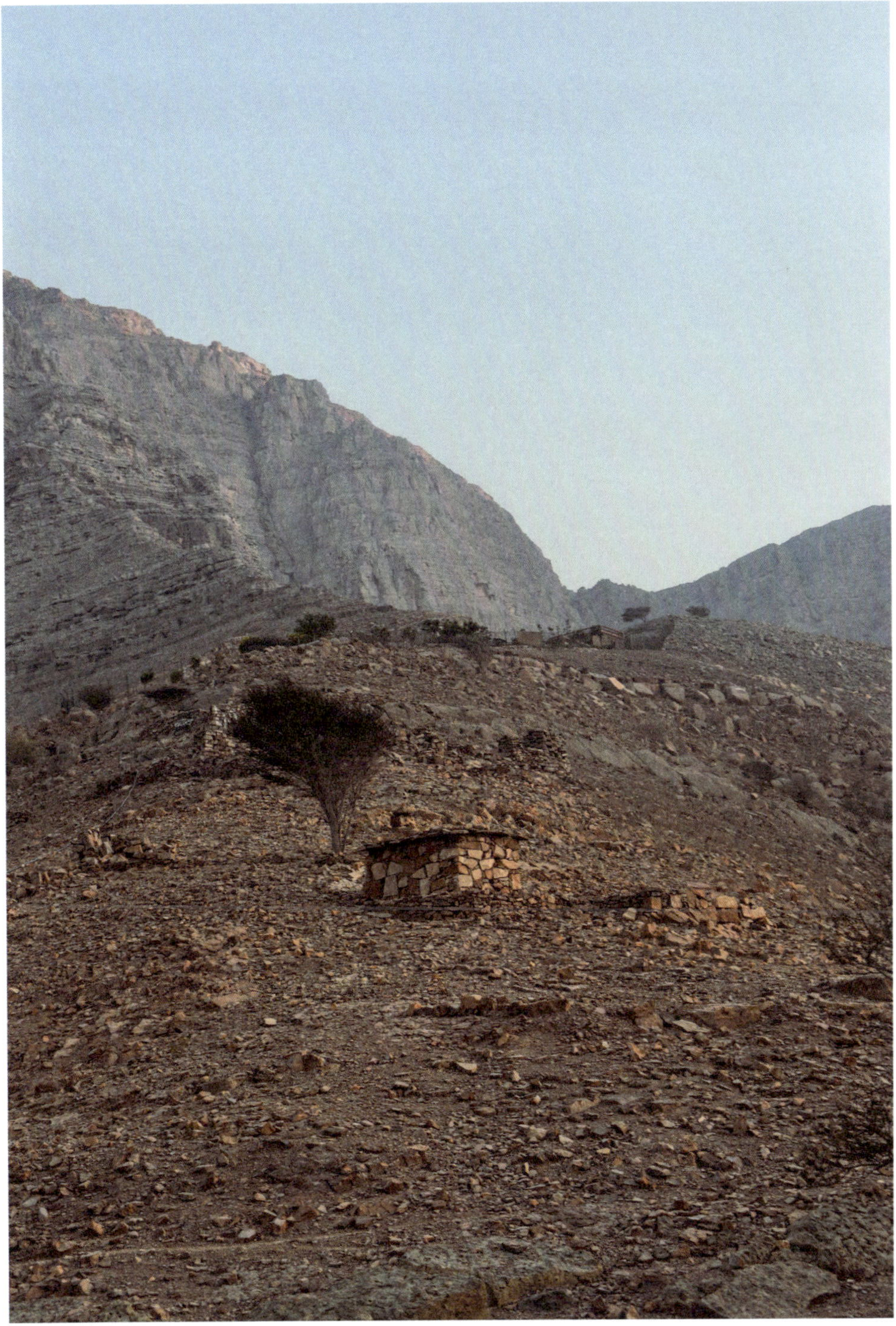

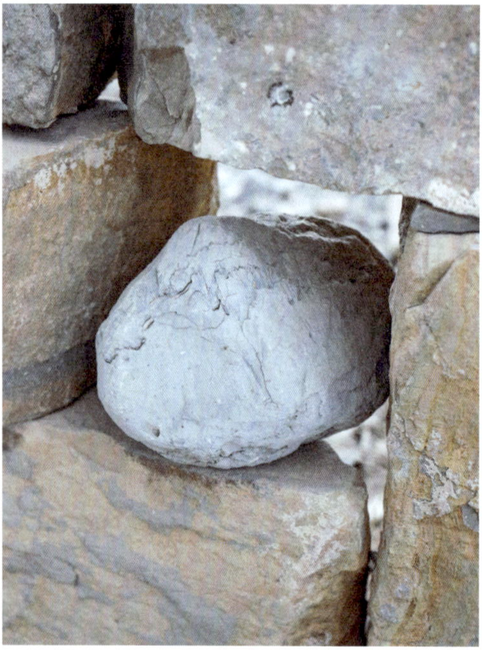

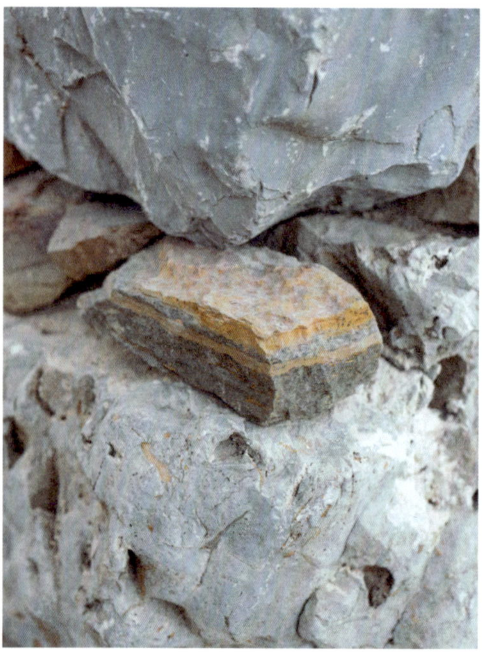

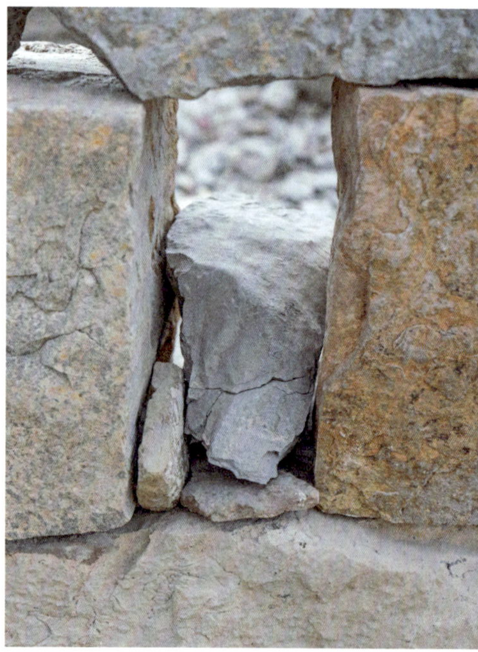

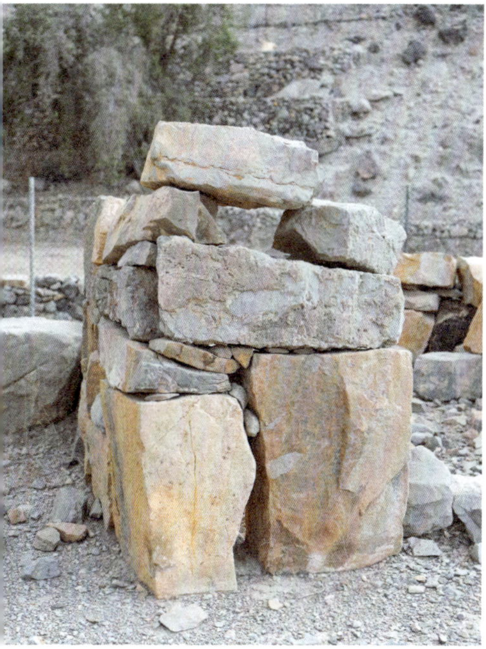

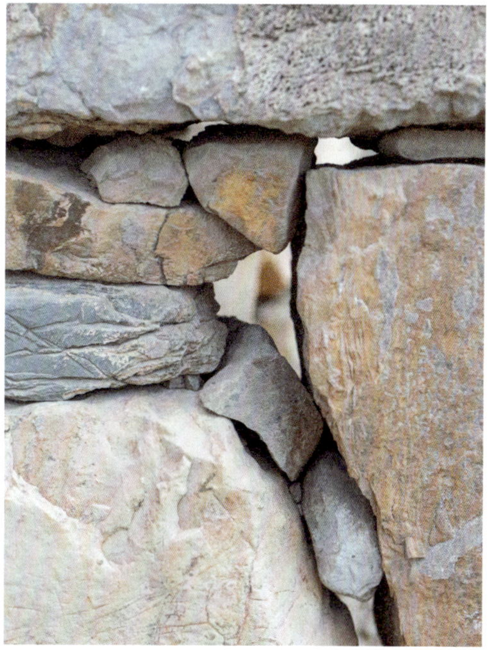

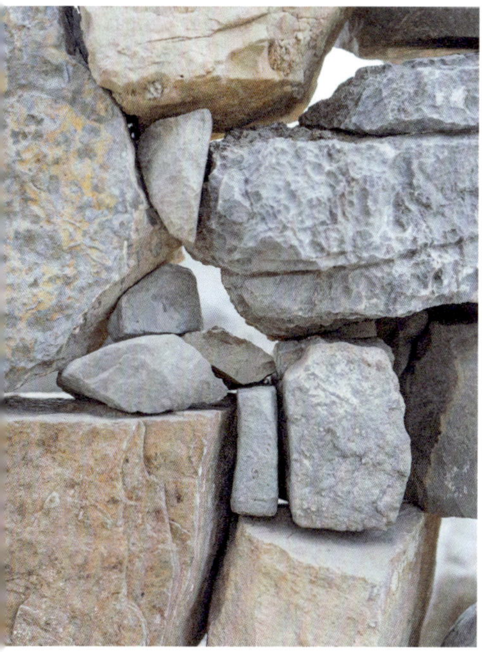

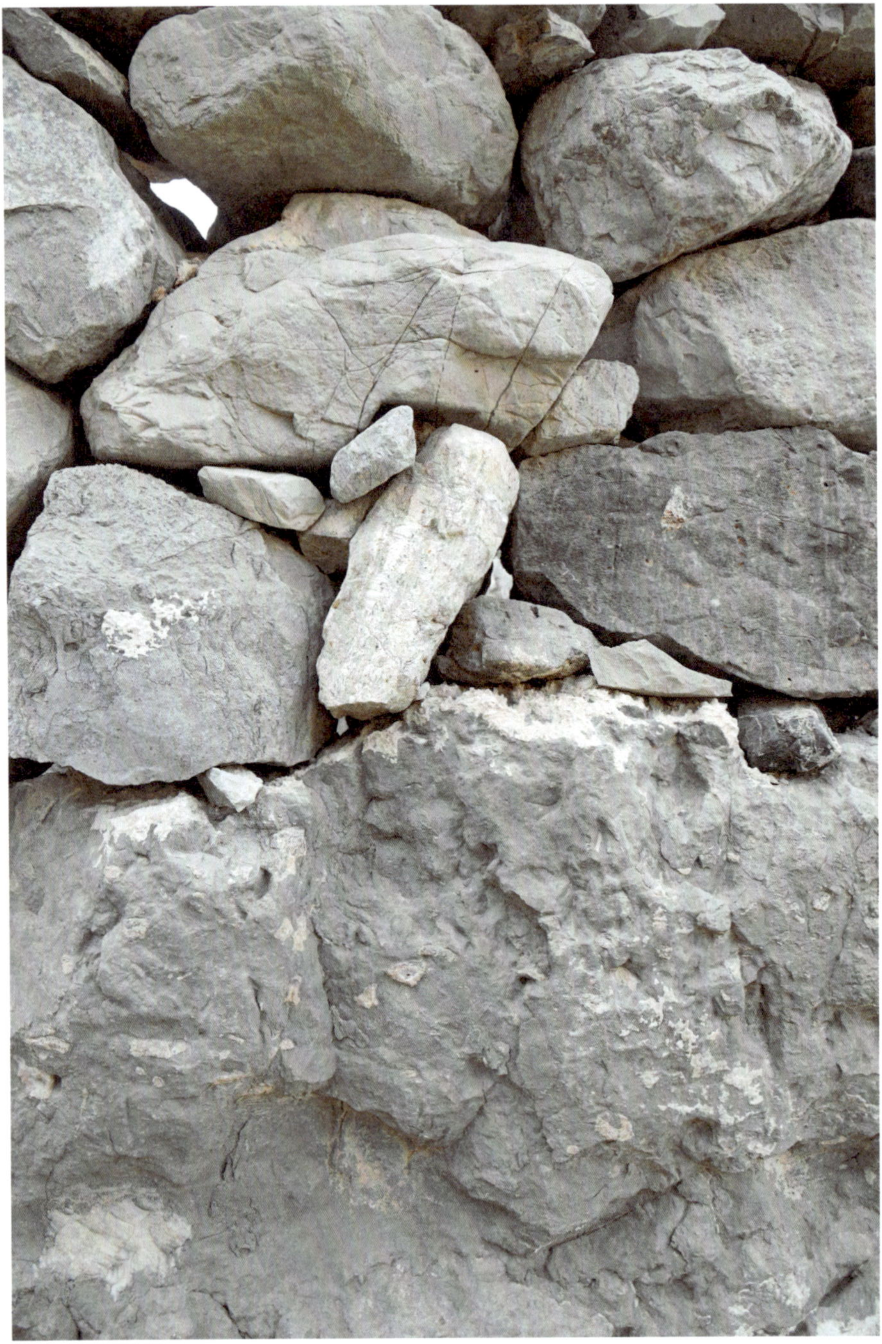

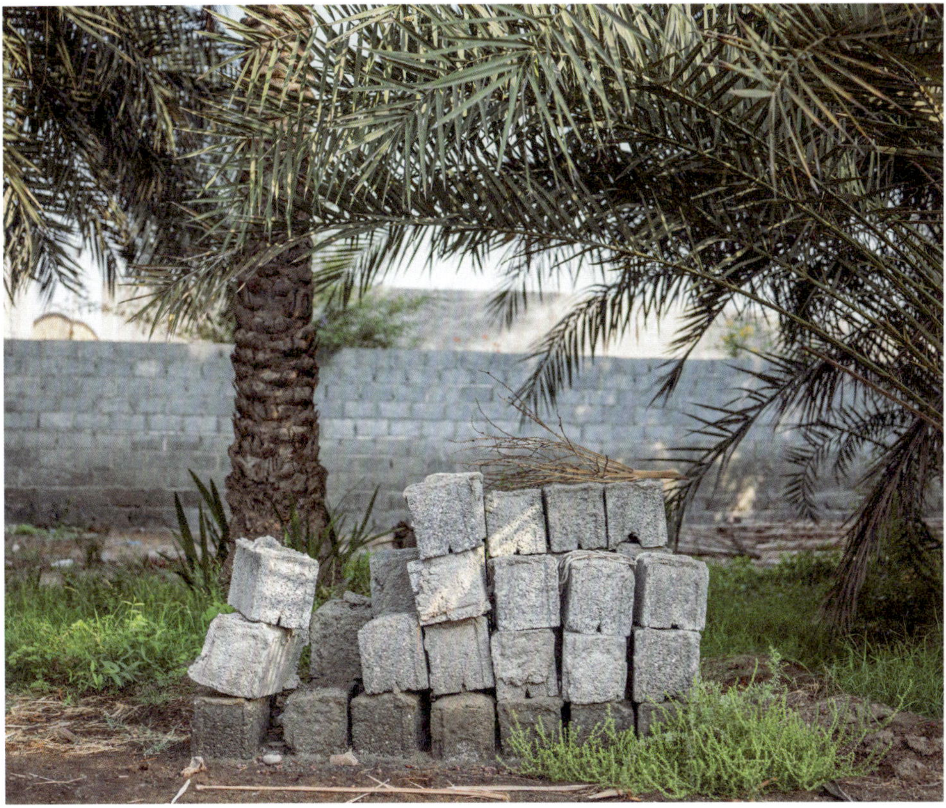

Faysal Tabbarah

A Note on Stacks, Terraces, and Clay

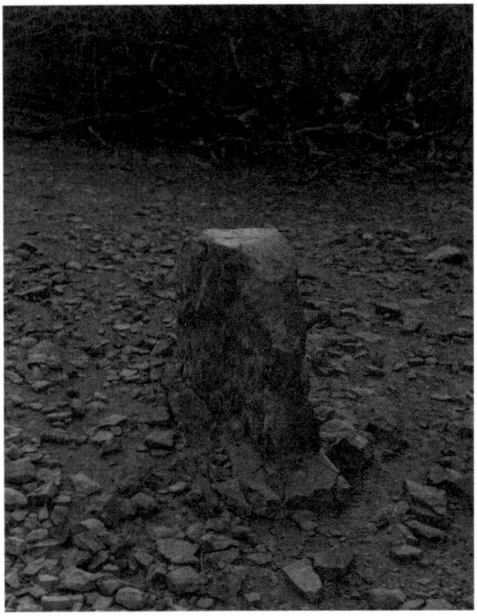

fig. (001) Relatively flat pieces of stone (approximately 50 x 50 x 20 cm), are found in abundance across Al Hajar Mountains, and are the building blocks for dry-stack assemblies. Photo by Reem Falaknaz.

From the urban centers on the west coast, there are two ways to reach the wadis which are sandwiched between the coastal city of Ras Al Khaimah and Jabal Jais, the highest point in the United Arab Emirates (UAE). On one hand, one could drive the almost-coastal E11 highway, which connects Ras Al Khaimah in the northeast to the UAE-Saudi border in the west. On the other hand, one could take the route that goes through the desert plateau and heads north after Al Dhaid, on the E18 highway. This route goes through Al Hajar Mountains' foothills, oasis towns, and agricultural fields. After I began an ongoing series of field trips in 2018, I realized that I am drawn to these sites not only because of the abundance of dry stack-stone construction, but because here, unlike elsewhere, there is clay. The confluence of these two elements was one of the reasons for my first series of trips here almost five years ago. I also have a reason for preferring the E18 north-south highway: it mirrors a historical caravan route that connected
[01] Ras Al Khaimah and its environs to Al Ain and the oasis around it.†

In late November 2022, while on my way to research sites in various locations along E18, I stopped by a gas station for some supplies. On my way out, I happened to catch the headlines that coincidentally connect to my research, populating a number of local newspapers. They all announced the launch of the first phase of the Mleiha Wheat Farm, close to Wadi Shawka and Shawka Dam, southeast of the city of Sharjah. Part of a wider food security initiative, the project
[02] is meant to encompass 1,400 hectares by 2025.† Mleiha is a strategic location with a history of agricultural development. Borrowing its name from the Arabic word for salt, *melh* (ملح), Mleiha was chosen as the site for a 10-acre agricultural experiment station in the late 1960s
[03] given its "favourable hydrological and soil prognosis."† Furthermore, the name in which Mleiha appears in the archives is Tawi Mleiha (طوي مليحة), where *tawi* is a local word for well.

As it happens, I was on my way to historical sites in which dry-stack stone assemblies were perched on the side of decommissioned terraced wheat farms.

Terracing for Wheat

Traveling along the historical caravan road, nowadays a major artery, in a southwesterly fashion beginning from Sha'am, a town in northern Ras Al Khaimah and ending less than 1.5 kilometers from the border with Oman, one experiences an abundance of *wu'oob* (singular: *wa'b*), a local word used to describe terraced farms that have virtually ceased cultivation in recent years. Sha'am is a particularly complex example as it exists along the mountain's foothills and immediately transforms into a fertile *sayh,* or coastal plain, in which flood waters flow into date gardens.† Continuing along that [04]
direction, one crosses through Wadi Ghalilah, another wa'b rich area, and passes by a *sabkha* (wetland), Dhaya Fort, the highest hilltop

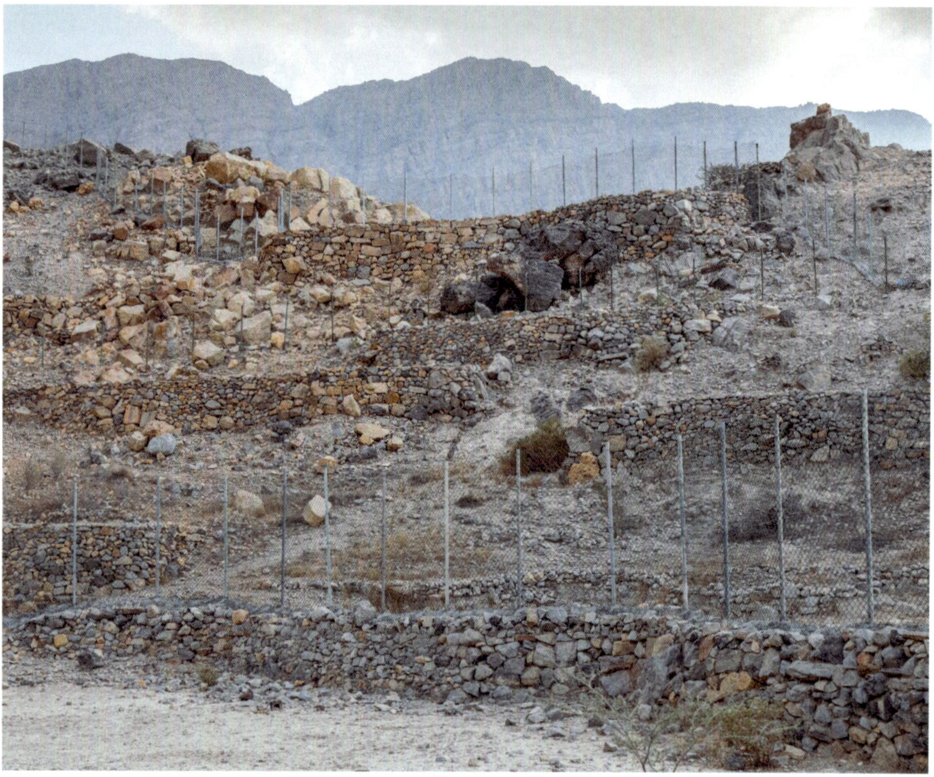

fig. (002) Relatively flat pieces of stone (approximately 50 x 50 x 20 cm), are found in abundance across Al Hajar Mountains, and are the building blocks for dry-stack assemblies. Photo by Reem Falaknaz.

fort in the UAE, before arriving at Shamal. This fertile area is adjacent to the modern-day city of Ras Al Khaimah, "where a network
[05] of tracks link up the hamlets scattered among the date groves,"†
a scene as evident today as it was in the early 1970s. From here, the route pivots due south along the western foothills of Al Hajar towards Khatt, passing by Al Dhaid, another key agricultural town and site of agricultural experimentation in the 1950s, before finally arriving in Al Ain Oasis. Throughout this southward route, there are many entrances to a number of important historical routes that exist along the wadis which allow for passage through to key towns on the fertile Al Batinah coastal plain such as Dibba. One example of a route that has both historical and contemporary importance, exists between Shamal and Khatt. Its entrance through Wadi Haqeel exhibits a number of abandoned and repurposed stone houses of varying sizes and layouts, including a stone house with its roof almost fully
[06] intact.† Today, this is the site of a major new road that cuts travel
[07] time to Jabal Jais by 75%.†

In their comprehensive oral history of life before oil in the northern UAE, William and Fidelity Lancaster recount a story about a man whose grandfather "exported wheat from the mountains here. The mountain men sold or exchanged some of their surplus grain here on the coast and all these small amounts were collected up by small traders like us, and sold further up
[08] the Gulf."† Similarly, archeologists Beatrice de Cardi and D. B. Doe, in a study of the same area published in 1968 described that within the "mountains, settlements are even more infrequent than in the foothills and are usually found only on small terraces cultivated with the help of ingenious irrigation systems designed to harness flash-floods and apportion whatever perennial water is available...the most notable feature of the settlement is the use of massive stone retaining walls built across narrow clefts and following the contour of the hills at dif-
[09] ferent levels to provide a series of small cultivable terraces."†

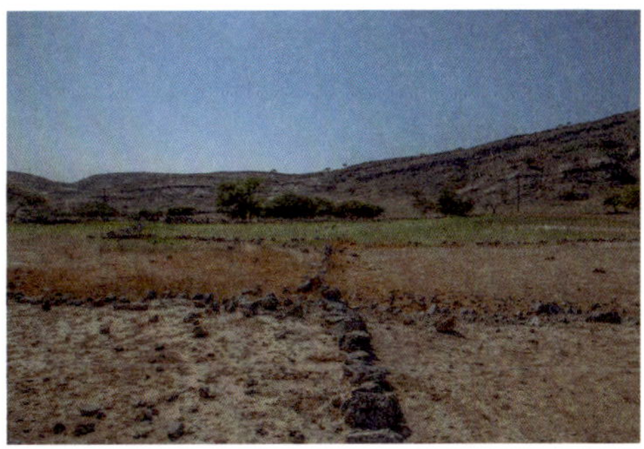

fig. (003) A typically shallow wa'b in the Habhab Plateau, a relatively isolated area within Al Hajar's interior. The view is towards the west, while a settlement of around 15 constructions of various sizes and functions is behind this view on the eastern foothills of the plateau. Only once in more than five years of fieldwork, I have glimpsed three gazelles hopping in the distance, disappearing into the eastern terrain. Photo by author.

Throughout this route, one could have found date trees and
grains such as red wheat and barley (which are typically sown in the
fall season around October, and harvested in March), while in the
summer, one could find limes, oranges, watermelons, and other kinds
of grains such as millet.† For the grain crops to succeed, the land [10]
must receive the *sayl* (storm surge or flood) twice in the season. Even
then, a local of the area describing the relationship between rain and
terraced farms had told the Lancasters that “rainfall by itself would
never, or hardly ever, provide enough water. We have to bring enough
rainwater to the field, and that is why we build channels to divert water
across rocky slopes to the fields we have built to hold silts.”† Another [11]
has noted that “water wasn’t a problem.”

Tangentially Searching for Julfar Wares† [12]

Searching for stone construction in Al Hajar is a contin-
uous game of *trompe l’oeil* (optical illusion), given the degree to
which assemblies assimilate, and sometimes disappear, into their
surroundings. Equally hard is the search for clay, a primary compo-
nent needed for earthen construction; the action feels like one is
tilting at windmills. On the surface, it appears as if Al Hajar is not rich
in clay. However, archeological evidence around the medieval port
city of Julfar (close to present-day Ras Al
Khaimah) suggests that this view can be
challenged, since recent findings indicate
an abundant production of Julfar Ware† [13]
suggesting deposits of clay can be found
within Ras Al Khaimah’s environs.

Julfar was a medieval port town
and had been mentioned by travelers as
early as the eighth century.† In 1516, Por- [14]
tuguese writer and officer Duarte Barbosa
wrote of Julfar that “here dwell persons
of worth, great navigators and wholesale
dealers. Here is a very great fishery as well
of seed-pearls as of large pearls, and the
Moors of Ormus come hither to buy them
and carry them to India and many other
lands.”† Within this context, it is between [15]
the fifteenth and seventeenth centuries
that local Julfar Ware production seems
to have peaked, occupying a space in
tandem with Chinese porcelain imports.† [16]
Julfar Ware was an unglazed and coarse

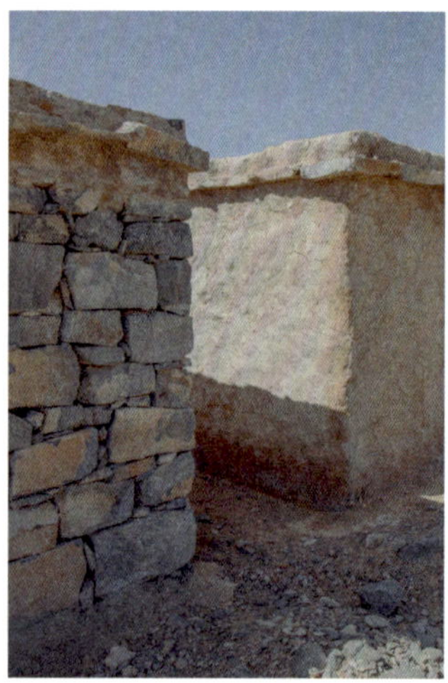

fig. (004) Two adjacent structures, comprising part of a building complex in Wadi Hayyah, show the different walls with and without an external mud application. It is likely that this application is relatively recent given its pristine condition. Photo by author.

earthenware oscillating between dark orange or gray, and decorated
[17] with dark red or purple paint.† Of note within the Julfar Ware repertoire are the slender ablution jugs with their narrow spouts, with "characteristic ornament... is a band of horizontal rust-red stripes painted
[18] around the upper portion of the neck."† The port of Julfar thrived in ebbs and flows, until it was bombarded in 1819 one final time, which
[19] led to the emergence of modern-day Ras Al Khaimah.†

As it stands, there is no written evidence that substantial rammed earth construction existed in and around Julfar
[20] other than some cursory references† as well as the existing physical evidence of the use of mud-brick. Mud-brick is currently found still standing as far south as Al Bidya Mosque in the Emirate of Fujairah on the eastern Al Batinah coast, as well as inland around Al Ain, such as in a recently discov-
[21] ered mud-brick mosque said to be 1,000 years old.† This, however, does not negate the provocation that the history of Julfar Ware suggests that developing rammed earth construction, as a strategic practice within this region, is immediately possible with potential impact.

Stacking Stone

One of the many places in which one can engage with this game of trompe l'oeil is the historic agricultural area within Wadi Sha'am, a village north of Ras Al Khaimah. In this area, there is a complex relationship between wadis, mountainous foothills, terraced

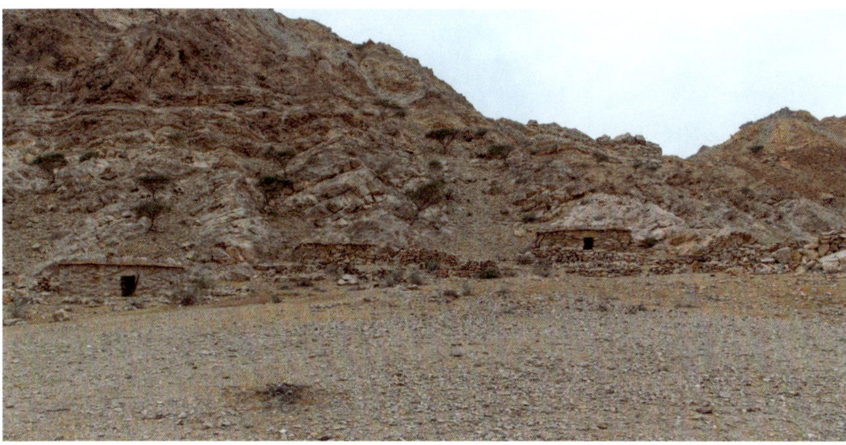

fig. (005) A photograph of the western foothills of Wadi Haqeel that reveals a series of embedded flat-roofed stone houses and their storage annexes. On the southern end of the row (the left side of the photograph), one can see a mud treatment on the exterior wall, while remnants of a round house can be seen on the northern end (the right side of the photograph). Photo by author.

grain fields, stone houses, and stone granaries, or *yunooz* (singular: *yanz*), which were able to store unthreshed grains for up to seven years.† [22]

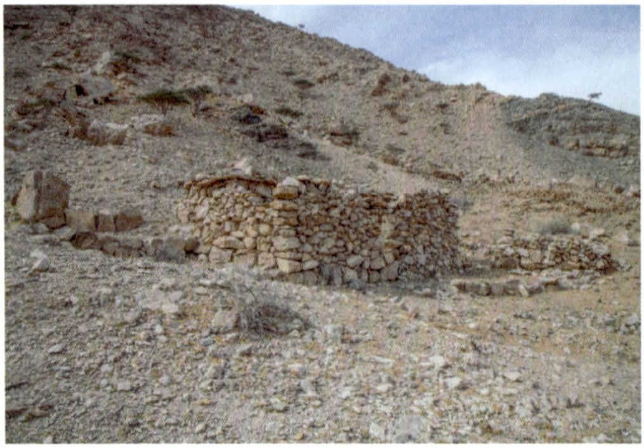

fig. (006) A free-standing flat-roofed stone construction on the western foothills of Wadi Haqeel. With its floor plan measuring approximately 9 x 6.5 meters, one can discern that it was structured as two primary spaces given the central wall running along the entire length is still intact. To the north (the right side of the photograph) is a storage space, while on the southern edge is an exterior platform. Photo by author.

In general, there are three microclimates within Al Hajar, each influencing its own variations on stone construction. These microclimates include the coastal area, the relatively flat plains (between the coast and the mountains in the east, and between the desert and the mountains in the west), and finally the mountainous region itself. While all regions experience really hot summer months, the plains and the mountains experience relatively less humidity, and the mountainous region experiences the most rainfall in the winter.† Beyond Al Hajar and within the desert landscape, [23]
one experiences a radically different set of microclimates. Hence, a particular type of construction abounds in the shape of *arish* or palm-leaf construction, similarly influenced by both environmental and resource factors.† [24]

Given the humid conditions on the coast as well as the availability of resources, coastal structures are built, in large part, using mud and coral stone, preferred for their porosity which enables air circulation into and outside the enclosed spaces. On the plains, an integrated earthen-vegetal construction occurs through mud-brick walls and arish roofs.

Based on surveys conducted during excursions in 1970-1971 and another one in 1977, Austrian social anthropologist Walter Dostal has extensively described four types of construction in the mountains that were intended for winter use, and two for the summer.

He described the following, intended for winter use: 1. flat-roofed stone houses (stone walls, timber, and earthen roofs); 2. gabled houses (stone, timber, and palm-leaf); 3. gabled huts (plant material, usually palm-leaf); 4. round houses (stone walls and plant material roofs, usually palm-leaf). As for the summer houses in the mountains, Dostal has described: 1. the *sofeh* or *saifeh* type (stone walls, timber and earthen roofs); 2. the arish hut (palm-leaf). What distinguishes the summer stone houses (the name is likely derived from *sayf,* the Arabic

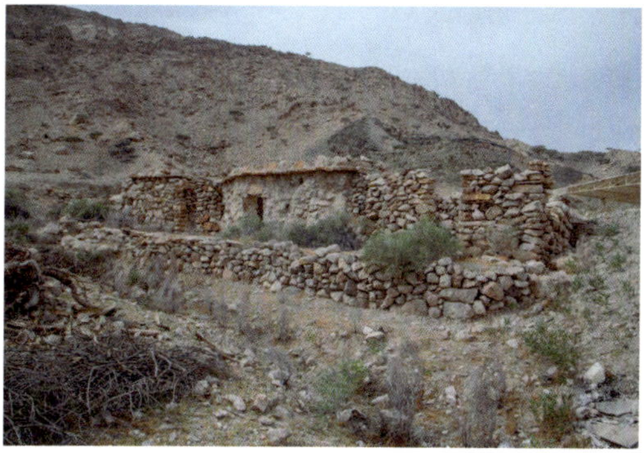

fig. (007) A building complex on the western plain of Wadi Haqeel, oriented perpendicular to the mountain's edge and parallel to a wadi, measuring around 20 x 4 meters. The house is composed of five discrete spaces. Its back wall is embedded in the earth, and it has an exterior platform running along its entire length. Its central and largest space has its exterior mud finish and roof partially intact. Photo by author.

word for summer) from their winter counterparts is that they have relatively more openings of various sizes and are, at times, constructed with only three walls, leaving the fourth
[25] side open for ventilation.†

These different types are dotted along Al Hajar's landscape, and while they sometimes do co-exist adjacent to one another, they are more often than not mutually exclusive, as their locations depend heavily on existing natural resources at a particular site. Moreover, given the relative transience of palm-leaf, the most visible type of construction today is the flat-roofed stone houses. While remnants of the other kinds of houses are still visible, the stone remainders are the most common. Typically, these were made of dry-stack stones and did not use any mortar, as the local mortar, *saruj*, a waterproof lime-based mortar, did not stick to the stone in the same way
[26] it did with coral stones built on the coast.† As a result, mud was used to cover the inside, and occasionally the outside, while compressed mud was used as flooring. The roofs were constructed first by laying wooden beams, about 20-25 centimeters in diameter, then a mat woven out of palm fronds would be placed on them and a thick layer of earth would be added. A hallmark of this type of roof construction is the flat stones placed on the roof's edges to keep the earthen layer in place. All in all,
[27] the roof structure would measure around one meter in depth.†

As for their sizes, spatial distributions, and functions, there is a radically wide spectrum within each type of construction. For example, within flat-roofed stone houses – the typology most easily discernible in today's landscape given the relative robustness of its materials and construction methods – one can find something as small as a single rectangular unit to large complexes. Single-unit houses measure between 9 x 3 meters to 12.5 x 5.5 meters and have around 2.1 meters in internal clear height correlating to around 3 meters on the exterior. William and Fidelity Lancaster have recorded an elderly man telling them that in the 1940s, "[we] built our houses from our own
[28] materials. We had *yarid*,† we had the trunks of date trees, stones were
[29] lying about, and a house eight meters by four took about a day."†

On the other end of the spectrum, building complexes of 20 units (or more) of varying sizes, proportions, and shapes can occupy an area around 35 x 25 meters.

The complexity of stone construction within the mountains, but also on the coastal plains, be it for shelter or for agriculture, is a stand-in for the environmental and ecological complexity of the region. Never the same, but sharing a particularly tactical spirit, they embody the essence of land-based practice.

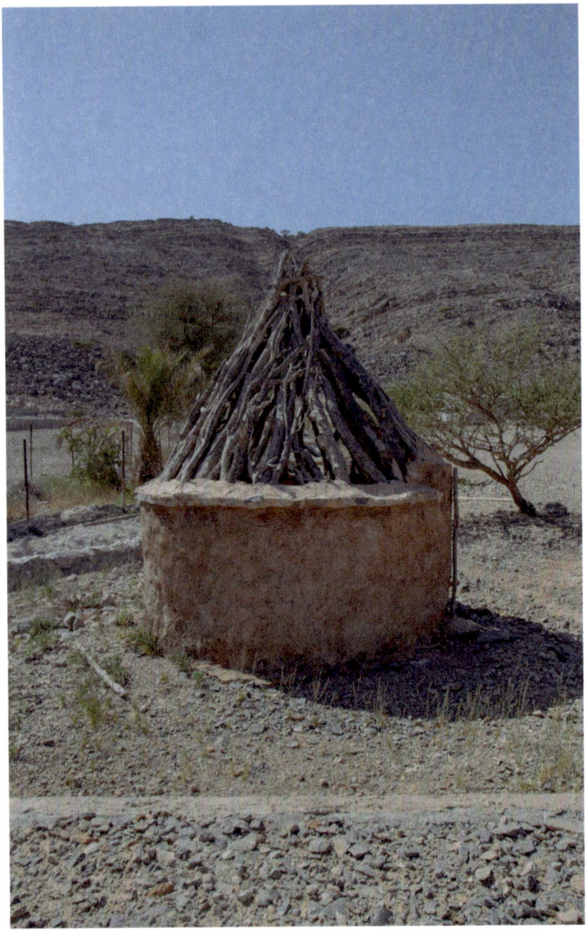

fig. 008 A gabled hut structure, most likely a yanz (grain storage) due to its size, in Wadi Hayyah along a series of terraced fields. Photo by author.

01

Beatrice de Cardi and D. B. Doe. "Archaeological Survey in the Northern Trucial States," *East and West* Vol. 21, No. 3/4 (September-December 1971): 227.

02

"Sharjah Ruler Launches 1,400-hectare Wheat Farm in Mleiha to Boost Food Security," *Gulf News* (Dubai), November 30, 2022, https://gulfnews.com/uae/environment/sharjah-ruler-launches-1400-hectare-wheat-farm-in-mleiha-to-boost-food-security-1.92384317

03

Harbour Development and Water Survey, 1967, FCO 8/861, 35, Arabian Gulf Digital Archives, UAE.

04

See William Lancaster and Fidelity Lancaster, *Honour Is in Contentment: Life Before Oil in Ras Al-Khaimah (UAE) and Some Neighbouring Regions*, (Berlin: De Gruyter, Inc., 2011). In the book, the spelling used is sayh, while it seems that another word publicly used is seeh.

05

de Cardi and Doe "Archaeological Survey," 227.

06

de Cardi and Doe "Archaeological Survey," 225-289.

07

Waheed Abbas, "UAE: New Jebel Jais Road to Reduce Travel Time by 75 percent for Motorists," *Khaleej Times* (Dubai), January 12, 2023, https://www.khaleejtimes.com/uae/uae-new-jebel-jais-road-to-reduce-travel-time-by-75-per-cent-for-motorists

08

William and Fidelity Lancaster, *Honour Is in Contentment*, 51.

09

de Cardi and Doe "Archaeological Survey," 227-238.

10

William and Fidelity Lancaster, *Honour Is in Contentment.*

11

William and Fidelity Lancaster, *Honour Is in Contentment*, 137.

12

Elements of this section will appear in a publication by Irthi Contemporary Crafts Council in 2023.

13

The name Julfar Ware seems to have been first used by Beatrice de Cardi and D. B. Doe.

14

Robert Andrew Carter et al, "The Rise and Ruin of a Medieval Port Town: A Reconsideration of the Development of Julfar," *Arabian Archeology and Epigraphy*, 31, (2020) 501-523.

15

Duarte Barbose, *The Book of Duarte Barbosa Vol 1,* (London: Haklyut Society, 1918), 73.

16

de Cardi and Doe "Archaeological Survey," 225-289.

17

Gen Mitsuishi, Derek Kennet, Jeffrey Szuchman and Ronald Hawker. "Kiln sites of the fourteenth-twentieth-century Julfar ware pottery industry in Ras al-Khaimah, UAE" in *Proceedings of the Seminar for Arabian Studies 2013*, Vol. 43, (2013), 225-238.

18

de Cardi and Doe "Archaeological Survey," 269.

19, 20

de Cardi and Doe "Archaeological Survey," 255-289.

21

Remains of 1,000-year-old Mosque Reveal a Rich Past, Accessed February 3, 2023. https://www.emirates247.com/news/emirates/remains-of-1-000-year-old-mosque-reveal-a-rich-past-2018-09-10-1.673063

22

William and Fidelity Lancaster, *Honour Is in Contentment*, 160.

23

Along with the fieldwork conducted and the collection of oral histories, and given the fieldwork has encountered largely abandoned stone constructions in the region, this section owes a great deal to the following: Walter Dostal, *The Traditional Architecture of Ras al-Khaimah (North)* (Wiesbaden: Dr. Ludwig Reichert Verlag, 1983); Beatrice de Cardi and D. B. Doe, "Archaeological Survey in the Northern Trucial States, East and West," September-December 1971, Vol. 21, No. 3/4 (September December 1971), 227-289. Specifically, Dostal's categorization is key in understanding the diversity of construction as well as the relationship between environmental conditions and available material resources.

24

For more on palm-leaf construction in the UAE see Sandra Piesik, *Arish: Palm-Leaf Architecture* (London: Thames & Hudson, 2012).

25

Dostal, *The Traditional Architecture of Ras al-Khaimah*.

26

Dostal, *The Traditional Architecture of Ras al-Khaimah*, 79.

27

Dostal, *The Traditional Architecture of Ras al-Khaimah*, 19-20.

28

Date-leaf stems.

29

William and Fidelity Lancaster, *Honour Is in Contentment*, 87.

Tactics of Enclosing

Enclosures of all types, materials, sizes, and characteristics abound in Al Hajar Mountains. Sometimes these are fully transparent, such as the contemporary wire fences, and at other times, these are relatively solid such as the stacked stones or walls made out of concrete masonry units (CMU). Most of the time, however, enclosures in Al Hajar can rarely be categorized as one thing or another, as they exhibit an ad-hoc and multi-material attitude towards construction.

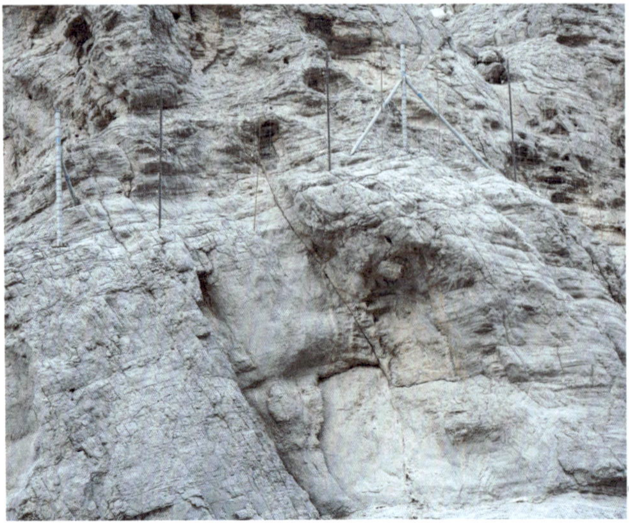

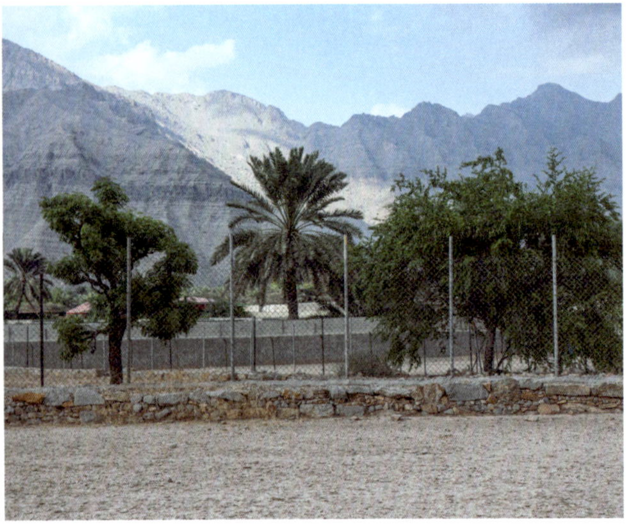

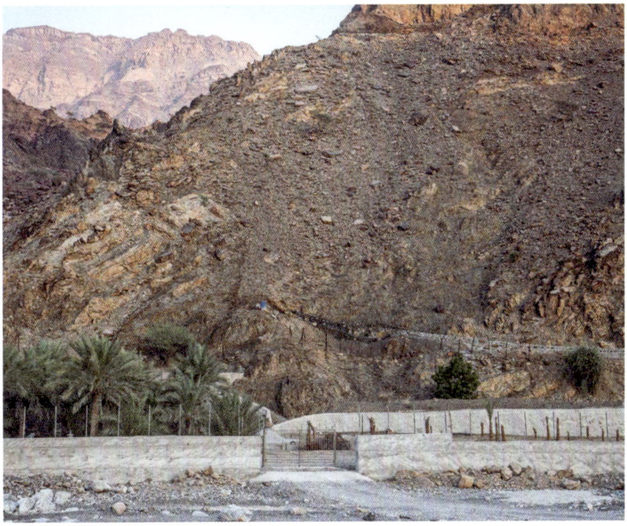

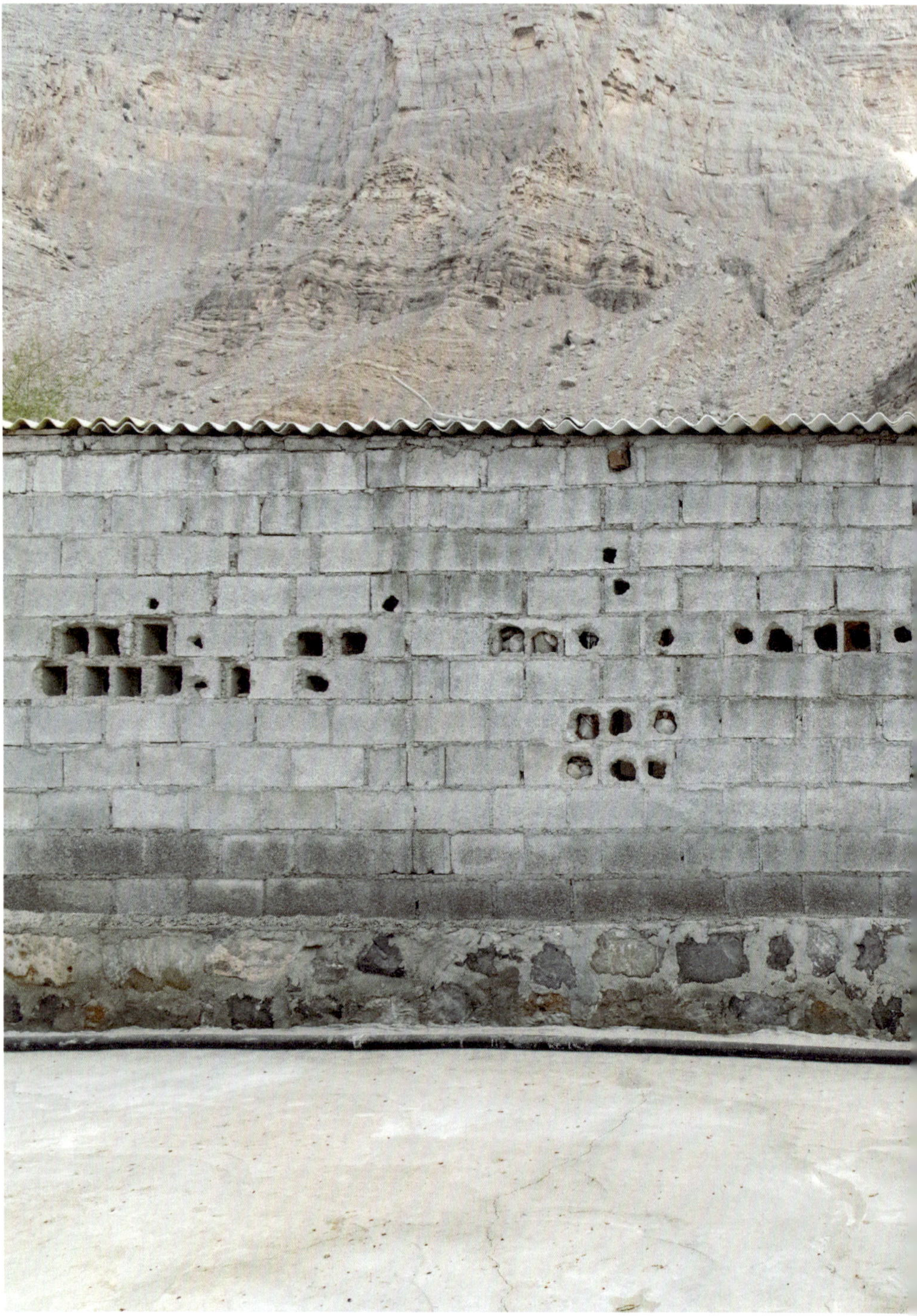

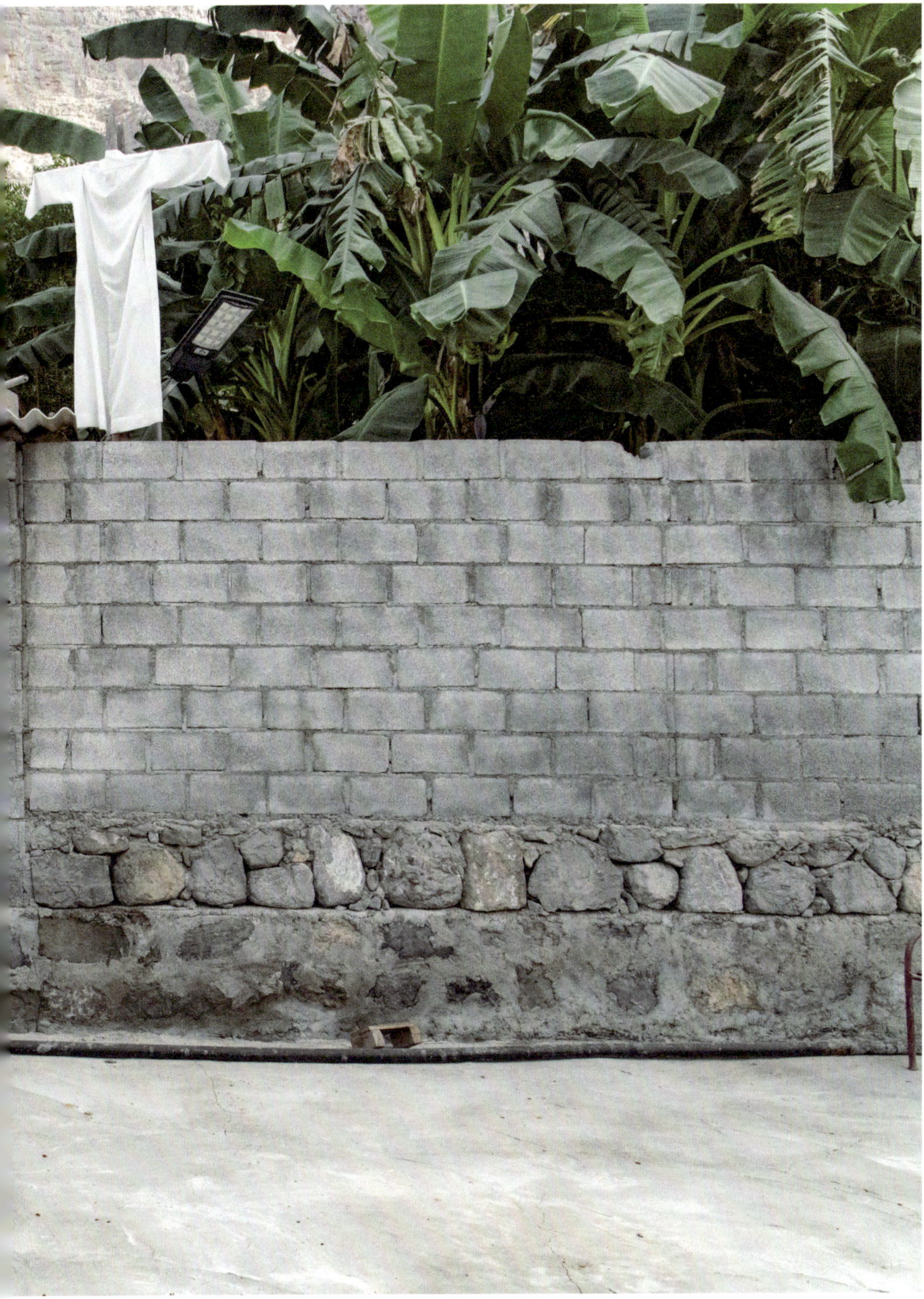

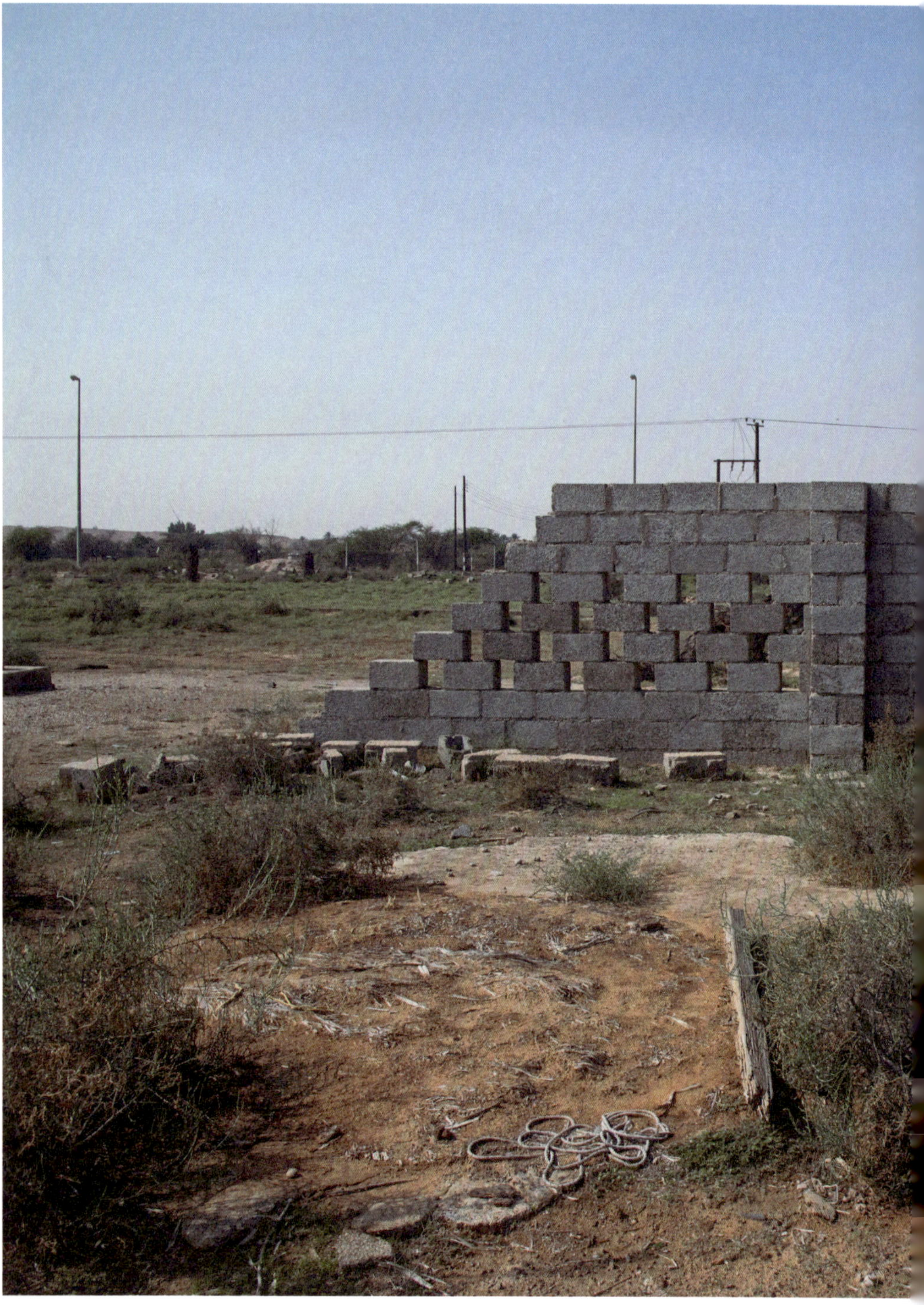

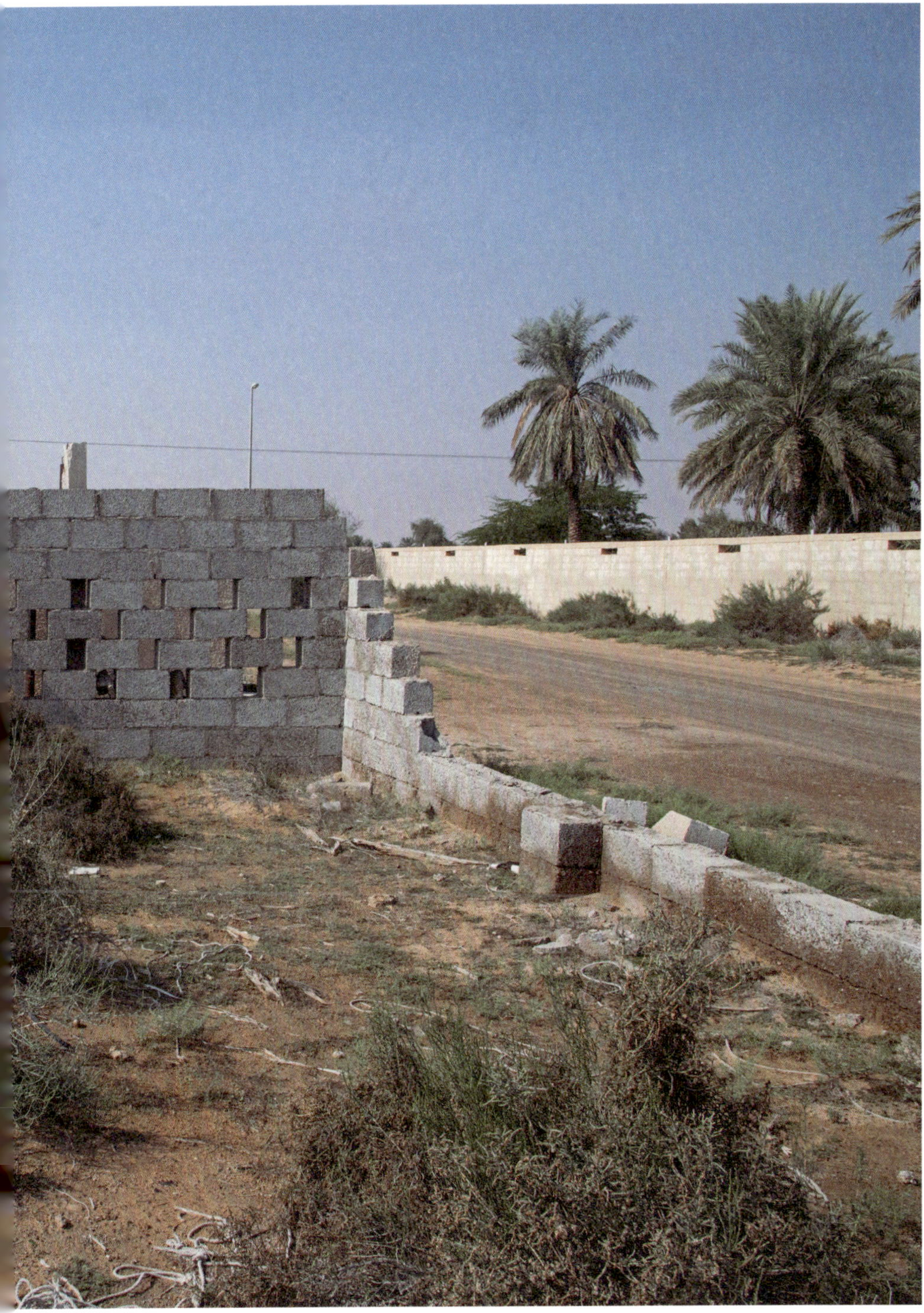

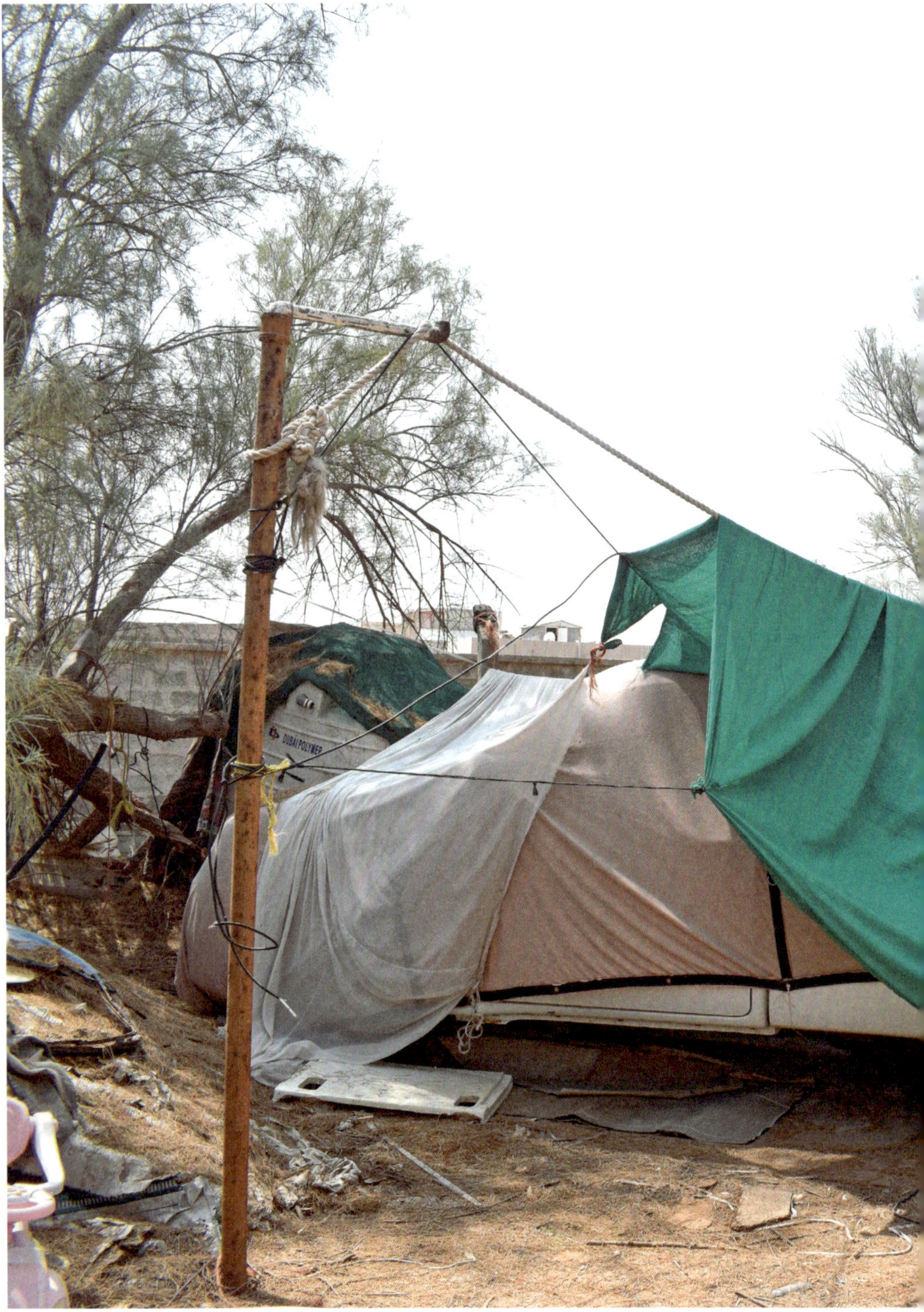
DUBAI POLYMER

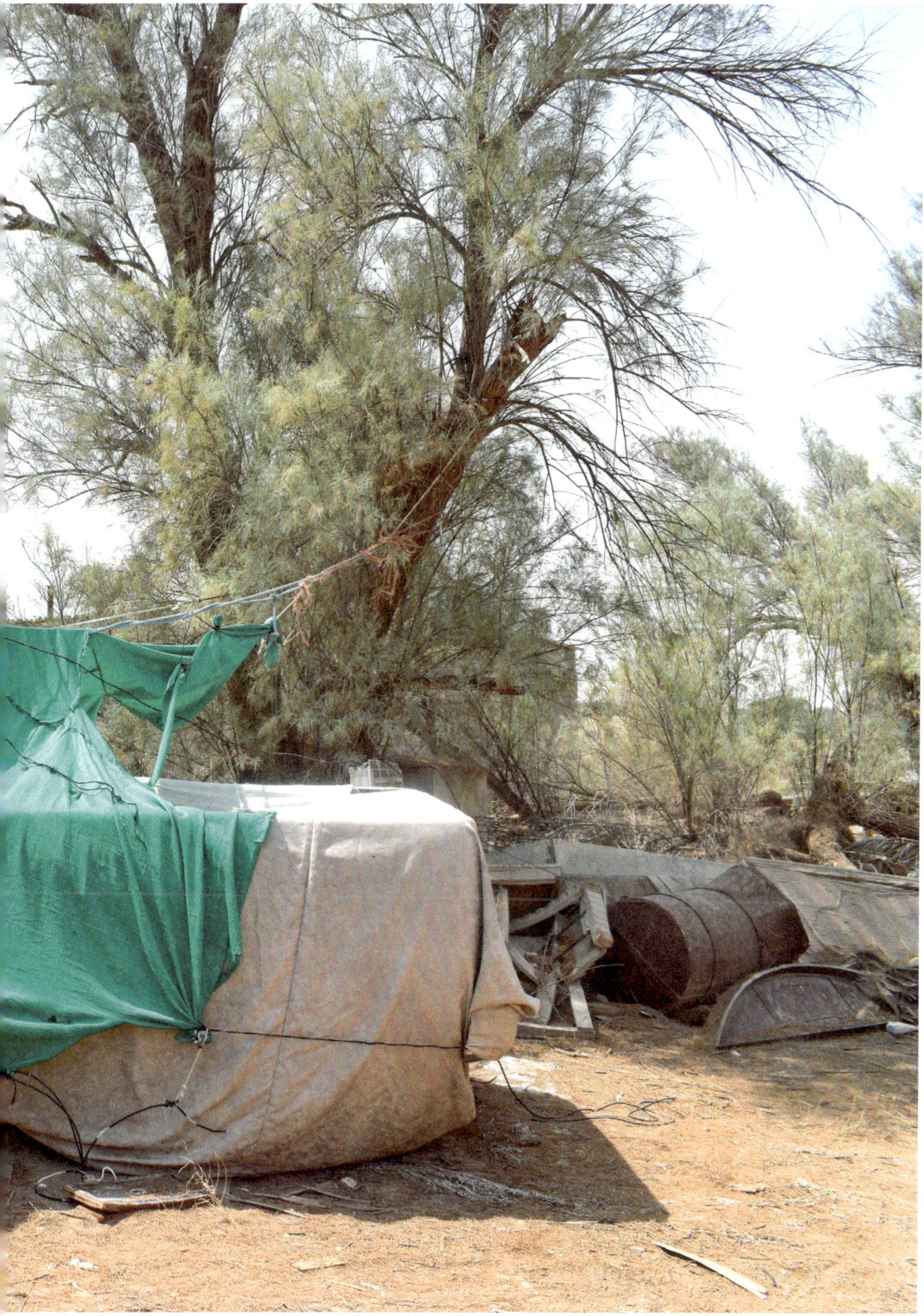

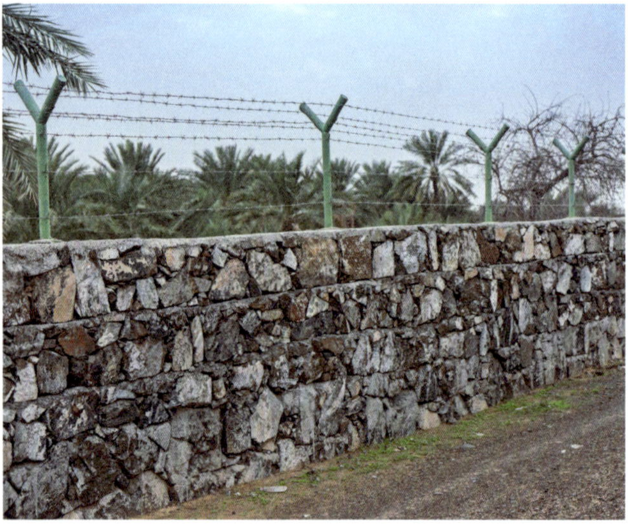

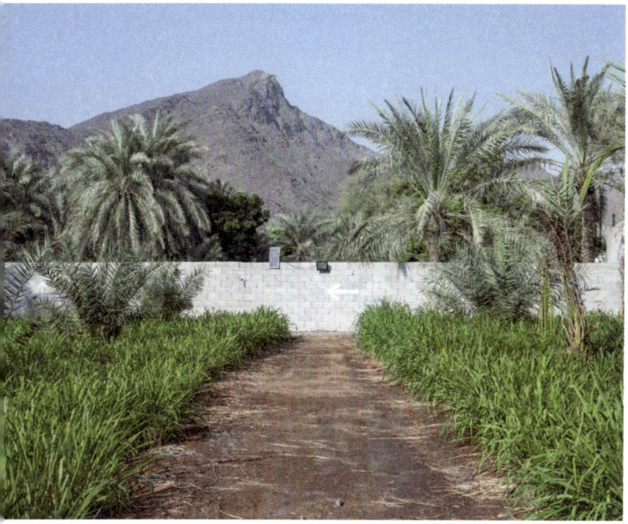

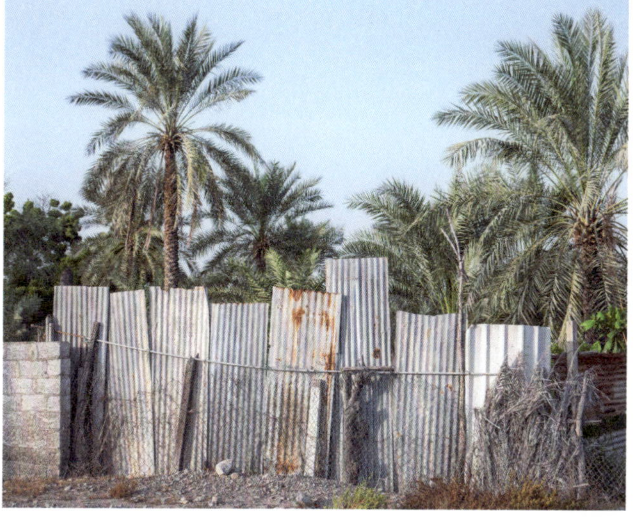

Where it can be mistakenly assumed that Al Hajar Mountains are continuously starved for water, reading the landscape closely reveals complex water management systems that oscillate between the permanent and the fleeting. Water reservoirs of different sizes, nowadays in concrete and rarely, in stone, are built in the landscape, sometimes in plain sight, and at other times hidden in a grove of trees under their shade. Occasionally, water is revealed through the places it has already passed through, such as through a rock, or through empty plastic pipes.

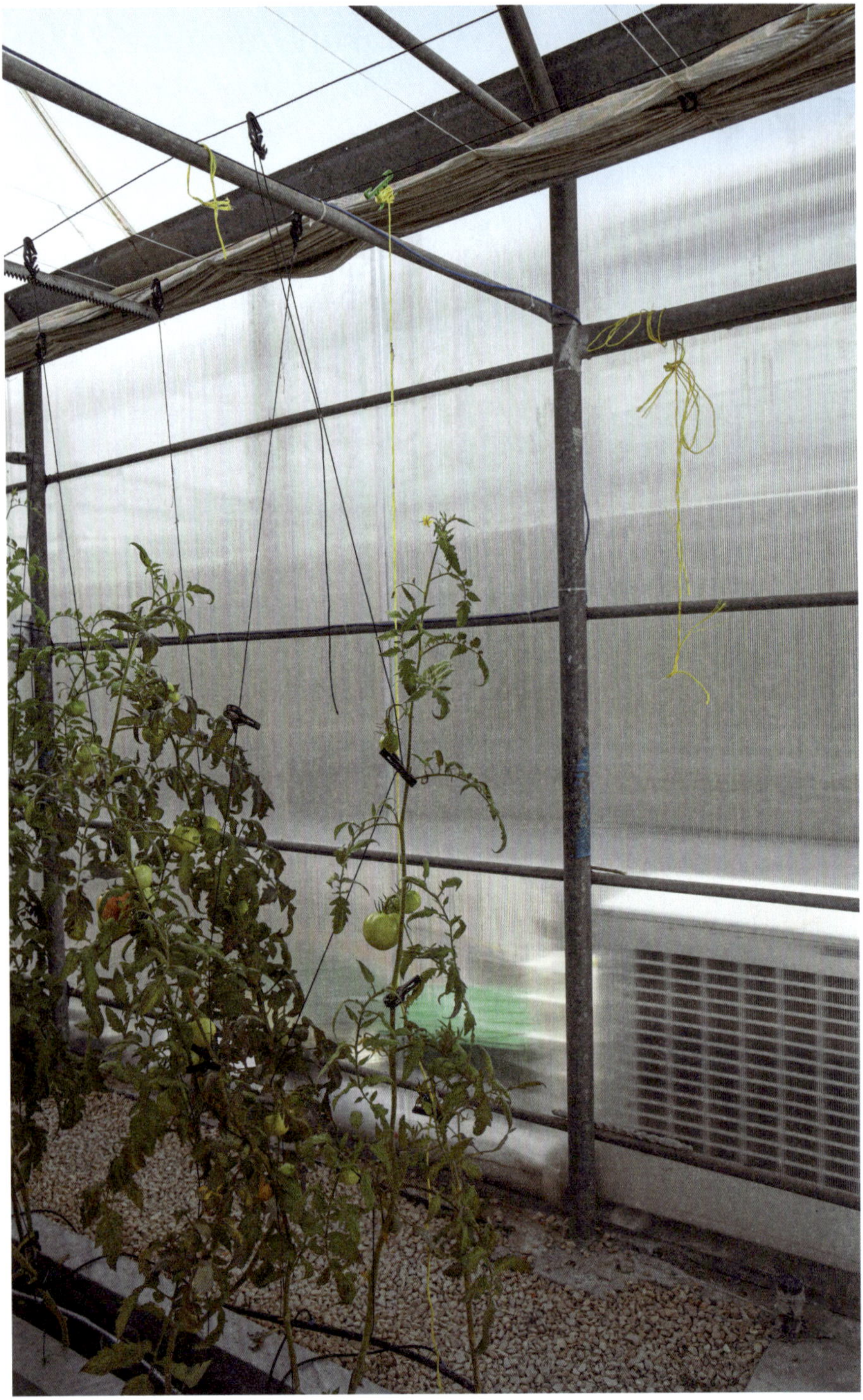

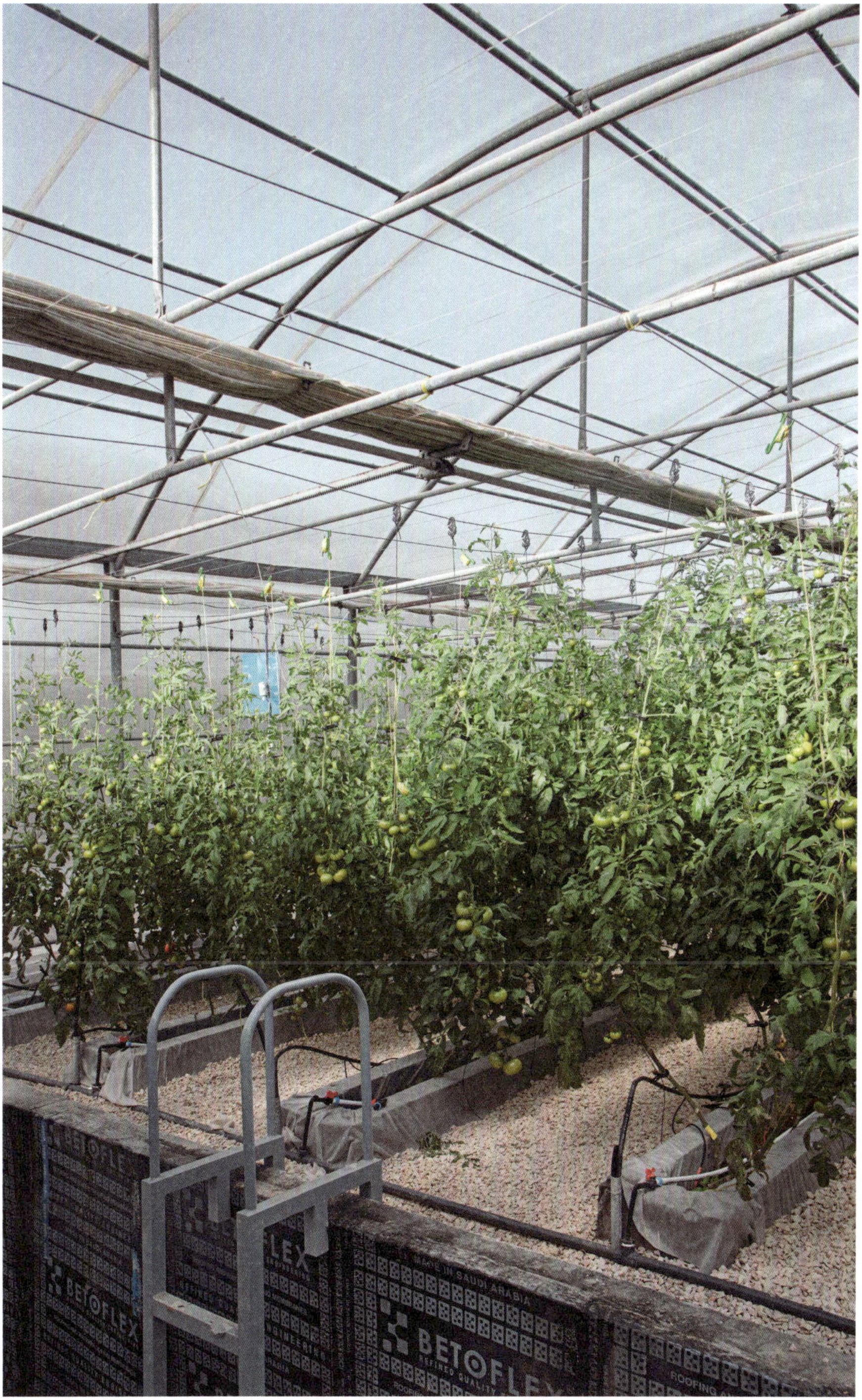
BETOFLEX
MADE IN SAUDI ARABIA
BETOFLEX
BETOFLEX

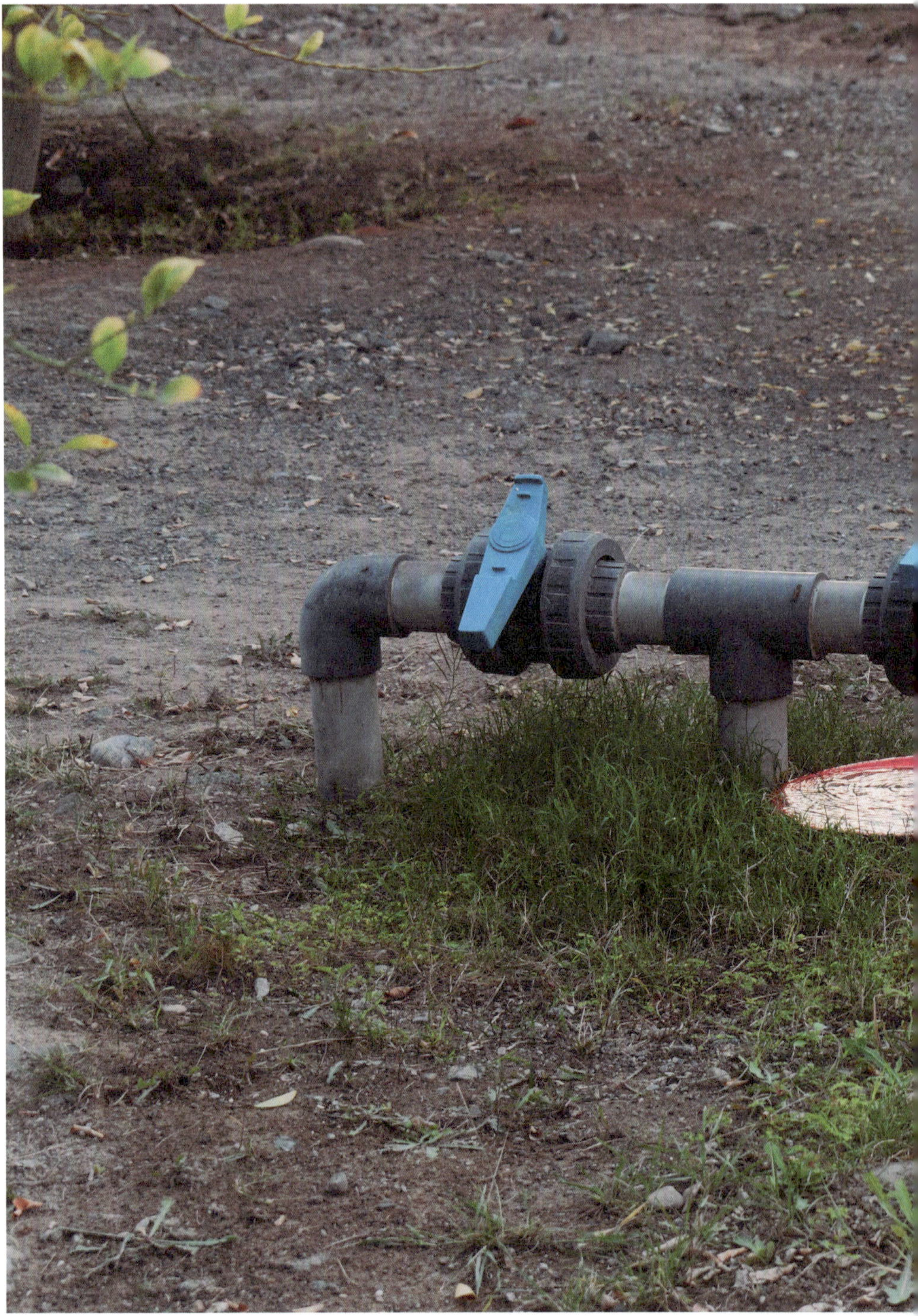

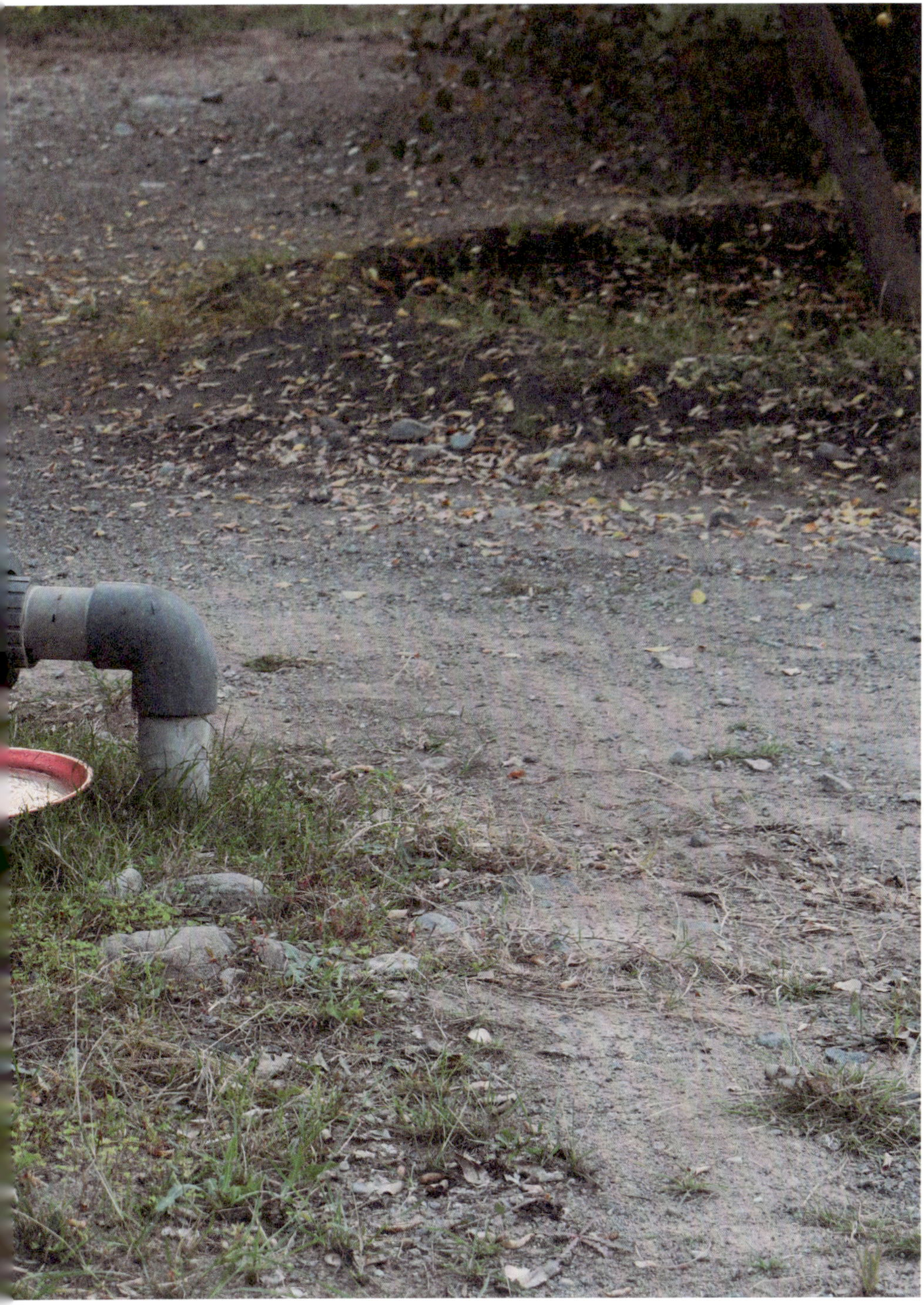

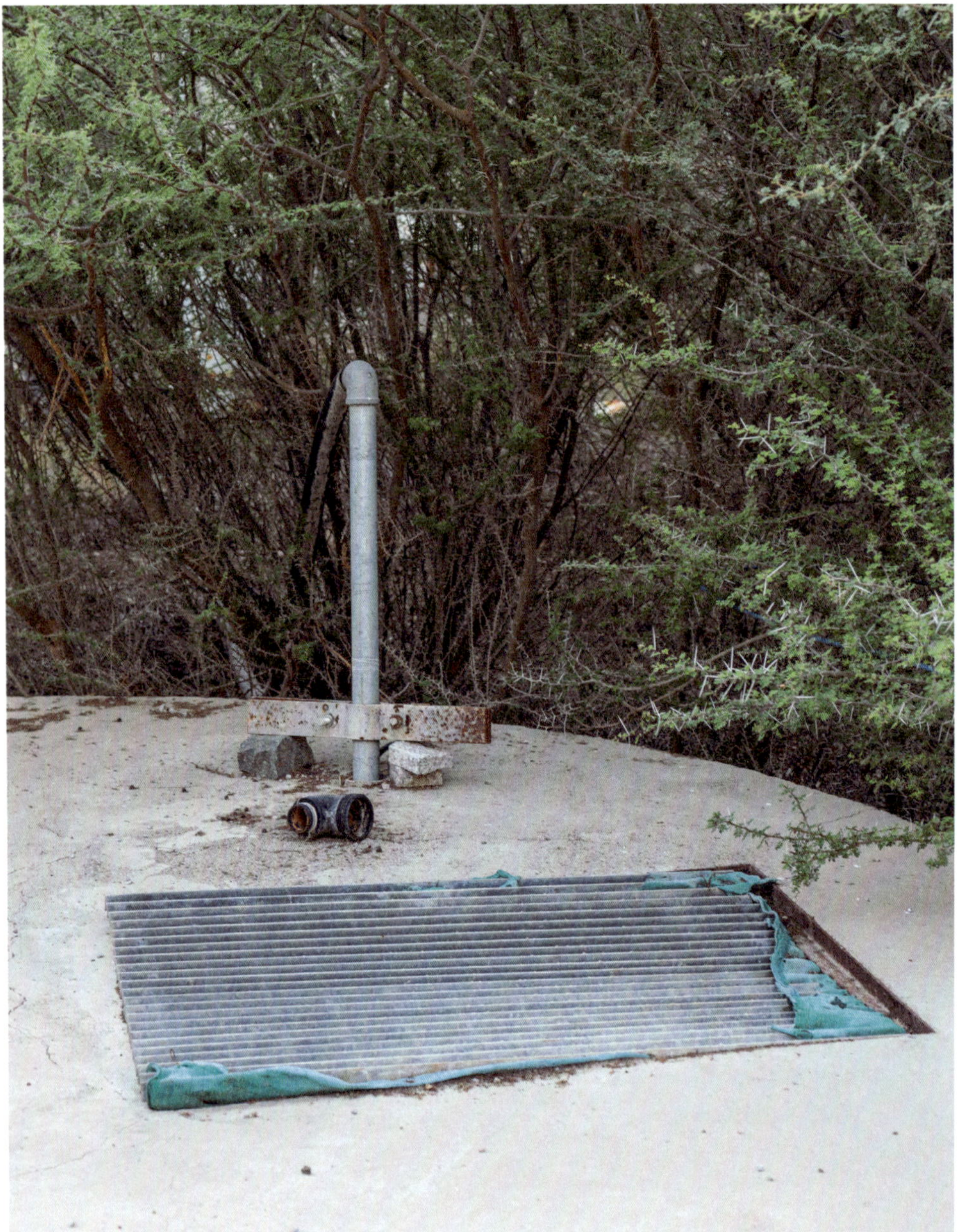

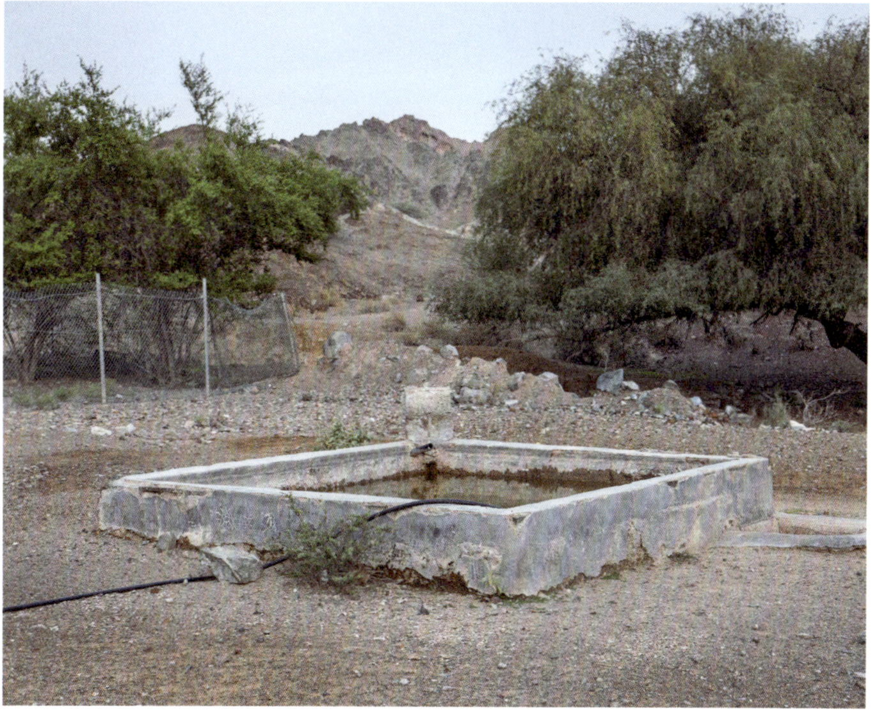

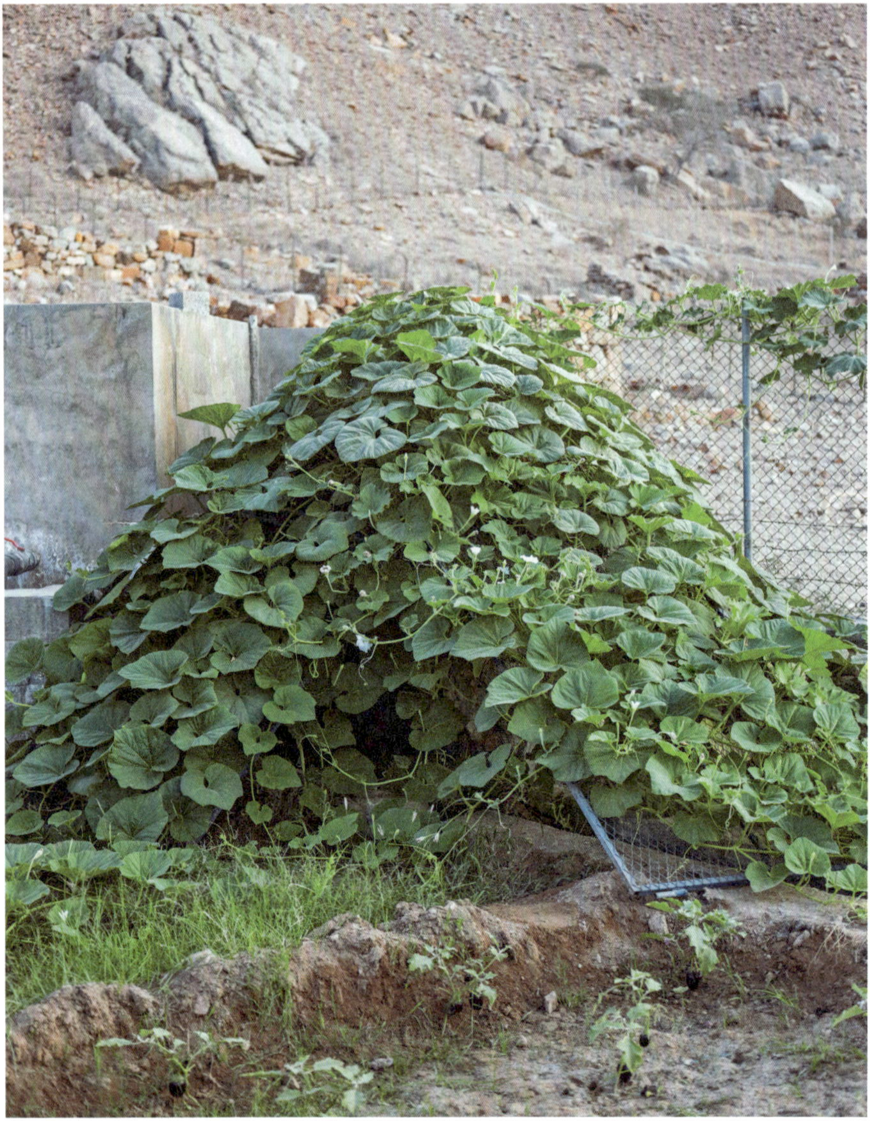

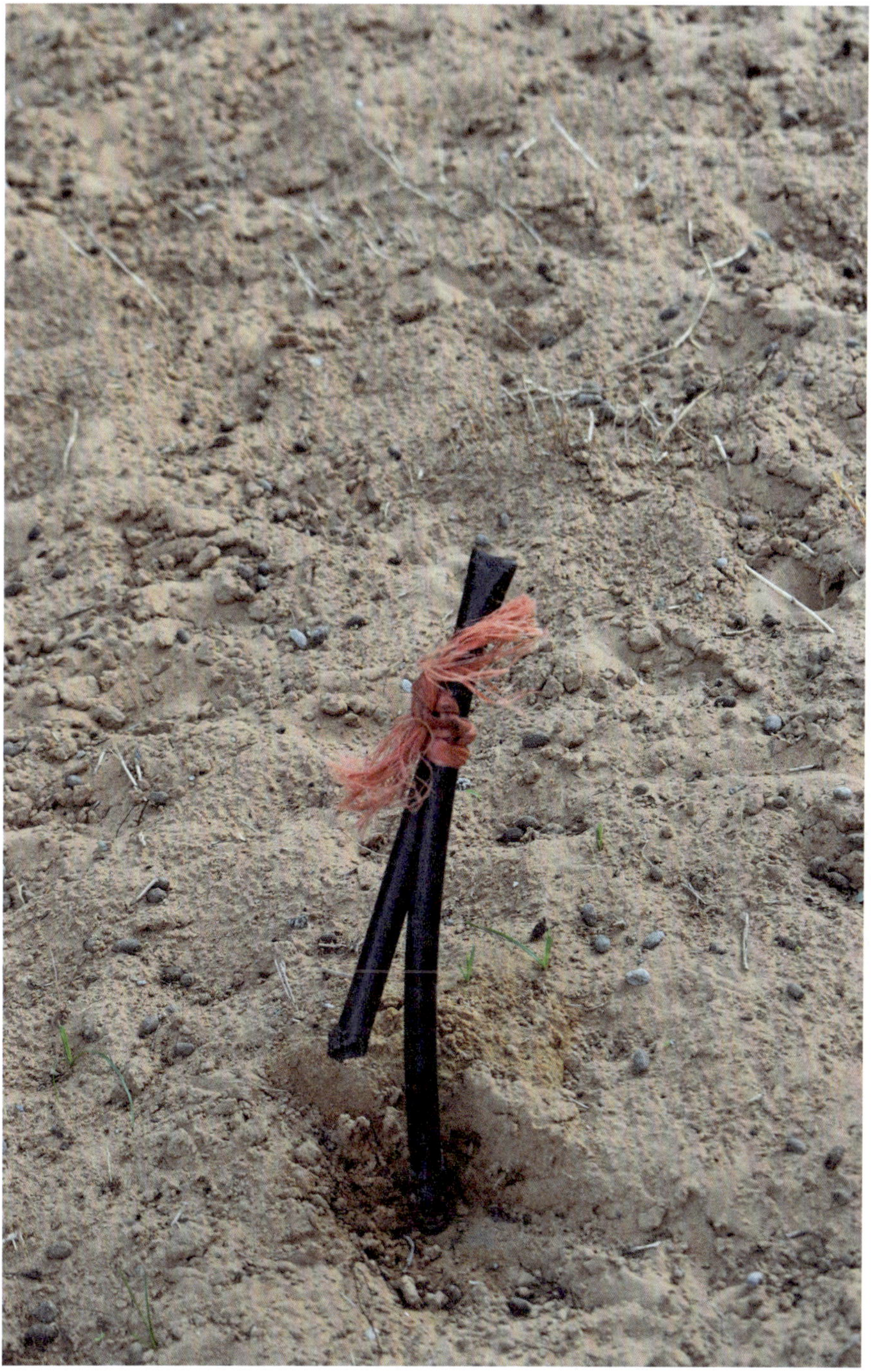

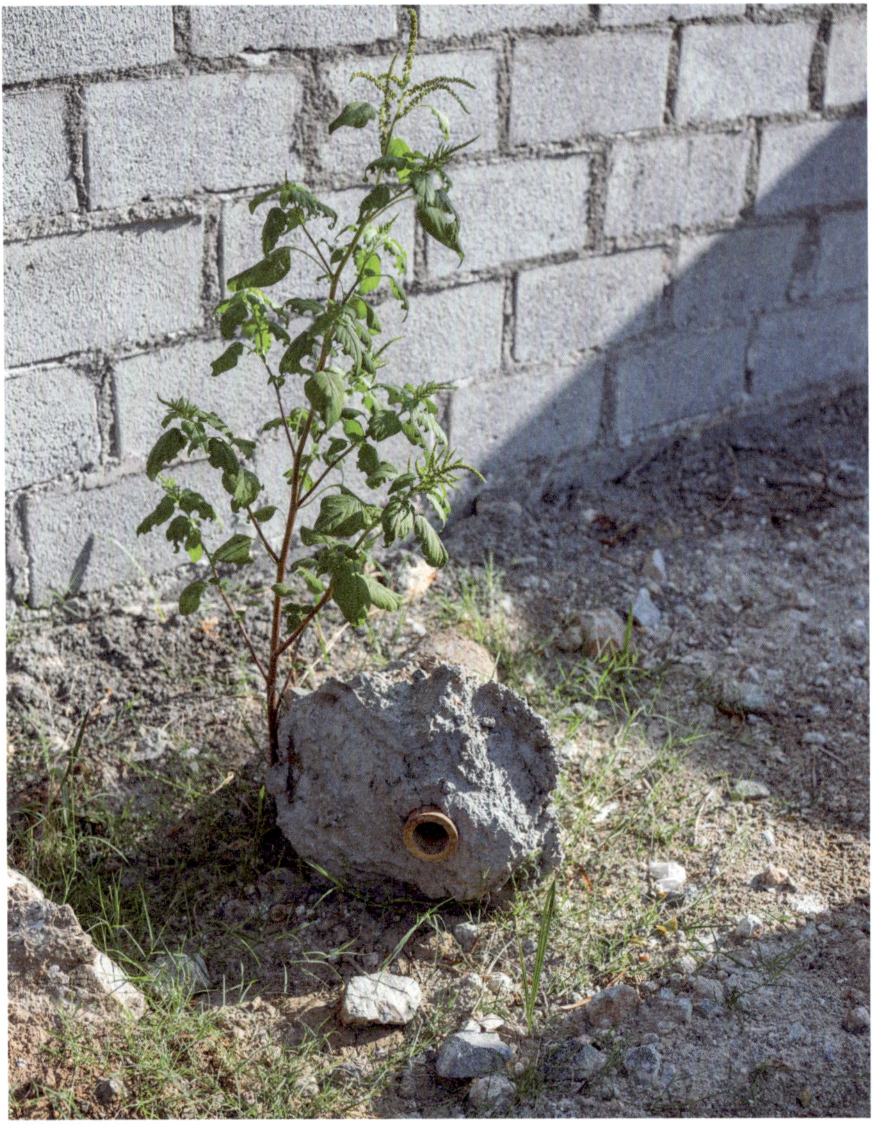

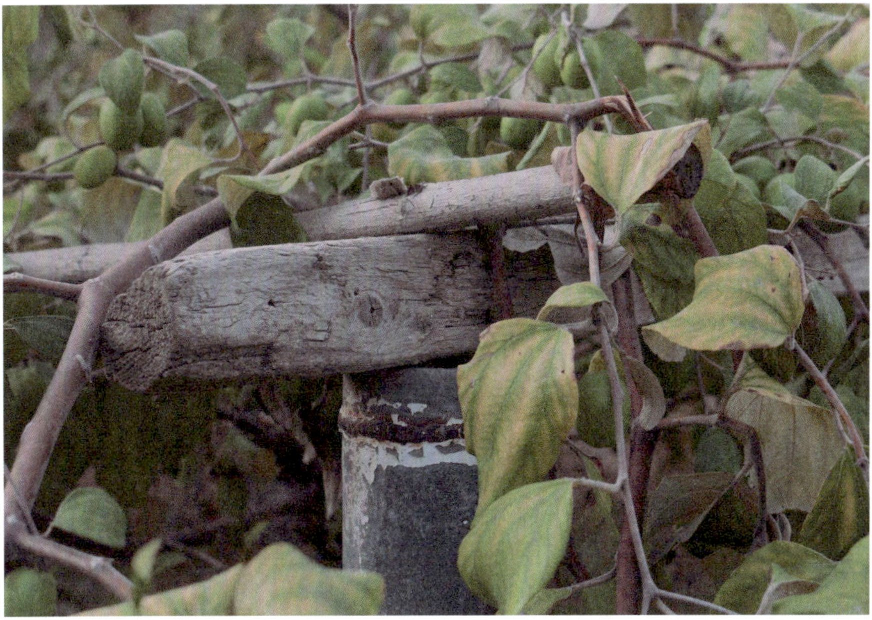

Samar Halloum

A Note on Flows

As our research team started making the initial exploratory field trips through and along Al Hajar Mountains, the ambition to follow a pre-planned route starting in Sharjah and ending on the east coast in a single-day trip was often interrupted by curious excursions and inquisitive stops along the way. The appearance of the mass of rocky mountains topped with layers of ridges looming in the horizon may, from a distance, imply a homogeneous landscape. However, as one travels through the highway connecting Mleiha in the western gravel plain of the mountain to Fujairah on the eastern coastal fertile strip, pockets of arable lands tucked away between the mountains reveal themselves to the traveler. The pockets aggregated into towns and villages, were often carved out of receding platforms in the mountain terrain, showcasing complex integrations of human, animal, and vegetal lives that are deeply embedded in the ecology of their surroundings.

Realizing that the diversions were more recurring than I had initially thought, I started methodically pinning them onto a live map in an attempt to keep track of the endless questions and ideas that these locations sparked. Simultaneously, I had been working on a map with locations of green pockets identified with archival satellite imagery between 1985 and 2023. Some of these green pockets spanned over an extended area forming large towns, while others seemed to consist of a few farms occupying areas that follow the mountain's topographies. When the two maps are overlapped, interesting connections appear along with the matching of exploratory routes and the locations identified with satellite imagery. Despite this, satellite imagery also revealed concealed pockets of agricultural production that a traveler might miss on a regular drive using a direct route towards the east coast. The field trips, loosely planned with the overlapped locations in mind, continued to populate the map, marking places shaped by spatial, social, and environmental tactics that enabled production that depended on and adapted to its context. A common attribute between varied locations is that they congregated around Al Hajar's wadis. The beds of the wadis are replenished with torrents of rainwater that, despite being intermittent, formed a crucial force that shaped human settlements and activities in Al Hajar. The wadis, restricted by the topography of the mountain, often extend into alluvial basins either westwards to Al Batinah gravel plains, or eastwards to the fertile strip along the coast.

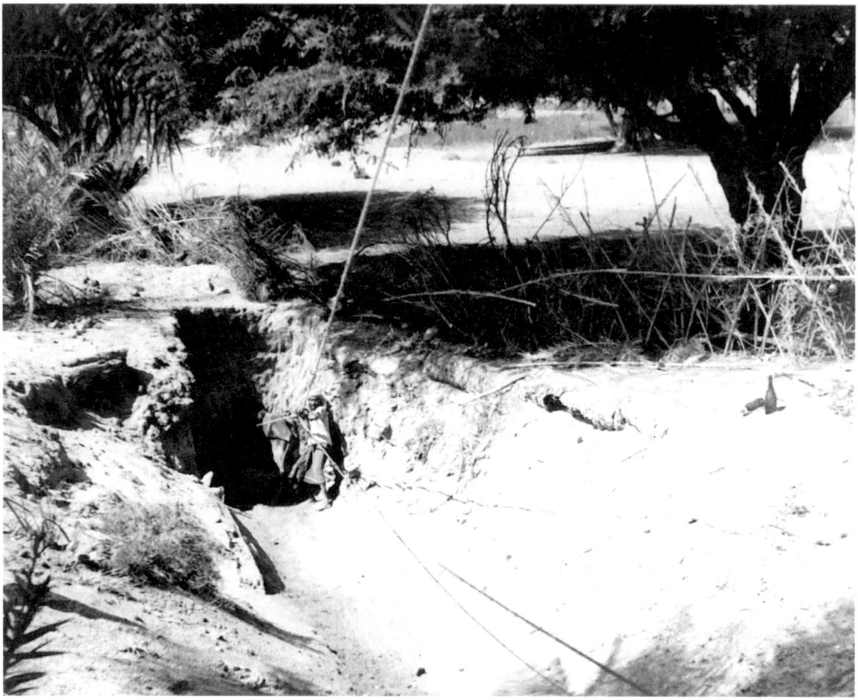

fig. (001) A laborer drawing water using a traditional method in Al Ain, 1954. Photo by Julian Walker © UAE National Library and Archives.

The efforts to trace, examine, and utilize surface and underground water resources predated the earliest available satellite imagery from 1985 and these recurring endeavors of tracing water in the recent history of Al Hajar are found in archival documents and oral histories. Simultaneous to the discouraging reports written in various hydrological surveys carried out by foreign travelers, diviners, and consultants, local efforts by individuals and collectives were working with the fluctuating presence of water resources within Al Hajar. The efforts are evident, first, In the map locating various agricultural activities across the mountain, and second, in the infrastructure that supports irrigation systems that one comes across frequently when exploring the environs of the wadis.

When I ask farmers and farm workers about the source of irrigation water for their farms located in proximity to wadis and dams, they usually point me to their mother well that feeds their land. These wells, reaching secret stashes of underground water accumulating in the rocks of the Semail Ophiolite Aquifer, are connected with pumps that supply water through subterranean channels, usually into a raised water reservoir that sits in the shade of fruit trees.

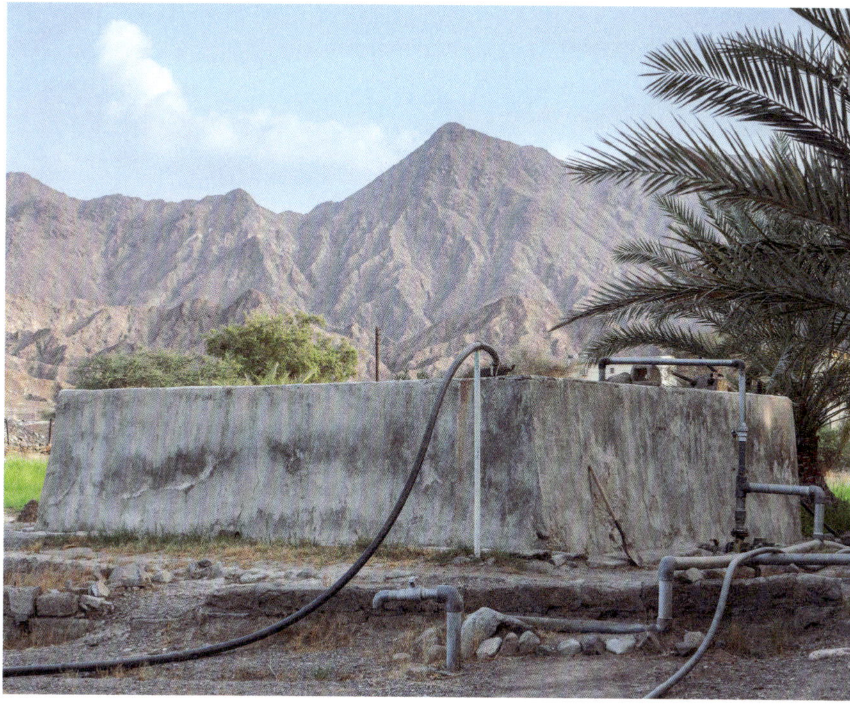

fig. (002) A concrete water reservoir pulls water from a mother well through PVC pipes then supplies its farm with water flowing through its falaj ghayli. Photo by Reem Falaknaz.

From the reservoir, like the one seen in *fig.* (002), a network of channels, furrows, or pipes are established by farmworkers to carry water flows across the farm. The spatial production of networks of water infrastructure located within the boundaries of each farm reveals deep reserves of land-based knowledge that farmers accumulate by working *in*, *with*, and *for* their agricultural lands.

Flawed Archival Notes on Flows

In 1945, correspondences between the political officer in Sharjah and the British Political Agency conveyed an
[01] urgency in initiating maintenance for Al Dhaid Falaj. † A letter shown in *fig.* (003) dated March 14, sent to the political officer in Sharjah labeled the required *falaj* (irrigation channel) maintenance as "of first importance" followed by the response sent on the following day confirming that work had already started. Three days later, the letter in *fig.* (004) confirmed that 60 local workmen were maintaining the falaj in a process that took two weeks for the water flow to continue

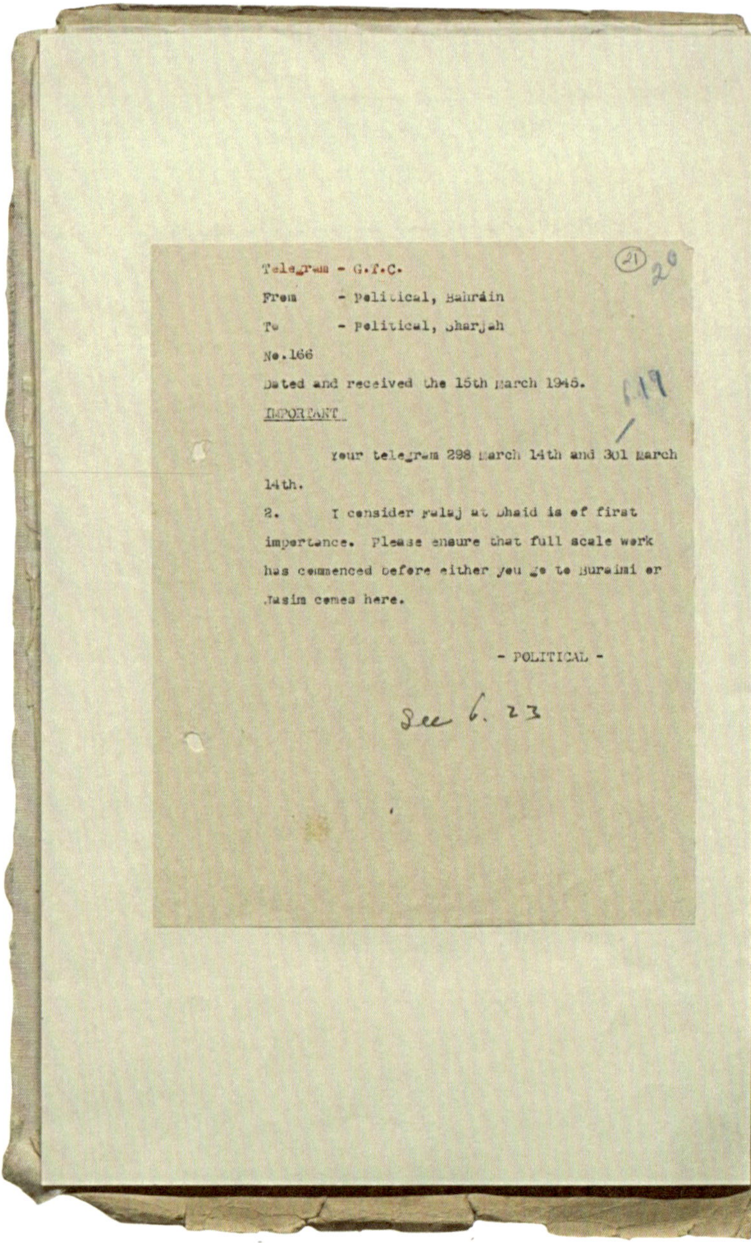

Telegram - G.T.C.

From - Political, Bahrain

To - Political, Sharjah

No.166

Dated and received the 15th March 1945.

IMPORTANT

Your telegram 298 March 14th and 301 March 14th.

2. I consider Falaj at Dhaid is of first importance. Please ensure that full scale work has commenced before either you go to Buraimi or Jasim comes here.

- POLITICAL -

fig. (003) A letter dated March 14, 1945 discussing Al Dhaid Falaj reparation work. File 0205 Sharjah Affairs (Including Bani Qitab), [21r] (41/104), British Library: India Office Records and Private Papers, IOR/R/15/4/1, in Qatar Digital Library.

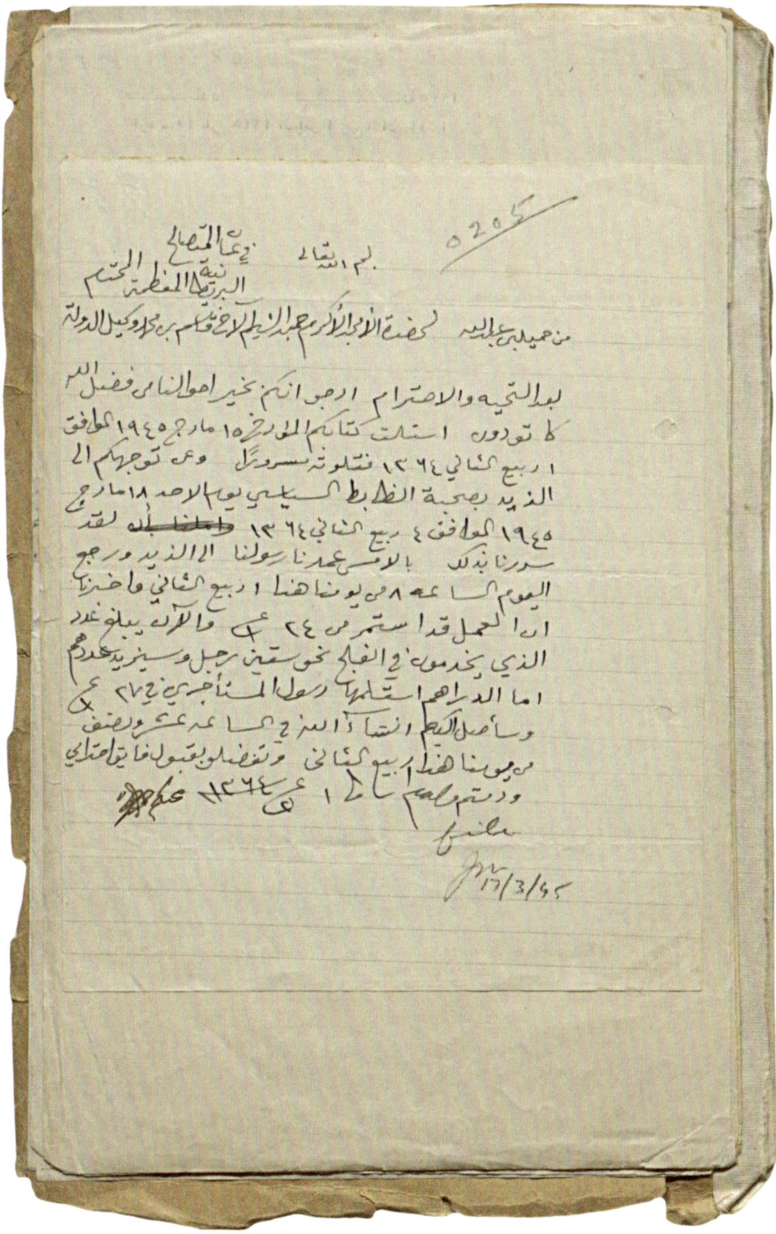

0205

بسم الله تعالى

في عمان المصالح

البريطانية المعظمة المحترم

من حميد بن عبدالله لحضرة الأجل الأكرم عبدالرحيم الأخ قاسم بن محمد وكيل الدولة

بعد التحيه والاحترام ارجو انكم بخير احوال الناس فضل الله

كما تودون استلمت كتابكم المؤرخ ١٥ مارج ١٩٤٥ الموافق

١ ربيع الثاني ١٣٦٤ فتلوته بسرور وعن توجهكم الى

الذيد بصحبة الظابط الكبير يوم الاحد ١٨ مارج

١٩٤٥ الموافق ٤ ربيع الثاني ١٣٦٤ لقد

سررنا بذلك بالامس عمدنا رسولنا الى الذيد ورجع

اليوم الساعه ٨ من يومنا هذا ١ ربيع الثاني واخبرنا

ان العمل قد استمر من ٢٤ ع والآن يبلغ عدد

الذي يخدمون في الفلج نحو ستين رجل وسيزيد عددهم

اما الدراهم استلمها رسول المستأجرين في ٢٧ ع

وسأرسل الكم انشاء الله في ساعه عشر ونصف

من يومنا هذا ١ ربيع الثاني وتتفضلوا بقبول فائق احترامي

ودمتم والسلام ١ ع ٢ ١٣٦٤

file

17/3/45

fig. (004) A letter dated March 17, 1945, discussing Al Dhaid Falaj reparation work. File 0205 Sharjah Affairs (Including Bani Qitab) [22r] (43/104), British Library: India Office Records and Private Papers, IOR/R/15/4/1, in Qatar Digital Library.

uninterrupted. The local knowledge used in building the *aflaj* (plural of falaj) combined with the detailed understanding of the terrain and its *falaj ghayli* (open-air irrigation system) were crucial in getting the maintenance job done.† [02] Despite the utilization of local knowledge and labor of the land, its terrains, and resources, perception towards local knowledge continued to be undermined in value. Almost a decade later, the survey on water supply development in the Trucial States† [03] conducted by Colonel Merrylees, a British water diviner, promised that a three-week trip between Kalba, Fujairah, Khor Fakkan, and Buraimi would allow him to evaluate existing wells and propose locations for new ones. The report that evaluated wells' water levels during his brief trip reveals a tone of surprise at the quality and workability of the networks of wells and aflaj that were established and dug by farmers and farm workers in the areas stretching along the western foothill of Al Hajar:

[...] but it is a remarkable fact that in all the falajs visited, the mother-well had been, in every case, sited in or near the best possible position on a subsoil flow. No traces of trial wells elsewhere now remain but it is unlikely that these falajs could have been so sited by trial and error or by chance and it is thought that the builders must have known some way of locating subsoil flows. Later owners have had no such faculty and some of the abandoned falajs could have been brought into use again by an extension above the "mother well" in the correct direction.† [04]

Merrylees evaluation of the physical quality of the aflaj that were locally built and maintained notes the dependency on materials from their natural surroundings:

The existing falajs (aflaj) built by the farmers do not require lining as the upper part of the alluvial fill is a firm mixture of small stones and a clayey earth and the lower stratum is of water worn gravel in many places consolidated into a hard mass by a calcareous white deposit from the very hard, and warm, water.† [05]

The survey concludes with sketches of trial well locations drawn by Merrylees.

The dispersed, and often concealed, occurrences of water abundance, mapped in *fig.* (005), borne out by the presence of human settlements and agricultural activities within the central zone of Al Hajar, were repeatedly painted negatively, discouraging investment in water infrastructure in reports by assigned travelers. In the Hydrological and Groundwater Survey report dated 1965, the survey party consisting of three British hydrologists of the British consultant engi-
[06] neers Halcrow & Partners noted the flooding within Al Hajar's wadis.†
The three men spent slightly more than three months in the UAE evaluating the persistence of groundwater and noting their findings. The survey divided the range of Al Hajar into ten different zones. In what was identified as the Central Mountains zone, the report described the wadis within the mountains as "deep with steep rock sides and with beds in-filled with gravel derived from the mountains." It continued to note that despite the varied depths and widths of the wadis depicted in the photographs in *fig.* (006-008), the gravel bed was "usually sufficient to absorb considerable quantities of flood water" which would eventually leave the mountain area, streaming into the
[07] surrounding eastern, or western plains days later.†

Despite the observed presence of water floods and flows, the report unfolds to advise against utilizing the flood water stating that "it is unlikely that it will ever prove economic to utilize this flood
[08] water by means of storage in surface reservoirs..."†

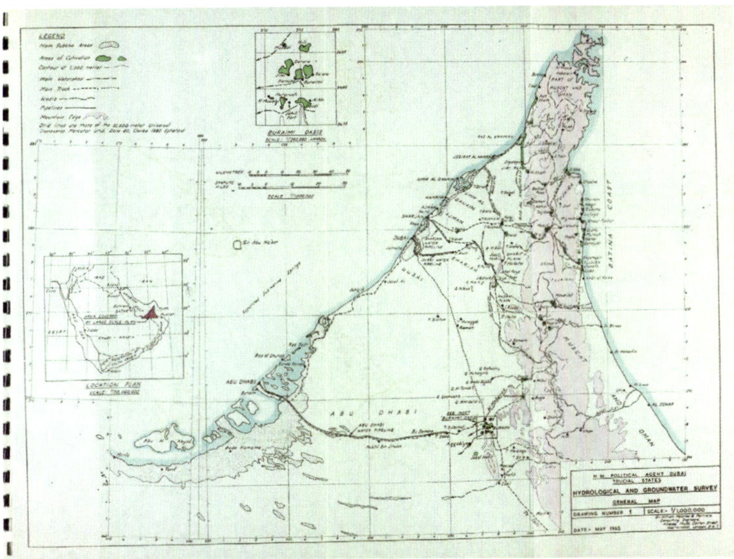

fig. (005) Areas of cultivation mapped in the Hydrological & Groundwater Survey, 1965. FO 1016/840. © Images reproduced by permission of The National Archives, London, England.

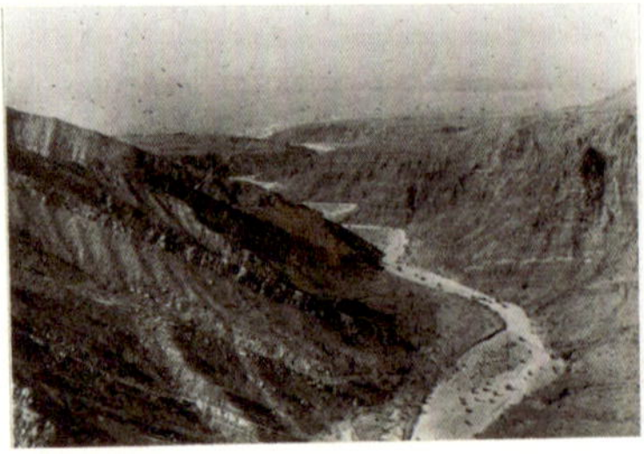

2A. "Limestone Mountains. The gravel bed of Wadi Bih leads from the mountains towards Ras el Khaimah."

fig. (006) A photo showing the gravel bed of Wadi Bih nested within Al Hajar and running towards Ras Al Khaimah. Photograph from the Hydrological & Groundwater Survey, 1965. FO 1016/840. © Images reproduced by permission of The National Archives, London, England.

Less than two decades following the Hydrological and Groundwater Survey and in response to frequent floods that are recorded across various wadis in Al Hajar, the first three dams (Wadi Ham in Fujairah, Wadi Al Beeh in Ras Al Khaimah, and Wadi Gulfa in Masfout) were established in 1982.† [09]
These dams were prioritized due to the need to protect their surrounding areas from the damage caused by the floods. The three dams that were built from earthy material available in the surrounding ground plain, harvested the rainwater and increased the water rate seeping into the aquifers.† These dams continue to supply the agricultural practices near [10]
them with fresh water. Today, the Ministry of Water and Energy manages and maintains 182 dams that it has established over the past 40 years, benefiting hundreds of agricultural practices that depend on underground water for irrigation. During rainy seasons, rainwater floods the dams, and their gates are frequently opened to prevent overflowing and to release excess water into smaller adjacent wadis.

Environmental Interdependence in the Field

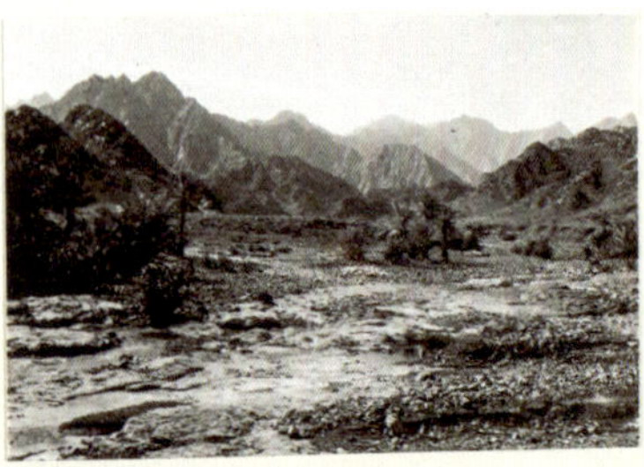

2B. "Igneous Mountains. A 'rock bar' across a gravel wadi bed in the mountains brings water to the surface."

fig. (007) A photograph showing an instance where the bed rock reaches close to the surface causing water to percolate and emerge forming a stream. Photograph from the Hydrological & Groundwater Survey, 1965. FO 1016/840. © Images reproduced by permission of The National Archives, London, England.

During one of the field trips, I visited the farms surrounding Mamdouh Dam, which is an earthy dam built with a 210,000 cubic meter storage capacity lying between the mountain ridges and along the road from Mleiha to Fujairah. I arrived at a farm surrounded by a low-stone stacked wall supporting evenly spaced vertical wooden poles with layers of fabric stretching between them. Crowns of palm trees protruded from the fence into the road, revealing a fragment of what was hidden inside. The farm contains two wells that benefit from the dam and perennially supply 33,000 square meters of agricultural activities with freshwater, mothering hundreds of trees that produce crops that will feed the farmers and their families.

I entered the farm on a narrow sand track, its grooves etched by the succession of wheelbarrows. The track, defined by the palm grove on one side, and a low wall forming an embankment on the other side, runs the length of the farm, overlooking two lower terraces. On the lowest terrace, a distinct break in the rows of trees reveals two holes in the ground; the wells. A quick glance might not have been enough to notice them; the layers of rugged rocks collected from the mountains allowed the wells to camouflage within the landscape. An estimated 5 by 4 meters and 3 by 2 meters respectively, the wells are each retained by four walls of stacked rocks. Since it was dug more than 60 years ago, the larger well has been sufficient in irrigating the highest level of the terraced agricultural land. Two of its retaining walls are vertically ruptured, inducing divergent segments that withstood forces of ground movements and water pressure over the years. But more importantly, the farm owner proudly tells me that unlike CMU-block wells seen in the area, the walls of their well have withstood the natural acids in the underground water without dissolving or erosion. Over the years, and as the farmer's family grew, the farm expanded, necessitating digging a second well around 25 years ago. Similar to the older well, the newly built one reflects a judicious use of layered rocks collected from the immediate surroundings.

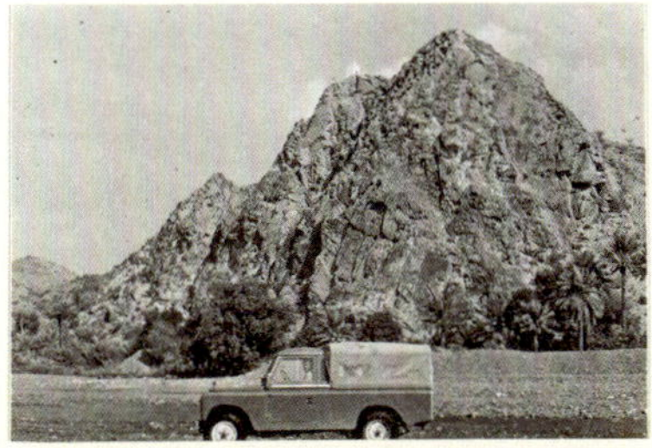

2C. "Mountain Wadi and Gardens. Water from the gravel river bed in the igneous mountains is used to irrigate the gardens at the foot of the rock."

fig. (008) Pockets of agricultural land appear at the foot of the mountain. Photo from the Hydrological & Groundwater Survey, 1965. FO 1016/840. © Images reproduced by permission of The National Archives, London, England.

Once the water is pumped from the mother well into a reservoir on the farm, it sits waiting for a barrier (مردّات الفلج) to open, allowing it to flood the falaj ghayli. I stand observing Khadem, who has worked on this farm since his arrival from Bangladesh 16 years ago. His calloused hand stretches down to pick up a rock that has been carefully placed on top of a wrapped bundle of woven fabric. The fabric bundle, which is made of an emptied fertilizer bag, is deliberately folded, wrapped, and cinched with jute rope to correspond to the width of the outlet where it has been placed. While it still holds the residue of printed ink from when it was made, it is now folded into multiple layers that overlap to prevent water from flowing through the gaps of its interlacing threads.

Khadem's hand *dis*locates the rock to the side and the bundle follows it receding the moment the rock wasn't anchoring it against the pressure of water flowing through the channel. The size and weight of the rock, which has been picked from the farm ground, is proportional to the size of the bundle and is heavy enough to hold it in place; sometimes, as a substitute, two smaller rocks are placed to anchor a bundle. Together, the rock and the wrapped fabric control this outlet in the falaj. Their *dis*location diverts the water through the unblocked outlet and into the soil of a sunken bed.

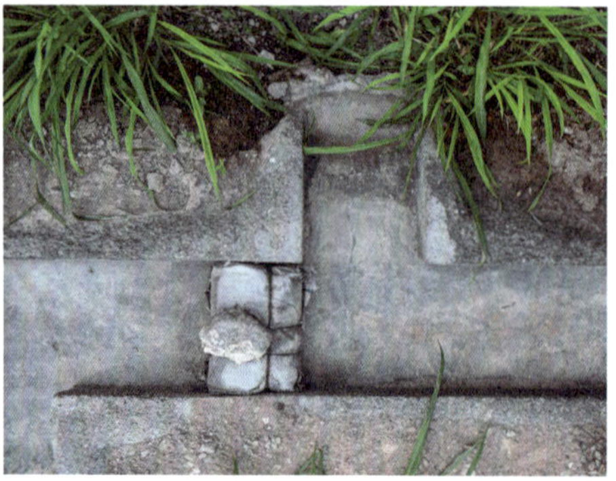

fig. (009) A rock picked from the surroundings placed on top of a folded emptied fertilizer bag fabric to redirect water into an adjacent sunken bed. Photo by author.

Over the years, Khadem acquired knowledge and experience in distributing water flows through irrigation channels on the farm. He stands by the side of the falaj while the water permeates the desiccated ground and quenches the soil filling its pores with water and depriving them of air. He crouches to *re*locate the assemblage back in its place, sealing the outlet and redirecting the water into the main channel. Moving along the irrigation channel in the direction of the water flow, he continues to *dis*locate and *re*locate one assemblage at a time; sometimes, he rotates them in their place, allowing a narrow gap for less water to trickle into a particular sunken bed with one single tree at its center.

*Dis*locations and *re*locations of these assemblages seen in *fig.* (010) block, control, and divert water through a falaj channel network that runs in the shade of a palm grove and between rows of sunken beds. The sunken beds, each approximately 4 meters by 4 meters, are created by removing the topsoil layer and adding it to other earthy components to form berms surrounding the falaj ghayli channels running between these sunken beds. These berms are effective in retaining the irrigation water within the bed and, thus, reducing the frequency of irrigation. The sizes of the sunken bed ensure that each palm tree planted at its center is around 8-9 meters away from other trees. The grid of the

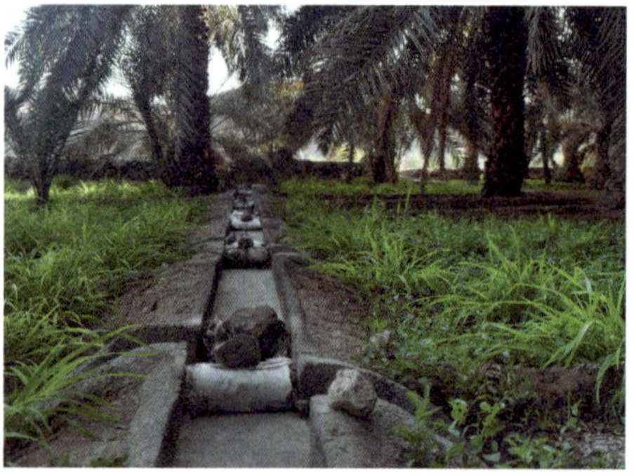

fig. (010) Water flow is controlled and diverted by the dislocations of ad hoc assemblages. Photo by author.

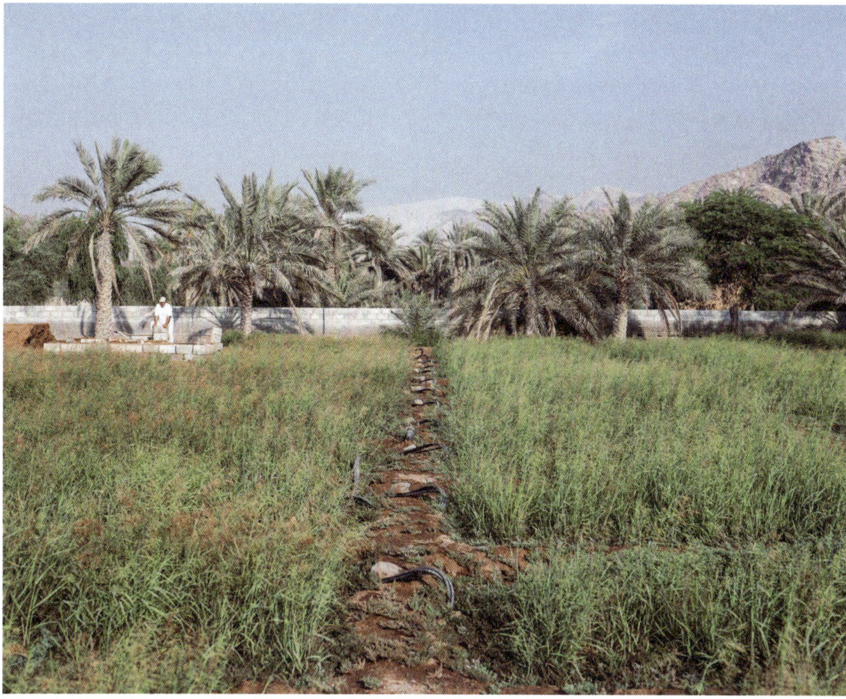

fig. (011) Irrigation pipes anchored using rocks picked from the farm ground. Photo by Reem Falaknaz.

sunken beds ensures that the palm trees are dispersedly planted, which is essential for their growth and productivity. Between these beds run the falaj channels with an outlet opening to each sunken bed. While talking to Khadim, I learned that the berms of the sunken bed are essential in protecting the topsoil layer from wind running close to its surface, which reduces soil erosion and deposition at the scale of the grid.

Although the falaj ghayli is a frequently used irrigation technique, the assemblages forming water barriers, consisting of emptied fertilizer bags and rocks, in this case, seem to take an infinite number of forms and consist of a wide variety of materials in different farms. The more farms I visited, the clearer it became that what distinguishes the utilized material in each case was often a byproduct of the immediate surroundings (e.g., rocks or tree branches), and activities and products used in the farms (e.g., material waste like old fabric or emptied fertilizers bags).

A common criteria for these assemblages is the need for a material with characteristics of malleability that, once pressure is applied, allow it to congest and block the inner part of the channel it sits within, combined with a relatively heavier object that is placed above to anchor it in place against the pressure of the water flow. In some cases, a tying material is used to keep the lower malleable bundle of material together. The falaj ghayli, the rock-and-fabric assemblages, and the sunken beds bear witness to approaches that reflect an understanding of material morphological features, and challenge mainstream supply chains.

In other farms, more recently distributed networks of pipes are in place. Although using synthetically manufactured products, the ways their pipes are laid out, assembled, and installed applies tactics that mimic the channeling of water through the falaj. An example seen in *fig.* (011) might be: a rock is placed on a curving pipe to stabilize the pipe on the ground allowing the water to flow. When the rock is displaced, the curved pipe rotates upwards, reducing the intensity of the flow against gravity through the pipe. What is fascinating about the complex irrigation systems that vary between the historic aflaj and the more contemporarily built channels and networks of water pipes, is that all these networks require constant human involvement, keeping a close bond between the farmworkers and their environment.

Tracing the waterflow through wadis, dams, wells, furrows, canals, and outlets reveals intricate layers of labor that deploy accumulated knowledge of the land and its resources to enable systems and assemblages that together distribute and manage flows within agricultural lands. Looking around the farm, I start to notice how the level of dexterity demonstrated in the assembly that channels and controls the flows, is found at varying scales shaping the social, and physical environment within the farm. The collection, extraction, distribution, and utilization of water requires land-based knowledge and skillful management that enables rich and productive social and agricultural lives in landscapes that would otherwise be impossible.

An Arabic term that comes to my mind as I scrutinize the use of materials across different farms is *istislah*(استصلاح), which is used to describe a process of redeeming objects or materials that are often overlooked or regarded as useless in mainstream processes, then employing them to achieve an intended purpose. On the farms, people's resourceful attitudes in utilizing the materials manifest their knowledge of the potential in their surroundings to address water-scarce conditions.

01

'File 0205 Sharjah Affairs' [25v] (50/104), British Library: India Office Records and Private Papers, IOR/R/15/4/1, in Qatar Digital Library, https://www.qdl.qa/archive/81055/vdc_100025675333.0x000033.

02

See "Note on an Oddly Natural History" for the differences between the three main aflaj systems.

03

The Trucial States originally consisted of six sheikhdoms on the southern coast of the Arabian Gulf and later became the UAE in 1971.

04, 05

Improvement of water supplies in Trucial Coast States, 1954, FO 371/109892, Arabian Gulf Digital Archives, https://agda.ae/en/catalogue/tna/fo/371/109892

06

Correspondences on water resources between January 1965 and December 1965, "Trucial States: Water Resources; with hydrological and groundwater survey", (March, 1965), FO 1016/840, Arabian Gulf Archive, https://www.agda.ae/en/catalogue/tna/fo/1016/840

07

Correspondences on Water, 123.

08

Correspondences on Water, 124-125.

09

A. S. Alsharhan, et al. *Hydrogeology of An Arid Region: The Arabian Gulf and Adjoining Areas. Elsevier Science,* (Amsterdam, The Netherlands, 2001).

10

Gerard Lods et al. "Groundwater Flow Characterization of an Ophiolitic Hard-Rock Aquifer from Cross-borehole Multi-Level Hydraulic Experiments. *Journal of Hydrology* 589, (2020) 125-152.

Tactics of Channeling

Al Hajar Mountains asks one to look a little bit lower than usual at the more immediate ground, revealing the complexity of activity within and on the surface of the ground itself. This, in turn, pokes at questions about what exists deeper in the ground. Tilting one's gaze lower reveals networks of water, which can be historic such as the falaj networks, or sometimes mimicking historic networks but made more recently with concrete or PVC pipes. Frequently, a rock appears in the story, aiding in the channeling of water.

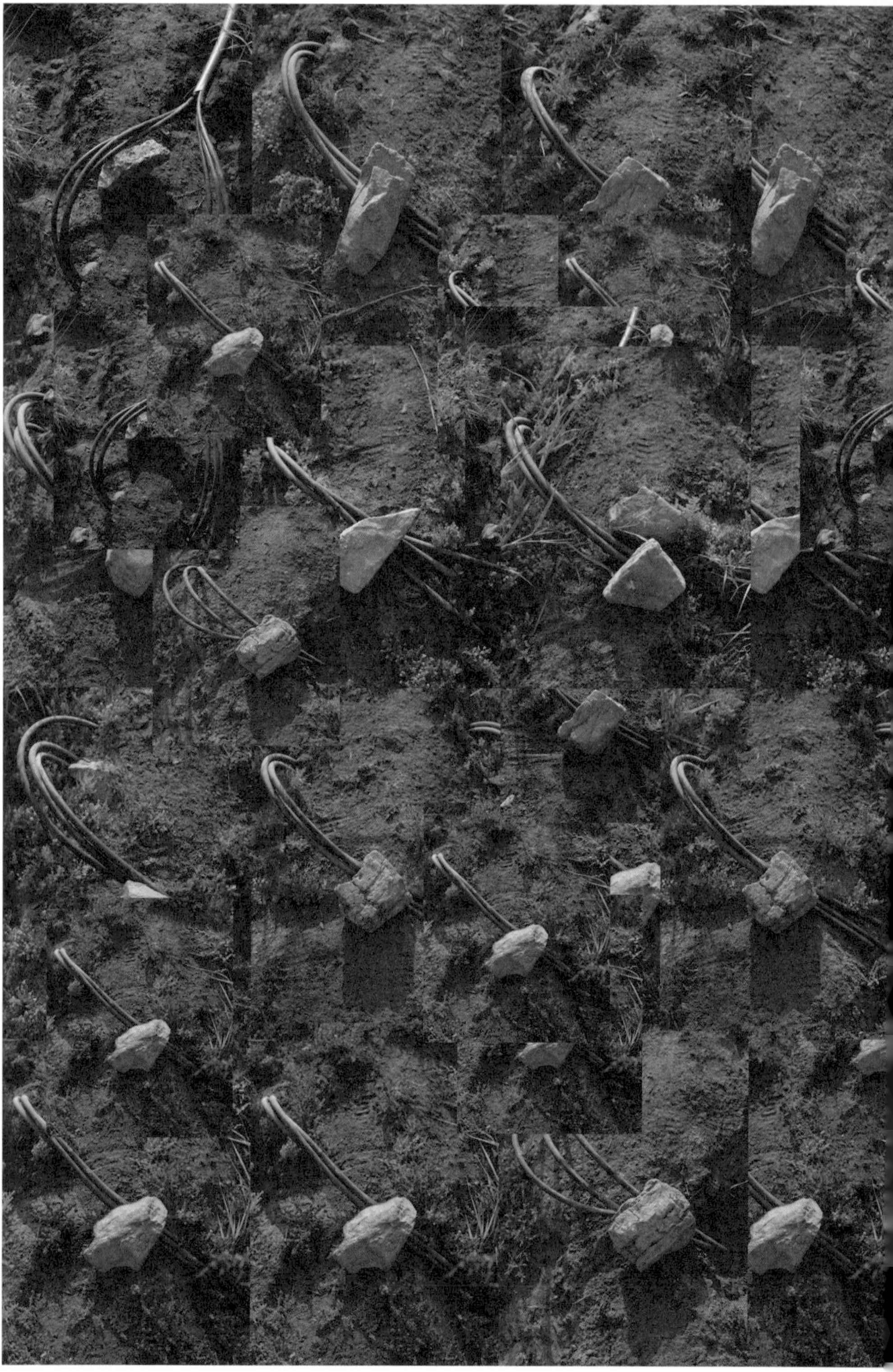

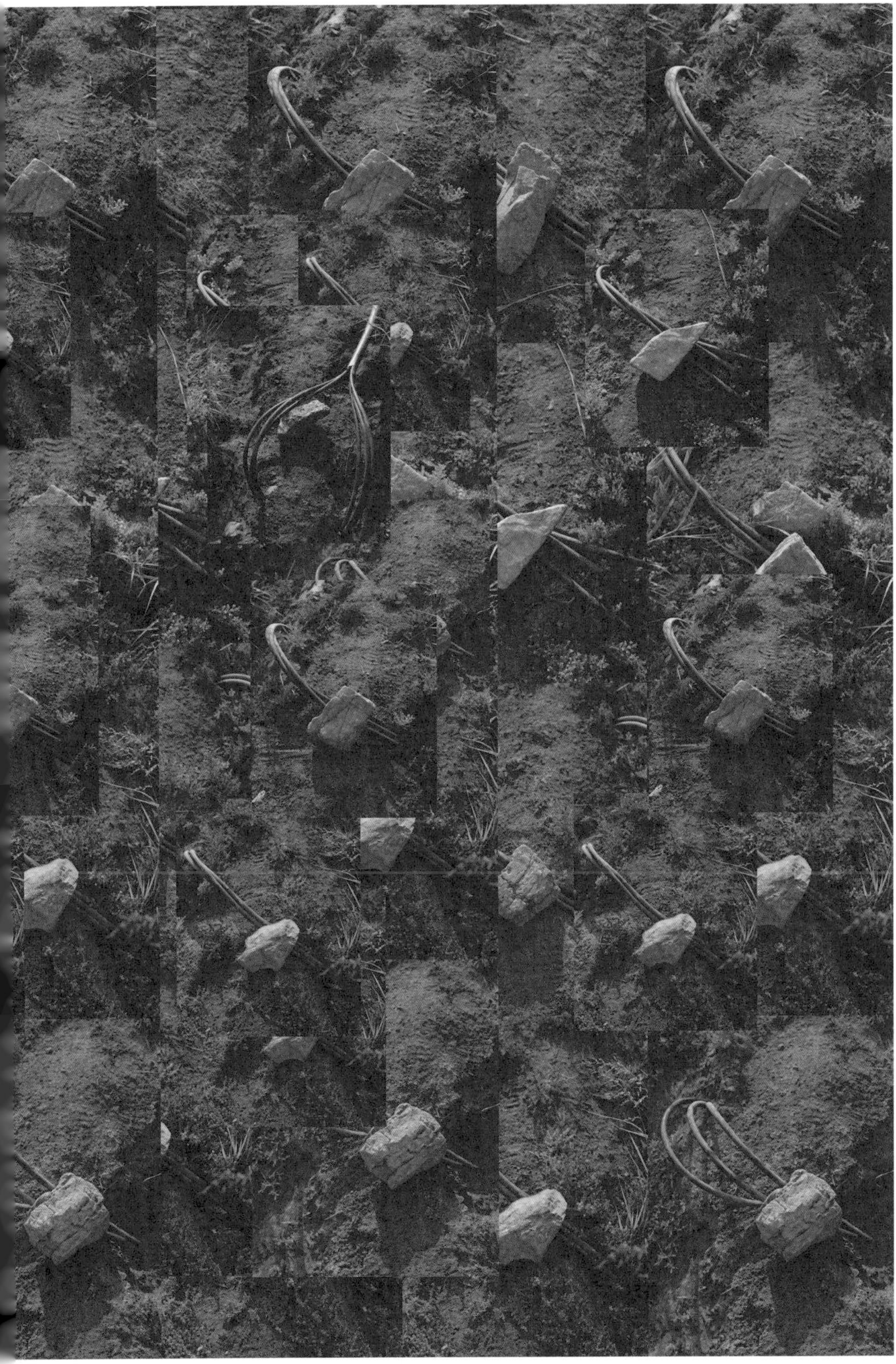

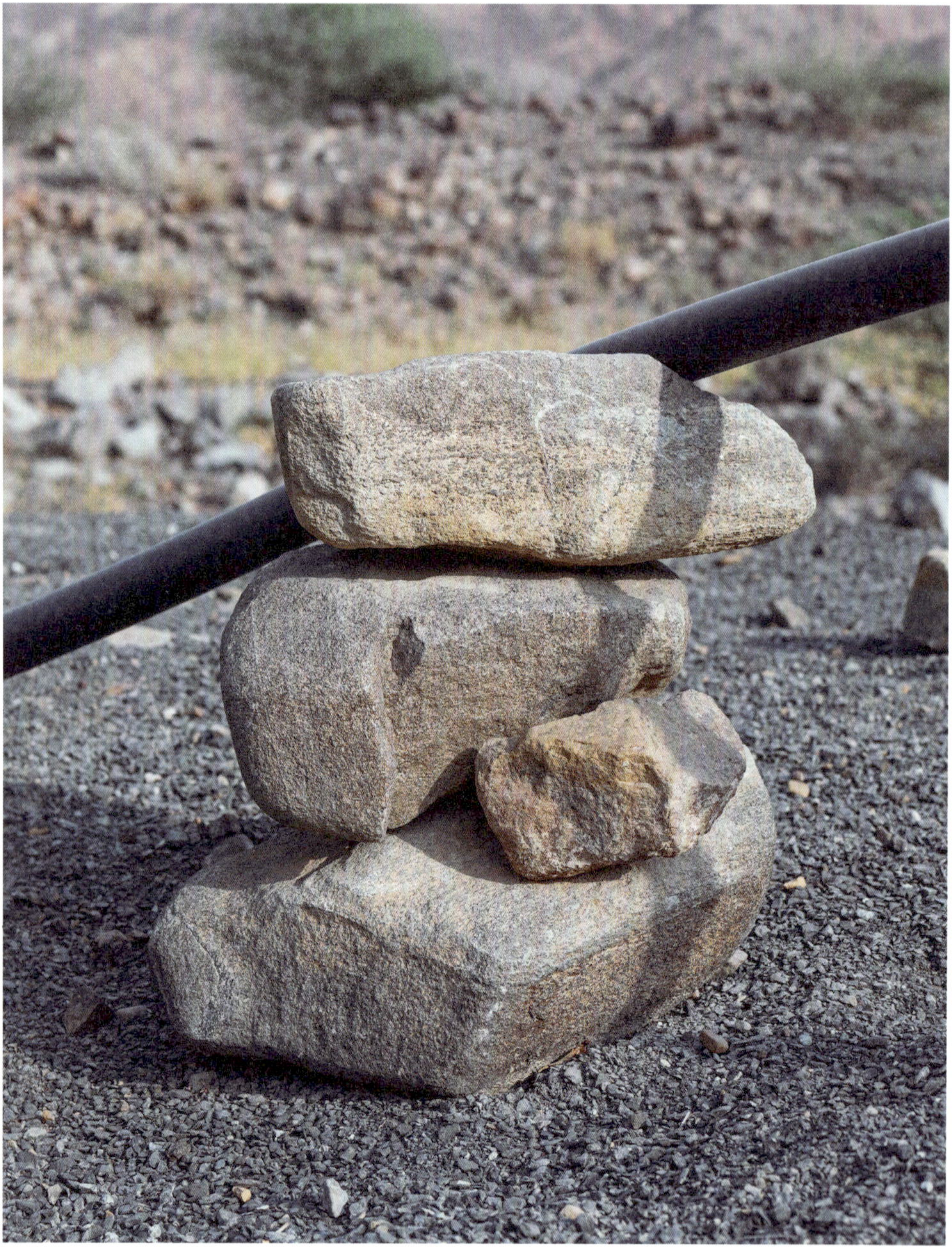

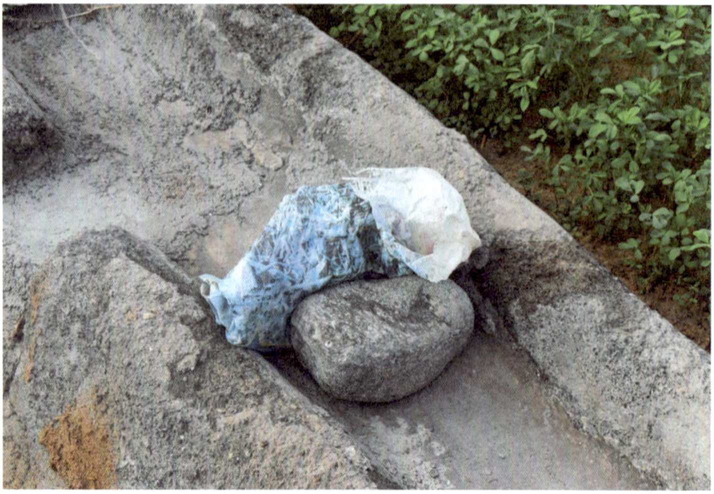

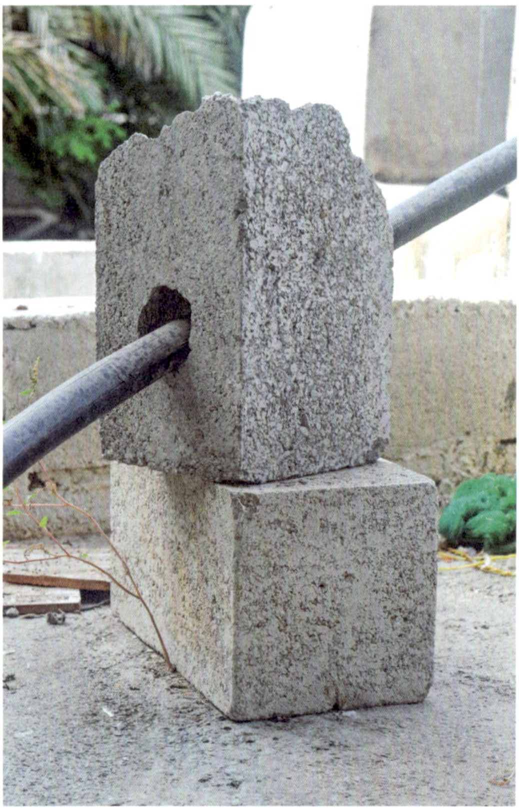

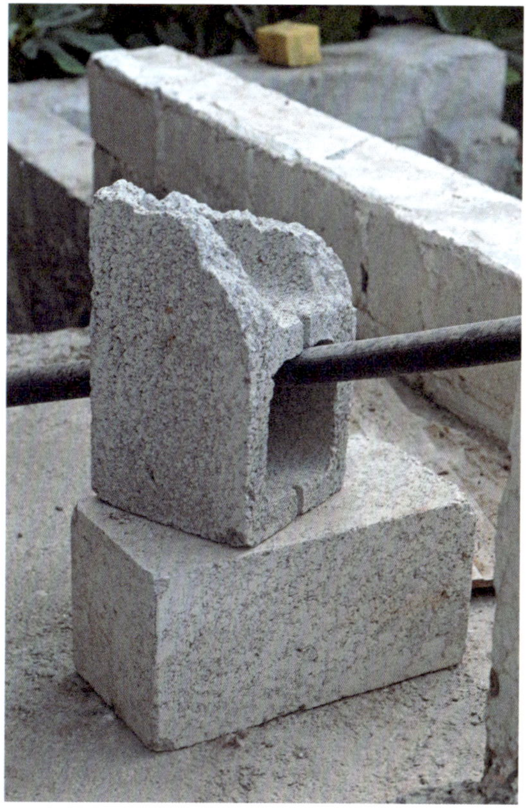

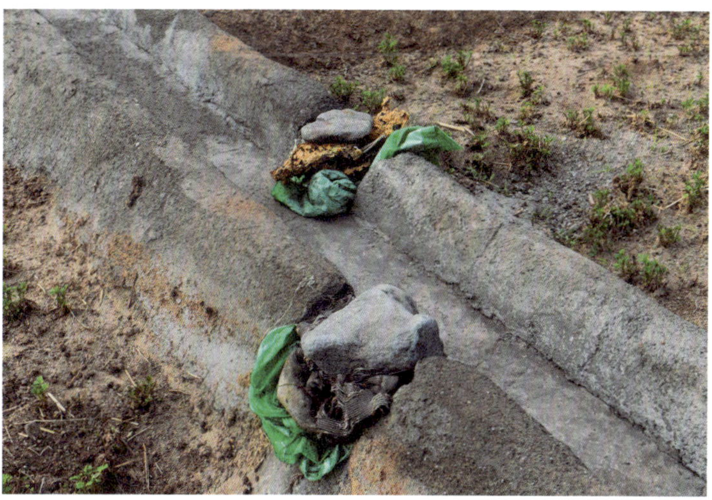

The sheltering of plant material in Al Hajar Mountains from extreme sunlight and insects suggests an architectural use of fabric that points to an adaptive form of scalability. From sheltering a full vegetable patch to that of a single flower, the architectural relationships between fabric, rigid elements, and sheltered material exhibit relatively loose physical relationships between the shelter and the sheltered.

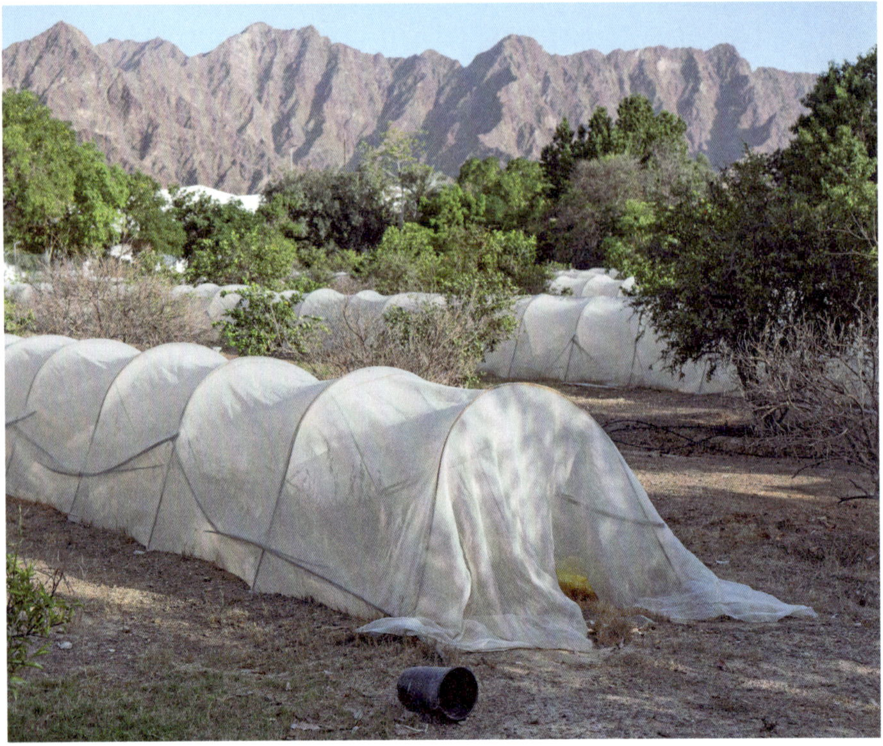

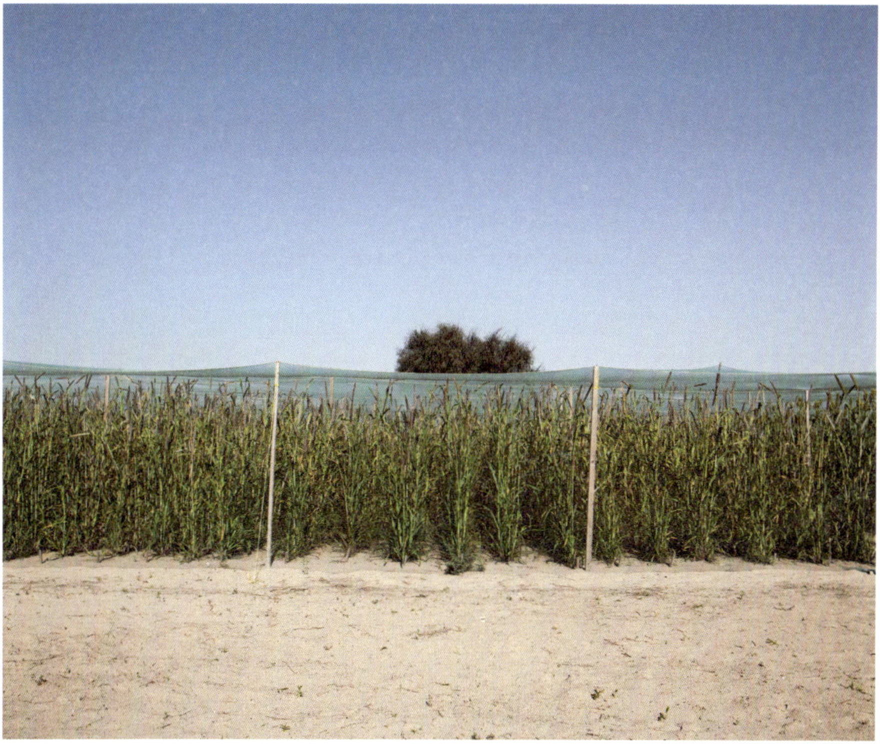

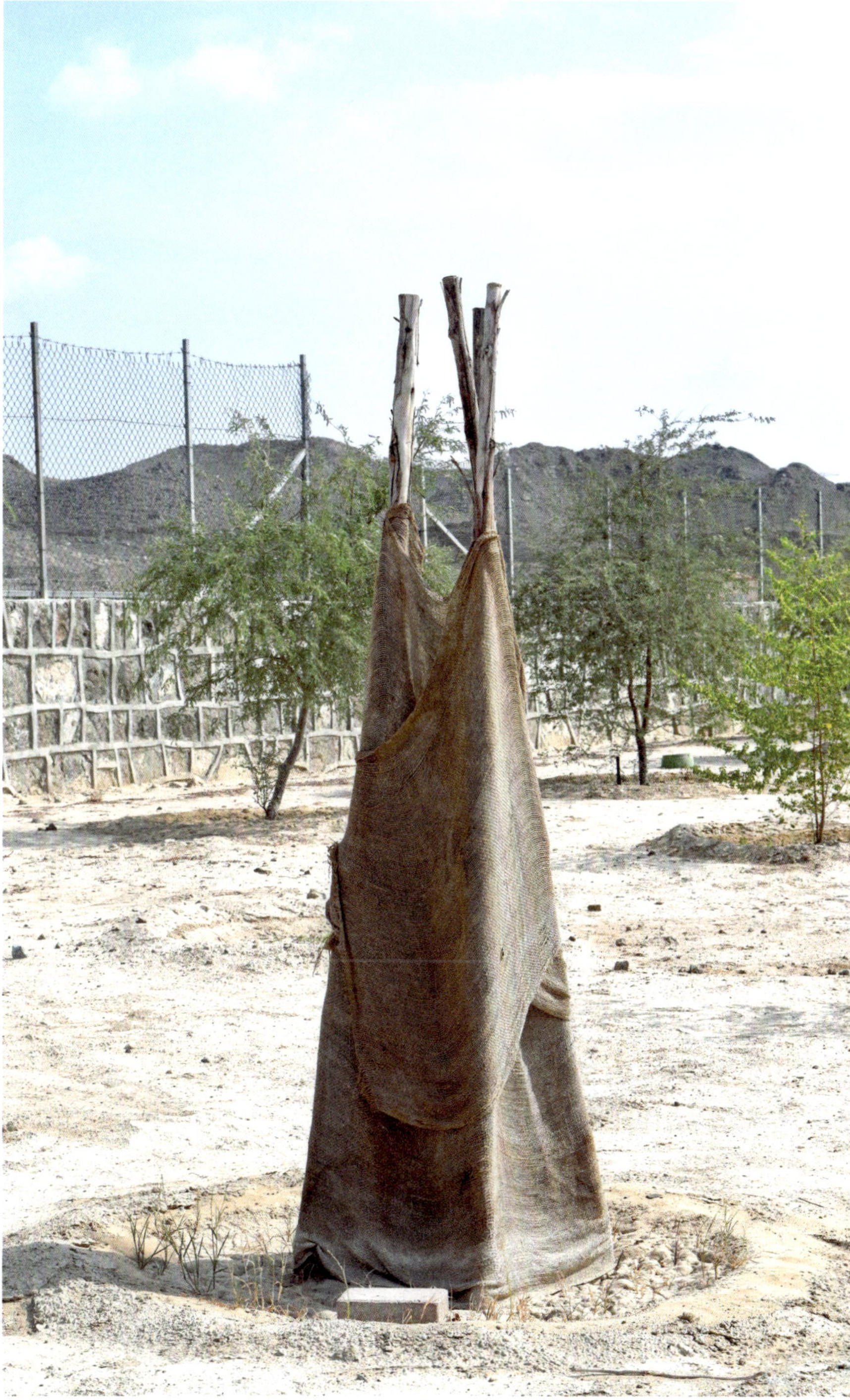

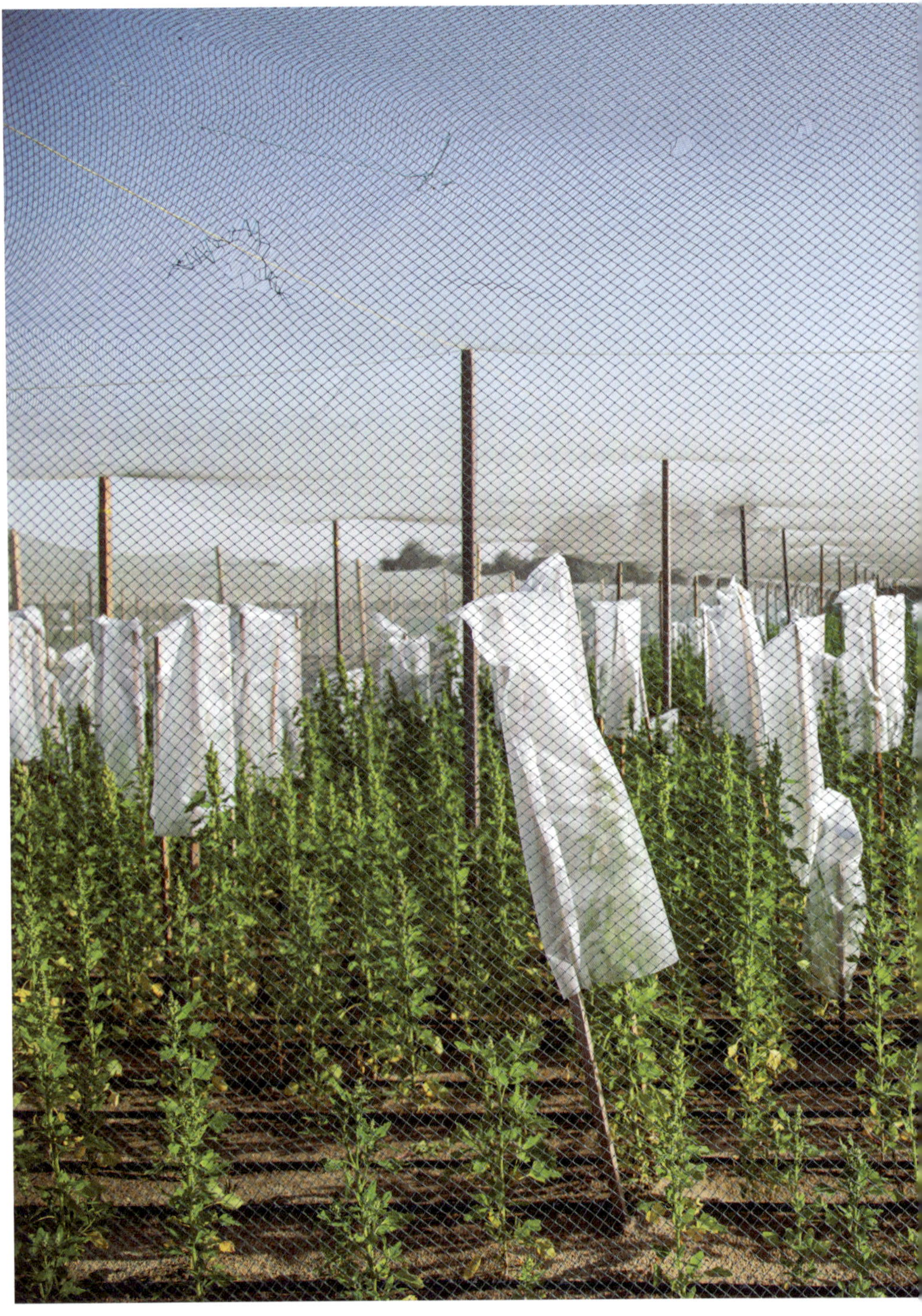

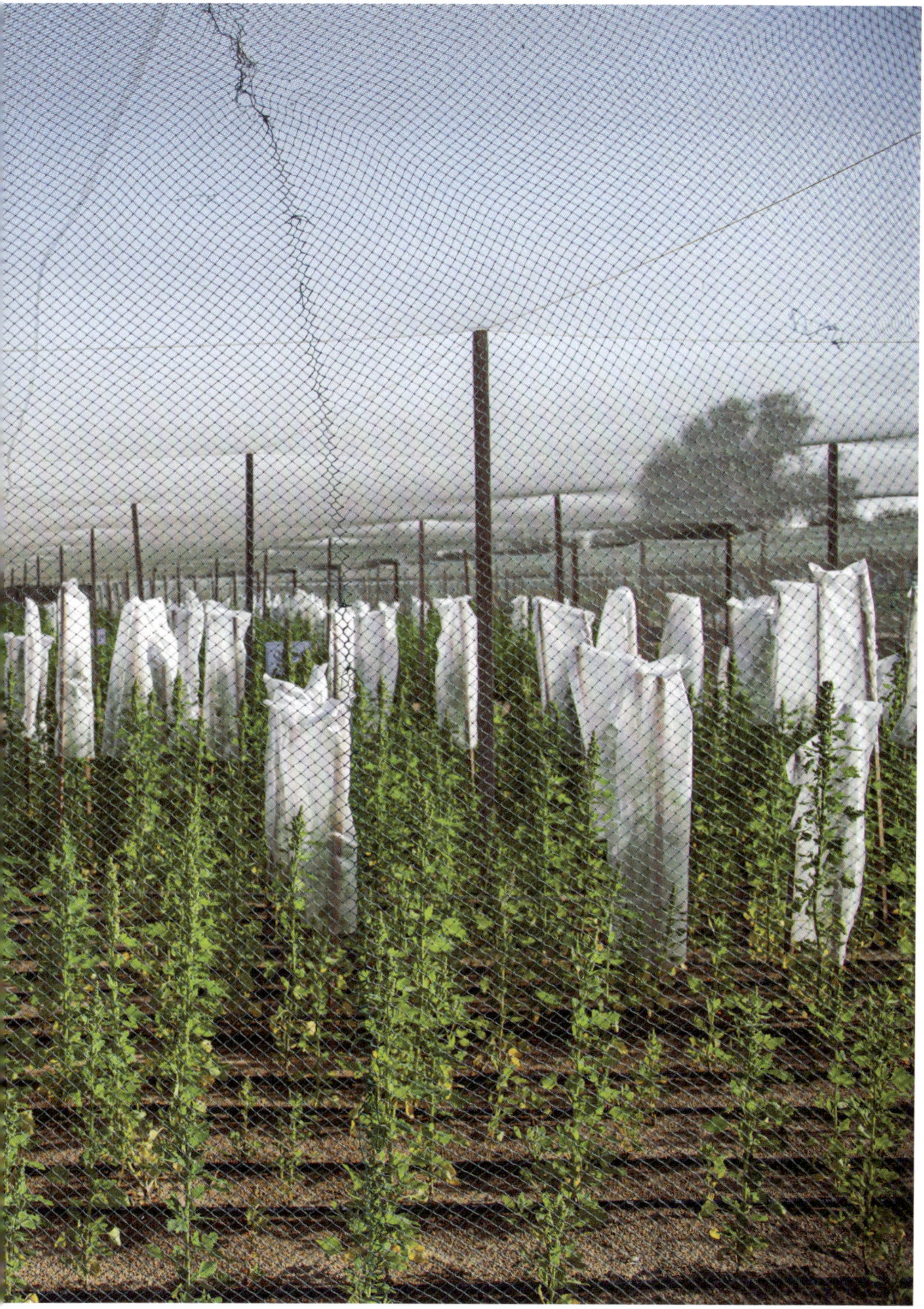

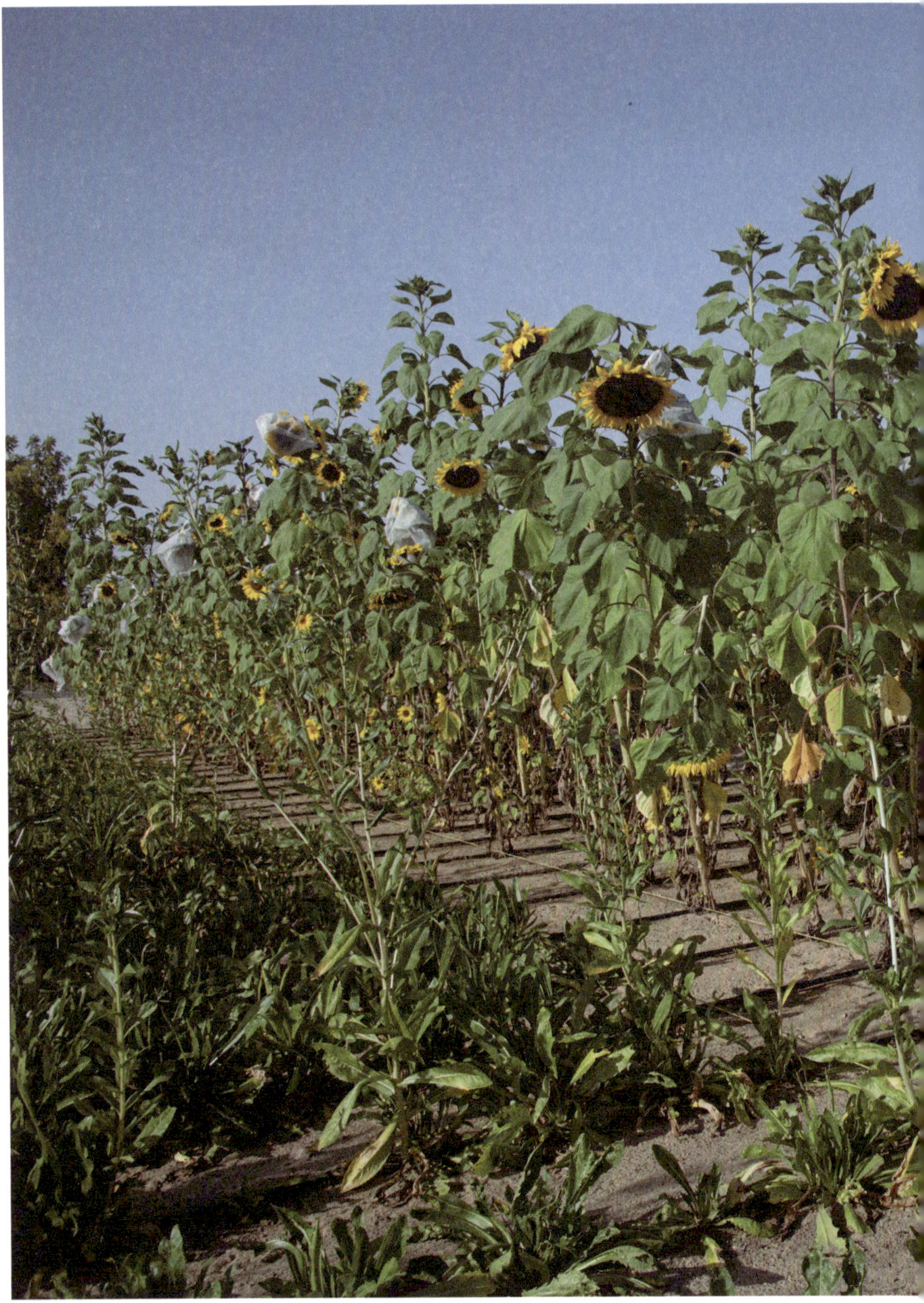

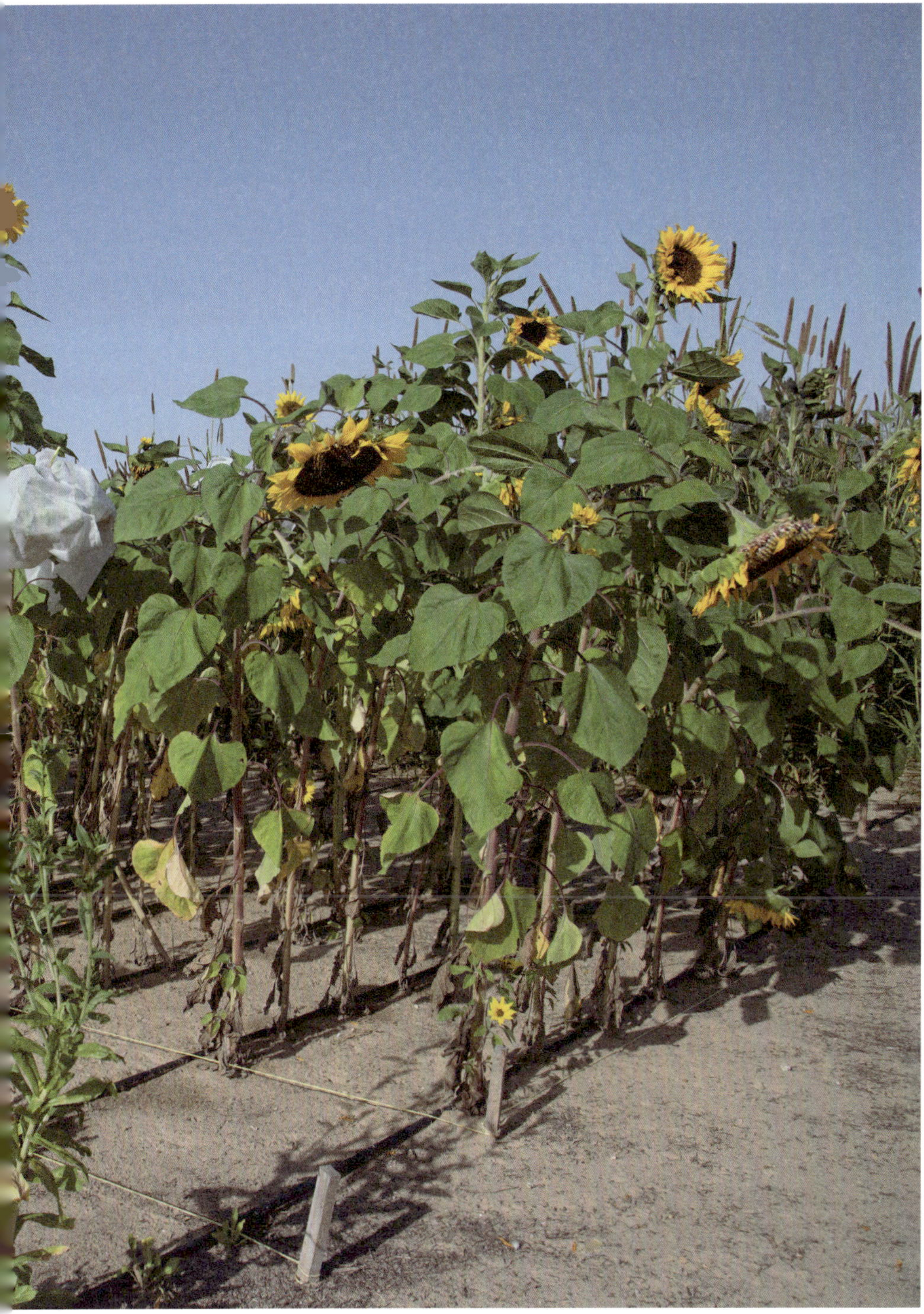

Faysal Tabbarah

A Note on Growing Food and Transforming Spaces

The pockets of agricultural activities within Al Hajar Mountains have been recorded by Al Maqdisi and other travelers for over a millennium. There is no doubt that they existed. However, in an effort to provoke architectural attitudes borne out of experimentation in integrating land-based practices with technology, I will focus on a series of relatively recent and contemporary agricultural episodes that are filled with the fervor of experimentation.

These episodes include the development of the Agricultural Trials Station (ATS) in Al Digdaga which was inaugurated in 1955 and the agricultural experiments that took place on Saadiyat Island between 1969–1974 under the name of Arid Lands Research Center (ARRC). Afterwards, you will find vignettes from the field that suggest that contemporary agricultural spaces within and around Al Hajar are socially reclaimed and exhibit a deeply adaptive spatial imaginary that bridges the technological and the land-based.

Divining Water

In 1953, British Diplomat Robert Stewart Crawford surveyed water infrastructures in the Trucial States, the modern-day United Arab Emirates (UAE), and reported that in Dubai and Sharjah, "a cycle of poor rainfall over an unknown number of years [I was unable to get an exact figure but it seems to be from 15 to 20] has resulted in the virtual disappearance of fresh water at shallow depths...there are the remains of extensive date gardens... some very poor vegetable gardens round Sharjah where the supply of fresh water is
[01] practically measured by the bucketful;"† a far cry from the flowers that grew in luxury documented by Samuel Marinus Zwemer half a century earlier.

Around the same time, in February 1953, Colonel K.W. Merrylees, a British
[02] professional "water diviner,"† indicated that he was willing to perform a survey for water in the Trucial States and was promptly asked by the Eastern Department of the Foreign Office to undertake an inspection
[03] trip.† Merrylees arrived in Dubai in late

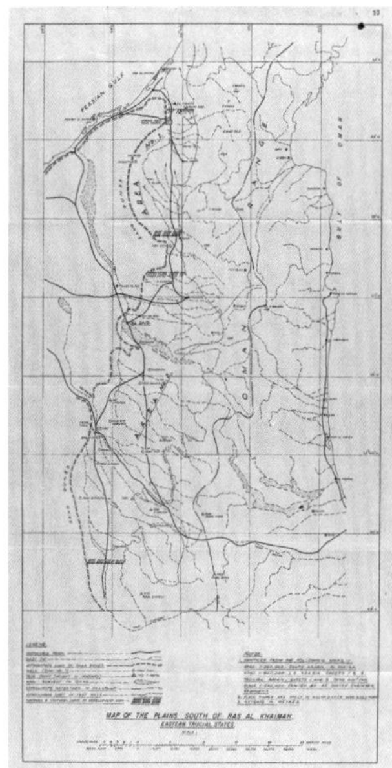

fig. (001) A 1961 map of the plains south of Ras Al Khaimah identifying motorable tracks, wadis, wells, flood plains, and watersheds. Water Supply FO 371/163058/33. © Images reproduced by permission of The National Archives, London, England.

1954 to search – or as I have come to understand from the archives – to divine for water. In truth, there had already been a number of test wells being dug over the 18 months that passed between his expression of interest and his arrival.

In imagining development in the UAE, – of which the development of commercial agriculture was key – British "conceptualization included no diagrams, no maps, and no specific timetable. It took shape, rather, over proposed typed-up budget tabulations – adjusted, readjusted, and most often scrapped."† Merrylees' arrival was part of [04]
the British development plan for the Trucial States for the financial year 1954–1955. This year 25,000 GBP (equivalent to approximately 730,000 GBP today) were earmarked for development projects including "education, hospital subsidies, harbor improvements, and the survey of water resources."† To highlight the importance of water [05]
drilling, about 60% of this budget was allocated directly to these projects. The other 40% of the annual budget included the maintenance of a *falaj* (water channel) in Buraimi, creek surveys for Dubai and Sharjah, a hospital in Dubai, a school in Sharjah, and windpumps.† [06]

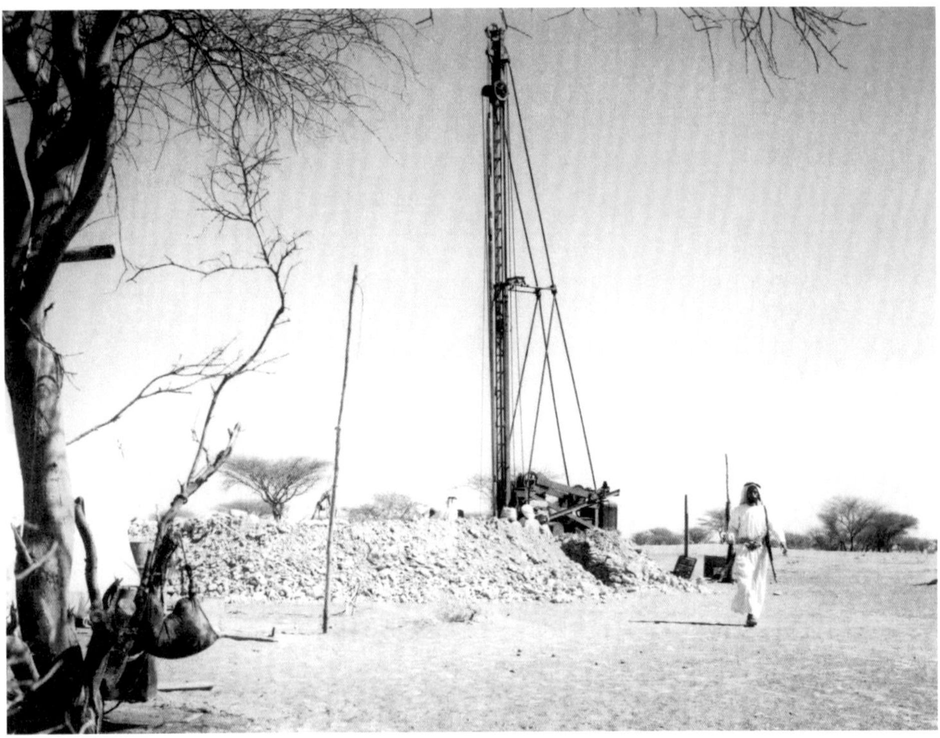

fig. (002) Drilling for water in Al Ain, September 1958 © Edric Worsnop.

By December 2, 1954, Merrylees' test well struck no water
[07] at 600 ft.† A telegram from that period ends with the fol-
lowing note: "Please telegraph as soon as water is struck
[08] or the decision taken to abandon the site."† Three days
later, on December 5, Christopher Pirie-Gordon, the politi-
cal agent in Dubai, sent a telegram confirming that the site
[09] was abandoned at 645 ft.† In a letter dated August 26,
1954, written by British Political Agent W.S. Laver from the
British Residency in Bahrain, we see hints of recognition
that a gap in knowledge exists between corporations from
the UK and operators on the ground in the Trucial States.
Laver writes that:

**I hope you will not be unduly depressed by Consolidated Pneumatic's
remarks... about the difficulty of clearing the rock without blasting.
These are clearly based on complete ignorance of present methods
[10] of work in the aflaj.†**

In relation to this lack of bridging between the historical
condition and the rapid pace of modernization, historian
Matthew Maclean, whose work offers a wealth of insight
into the context around the development of ATS, makes
a particularly cogent remark when he writes that "the
date palm was the key to livelihood in the northern Tru-
cial States, which was totally ignored in British attempts
to commercialize the economy of the northern Trucial
[11] States"† This attitude did not dissipate with further agri-
cultural interactions in the region. J.C. Eyre, an agricultural
adviser stationed in Bahrain, visited the ATS a number
of times after its establishment in 1955 and pushed for
a complete modernization in irrigation. Maclean sug-
gests that "Eyre's emphasis on fixed water sources (wells)
rather than flows (aflaj and floodwaters) suggests that
the dense, decentralized networks of the local economy
were illegible to him and would fade away in the face of
[12] modernization."†

Given that the other wells being dug or earmarked to be dug in the
[13] area were based on the same "faulty information"† provided by Mer-
rylees, the failure to find water in Dubai begins the story of water
divining in Ras Al Khaimah.

Pumping Water

In May 1955, eight successful wells were dug in Ras Al Khaimah, and "a pump was installed on the first well and produced excellent drinking water with a steady flow."† [14]
At this point, ATS was established and Robin Huntington, a man with military experience and a command of Arabic, was appointed to run it. Huntington lays out a clear four-part plan for the wells at Al Digdaga: 1. establishing experimental plots; 2. maintaining the plots for a period of at least 10 years to be able to fully achieve their potential; 3. centering Al Digdaga as a commercial agricultural center; and 4. integrating an educational component into the experimental plots in the form of an agriculture school. His plan was approved in September 1956 on a pilot basis but seems to have been considered a success in its early years.† In Fidel- [15]
ity and William Lancaster's *Honour is in Contentment: Life Before Oil in Ras Al-Khaimah (UAE) and Some Neighbouring Regions,* there is a reference to how "Mansur, the Englishman at Digdaga... started the digging of wells with a drilling rig and the water was raised by diesel pumps...Mansur at Digdaga really pushed commercial agriculture; machines for farming, new vegetables for markets in Sharjah and Dubai, and companies or partnerships for production and market- [16]
ing."† Presumably, this is a reference to Huntington.† [17]

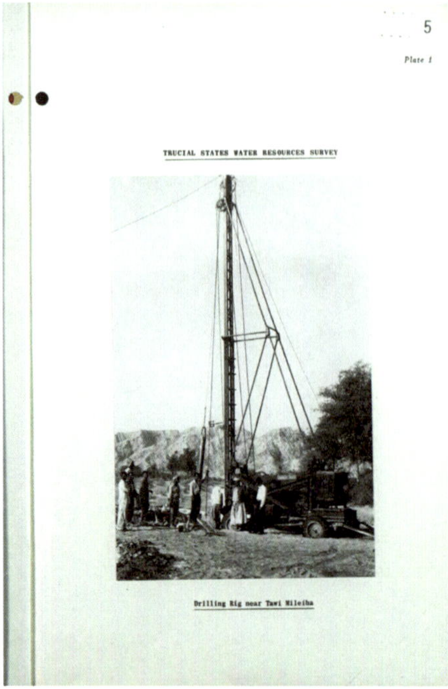

fig. (003) A plate from the 1967 Water Resources Survey conducted by Halcrow. Drilling rig near Tawi Mleiha. Harbour Development and Water Survey FCO 8/858/5 © Images reproduced by permission of The National Archives, London, England.

The period between 1956, the year of the first harvest, and 1971, the establishment of the Union, saw the ATS go through a cycle of expansion and contraction. In the background, agriculture grew in general, and the school first proposed by Huntington thrived, especially as oil drilling began to reap its rewards after 1966. The ATS continued to operate beyond the establishment of the UAE in 1971 until the late 1970s.† [18]

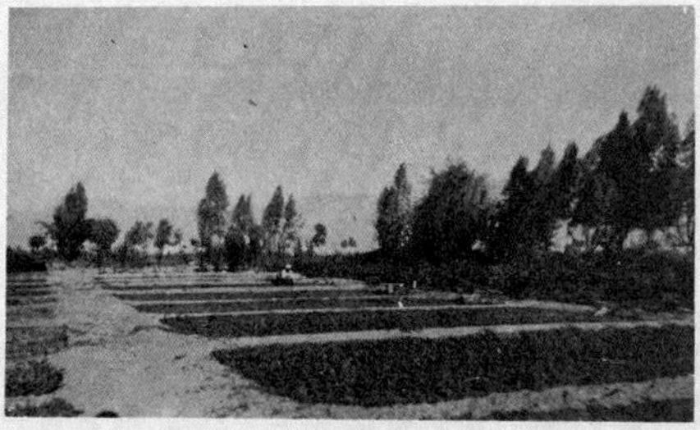

Figure 5.
A garden of the Agricultural Trials Station

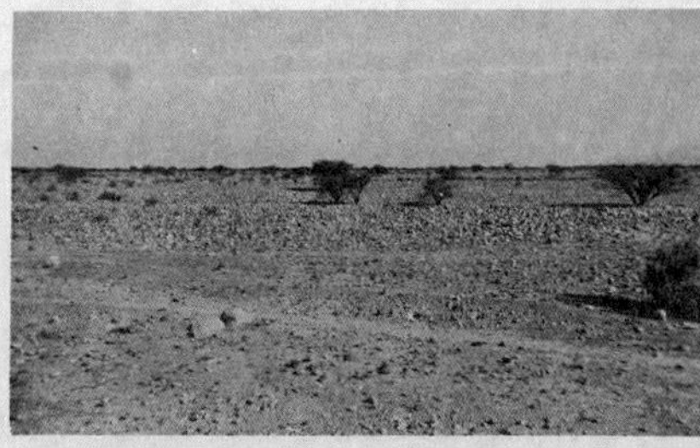

Figure 6.
The gravel plains - No.2 area

fig. (004) A photo showing the ATS and adjacent gravel plains, 1962. Water Supply FO 371/163058/35.

Magic in Al Saadiyat

Overlapping ATS was another project called the Arid Lands Research Center (ARRC), born in entirely different circumstances. In Al Saadiyat, an island in Abu Dhabi, there existed an experimental project in the late 1960s and early 1970s.

Buried deep on page 25 of the February 27, 1969 issue of
the Tucson Daily Citizen, a local newspaper in the city that is home
to the University of Arizona (UA), we read that “UA Team To Build
[19] Arabian Plant.” † In this article, we learn that “green vegetables soon
will emerge out of the beach sands of the Arabian Peninsula desert,”
thanks to a team of researchers from the UA Environmental Research
Lab (ERL). Based on an already completed project in Mexico on the
[20] Gulf of California branded under the title of Food, Water, Power, † the
Saadiyat experiment was 10 times larger and aimed to feed all 40,000
residents of Abu Dhabi. The central premise of the Food, Water, Power
project was an integrated system of these three elements that is exis-
tentially linked to coastal landscapes. In this system, heat from gen-
erators would be used to desalinate seawater transforming it into
[21] 120,000 gallons of fresh water daily, † which, in turn, is used to irrigate
[22] crops inside controlled-environment plastic greenhouses. †

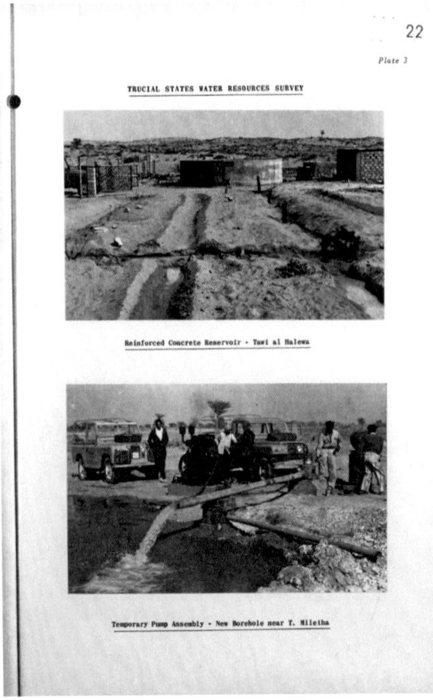

fig. (005) A series of plates from a water survey study compiled in 1967. The first plate shows a reinforced concrete tank with an 8000 gallons capacity at Tawi al Halewa near Al Digdaga. The second plate shows a temporary pump assembly near Tawi Mileiha, within modern-day Sharjah. Harbour Development and Water Survey FCO 8/858/22 © Images reproduced by permission of The National Archives, London, England.

In an interview, Dr. Alamira Reem Al Hashimi, an urban planner based in Abu Dhabi and Dr. Merle Jensen, who was part of the Saadiyat Project, tell us that the team "went over there and we built a small experimental unit to make electricity to desalinize the water, and a small greenhouse to prove that we could do there what we did in Mexico on the Gulf of California."† [23]

A document published by the UAE's Ministry of Farming and Fisheries (potentially sometime in the late 1980s) clearly identifies the three-fold goals of the project. First, it was to conduct research to modernize agricultural production and to become a center of research for agriculture in arid lands within the Gulf region. Second, it aimed to produce high-quality crops that can assist in minimizing food imports. With this in mind, 80% of the project's space was allocated to this goal, which suggests that the highly experimental research component – i.e., the first goal – would have taken up the remaining 20% of space.† Thirdly, [24] the ARRC was to act as a training ground for local technicians, operators, and administrators in the field of agriculture in arid lands.

A very brief documentary (2 minutes 39 seconds), titled "Vegetables Grown in the Desert - In Colour," was produced by the Associated Press (AP) in 1972. It can be easily found on YouTube and starts with a shot looking directly at the glaring sun, before the body of an adult male, potentially in his thirties, appears in the frame, followed by the narrator telling us that "the light and the heat play strange tricks."† Immediately, we see in the distance the silhouettes of con- [25] trolled-environment greenhouses, and while the man rubs his eyes, the narrator tells us that "this is not a trick, not even a mirage."† As [26] the person enters the greenhouse (the reference to "Open Sesame" when entering the greenhouse will not be lost on most), the clip cuts

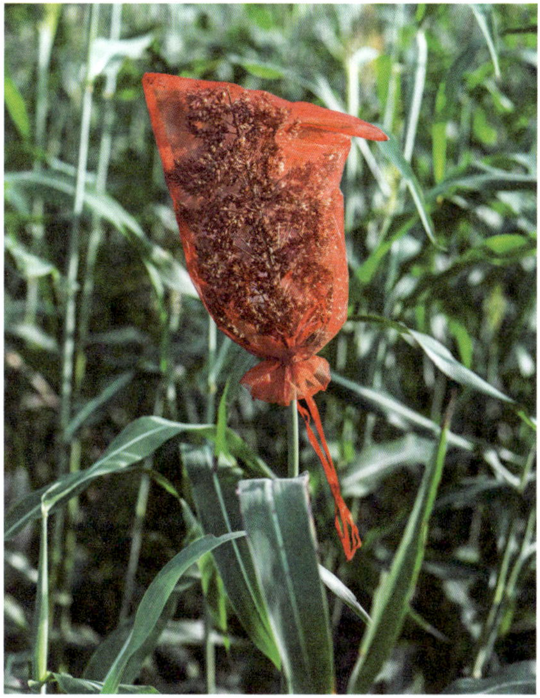

fig. (006) An example of the careful sheltering of plant material, a common occurrence on experimental plots. Photo by Reem Falaknaz.

to scenes inside in which we see endless rows of unripe vine tomatoes and a combination of manual labor and mechanical machines. The narrator tells us that the "plants themselves seem to appreciate
[27] this artificially induced life,"† backing the claim with an indicator that 71 tons had been recently picked up from only 1 acre, out of a 5-acre proj-
[28] ect.† While the stated numbers might appear to be abstract, archival

documents tell us that at the height of the project in the early 1970s, its success meant that crops were exported as far as Kuwait.† For context, [29] in 2019, the UAE exported 102,603 tons of tomatoes (an almost 1500 times increase from the single acre yield).† Curiously, those 71 tons of [30] tomatoes could have been of a variety "developed in Hawaii under very tropical conditions, and those varieties worked the best over all of the other varieties in the world. They did very well for about eight months during the growing season in Abu Dhabi."† [31]

After a few clips showing farmers washing and packaging food, the camera cuts to an exterior view of the greenhouses, before panning into the "arid and inhospitable area [where] man has accepted nature's challenge."† [32]

Revealing a nuanced and scientifically objective approach to this project, in contrast to the ATS, the model tested and refined in the Gulf of California was not implemented without necessary transformations. One example of this is the immediate recognition of the high calcium content within Saadiyat's shores. Thus, the sand operated more as a structural armature for the plants, while an integrated fertilizer solution provided the requisite nutrients. As for the physical makeup of the greenhouses, which can be deduced to a certain extent from the AP's documentary, Dr. Jensen described the following:

Half the greenhouses were steel structures that were covered with fiberglass on the sides. We had a central aisle, and on both sides we had greenhouses that extended about 30 meters. At the end of those greenhouses, we had these pads that would allow us to flow seawater over them, and then bring air through there with fans to give us cooling. Now, the lower the humidity, the more cooling you would get, because that's just the process of physics, but in the summertime, when it was so humid, we would only get a temperature drop of four or five degrees. The other two and a half acres, we decided to make them very simple. We blew them up with air. We had fans that would blow them up with air, like a balloon, and they were attached along the side and on the end.† [33]

It is yet unclear to me what the ultimate fate of the Saadiyat center was, but it appears to have remained operational for some time during the 1970s, with a transfer in management from ERL towards local administration,† [34] before finally being decommissioned or moved elsewhere,

[35] with some references pointing to a complete relocation to Al Ain. † However, what remains rather clear is that this form of experimentation that has evolved from imported models towards one that acknowledges the nexus of environmental and cultural conditions continues to reveal itself today.

Looking for Water, Today

On a January visit to a subsistence farm close to Al Halah, – a town on the western edge of the E89 highway (also known as the Dibba-Masafi Road) – a middle-aged landowner and principal farmer of his subsistence farm described how his decisions are driven by a potential future water shortage. His extensive network of PVC pipes tapping water from deep water wells located on his land has displaced a rather extensive *aflaj* (water channel system) visible throughout his farm, rendering them a physical relic. With the advent of deep-well drilling and intermittent rains, much of the historical physical infrastructure and associated farming practices have been transformed. His 70,000 meters squared land was first sowed some time after the UAE's formation in 1971. Today, the farmer sells minimal quantities to vegetable retailers in Fujairah, as his primary motive is to grow food for his family, kin, and community.

Around 15 years ago, increasing wells' depths and intermittent rains resulted in abandoning flood irrigation through the *falaj* (water channel) in favor of the efficient PVC network. The landowner no longer floods 60–100 meters squared rectangular basins holding around 10 palm trees. He adopted a localized condition with round basins hosting up to three trees as seen in *fig.* (007). While he still floods these basins, the approach is more efficient than the historical practices recorded in the archives and still in use in other farms. Located some distance from the foothills, the relatively flat topography of the farm facilitated the transition to the mechanized water network.

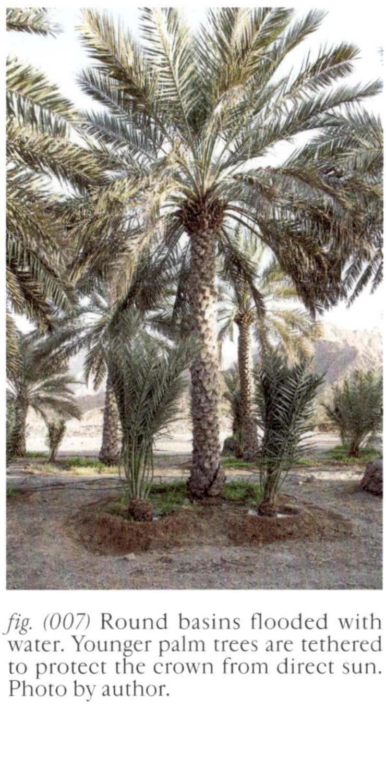

fig. (007) Round basins flooded with water. Younger palm trees are tethered to protect the crown from direct sun. Photo by author.

Beyond subsistence farming, his land is a familial and social space. While he does have a freestanding single-story *majlis* where he receives his family and friends, it is primarily used in the summer or when watching football on TV. From the verb "to sit," a *majlis* denotes a space for gathering and hosting people and is used interchangeably between domestic, social, and political settings. At other times, he meets with his friends outdoors on the farm grounds, expanding the spatial definition of the majlis. Here, the agricultural space is imagined, designed, and inhabited as a generative extension to domesticity, not hidden, and not relegated to food production or sensorial aesthetics, despite also being both of these things. In blurring private, public, and production spaces, this spatial imaginary and the practices it enables actively resist overtly categorized forms of spatial organization – no space serves a single function only. Upon my departure for the city of Sharjah, I was sent back with at least two weeks' worth of coriander, parsley, tomatoes, chili peppers, buckthorn, and a cabbage.

On the same day, I visited a leisure farm in Al Bithnah, on the eastern edge of the mountain range. Upon entering the farm unannounced, I found a middle-aged landowner – in what I surmised were his work clothes, blue pants and a thin white t-shirt – instructing a couple of workers building an exterior bathroom. The landowner mentioned that his water is brought to the farm in 2000-gallon tanker trucks where it is then stored in two concrete tanks, one on the entry-level, and the second about 8 meters above, at the top of a terrace.

Adapted to its complex site, the farm's deliberate terracing exhibits an extreme form of subverting contemporary farming organizations or even gardens as seen in *fig.* (005). On top of the differences in relative flatness and farm sizes, crops are another key variable. Where the subsistence farm grows key fruits and vegetables at some volume, this leisure farm has a small number of fig, papaya, and mulberry trees to supplement the palm trees. The landowner also grows a number of ornamental flowers purely for their colors. When I asked about new water-saving techniques such as drip irrigation, he told me that it does not produce strong trees –accompanying this response was a full-body gesture akin to a flexing bodybuilder. I understood from him that traditional flood

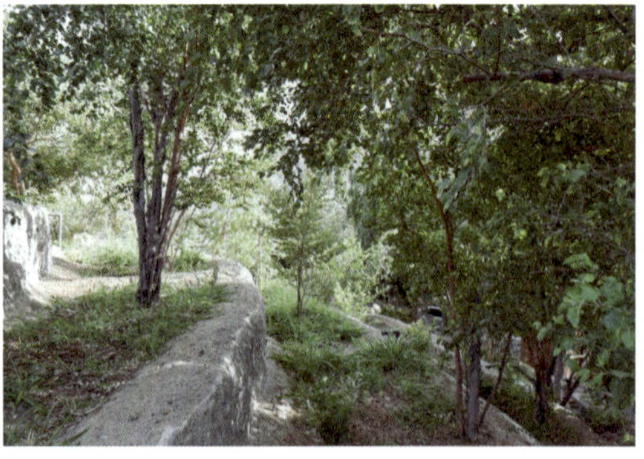

fig. (008) Terracing within a leisure farm in response to its existing topography. Photo by author.

irrigation is very hard to replace and I also inferred a relationship between water volume, tree health, and its perceived productivity. Given the size of his farm as well as his planted basins, no more than three to four palms per 10 metres squared, his irrigation strategies are, in principle, not very different from the subsistence farmer.

Both farmers described a 50-year transition from stone dwellings very close to their farm grounds, to a *sha'bi* residence
[36] within a *sha'biya*,† to their current residences which they referred to as villas. By villas, they mean free-standing one or two-story houses within walled boundaries, sometimes with other smaller annexes. They both told me that they prefer spending time on the farm, even during the summer. In conversation, I was able to infer that the tactical and adaptive reclaiming of communal ways of living has become increasingly difficult, if not impossible, with the advent of concrete frame constructions with rigidly cellular space planning strategies. As with many landowners, they privilege an informal spatial condition and an environmental imaginary that reminds them of their childhood dwelling in the mountain's interior over the efficiency exhibited by even the most amateur farmers elsewhere. What is rather striking about the leisure farm I am describing is the mobility of its social spaces throughout the day. Arriving mid-day, we sat down close to the entrance on a semi-formal seating setup of a couple of wooden benches with cushions and the landowner described to me how he would sit elsewhere when it gets closer to sunset, but that also depends on how many people, and who, he would be hosting. On the weekend, when his family comes for a Friday barbeque, they would occupy the larger spaces, but if he is alone or with another guest, they would sit within the groves. Within his relatively small plot, I counted at least six different social spaces, each radically different from the other in size, seating arrangement, and solar orientation.

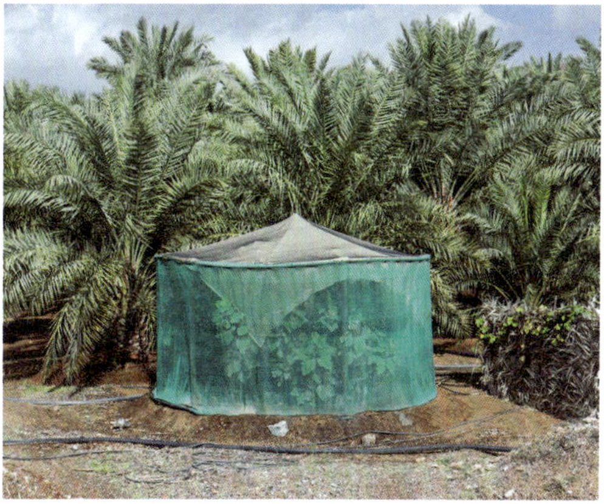

fig. (009) Water channels and plant shelters. Photo by Reem Falaknaz.

On the other end of the agricultural spectrum is the farm across from the leisure farm described above, a 12,000 meters squared, wedge-shaped, 3,500 palm tree-strong subsistence farm. I spoke to one of the landowner's sons, a young man in his twenties, who is responsible for the farm's upkeep. He pointed to a stone wall close to the well where his grandfather lived. Essentially, his grandfather's farm was both a space of production and domesticity, an attitude that contemporary landowners are trying to reclaim. He described the 150 meter deep well just outside of the main gate and the invisible subterranean PVC infrastructure that irrigates his farm, referring to it as *aflaj.* This illuminates an attitude that thinks through the performance of systems as opposed to a rigid historical definition based on what something is made of or how it is made, for instance, a subterranean channel is a falaj, be it earthen or PVC.

His attitude about the performance of systems parallels a conception of space through performance. In Al Hajar, a space is primarily described through what its inhabitants do within it. He referred to different areas within the farm as majlis where he congregates with his family and friends, regardless of the spatial organization and orientation. He also told me that he prefers to occupy the temporally constructed space on the farm as opposed to discrete ones in their villa. The relationship between environmental and spatial imaginaries in Al Hajar produces a temporal and adaptive space, one that silently rejects the villa that represents capitalistic rigid spatial organizational strategies, even if they are purported to be flexible. All of these spaces are spaces of temporal and performative interactions. What I mean by this is the inhabitants react to these spaces in a temporal way, reflecting their relationship with spaces based on the times of day or seasons. He asked me to come again in the summer because I wouldn't believe how cool it could be, as these spaces and associated agricultural practices exhibit microclimate changes throughout the day and year. From where we were sitting within the sprawling date palm orchard, one could almost forget that the western edge of the farm is defined by a major highway running along the edge of the mountains.

01

Social and economic development in the Trucial States, 1953, FO 371/104332, 146-148, Arabian Gulf Digital Archives, UAE.

02

Water Supply, 1962, FO 371/163058, 79, Arabian Gulf Digital Archives, UAE.

03

Improvement of Water Supplies in Trucial Coast States, 1954, FO 371/109893, 41, Arabian Gulf Digital Archives, UAE.

04

Todd Reisz Todd, "A Seed Sown in Digdaga for a Stomach in Dubai," in *On Foraging: Food Knowledge and Environmental Imaginaries in the UAE's Landscape,* ed. Dima Srouji, Faysal Tabbarah, and Meitha Almazrooei (Abu Dhabi: Warehouse421, 2020), 39.

05

Social and economic development in the Trucial States, 1953, FO 371/104332, 83, Arabian Gulf Digital Archives, UAE.

06

Improvement of Water Supplies in Trucial Coast States, 1954, FO 371/109893, 197, Arabian Gulf Digital Archives, UAE.

07, 08

Improvement of Water Supplies, 147.

09

Improvement of Water Supplies, 158.

10

Improvement of Water Supplies, 6.

11

Maclean, Matthew, "Spatial Transformations and the Emergence of 'the National': Infrastructures and the Formation of the United Arab Emirates, 1950-1980" (PhD diss., New York University, 2017), 51; Maclean's work is key in understanding the development of the Agricultural Trial Station at Al Digdaga and the context within which it emerged.

12

Maclean, "Spatial Transformations," 57.

13

Improvement of water supplies in Trucial Coast States, 1954, FO 371/109893, 182, Arabian Gulf Digital Archives, UAE.

14

Efforts to improve water supplies in Trucial States, 1955, FO 371/114699, 44, Arabian Gulf Digital Archives, UAE.

15

Ibid, 118-119; Development programme of Trucial States, 1956, FO 371/120611, 62, Arabian Gulf Digital Archives, UAE.

16

Fidelity Lancaster and William Lancaster, *Honour in Contentment: Life Before Oil in Ras Al-Khaimah (UAE) and Some Neighbouring Regions* (Gottingen, Germany: De Gruyter, Inc., 2011), 438-439.

17

Matthew Maclean makes a similar assumption which might be further informed by his fieldwork.

18

Maclean, "Spatial Transformations," 98.

19, 20

Nyla Crone, "UA Team To Build Arabian Plant," *Tucson Daily Citizen*, February 27, 1969.

21

Farming in the UAE, 43, Abu Dhabi: by the Ministry of Farming and Fisheries.

22

S. M. Zwemer, "Three Journeys in Northern Oman", *The Geographical Journal* Vol. 19 No. 1 (January 1902): 62.

23

Hessa Al Romaithi, "A Vain Hunt for Water", *The National*, (December 28, 2008), https://www.thenationalnews.com/uae/a-vain-hunt-for-water-1.589945.

24

Penelope Tuson, *Records of the Emirates 1820-1958*, (London: Archive Editions, 1990), 714.

25-27

British Movietone "Vegetables Grown in the Desert - In Colour," YouTube, March 16, 1972.

28

Farming in the UAE, 42, Abu Dhabi: by the Ministry of Farming and Fisheries.

29

Natural Resources Institute in United Arab Emirates, 1977, FCO 8/2901, 43, UAE National Archives. https://www.agda.ae/en/catalogue/tna/fco/8/2901.

30

"United Arab Emirates (UAE) Tomato Market Insights." Selina Wamucci. 2023 https://www.selinawamucii.com/insights/market/united-arab-emirates/tomatoes/

31

Al Hashimi, "The Saadiyat Experiment," 112-113.

32

British Movietone, "Vegetables Grown in the Desert - In Colour."

33

Al Hashimi, "The Saadiyat Experiment," 112-113.

34

Farming in the UAE, 44, Abu Dhabi: by the Ministry of Farming and Fisheries.

35

Al Hashimi, "The Saadiyat Experiment,"

36

A *sha'biya* refers to a residential neighborhood, and in this context, also refers to a *sha'bi* house, best translated as the people's house. These neighborhoods and houses exhibited elements of informality and communality. See: *Transformations: The Emirati National House*, ed. Yasser Elsheshtawy, Abu Dhabi: National Pavilion UAE, 2016.

While it might appear that the primary visual expression within Al Hajar Mountains emanates solely from its intense visual mass, moments of extreme precarity abound, requiring tactics that tether two or more elements together. Sometimes, this is two plants that need to support each other with the help of a strip of fabric. At other times, two tethered metal pipes work together to support a tree or a larger set of trees. What emerges is a complex relationship between rigid (metal or timber), semi-rigid (plants), and flexible (rope or fabric) linear elements.

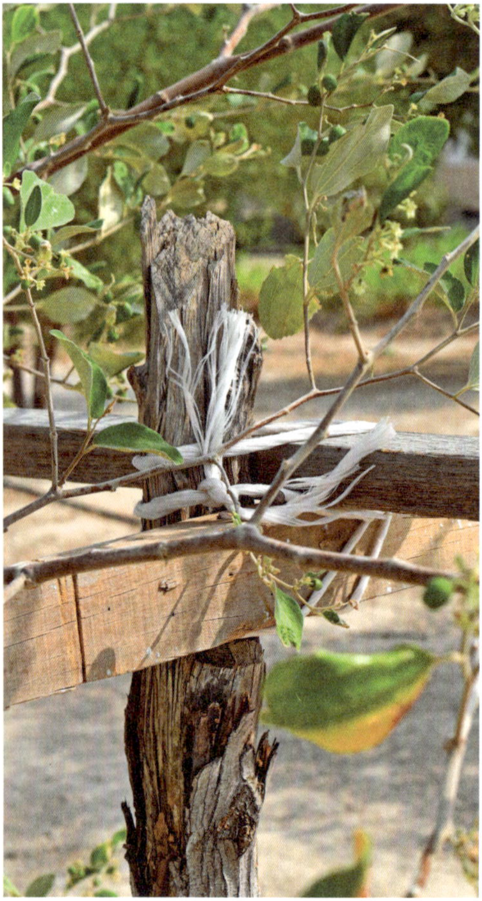

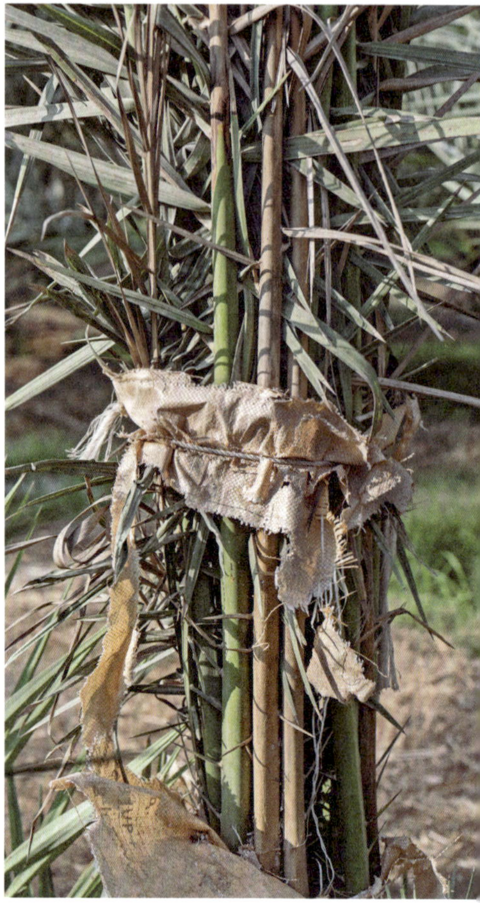

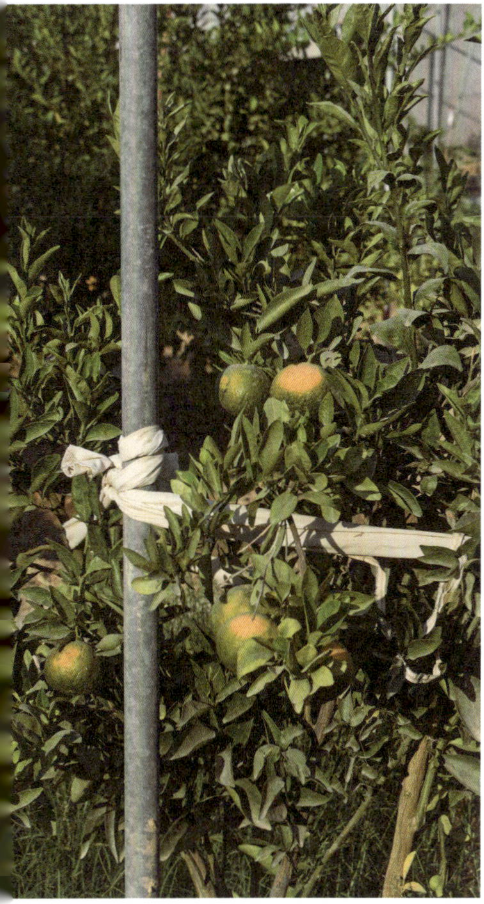

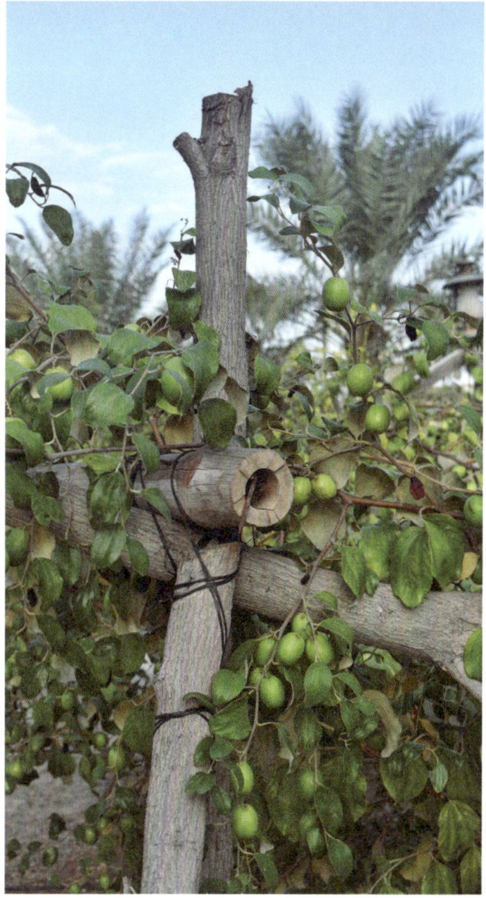

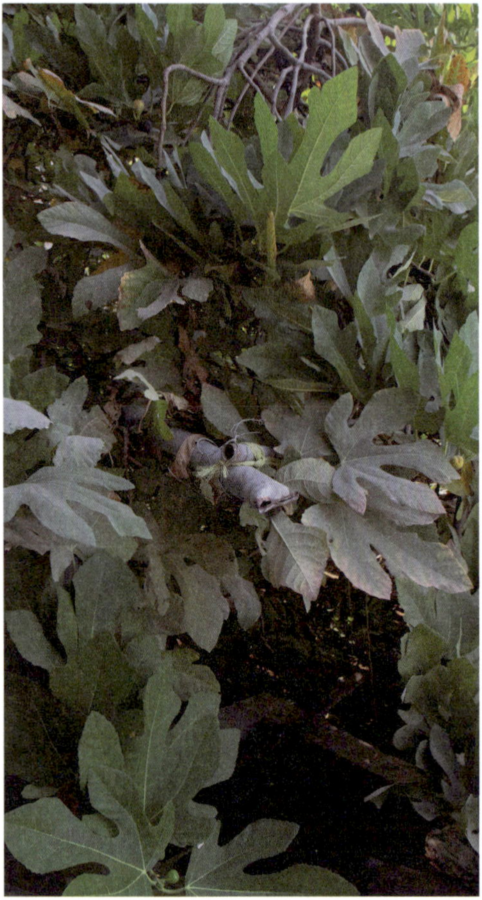

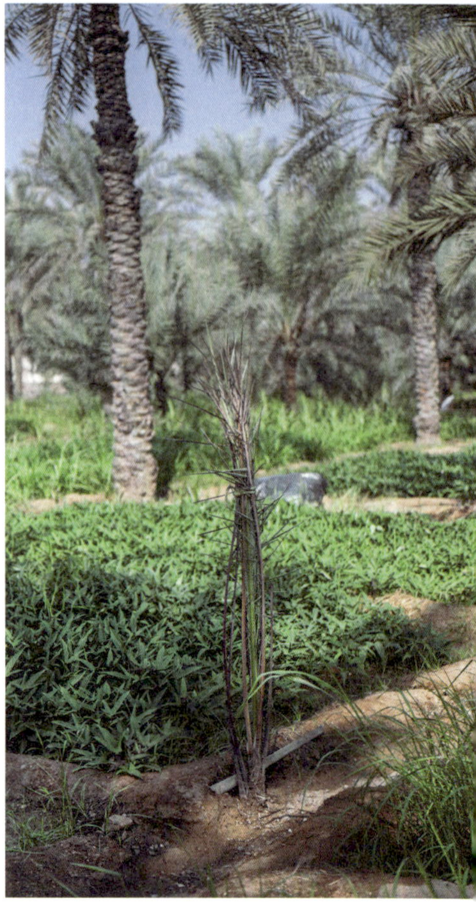

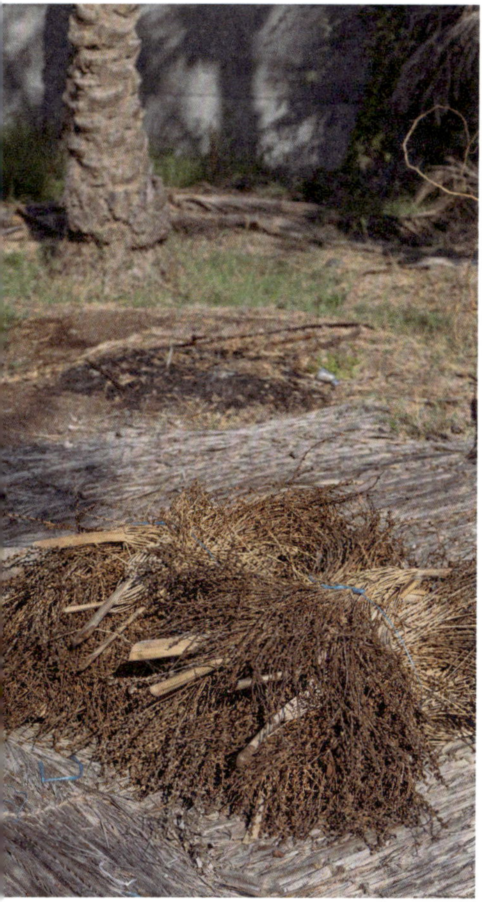
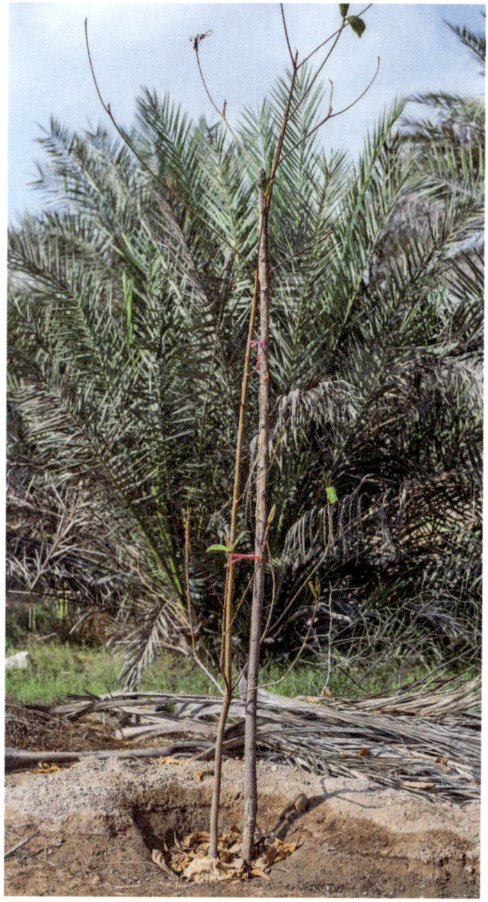

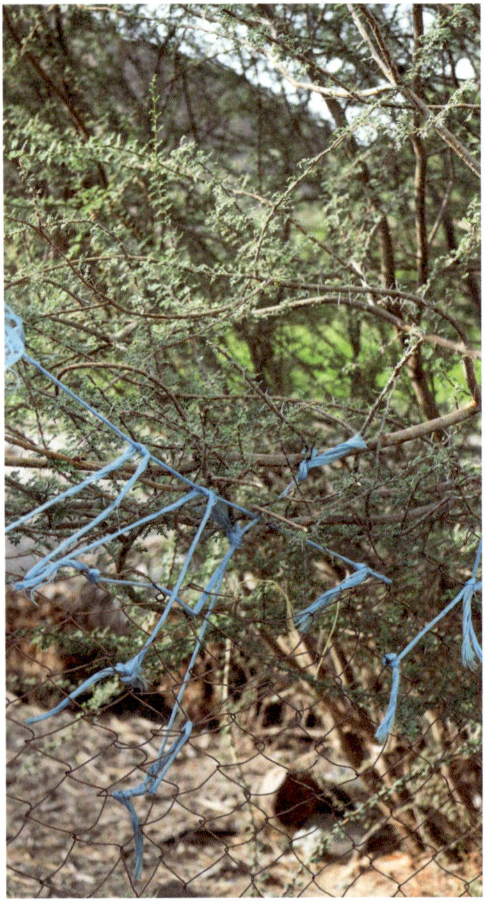

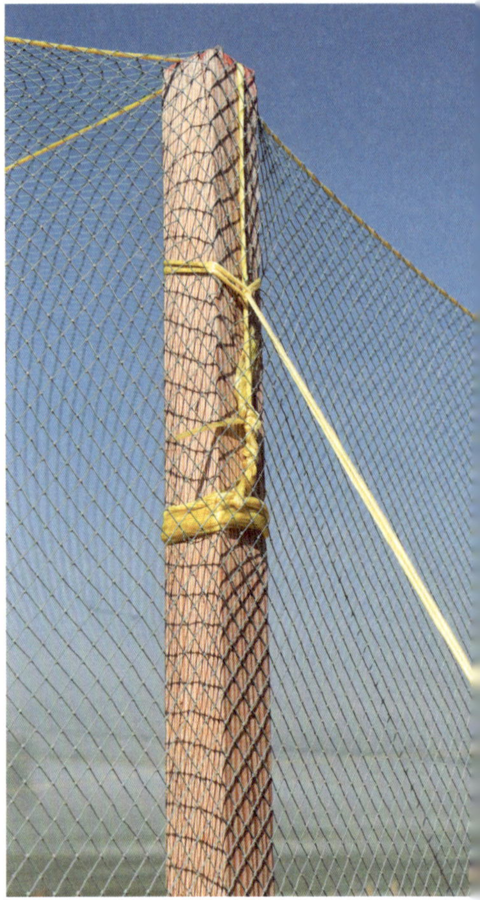

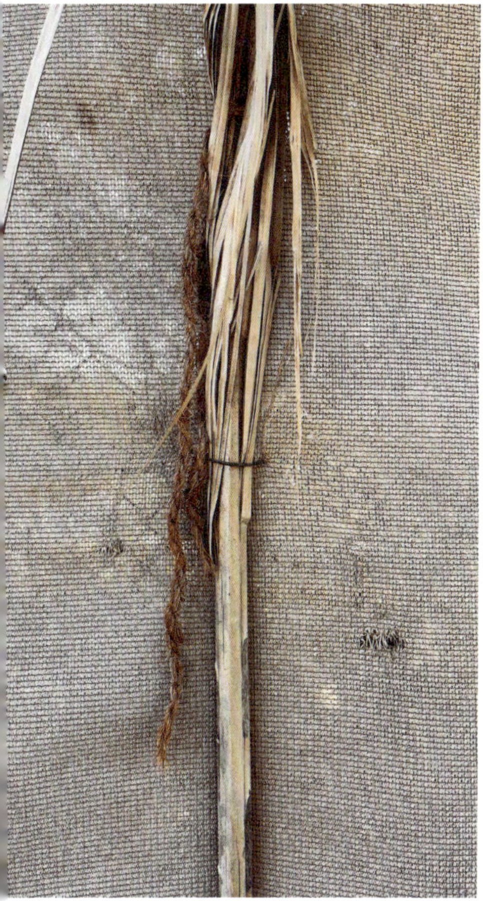

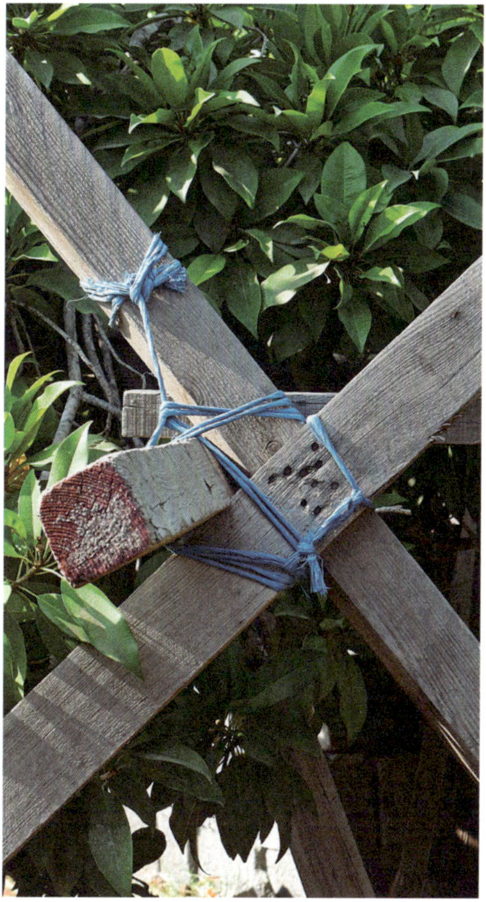

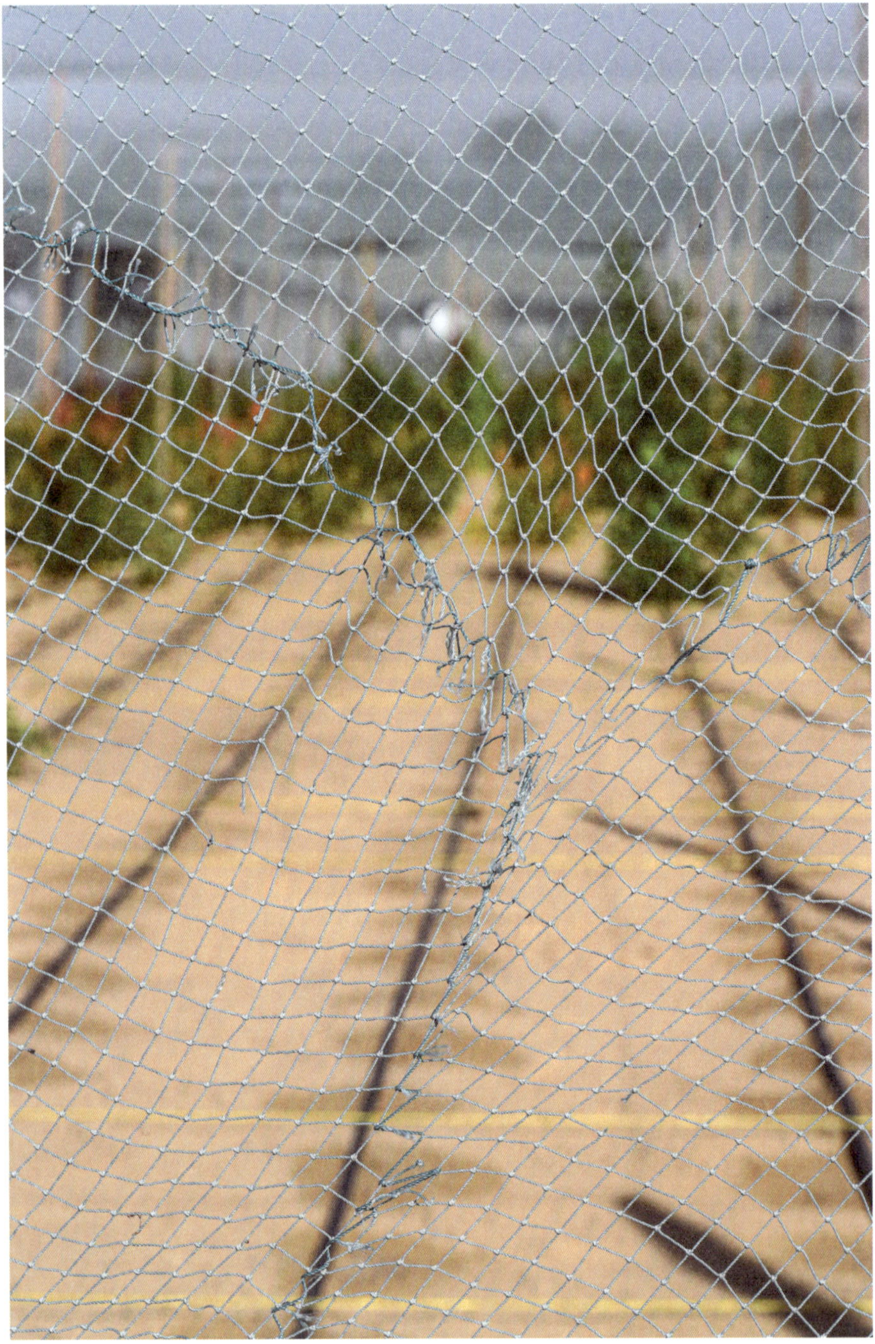

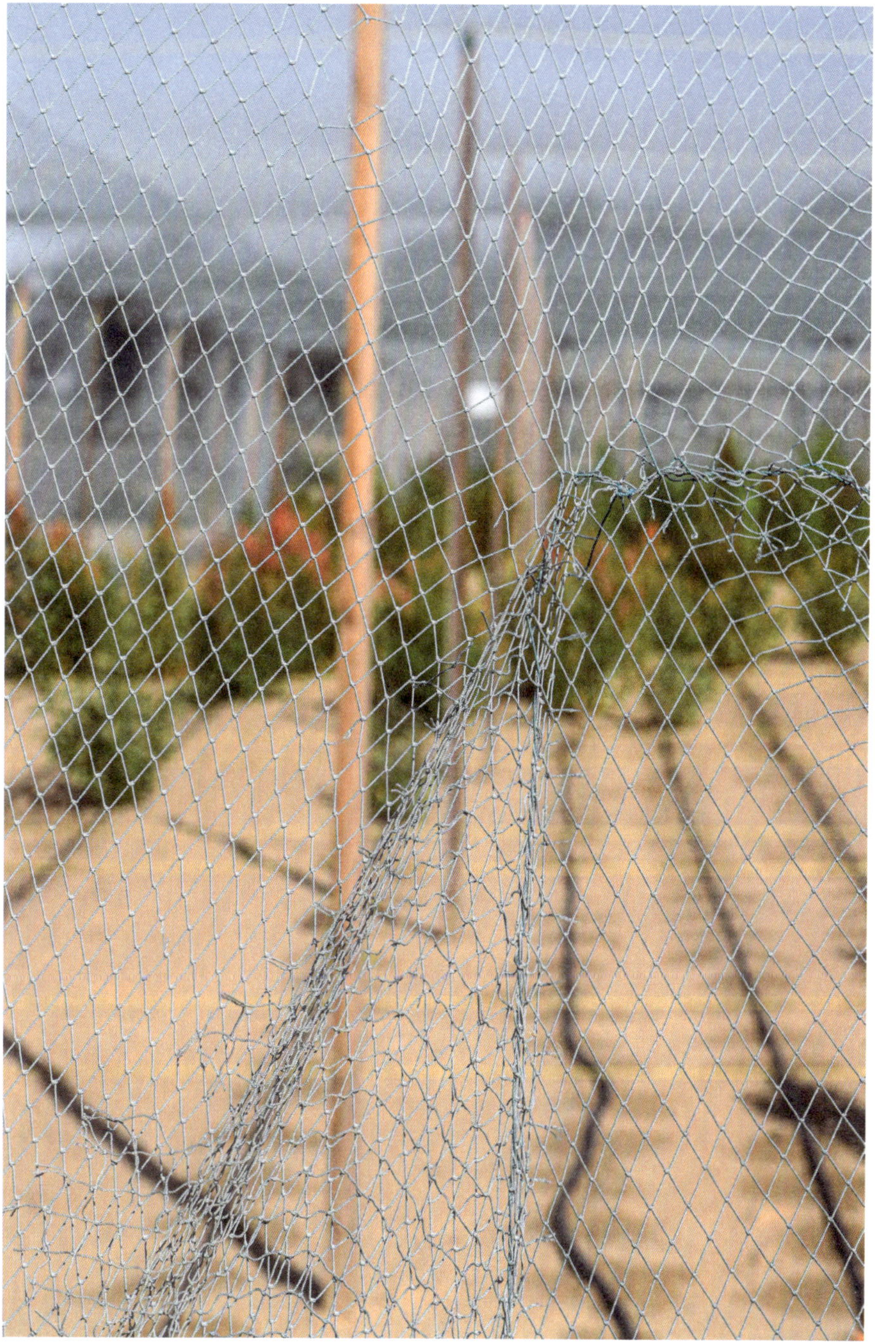

In the Arabic language, there is a very specific word used for supporting a tall and generous palm tree that has yielded a substantial harvest in order to assist it in staying upright. Based on the root word **rajaba** (رُجَّبَ), which describes the building of a small stack under a generous palm tree to support it, **Al rujba** is the word used to define implements that support palm trees and it follows that **al tarjeeb** is the act, or tactic, of supporting generous palm trees. Al Asma'I (b. 740 CE), a philologist from Basra adds more nuance, telling us that **al rujba** refers specifically to the use of a forking piece of wood to support a generous palm tree, while **al rujma** refers to the use of stones in supporting palm trees.†

01 "P412, كتاب لسان العرب," https://shamela.ws/book/1687/412#p1

In Al Hajar Mountains, we have seen both, as well as the use of concrete masonry units (CMU).

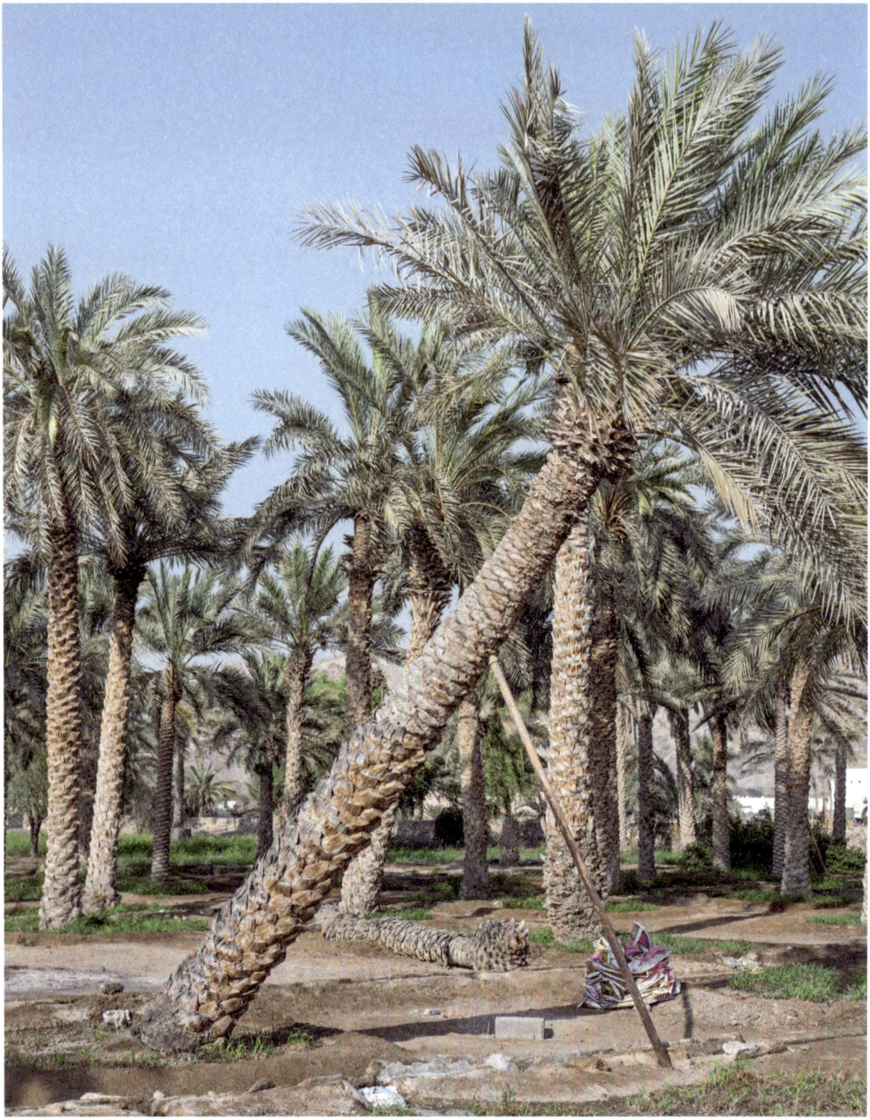

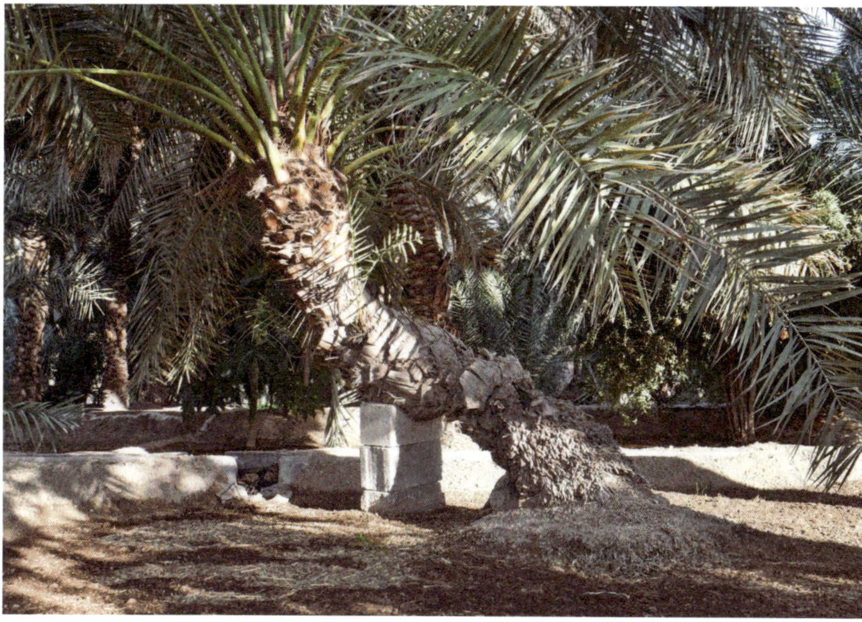

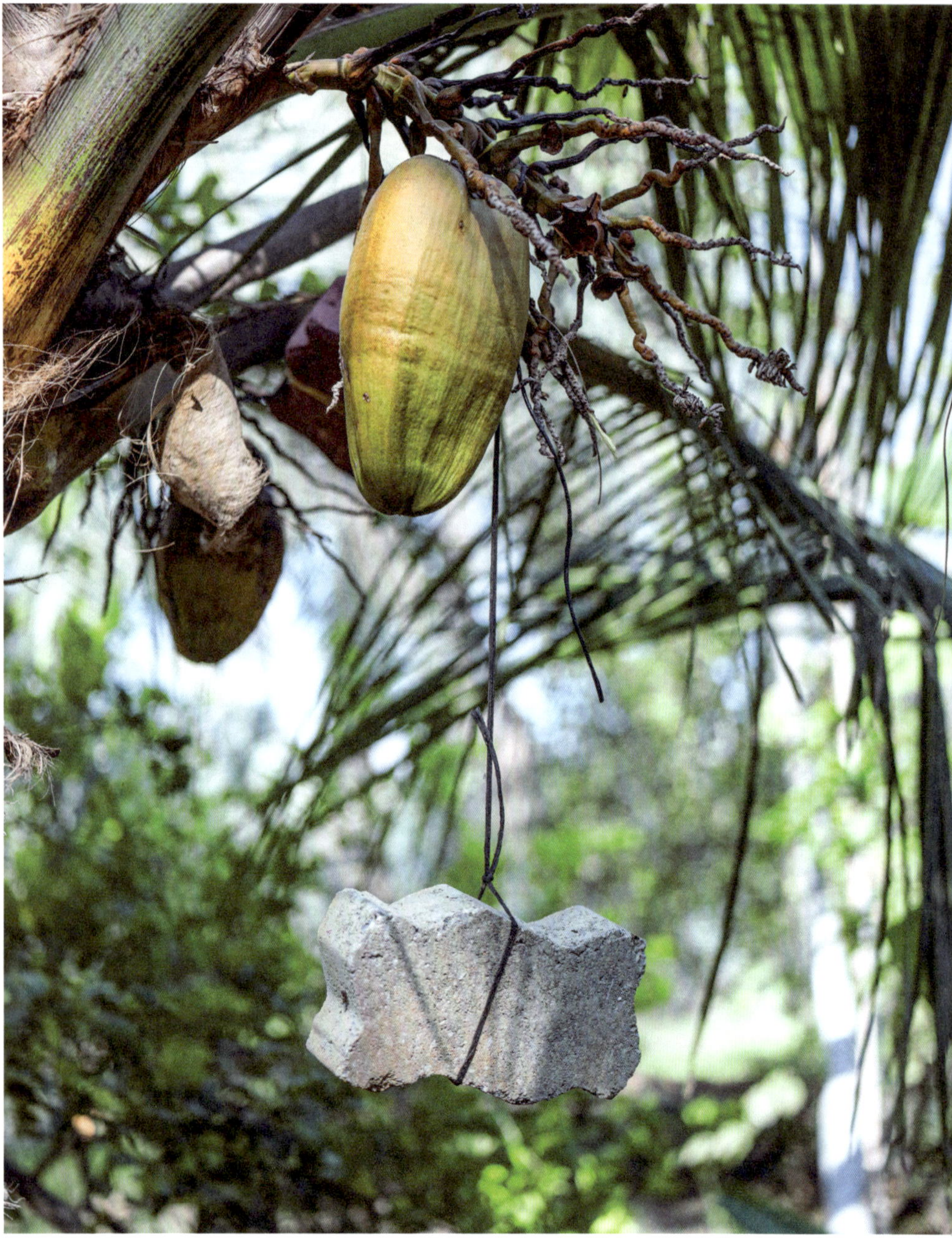

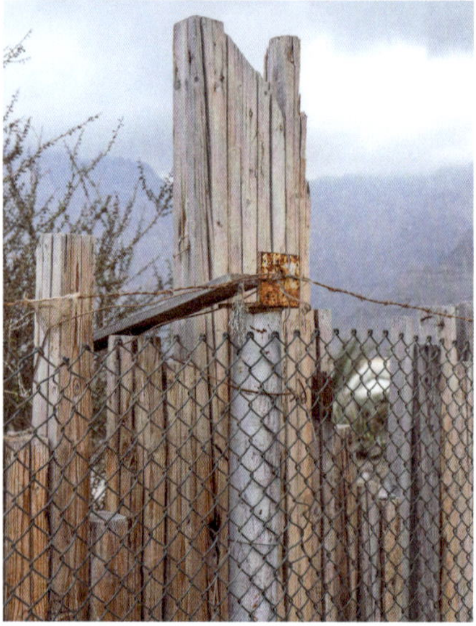
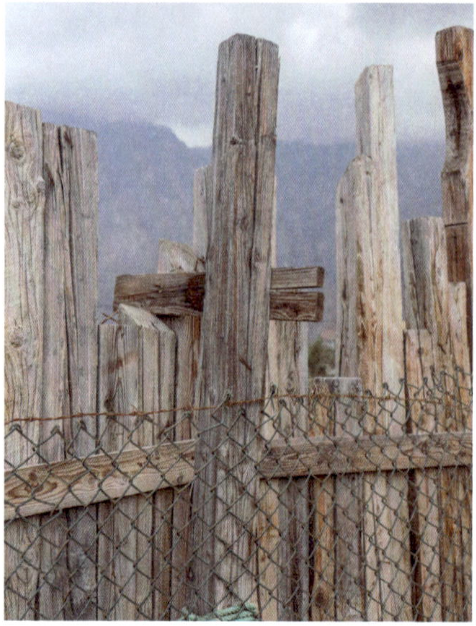
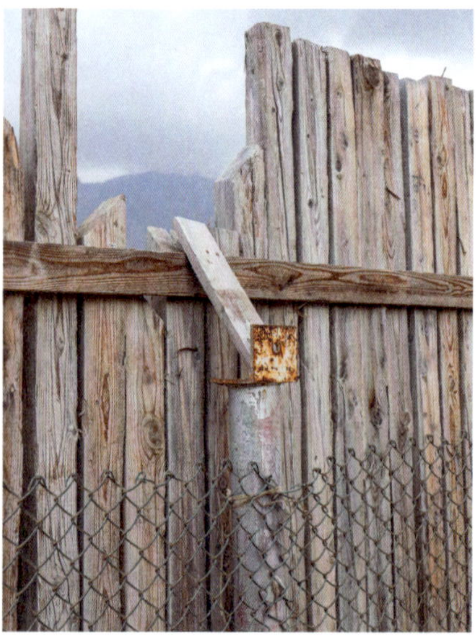
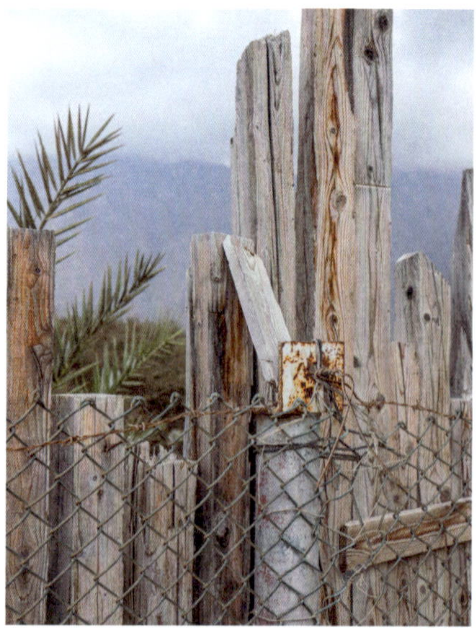

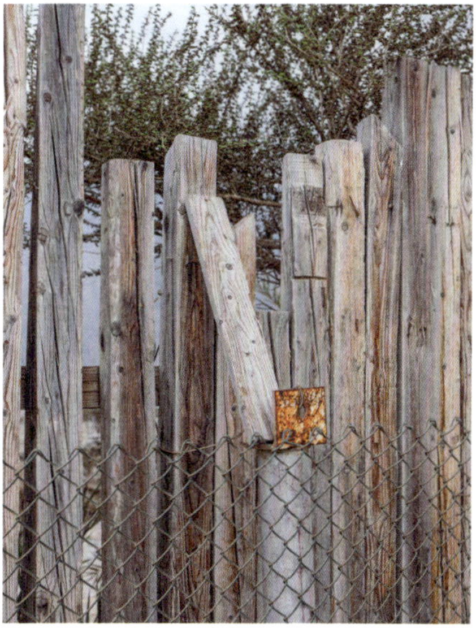
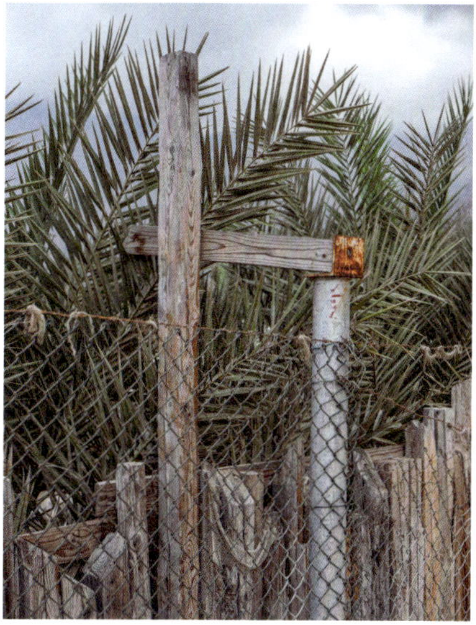
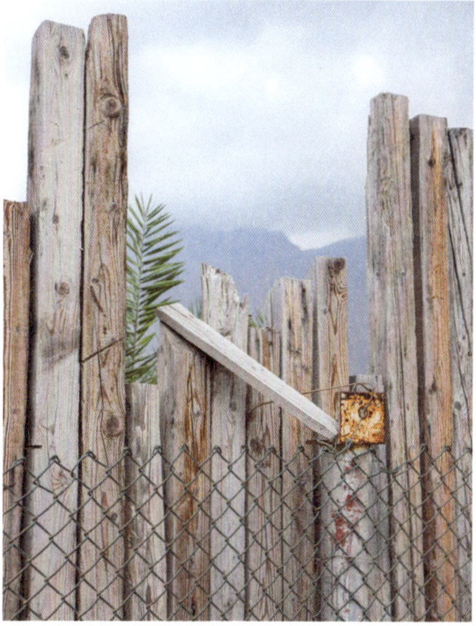
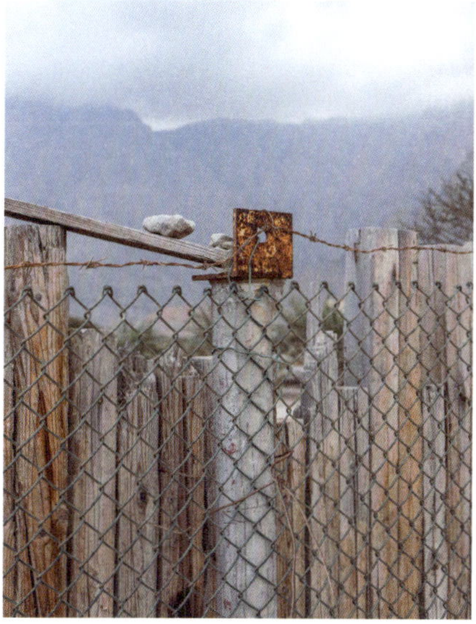

Faysal Tabbarah

A Final Note on Misfit Assemblies

While I have been making trips to Al Hajar Mountains to uncover and understand the tactics used in constructing its contemporary built-environment since 2018, documenting, exploring, and deploying what I have come to describe as misfit assemblies, my understanding of what I continue to see there seems to have crystallized somewhere entirely different: in Denmark.

A few days after temporarily moving to Denmark in the summer of 2020, I was walking down a main street in Aarhus, Denmark's second city after Copenhagen, and saw what appeared to be a fairly large earthen-colored solid sheet curiously floating in the air. It took me a few moments to realize that I was walking by a construction site, and that the gravity-defying object was, in fact, a prefabricated clay brick panel measuring around 4 x 1 meters, with a thickness of a single course of bricks, a mere 5.4 centimeters. Suspended by a crane, the clay brick panel appeared blade-like and was moving ever so slowly in the air on its way to being installed next to its peers, claiming its spot as part of a strangely thin façade.

Six months later, while sharing my increasing curiosity
[01] about the Danish *skalmur,* † clay brick panels, one of my colleagues asked if I had seen how they are transported, describing the process,
[02] with some irony, as a parade. † My curiosity was obviously tickled, and I set up camp on a bench on a typically crispy March morning along the road she mentioned. After less than an hour of waiting, I was lucky to witness this odd parade, a 48 foot flatbed truck transporting a single precast concrete wall panel with a traditional Danish red brick finish on one of its sides. It was on its way to the construction site of an upcoming residential project along the Bay of Aarhus.

Architects are cynically trained to be critical of materials that pretend to perform in particular ways, and within this logic, the brick panel is a perfect nemesis. In contrast, the single-fired traditional clay brick communicates deeply historical human-land entanglements; it is a carrier of chemistry, physics, history, economics, and culture. On the other hand, its descendent, the clay brick panel, is a strange confluence, abstraction, and alienation of all of these things; in fact, it is largely a machine-land entanglement. Despite this, the clay brick panel currently plays a central role in shaping the contemporary Danish architectural imaginary and elsewhere, given its prevalence in new and ongoing construction. This poses difficult questions about ideas such as truth to materials and their relationship to the tenets of precision and accuracy that are hallmarks of contemporary material supply chains and construction.

The relatively recent entrenched attitudes towards construction have privileged homogeneity and precision through economies of scale resulting in a rather uniform built environment. Thus, when thinking about arid spaces, it is through this object of contemporary construction and economy, the clay brick panel, that moves across vast territories before it is precisely assembled and installed on buildings, that I turn to Al Hajar's built environment and its misfit assemblies to provoke architectural conditions that are simultaneously contemporary and rooted in the material, cultural, and historical contexts. Disruptive to the homogenous built environments, misfit assembly is extremely generative, less costly on resources, and provides avenues for new technologies to deliver on their paradigm-shifting promises.

When explaining misfit assembly, I describe the arranging of materials in tactical ways that challenge precision in their visual expression, but deliver on the functional needs they were conceived for. Sometimes these materials are self-similar such as a stone wall and sometimes radically different as the case where stone meets concrete masonry units (CMU), corrugated metal sheets, twine rope, and vegetal matter. These assemblies are not bound by a particular size or by time. They appear at the scale of an assembly that can be carried and executed by a single hand, or at the scale of a multi-storied building. They are sometimes meant to be permanent, and at other times purposely transient.

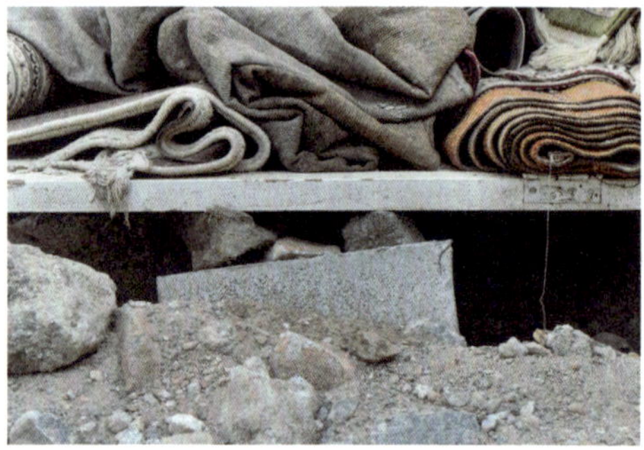

fig. (001) A misfit assembly in Al Hajar including a CMU, stones, and a repurposed wooden door. Photo by Samar Halloum.

Al Hajar is abound with misfit assemblies. Before describing them further, I will spend some time in Denmark to describe the ways in which material is procured, processed, and deployed to create a clay brick panel, an antithesis to the misfit assembly in Al Hajar and its resulting spatial conditions.

The Teglværk as a Botanical Garden

A twenty-first-century *teglværk*, Danish for a brickwork yard, shares many physical, cultural, and economic similarities with botanical gardens. Culturally and economically, the teglværk and the botanical garden are sites of significant cultural production through material extraction. Where they differ, to a certain extent, is that the teglværk initiates the movement of material across vast territories, while the botanical garden is, most of the time, the final location in a plant material's journey. Here, one has to wonder whether the name teglværk, or brickyard, still applies today as it points to spaces and processes that have disappeared. Spatially, they are both an aggregation of discretely controlled interior and exterior spaces that cater to the extremely particular requirements of their hosted material, oscillating between the cold, tropical, dry, and humid. They are also both non-linearly experienced; in a teglværk, one does not have to follow a particular path, even though the material does, just as one does not have to move through the whole of a garden.

In the contemporary globalized networks of material movements across vast territories, a teglværk is no longer a place for the exclusive production of clay from raw material to a single brick. While it still serves this role, this is far from being its only one. I experienced these conditions vividly when visiting a leading teglværk in Midtjylland where I walked through a collection of interior manufacturing spaces, administrative spaces, interior and exterior storage, loading bays, as well as a clay extraction site across 120,000 meters squared. This particular facility has three main types of brick production lines alongside its brick beam panels. First, it produces special-colored bricks from clay sourced both locally and elsewhere. Its second product is a fully automated extruded brick. Finally, it produces hand-struck and hand-made bricks in processes that integrate traditional and contemporary techniques and machines. Part of a 110-year-old brick manufacturer, this particular facility was built in 1953 and currently has an annual production capacity of a staggering 70 million bricks; more than 12 Grundtvigs Churches.

A walk through the interior landscape of the teglværk means experiencing radically different environments in a fairly short period of time. Just like in an enclosed botanical garden where different plants require different microclimates, not all clay is stored the same, nor does all clay thrive, and become a brick, in the same environment. First, I entered a large warehouse space and had to put on a warm jacket as the temperatures were around 5 degrees Celsius.

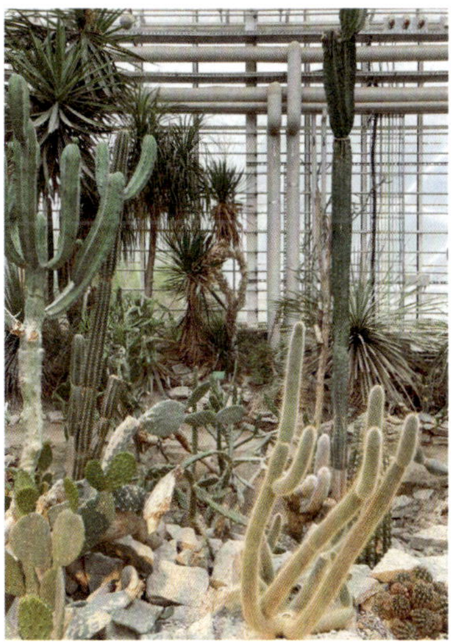

fig. (002) An interior botanical garden in Aarhus, Denmark, exhibiting a desert garden. Photo by author.

Here, clay is stored before it gets screened and filtered. Journeying through this process, I walked alongside what seemed like an infinitely long belt, punctuated at times with a vibrating surface to ensure the filtering process results in the desired clay sizes. As you walk alongside the belts, the temperatures rise to a more comfortable condition and you witness the blending process that requires meticulous chemistry to ensure the outcome of a uniform clay body with specific characteristics including durability, color, texture, size variations, compressive strength, and absorption.† [03]

Once the clay bodies are blended as desired, they are formed and cut along another belt, in a largely mechanized fashion. It is here that the micro-climate takes an immediate turn, as the next step is to load the bricks into a kiln. The kiln, of which the facility has more than one, is around 135 meters long and 20 meters wide with a production capacity of between 5,000 and 7,000 bricks per batch, depending on the type of clay and brick sizes. At temperatures approaching 1,000 degrees Celsius, the space becomes noticeably hotter near the kiln. There is also a topographical condition here, as to better understand the firing process and the kiln mechanism, one has to climb on top of it, where rows and rows of vents work to regulate the temperature. The most fascinating aspect of this microclimate is that it is variable across the kiln's length. While walking on top of it and avoiding the scorching steel inspection caps, one experiences an increase in temperature when approaching the center of the kiln, which reduces at a relatively quick rate once the center is crossed and the bricks begin to cool. Finally, the fired bricks are left to cool completely once they exit the kiln, and the temperature is again noticeably cold.

Outside, in teglværk's exterior landscape, the botanical garden metaphor continues. Here, instead of different plants, one experiences different clays, each stored in a way that suits its particularities. Some of it is covered and some of it is more resilient, left to weather in the elements such as the frequent rains. Each material is labeled, which includes its name and geographical origin. Inside a botanical garden, green can be said to be the primary performative color but here it is shades of red and yellow, and occasionally white. Instead of gardeners or botanists, there are miners driving

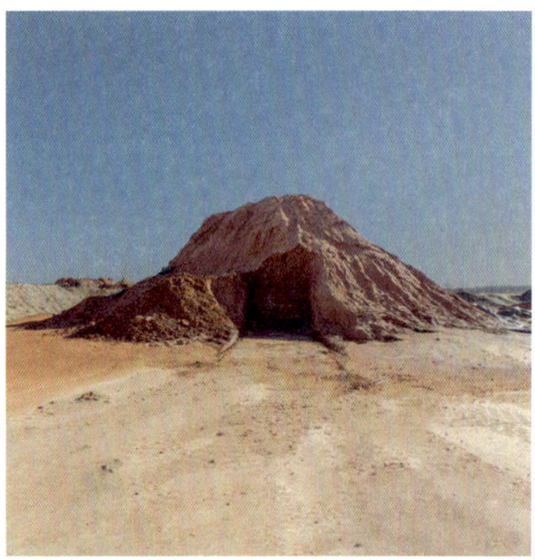

fig. (003) A clay mound within a mine in Jutland, Denmark. Photo by author.

mechanical equipment moving between the manufacturing, storage, and extraction sites. In fact, there is another extraction site 300 meters north of the current site that has been capped and decommissioned. Surrounded by agricultural land on all sides, this covered pit will be integrated into that system. These days, the clay is extracted either onsite, elsewhere within Denmark, or imported from places such as Germany, Sweden, and Finland. Manufacturers provide a full turn-key solution where raw material can arrive at the facility from Finland, undergo its journey through the manufacturing plant, get assembled as a panel, and be shipped back to Finland to assume its place on a façade. Sometimes, the raw material that is extracted on-site, travels as far as Australia. This is a far cry from the 50 kilome-
[04] ter average that a panel used to travel in 1969 in Europe.†

Landscape as Emporium

[05] Within the relatively techno-optimist† context described above, what remains unspoken for anyone who engages with contemporary technologies around construction is how much error still exists within construction and how laborious putting allegedly perfectly fitting elements together still is.

The promise of speedy precision remains difficult to achieve with no real paradigm-shifting construction methods. Therefore, integrating a land-based attitude with tactical uses of technology that privileges and amplifies misfit-ness and redundancy can challenge the inherently dubious search for speedy precision in constructing a sustainable built environment. This attitude also unpacks the potential of materials that exist outside of mainstream supply chains that have been deemed irrelevant for constructing a built environment, sustainable or not.

To borrow from Al Maqdisi, our ninth-century intrepid Arab traveler who has been referenced at length in this book, misfit assemblies result from understanding the landscape as a storehouse or emporium for its immediate built environment. In the case of the historical clay brick, it is no longer true that its production is located in proximity to its usage at construction sites, nor is it true that it makes up a majority of the Danish contemporary-built environment. To conceive of the landscape as an emporium, in ways that challenge contemporary notions of extraction, suggests changing one's perspective or ways of looking at landscapes. Whereas typical landscape representations privilege the horizon – maybe I am thinking about Turner's paintings here – fieldwork within Al Hajar forces one to look a little bit lower than usual at the more immediate ground. Perhaps this is a consequence of when one approaches Al Hajar, as hazy from a distance even in a car, or because its topographic complexity when one is within the mountains erases any sense of distance and horizon, or finally, because of the complexity of activity within and on the surface of the ground itself.

Towards the base of walls built around Al Hajar, and sometimes within the walls themselves, it is difficult to not notice the effects of salinity on the CMU. Eroding at different rates, walls made entirely or in some part with CMU begin to exhibit non-linear patterns. The solution to this is simple: find a rock that fits the gap where there was once concrete as seen in *fig.* (004); sometimes two rocks can do the job.

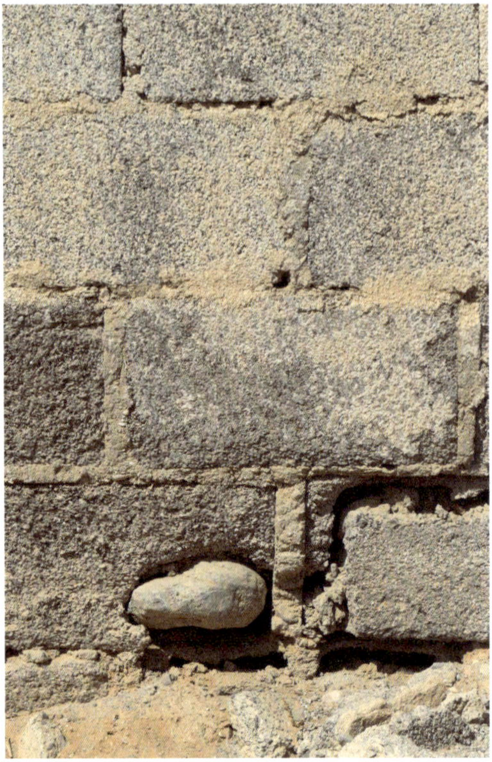

fig. (004) A stone covering a gap in a CMU caused by salinity. Photo by Samar Halloum.

The most common misfit assembly found in agricultural spaces – possibly even in your domestic space – is the plant support stake. Usually, this is a vertical thin element, sometimes made of metal, and at other times a piece of bamboo, struck into the ground with some gumption, and tied to a plant to provide support while the plant finds its place in the ground. Thus, misfit assemblies reveal themselves through three interconnected markers.

First, they are directly linked to an emergent need within a dynamic socio-spatial construct. For example, *fig.* (005) shows a relatively old dry-stack stone wall, at almost one meter high, might be reinforced with concrete before receiving ten new courses of CMU, extending its height by a further meter or a meter and a half. Most times, as I have seen, a corrugated metal sheet is used to roof these kinds of structures. Thus, misfit assemblies reveal dynamic social conditions that result in an equally dynamic and heterogeneous built environments.

Second, in their procurement method, misfit assemblies tap into the idea of a landscape as an emporium. As best as I can describe it, this attitude of constructing a place is akin to farm-to-table dining.† Both practices bypass typical supply chains and deploy [06] material with little processing. In dining, chemistry is at play, whereas in construction, it is largely physics. Thus, once a social or functional need emerges, the materials for these assemblies, which ranges from the natural, such as stone, to the synthetic, such as polycarbonate, are sourced from within the immediate natural or shaped landscape. An example of this might be: you need to raise some collected timber off of the ground to avoid rotting? Find a rock, some concrete interlock pavers, or both.

Finally, the assembly logics and resulting visual expression from these assemblies challenge contemporary construction methodologies through their ambiguous part-to-whole relationships. This also suggests an architectural project that is forgiving and potentially fast to put together. In all instances, what is required for assembly is an embodied action, requiring the use of a pair, or multiple pairs, of error-prone hands.

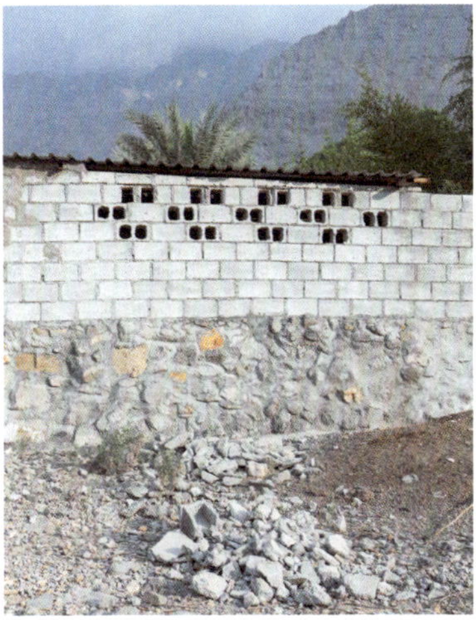

fig. (005) Relationships between stone and concrete appear to be symbiotic in the construction of tactical walls. Photo by Reem Falaknaz.

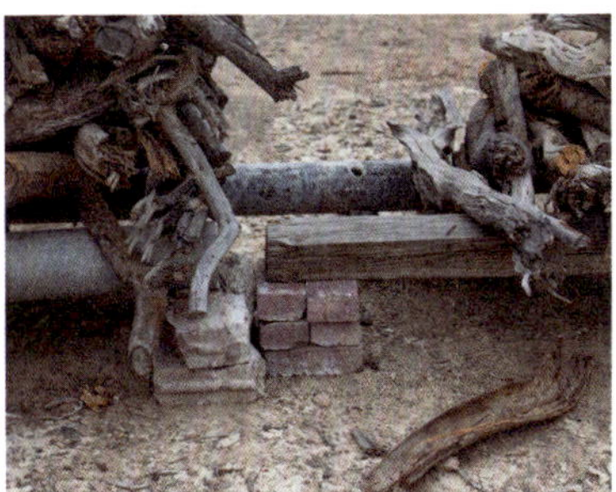

fig. (006) A misfit assembly of rocks, timber, steel lifting collected timber off of the ground. Photo by Reem Falaknaz.

Misfit Stones No Longer

For the National Pavilion United Arab Emirates (UAE) at Biennale Architettura 2023, La Biennale di Venezia, *Aridly Abundant* explores the idea of misfit assemblies through the construction of a wall. Conceived as a device that exhibits the multitude of misfit building tactics used within arid landscapes and described within this book, the wall is infused with technology to provoke alternative building systems that are rooted in material and cultural environments. Specifically, the wall is constructed out of foraged stone and fallen tree elements, typically existing outside of the repertoire of contemporary construction materials. As has been described in earlier notes in this chapter, the history of stone construction in Al Hajar abounds, however, overlaying this context with contemporary data about quarry waste makes this provocation all the more urgent.

There is evidence that approximately 30%–40% of quarried stone is considered waste and not used within the construction industry, even after significant

amounts of energy have been expended in its extraction. Within the construction industry, the understanding of quarry waste is nebulous in itself, as it includes fragments that are: too small to be used, oddly shaped, do not fit aesthetic thresholds, lack structural integrity, or are marked as undesirable by the industry. While some of this waste, especially in the case of limestone and marble dust, has been cycled into cement and concrete production to some degree of success, or crushed to be used as filler for terrazzo tiles, other elements are discarded altogether in landfills or left as debris in quarry sites, leading to serious environmental and health hazards.† In [07]
the case of using quarry waste in cement production and concrete construction as well as crushing it further, the implied reality here is that more energy, and therefore, more resources are needlessly expended. Thus, thinking about ways in which this stone becomes a viable construction material at a scale not currently adopted within the construction industry is essential for environmental, economic, as well as cultural reasons for areas of the world in which stone construction has historical roots.

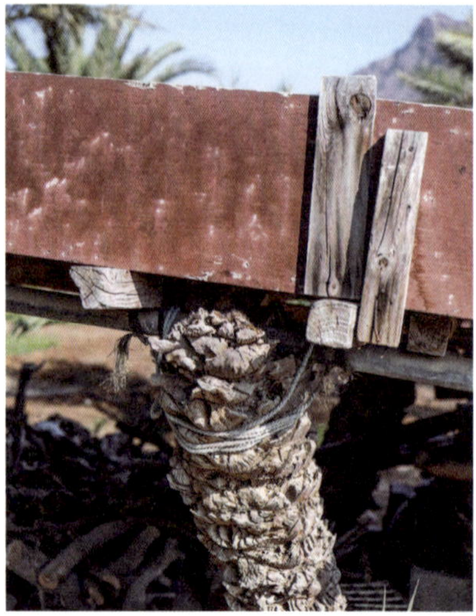

fig. (007) Ambiguous part-to-whole relationships. Photo by Reem Falaknaz.

A short pause for a tangent here: it is often assumed that stone construction is limited to a particularly modest scale not suited for rapid urban development; this is untrue, and one does not have to look far off in history to challenge this conception. A relevant example from the mid-twentieth century is Fernand Pouillon's Diar Es Saada housing complex in Algiers, built in the 1950s. Within this complex is the Totem Tower, a 20-story building constructed with a majority of

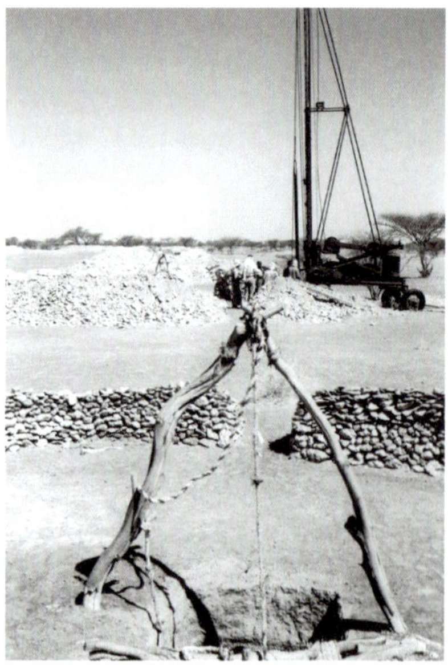

fig. (008) Drilling for water in Al Ain, September 1958. © Edric Worsnop.

structural quarried stone and integrated with reinforced concrete
[08] slabs.† Of note is the integration of structural and environmental functions in the structural building envelope through its thickness, varying between 40-80 centimeters, a relatively thick façade for even its contemporaneous constructions, as well as for today's standards given our reliance on energy intensive active
[09] cooling methods.†

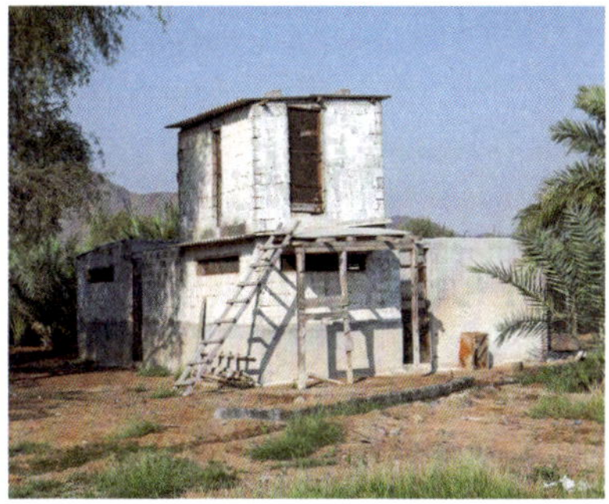

fig. (009) Misfit assemblies express themselves not only at the scale of the detail, but also that of spatial assemblies. Photo by Reem Falaknaz.

As we come back to the present, one might ask about stone technology today. Steve Webb suggests that "technological development in stone largely ceased with the advent of reinforced concrete
[10] and steel in the nineteenth century."† And so, building on these ideas and histories, led our research to think about ways in which technology can, in fact, amplify the use of discarded or ill-fitting stones - an idea latent with potential.

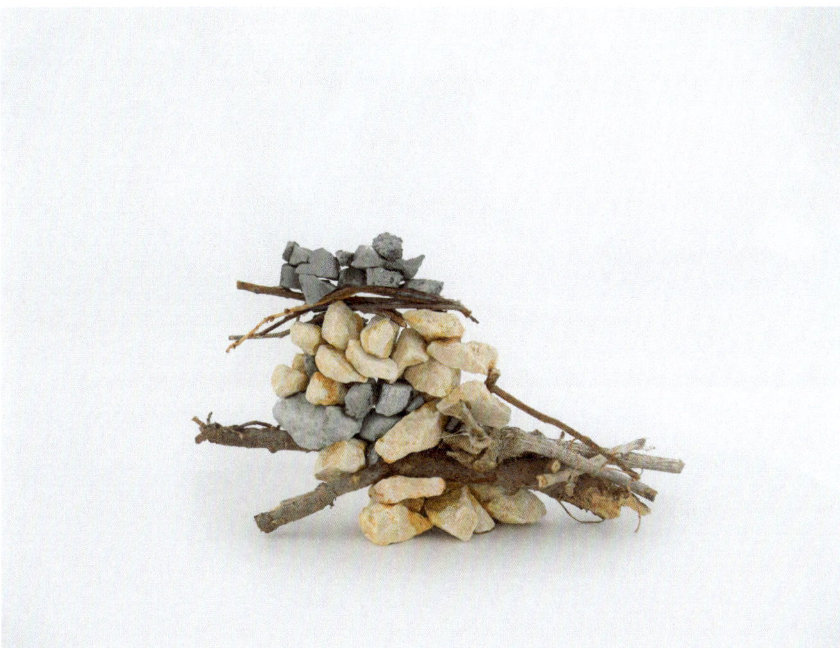

fig. (010) A relatively small prototype, on a table, of a misfit assembly wall incorporating stone and twigs. Photo by Rana Salah.

The central provocation lies in the minimal degree of intervention, including energy resources, to shape the found material. Using technology, the stones which would have typically not come together without transformation are digitally scanned to allow for the development of a 3D printed interface to connect and work them together to create a free-standing wall.

It is important to note that the stones and fallen timber used in this exhibition are all sourced from Italy to highlight how the tactics and processes documented within the arid landscapes of Al Hajar have universal applications in other areas in the world that are either facing similar conditions, or will very soon face them. This is doubly relevant given Italy's announcement, in the summer of 2022, of a state of emergency due to severe drought conditions in Northern Italy.† [11]

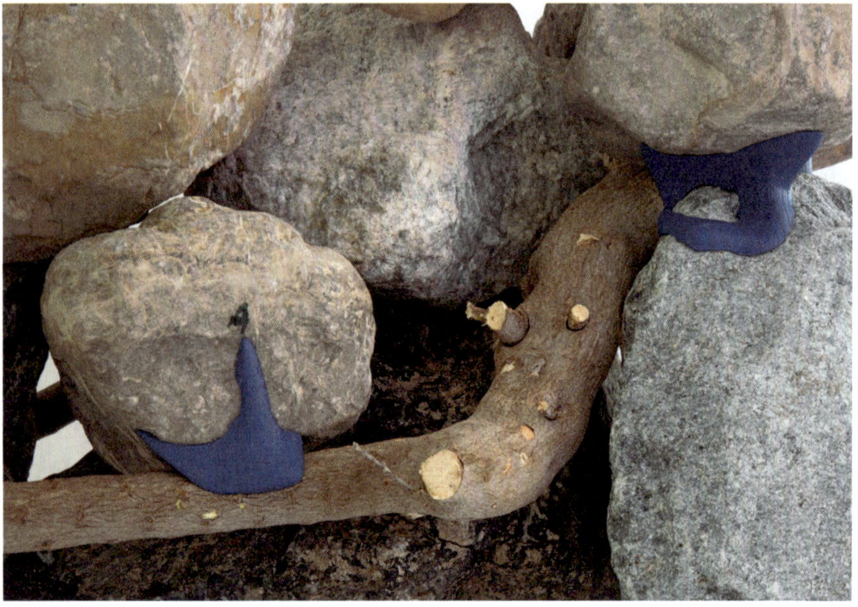

fig. (011) Augmenting collected stones with 3D printed interfaces allows for their expanded use within construction. Photo by Rana Salah.

01

Many thanks to Thomas Bo Jensen for the translation and suggestion.

02

Many thanks to Carolina Dayer for this discovery.

03

Manufacturing of a Brick. Technical Notes on Brick Construction. The Brick Industry Association. 2006. 5.

04

Jorgen Bryrup "Prefabricated Brick Facing Panels - An International Survey".

05

By techno-optimism, I specifically mean an adherence to the idea that technology is singular in the development of the built environment, overshadowing land-based knowledge.

06

Thanks to Adam Melonas for a lengthy discussion clarifying my misconceptions around farm-to-table dining.

07

Pradeep Kumar Gautam et al, "Use of Quarry Waste as Building Material: A Review," *Proceedings of 168th The IIER International Conference*, (June 2018): 1.

08, 09

Louiza Mohammedi et al, "Assessment of the Seismic Behaviour of Heritage Masonry Buildings Using Numerical Modelling: A Study of Fernand Pouillon's Totem Tower in Algiers, Algeria," *Journal of Building Engineering* Volume 38 (June 2021): 1,3.

10

Steve Webb, "Stone Age," *The Architectural Review* 1490 (April 2022): 7.

11

Reuters, "Italy declares state of emergency for drought-stricken north," *Reuters*, July 5, 2022, https://www.reuters.com/world/europe/italy-declares-state-emergency-drought-stricken-north-2022-07-04/

Landowners, farmers, and farm workers within Al Hajar Mountains constantly tend to plants, rocks, animals, and even other people. In some cases, they tend to the remnants of another's previous handiwork, such as in the stacks of tightly rolled palm frond mats. These tactics make the built environment within Al Hajar a dynamic and constantly transforming one. Everywhere one turns, tending hands are responsible for placing markers in the landscape, blurring the effects of the sometimes harsh sun, stacking to create various structures and enclosures, revealing and channeling water, sheltering plants, tethering precarious elements together, and supporting growth.

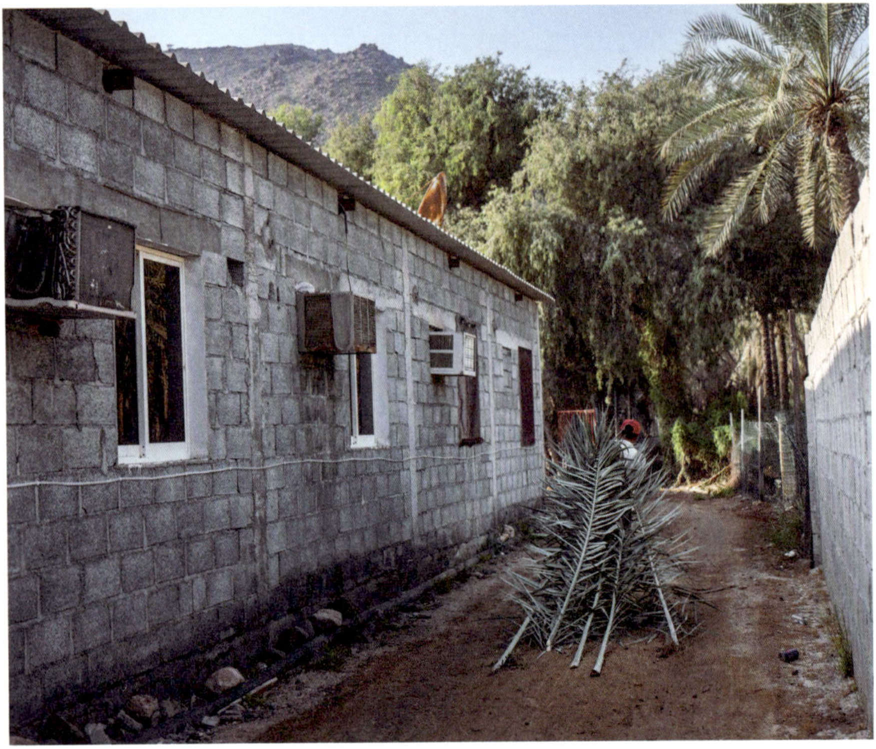

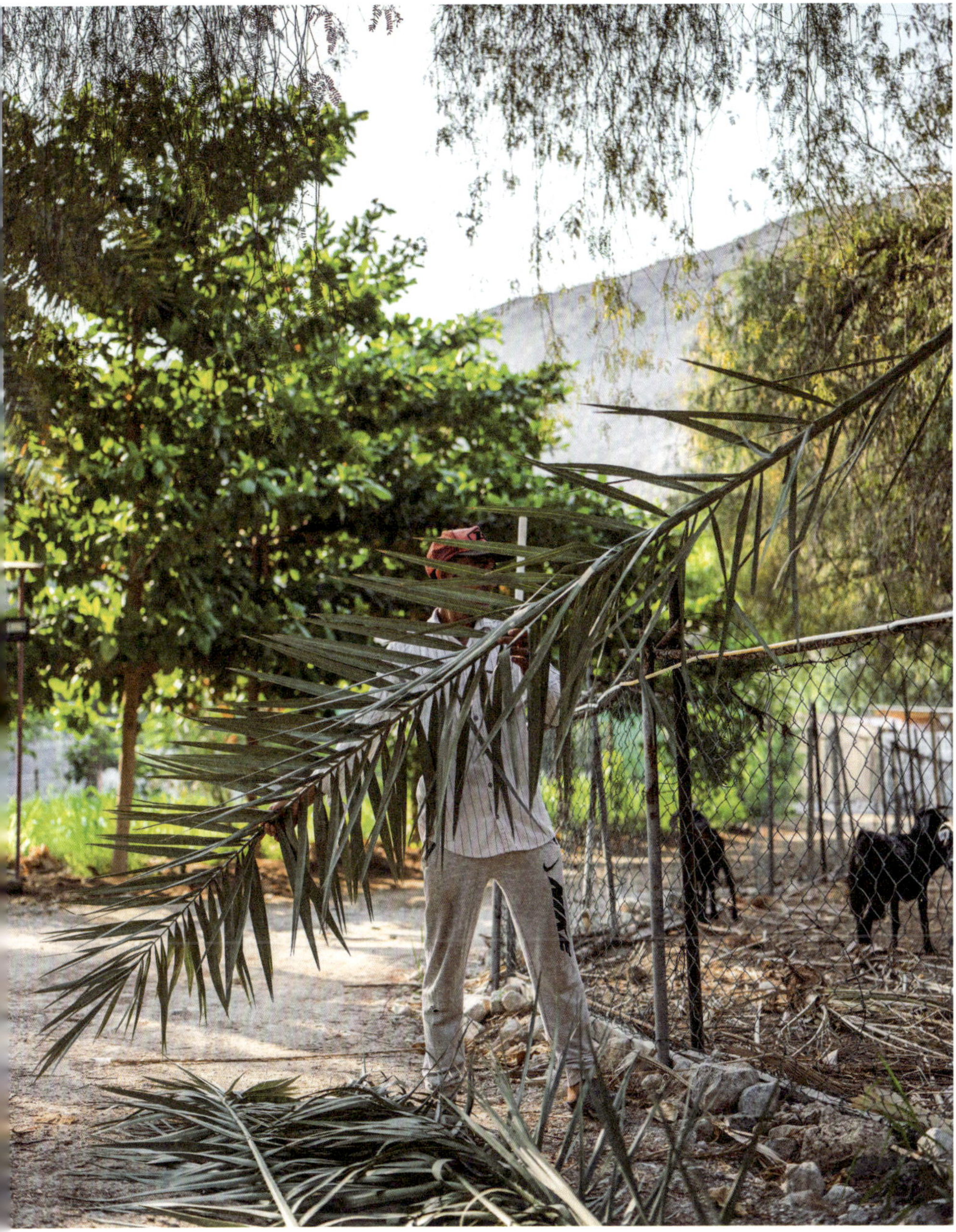

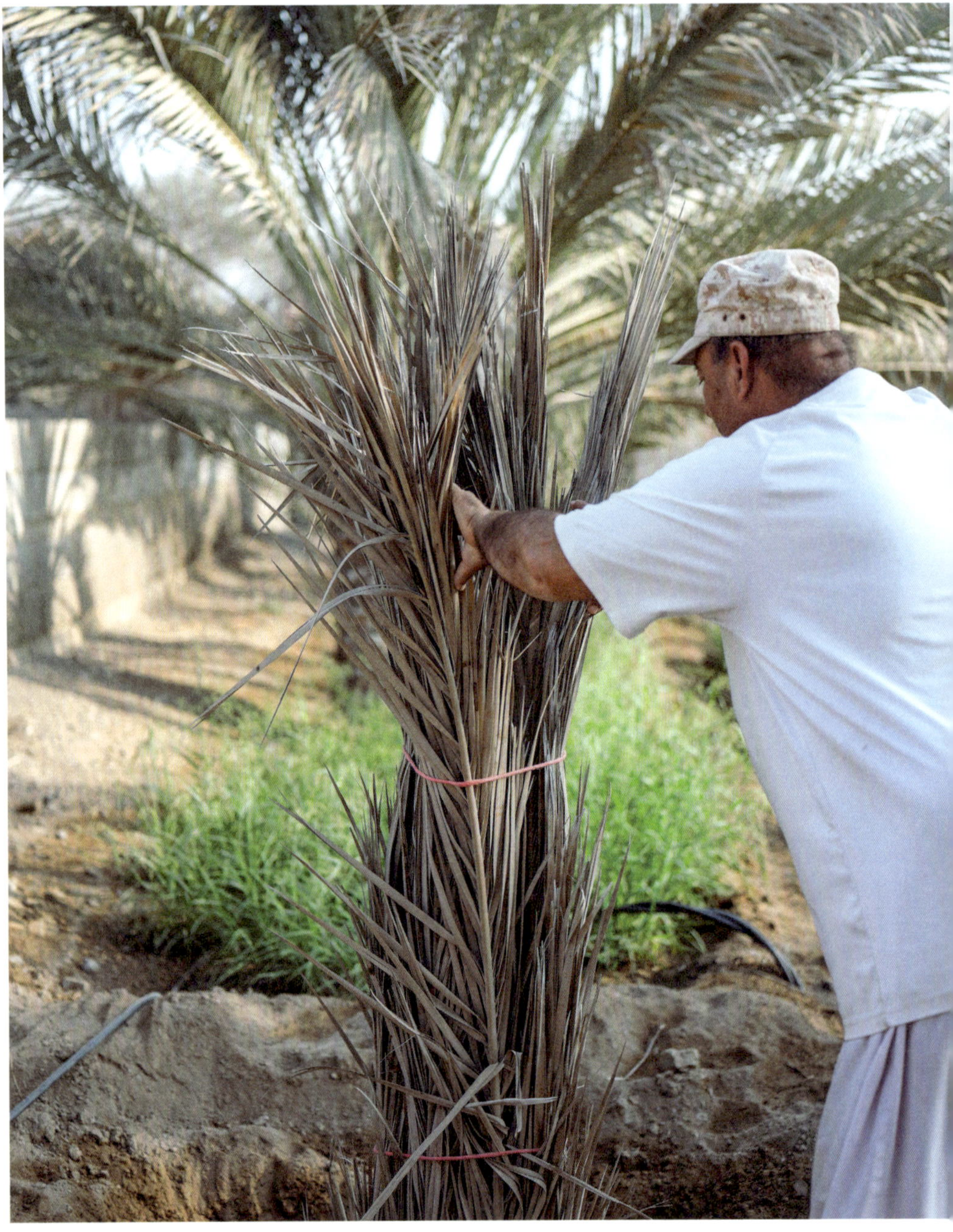

Field Notes: Index of Figures

Mohamed M. Elnagar

Life of a Rock

My knowledge of this universe was limited.

I had no awareness of how things began and what their end looked like; what a rise or a fall referred to; or how day and night followed each other. Despite this, hope from an unknown source flickered within me. My flat surface beamed when it approached, and my heart (if I had one) danced in joy. My home had always been between two giant rocks that conspired to restrain my movement on both sides, rendering me immobile. Instead, I watched and waited. Water surrounded everything. I had no clue when it began, or how it commanded control over the scope of my vision or perception. It extended its wings over endless rocky mounds, creating a blue-grey world that made me believe that no other colors existed or no movement could be felt other than the currents that kept me company in this simple world. On purpose, I chose to ignore some small dots that shone like barely seen far away stars. I was no stranger to the illusion that bears forth disappointment, born out of a trick conspired against me by the water and light. That was until the stars bloomed, revealing a new reality in the form of fresh lives stepping slowly into an empty universe. Surrounded by color never seen in my bound world, they grew and blossomed before my sight, my dazzlement, and my restricted motion. I almost screamed in joy at the good tidings, an oncoming companionship crawling into my silent world. Within the

ية الأشياء وكيف تبدو نهايتها، معنى الإشراق
، ولكن كان يلمسني أمل ملازم لنور مكسور
ط، ويرقص قلبي طرباً إن كنت أملك واحداً...

blink of an eye, this life gave birth to multiple creatures: minuscule and massive; peaceful and aggressive; recluse and predator. They all passed me quickly, rushing to leave very shortly afterwards. In their absence, my only consolation was their successors. One time, a struggle ensued between two giants and one of them sunk its sharp teeth into the other's short arm who pulled it away abruptly and painfully, then escaped by swimming away, moving its feet and torso sideways in slow motion. The victor extended its pointed mouth in celebration of the win, baring its teeth in ecstasy. It moved its tail and inadvertently slammed me and the two rocks, then it flinched and swam away. Soon after, an anonymous whale freed me from my chronic shackles, and for a few seconds, it seemed like I was living an impossible dream, where I drifted along the water current until I landed on a grey rocky mound. There, I looked from a distance towards my past which was reflected in the eyes of my two jailers whom fate had freed me from.

Gradually, the water retreated off of the sharp tips of the grey land, and I eagerly watched the water levels go down. Then, sunshine sparkled on my smooth surface uninhibited or mediated. I felt dryness for the first time, and whales disappeared from my sight, never to return. Another exquisite world that the ocean waters had deprived me of emerged. Creatures do not swim here, nor are they pulled by the current. Rather, they waddle on land with their flexible limbs, not unlike the one that landed on me and cast a shadow on my surface with its thin body and a tail twice the length of its form. The small creature looked around in panic, its instincts alarming it of impending danger. It froze in place, perhaps to look as if it was a part of me so its pursuer would not take notice of it. Its four limbs wrapped around me, each with five still fingers sprouting from it. Its belly was the color of the sky, ceaselessly rising and falling, making me feel its anguished pulse beneath its blue skin. Here, it remained the same until the cracks of light between the clouds receded, and night spread over and

لم أكن أعرف شيئًا عن هذا الكون بعد، ما هي
أو الأفول، تتابع النهار والليل، لم أدرِ أيًا من ه
مجهول المصدر، يرنو فيتهلل سطحي المنب

covered the sky, allowing darkness to prevail, and peace to take over. The fabric of quiet remained unsoiled, except for a sharp intermittent sound; a rhythmic wailing, pulsating steadily at times, and resounding with a continuous scream at other times, followed by the flapping of wide wings. After an extended stillness, the little creature lifted its head. Terror took over its body and it froze in its place. Soon thereafter, its little head collapsed and fell to my side when a long talon grazed my surface, carving a path through its blue skin. The incoming visitor from the sky took over my humble surroundings. Its ruffled feathers and outspread wings rendered it a mythical creature, parading its power and asserting its domain and rule. It continued to survey its surroundings with its wide eyes whose dark parameter was outlined by circular feathers. Moving its head, it could turn in a full circle without disturbing the stillness of its body, casting fear into the heart of whoever dares to even look at its prey. The creature stooped its head to examine its food with a small hooked beak, making sure it was no longer alive. Extending its wings, it then carried its loot to a nearby branch connected to a long tree trunk, and I could see the tree's roots two rocks away from me. The branch shook under the weight of the bird, and so it jumped to another thicker branch. The white feathers melted into the greenish white of the tree blossoms, uniting the two creatures into a single being. The aggressor put down its kill and sharpened its talons, then picking up the prey once more upon completing its task, it flew away, gradually disappearing into a foggy dot within the circle of the moon.

The following morning, the sun attempted to peer its head through the clouds but they refused to yield, continuing to slowly roam, creating dark gaps between them that looked like giant mouths which birds avoided in fear of being swallowed by the unknown darkness.

This is when the earth began to shake under the weight of strange herds arriving, walking on two talon-less limbs, their mouths holding two rows of small teeth, useless for cutting flesh or tearing any meat. Their skin appeared soft, fragile, easy to penetrate, and was sparsely covered with hair, devoid of any feathers or scales. They communicated in fitful sounds, stormed in herds and stocks, and began to prepare their abode in the expansive valley. They erected wooden pillars with roofs of palm tree fronds, sleeping and waking so many times that I became used to their existence. One day, they worked together to collect all the stones they could find in sight, preferring the large ones. I could not fathom where they were taking my mates, so I was filled with horror every time they came close to me until I understood what they were doing. They laid the stones over each other in a tall construction, leveling its surface and filling the gaps with wet mud. They created quarters that sheltered them from the dangers of the outdoors, carefully electing locations near the rows of palm trees as an added line of protection. Palm trees extend their fronds behind the walls, looking like they sprouted from the heart of the stacked stones. Their long necks extended forward to forecast danger, anticipating it from their great heights so the structure below rests in peace. Later on, the herds began tearing the earth with their bare hands to allow the passage of a beast that cascaded from the top of the mountain each time the sky wept. They directed the passage of running water according to each of their needs, so it flowed to whoever suffered from dryness, quenching thirst and alleviating drought, and the earth gave birth to supplies and harvest. One of them carried me to use me to block the current, but my small size was to no avail. He tried and failed again, so he left me giddy with the touch of water on my surface that I have longed since missed. Water became abundant, and so life flourished. Buildings replaced the emptiness that was, and so the herd settled. Walls of stone and mud with roofs of mud, wood, and fronds, kept them peaceful and protected. For some unknown reason, their peace brought me peace, and I became calm with my place beside one of the walls that I escaped being part of. That was until the first wall collapsed under the weight of the imminent calamity. Near the sea, small stars hailed on the quiet town, balls of fire fell like scorching rain, burning everything and everyone they touched. The peaceful herd was overcome with terror; screams grew loud and wailing filled the air. All who were left alive looked around, stunned. It was then that another herd arrived from where the fireballs originated. They walked in successive rows and were armed with long metal arms that roared in their hands, with one falling motionless each time the arm roared. Death roamed around the stone abodes, tirelessly harvesting with its sickle. The males of the village collected their wits and lifted metal swords in vain, and the offending herd continued to harvest souls. They were all of the same type despite the difference in their appearance: the heads of the aggressors shone with light hair, and their pale skin appeared burned by the midday sun. The dark complexion of the town dwellers appeared clear beneath their long beards. Close to me, the consecutive fireballs left a large hole, where the light of the flames shone with the power of a thousand suns. The hole was certainly unlike any other, and both warring ends collectively stopped for a breath in awe. A knight emerged from the bottom of the hole, riding a dust-colored creature, and continued to split the light of the hole, casting his image onto the moving clouds. The knight, with his tanned complexion and white turban, released a cry that shook the very earth where he stood and caused me to roll to another spot with a better view. The knight was followed by another herd that appeared to be his subordinates, who also emerged out of the hole to overtake the offending herd like a torrential flood. Once the offenders realized what was happening, the fighting ensued once more and had no end in sight.

One day, everything returned to what it was before. The offending herd disappeared, the knight dismounted, and each went their own way. I began to watch their lives with fascination, then as a daily occurrence, then with boredom, and finally, with indifference. In the meantime, they continued to move about within their temporary existence. Death lurked in each of their steps. As for myself, I always remained by the shore of this raging sea, sipping at the chalice of immortality that no longer tasted sweet.

Years passed by slowly, and the sun and moon alternated above the heads of those who bore witness to them. Movement subsided, and most of the buildings collapsed except for a few. The group left the valley, and the wild beasts moved back in. The ancient life that I had missed gradually returned, a beloved existence that sparked joy within. Life was never meant for hiding and fortification. An expansive land, an ample sky, and a wide sea all existed that way, without borders or conditions. It is only right that they remain this way. Life breathed into me once again, and I came to look forward to a promising tomorrow that follows each day. Limbs, feet, talons, wings, beaks, and tails, running tirelessly one after the other over my surface, leaving their traces, parts of their memory, and stories for me to carry, perhaps in the hope of revealing them one day. Here, you will never find a rock without a story, or a speck of sand without roots or recollections.

One morning, I felt a tame hoof familiar to my smooth surface. I had settled on a slanted terrain inside a large hole formed by the passage of time, where consecutive fits of wind, rain, and earthquakes had deposited me. The four-limbed hoofed creature stood effortlessly on the slanted surface, looking around, continuously chewing on something. It was scratching its curved horns on a rock near its head, its mane shaking along its neck from the movement. Its brown color jelled with its entire surroundings to a degree that made it hardly visible. In its eyes, one could see its peaceful nature without a doubt. There was a whole clan of them, one following the other, grazing carelessly in peace, until a thunderous sound boomed above the hole. The familiar sound startled the clan, which scattered in terror, beating the earth violently and chaotically. They kept striking me left and right until I was extracted from the hole amidst a cloud of horror and dust. The dust settled and I was able to see what being inside the hole had shielded me from for a while. There were walls built without stone or mud, well-leveled and uniform in color, some of them rising to match the mountain next to them. There were lands cultivated in straight lines with nesting identical plants in the distance. There were ponds, manufactured or mysterious in their nature. There were bowed, resigned animals, grazing within a fenced space. Similar to the strike of the whale that freed me from a prison, ushering me into an alternative world, the hoofs of the animal threw me into a new reality, where the two-limbed erect creatures ruled. Someone approached me, fanning the dust away from his face, wearing a cover on his head to protect him from the heat of the sun. He examined me with soft teeth that stuck out of the end of a wooden stick that he held with his fingertips. He extracted a round glass piece from his bag to look at me through, then declared victoriously: "A volcanic stone. I bet it is thousands of years old."

I would have smiled in pity, if I was able to. How naive you are, and how humble is your outlook. The man stood again to examine another bigger stone, followed by a youngster walking behind him, guided by his curiosity. The youngster stretched his hand out to collect me, smiling, then turned his head to the man to make sure that nobody was watching. He then extended his arm and threw me away in the direction of a pond. I crashed into the water and sank slowly, settling into the shallow bottom. A small cylindrical fish passed by me, laboriously swimming in the turbid water. That poor fish seemed to be lost, one way or another, to end up in this small pond. The fish did not have a giant tail to free me, and, in turn, I had no desire to be freed. The mud at the bottom of the pond slowly engulfed me until I was completely submerged by it. I felt reassured by the surrounding peace that I had long forgotten after a lifetime of noise. I surrendered to my new dwelling, and for the first time ever, tasted the sweetness of slumber and seclusion.

Characters, in order of appearance:

01

Volcanic Stone: A rock of volcanic origins from Al Hajar Mountains, anciently formed as a result of magma that cooled off when it reached the surface of the earth.

02

Whale (*aegicetus gehennae*): A primeval whale that represents the intermediate era between swimming using feet and tails.

03

Blue-Tailed Lizard: A medium-sized lizard known for its flat head. It prefers to live in rocky environments near water sources.

04

Arabian Eagle-Owl: A type of owl that prefers living in open forests and rocky hills with trees that have many tangled branches. It is generally active at night and feeds on small birds, reptiles, and large insects.

05

Arabian Ban Tree (Moringa Tree): Known as "The Tree of Life," it generally grows rapidly in hot and arid climates and thrives in droughts.

06

Human 1: The first human settlers in the lands of the Arabian Gulf. The groups transitioned from constant migration to settlement, creating small communities based on agriculture.

07

Stone Houses: Built as alternatives to penetrable tents, stone houses offer a more secure and protective housing.

08

Falaj: A channel dug in the ground to collect and regulate the flow of rain/flood/spring water, which people controlled by obstructing the flow of water and neutralizing it in the direction of need.

09

Human 2 (the offending herd): The Portuguese Army that colonized the Arabian Gulf regions to control the eastern trade corridors.

10

Human 3 (the knight and his followers): The Ya'rubid knights attempting to resist in an effort to reclaim the land from the Portuguese colonizers.

11

Arabian Tahr: A mammal that lives in Al Hajar Mountains and is considered the smallest species among the tahr bovines. It has a short body, hooked horns, and the males have a distinctive mane along the chin and neck.

12

Human 4: Contemporary humans interested in geological fieldwork.

13

Koi Fish: A type of colorful hybrid fish that is sought for decorative ponds in landscaped areas.

Wesam Al Asali

"As They Have No Wood:" Building Tactics for Arid Structures

[01] At the entrance of the desert, coming from Aleppo, I found a village built in a very singular manner; each room was a cupola, and resembled a haystack, some of them a sugar loaf. The whole was of earth, as they have no wood. The inhabitants said their town had been built by Abraham; that is, they did not remember when the oldest houses were built. They said they were never out of repair, but that they sometimes plastered the upper part, or rather beat earth on it. The walls were composed of clay and gravel and were exceedingly hard. The method they use is to beat each layer of earth till it is very hard.†

After years of living and traveling in the Near East, William Eton wrote his book *A Survey of the Turkish Empire* in the late eigh-
[02] teenth century.† Unlike usual travel books, Eton's book does not follow a chronological or geographic sequence. Instead, it contains several political, scientific, and social notes about today's Middle East, some of which were on construction and building techniques he associated with earthen materials. These techniques, however, are aligned along the travel route from Europe to India; the inland path that connects the Mediterranean Sea with the Arabian Gulf. There, the earth villages and structures between Aleppo and Basra intrigued him as much as other travelers before and after him. In this essay, I will be reading Eton's notes as I travel with him looking at earthen building tactics today, from the villages with domed houses near Aleppo to the methods of onsite building prefabrication in Basra and the remarkable domed mosque in Al Bidya in Fujairah, United Arab Emirates (UAE).

Where does aridity start and where does it end? In the built environment, aridity extends beyond geographical locations. It is a palette of specific resources and the knowledge on how to deal with them, both of which have been overlooked from the times of eighteenth century travelers' writing until today's architectural framing of earthen architecture in the Near East. This architecture resembles an evolving state of transnationality between permanence and temporality – a house is both a tent and a castle. Eton and other Western travelers mistakenly thought that for an earthen dome to exist in a house, builders must have come up against a scarcity of materials. However, we will counter this notion and reveal how these builders understood the abundance of resources, time, and gravity in these structures.

01

William Eton, *A Survey of the Turkish Empire* (London: Printed for T. Cadell, jun. and W. Davies, 1798) 229.

02

Eton, *Turkish Empire*.

Entrance of the Desert: Paths through Aridity

There were three main routes that connected Europe to East Asia: the Red Sea, the Caspian Sea, and the most ancient inland route of the Euphrates Valley in Mesopotamia.† The latter was revived in the sixteenth [03]
century with Portuguese and Venetian travelers exploring the Babylonian desert path to India. For those going from Europe to India, the Asian part of the route starts in Aleppo's port, Alexandretta. Travelers entered Aleppo from the northwest and left it from the southeast heading towards the Tigris or Euphrates, where they marched to Baghdad, and then Basra (Bassora). From Basra, travelers would take a ship to either the eastern coast of Arabia or the western coast of India. Eton does not provide specific details about his path from Aleppo to Basra. However, we know from other travelers that the section from Aleppo to the Euphrates is particularly known for being barren and desertic. For example, in 1745, William Beas described three ways to travel from Aleppo to Basra, the first is to ride with the caravans from Aleppo to Mosul and then to sail in water carriages to Baghdad and Basra. The second way is similar but heading to Bir, not Mosul, in which a traveler can sail on the Euphrates, but not the Tigris. The last route is all inland where caravans ran parallel to the Euphrates.

In many cases, caravans took the river route to descend to Basra "to avoid the great weariness of the desert journey," as the Venetian jeweler Gasparo Balbi described his journey in 1579. For return trips, travelers took inland routes like another Venetian traveler, Cæser Frederick, did in 1581. Frederick needed 40 days for his journey, 36 of which were entirely through the wilderness, where there were no inhabited villages.† Pietro Della Valle, an Italian composer who traveled exten- [04]
sively in this part of the world, also described in detail his return trip from Basra in 1625. He defined the desert between Basra and Aleppo as "a great Plain with very few inequalities." In this great plain, the soil changes from "saltish" to "stony" and from "Moorish" with reed to green with "thorny grass."† [05]

03

Douglas Carruthers, "The Great Desert Caravan Route, Aleppo to Basra," *The Geographical Journal*, (vol. 52, no. 3, 1918): 158. https://doi.org/10.2307/1779587.

04

Carruthers, "Caravan," 159.

05

Pietro Della Valle, *The Travels of Sig. Pietro Della Valle, a Noble Roman, into East-India and Arabia Deserta in Which, the Several Countries, Together with the Customs, Manners, Traffique, and Rites Both Religious and Civil, of Those Oriental Princes and Nations, Are Faithfully Described : In Familiar Letters to His Friend Signior Mario Schipano : Whereunto Is Added a Relation of Sir Thomas Roe's Voyage into the East-Indies.*, (2004) 272, http://name.umdl.umich.edu/A65012.0001.001.

For passersby like Della Valle, these variations of wilderness just appeared as desert landscapes, however, for the inhabitants, they were resources for building. Accordingly, the resulting built environment changed as much as the landscapes did. Unlike in cities where buildings were well documented, travelers rarely provided detailed accounts of the built environment in rural areas beyond the physical status of a building being maintained or ruined, inhabited or abandoned. For them, villages on paths through aridity are no more than scattered dots of potential resting points. The only exception occurs near Aleppo, at the entrance of the desert, where villages of houses with large pointed domes, so vividly different from other shelters on the journey, enchanted travelers like Eton.

Sugar Loaves, Haystacks, and Beehives: Metaphor as a Description

Between the Euphrates and Aleppo, mud villages with elongated domed ceilings are mentioned in travelers' writings as a first or last resting place to enter or exit Aleppo. While William Eton was more elaborate in explaining the construction of these villages, the shape of the domes was undoubtedly the focus of attention for many of his predecessors. On his way back from Basra to Aleppo in 1610, the Portuguese traveler Pedro Teixeira mentioned resting at three domed villages, Ackel, Melluha, and Sfiera. In Ackel, a village "standing at the foot of a pleasant hill, in a good meadow by the lake," he found houses that are " small, but well built, of sun-dried bricks, pyramidal over vaults." Then, he went to Melluha and Sfiera and both were "built like
[06] the last, but better."† Two centuries later, in
1825, the English journalist James Silk Buckingham mentioned passing several ruined villages, whose houses were "distinguished by a high-pointed dome of brick-work, rising from
[07] the square of their base."† Like Buckingham,
Bartholomew Plaisted and John Carmichael described domed-mud villages near Aleppo in 1750 and 1751 respectively. Both men noted the villages' small houses, writing that some
[08] were ruined while others were inhabited.†

06

Pedro Teixeira, *The Travels of Pedro Teixeira: With His "Kings of Harmuz" and Extracts from His "Kings of Persia"* (Hdeluyt Society, 1802), 110.

07

James Silk Buckingham, *Travels in Mesopotamia; Including a Journey from Aleppo, Across the Euphrates to Orfah, (the Ur of the Chaldees,) Through the Plains of the Turcomans, to Diabekr, in Asia Minor; from Thence to Mardin, on the Borders of the Great Desert, and by the Tigris to Mousul and Bagdad; with Researches on the Ruins of Babylon, Nineveh, Arbela, Ctesiphon, and Seleucia* (Colburn, 1827), 6-9.

08

Douglas Carruthers, *The Desert Route to India: Being the Journals of Four Travellers by the Great Desert Caravan Route Between Aleppo and Basra, 1745-1751* (Asian Educational Services, 1996), 6-8, 135.

In the absence of images, travelers used the shapes of ordinary objects exchanged globally across cultures to describe the houses. Eton used the shape of a haystack, which is pyramidic, and a sugarloaf, which is closer to a cone.† The term sugar loaf dome [09] was not only limited to the domed villages in Aleppo, but many travelers also used it to refer to the finely ornate *muqarnas* domes found in mausoleum architecture in Mesopotamia, like the dome in the eleventh-century Imam Dur Mausoleum near Samarra.† James Silk Buck- [10] ingham and Bartholomew Plaisted described the domed houses as beehives raised on a pedestal of mud and stone walls. This particular image continues to this day. Researchers call these houses beehive houses despite the awkwardness of the name for the inhabitants of these villages who simply call their houses, domed houses (*Byut el Qibab*).

The travelers' writings and their metaphors reveal a fascination with the shape of these domes whose silhouette was always described as singular and remarkable. Such fascination can be associated with how these structures were witnessed from a moving caravan as "aridscapes" (arid landscapes) standing near the horizon and emerging from the flatness of "the great plain with few inequalities," to remember Della Valle's words. As some domed clusters of houses were abandoned and only few were inhabited and safe for rest, all domed villages stopped being villages in the travelers' eyes and became aridscapes rooted in the barren, once prosperous land. As such, the ruins of a village are not very different from the desert of a bygone orchard.

As They Have No Wood: Homo Faber

If the concept of traveling in aridscapes is centered on the endurance to cross, then in construction, it is the effort to endure the lack of materials. Eton, a consul, politician, traveler, and a "man of facts" as he introduced himself in his book, spares no effort to illustrate the terrifying nature of the Turkish Empire and its governors, concluding that "expulsion of the Turks from Europe, and the re-establishment of the Greek Empire, would be more advantageous to Britain than even to Russia itself."† Such positioning is vastly pro- [11] jected on all chapters of Eton's book, including the one on the sciences and arts where he sees Near East architecture that although

09

The term sugar loaf is also used by Carmichael.

10

Jonathan Bloom and Sheila S. Blair, *Grove Encyclopedia of Islamic Art & Architecture: Three-Volume Set* (OUP USA, 2009), 251.

11

Eton, *Turkish Empire*, vii.

12

Eton, *Turkish Empire*, 202.

it is "grand and imposing, the particular parts are devoid of all proportion." His belief was that these architects never "conceived any idea of proportion, from the perfect [Greek] models they have daily
[12] before their eyes. In short, they have never studied architecture."†

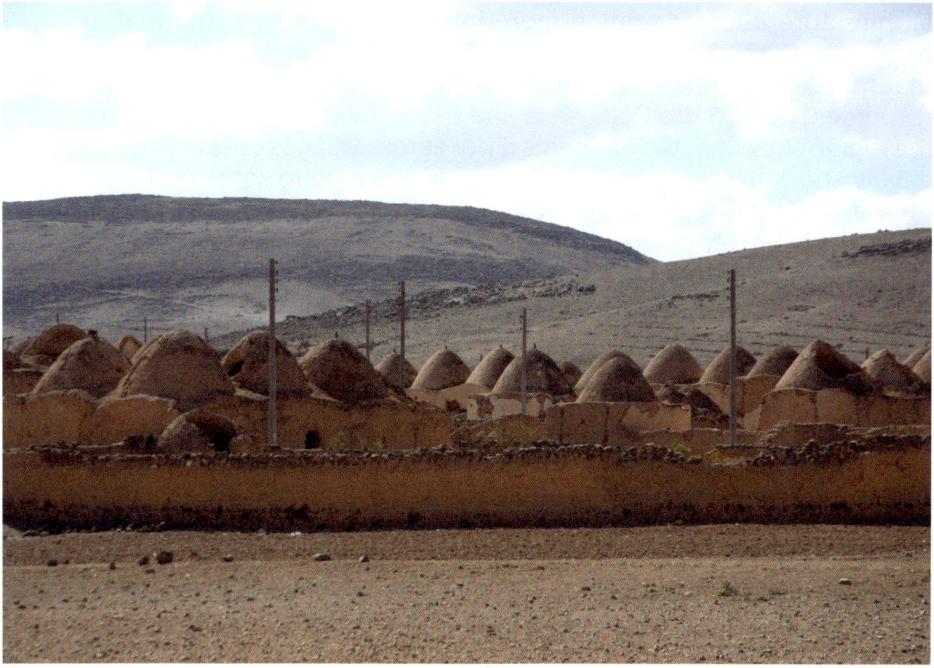

fig. (001) Domed houses villages as aridscapes. Photo by author.

It is from such a perspective that Eton disassociated "architecture" from the earthen construction techniques in his notes. The two are in different sections. Like other travelers who wrote something about the domed villages, their construction is depicted as a result of a lack of trees, precisely as Eton put it. However, little has been said about the materials and practices that made this architecture possible, except for some brief mentions of sun-dried bricks, their dimensions, or their uses. Similar explanations always appear when describing building techniques using domes in the Middle East and North Africa, such as those in Mali and Niger, the Nubian domes in Egypt and Sudan, the Manzil architecture in eastern Tunisia and the island of Djerba, and the mud building in the city of Yazd in Iran. With such reasoning, a dome, in an aridscape, is an exceptional case in which the deficiency of resources is the reason for producing the built environment.

But what if we were not travelers just passing by? What if we start looking at these domes based on the concept of abundance, not scarcity? And on rooted habitation knowledge instead of temporal adaptability?

With this change of scope from scarcity to abundance, earth-domed architecture becomes much more interesting than a sugar loaf. It becomes a premise and is an evolving knowledge of construction that has developed with the temporal and geographical variations of resources. Both Pierto Della Valle and Pedro Teixeira's descriptions of the region show that the materials differ across villages despite the relatively short distances between them, from stone to sand, and from reed and timber. Although, they have not really described how such a variation is manifested in the construction of these villages. While all the structures appeared as earth plastered, the material under this plastering, and in the interiors, vastly varied from village to village. If basalt stones were present, builders would frequently use them in foundations, quarried or found from shallow surfaces, and rarely cut them unless placed on windowsills, doors, or arches separating two rooms. In limestone areas near Hama, where stones become softer and the carving techniques become richer, limestone is usually cut and used in walls, especially in the lower part to protect the mud wall from humidity. The geometry of the mud domes also starts to change as they become shorter, resting on rectangular stone bases. When a fast-setting mortar like gypsum exists, as in Basra and Baghdad, a dome starts to become a vault because it will not need formwork to be erected. Finally, in wetland areas, where reed and poplar wood are abundant, domes start to be truncated using flat timber ceilings with a group of wooden posts anchored in the middle of the dome. Here, reeds or straw are placed on
top of the timber to be covered with mud and straw. † *[13]*

Resources, too, extend beyond materials to accommodate time and gravity – both more tangible for a dweller than a traveler. In his text, Eton describes the rammed-earth technique, where layers of earth and gravel are patted to make a solid thick wall. This is only one, very laborious, way of building a mud dome. In many other instances, the mud walls are made with mud bricks which would have been fabricated months before the construction, which was only possible if the brick production coincided with the cycle of activities of their makers. In a different instance, using specific materials can be time-saving. The truncated dome is a result of the shortening of construction time, as adobe dome construction takes more time than adding wooden posts. Similarly, when basalt or limestone stones are found, they are placed in the corners of the room as an alternative to the laborious making of dome pendentives and to reduce the number of circular coursing necessary to move from the square to the circle, from the base of the dome to its body.

However, the best depiction of the relation between time and construction is Eton's test in Basra. There, again, builders made arches without any frame because they "have no timber but the wood of the date tree, which is like a cabbage stalk." For a builder to make an arch, he starts with "a nail and a bit of string describes a semicircle on the ground, lays his bricks, fastened together by a gypsum cement..., except the crown brick." The arch is then "carefully raised, and in two parts
[14] placed on the wall." † What Eton is describing in this text is, in today's terms, an on-site prefabrication system of barrel vaults. This technique was used broadly in mudbrick architecture in present-day Iraq and Iran, where halves of the sequencing arch are placed along the room. The same technique of using gypsum mortar is also mentioned but for dividing domes into smaller parts, speculated as the genesis of the rib domes, a typology that extended from Bukhara to Cordoba.

13

For more information about the typologies and materials of earthen domes in Syria, see: L. Dipasquale S. Mecca, *Earthen Domes et Habitats. Villages of Northern Syria. An Architectural Tradition Shared by East and West* (Pisa: ETS, 2009).

14

Eton, *Turkish Empire*, 222.

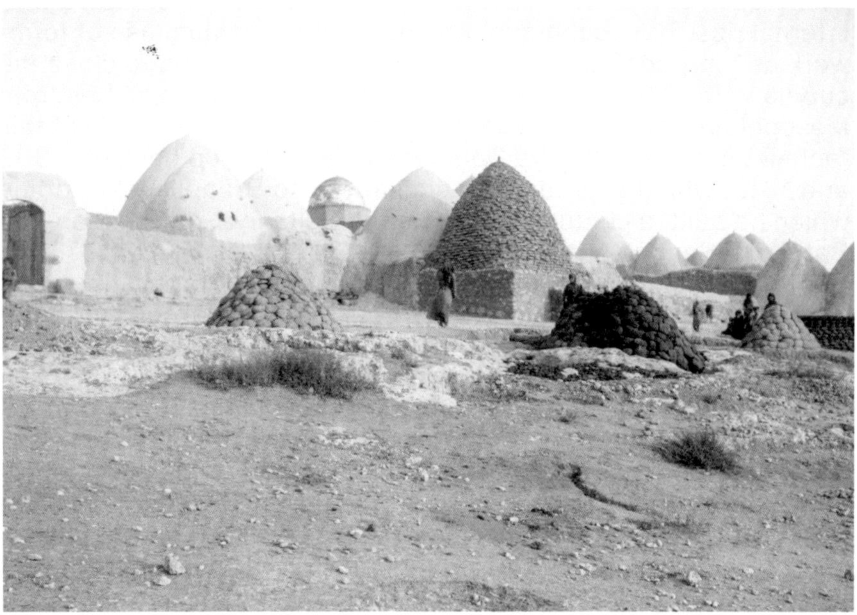

fig. (002) Bee-hive village [Moselmeih, Syria]. G. Eric and Edith Matson Photograph Collection. Courtesy of Library of Congress.

15

Eton, *Turkish Empire*, 222.

16

Marco G. Brambilla, "Construction Techniques of the Dome of the Mausoleum of Uljaytu in Sultaniyya," *Domes in the World – International Scientific Conference*, (2012).

In addition to time and with the absence of solid materials, geometry (and the craft of knowing how to deal with it) becomes yet another source of building. Curved lines that start such as arches and vaults begin to abound in geometry to transport loads safely to the ground. Here, knowledge and experience become necessary in construction by placing mud bricks in their correct places using different tools such as small formworks for windows and door arches, or flexible string systems as guide work to find the correct form of the domes during construction. Before his note on Aleppo's domed houses, Eton states that "In some parts of Asia, I have seen cupolas of a considerable size, built without any kind of timber support." He described a double compass system where two poles are fixed in the central axis of the copula but at two different levels. The first "describes the outer part of the cupola; lower down is fixed to the post [of] another pole...and describes the inside of the cupola, giving the difference of thickness of the masonry at top and bottom, and every intermediate part, with the greatest possible exactness."† What Eton is describing in this [15] section is the construction of the continuous double-shell domes, where each pole describes a shell, and the two are connected with internal ribs. This technique allowed for the minimum use of formwork as "only scaffolding for the workmen is required to close the cupola at [the] top," and the emergence of large-span domes from Mesopotamia to Central Asia. The oldest and finest example of this technique is the Sultaniya Dome in Zanjan, erected between 1302 and 1312, which shared many similarities to Brunelleschi's dome which he built, a century later after the Sultaniya, for the Florence Cathedral Santa Maria Del Fiore.† [16]

This evolving knowledge between geography, time, and geometry extends beyond the usual definition of local building methods as a set of techniques developed through transmission and repetition. This knowledge becomes the malleability that, when meeting new emerging scenarios, induces flexibility and risk-taking much more than the repetition of a physical or formative process. This flexibility is the basis for the persistence of earthen-building knowledge to the present day. It contributes to the accommodation of the change in resources and landscapes: from hilly limestone in Hama, a salty wetland with reeds and poplar trees near Aleppo, to the basalt volcanic tuff fields near the Euphrates River.

In the village of Sfiera, Al Hajj Ali lives in a mud house with multiple domes. The two main ones are used as a living room and a kitchen. A third, much smaller dome is called *matban* and is used to house stacks of hay after the harvest season when Al Hajj Ali and his brothers used to empty the bags of hay from an opening in the upper part of the dome. Today, the upper window is closed, and the room is used as storage. Next to the matban dome is another one of the same size, called *tannour*. It used to serve as the space for bread baking, but is now in ruin. On the other side of the smaller domes is a sleeping room with mud walls and a flat wooden ceiling of poplar wooden beams covered with wooden planks and mud.

After half a decade away from home, Al Hajj Ali returned to Sfiera in 2018, repairing the fence, re-cladding some of the walls, and replanting the yard. He dates the domes through people, saying that the central dome in the house had existed for more than 100 years because he did not attend its construction, but his father did when he was a child. As for the small domes of straw and the tannour, he mentions that they are nearly 60 years old because he helped build them.

To build a mud house, the foundation is laid with stone from a nearby hill, raising it above ground to at least the height of the builder's knee. On this base, rows of double mud bricks are laid. The bricks, called *toubb*, or *labneh* are usually made by the people of the house, and the process is called *darb al laban*. A mold called *jawzeh* is used to make bricks from clay and straw, with an average size of 25 by 30 centimeters and an average thickness of 10 centimeters. Al Hajj Ali mentions making adobe with his father starting at the beginning of spring to obtain the necessary bricks for the domes to be built in the summer. The soil is often brought from Melluha – where Pedro Teixeira stopped in the sixteenth century – because its black soil is stickier and is of better quality than Sfiera's red soil. Al Hajj Ali pulls out a brick from the ruined dome and says: "I made this brick a long time ago."

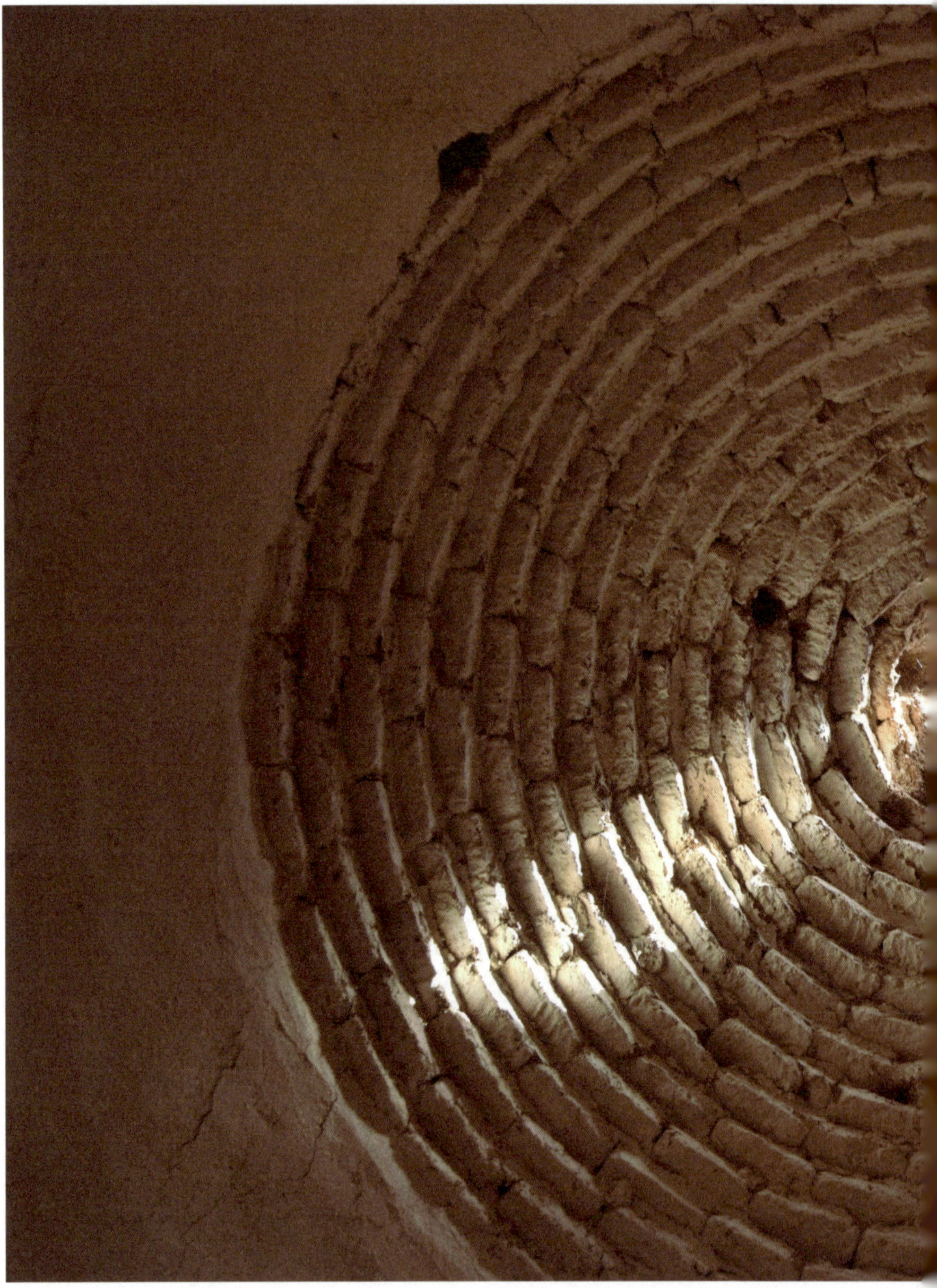

fig. (003) Domed house near Melluha, 2022. Photo by author.

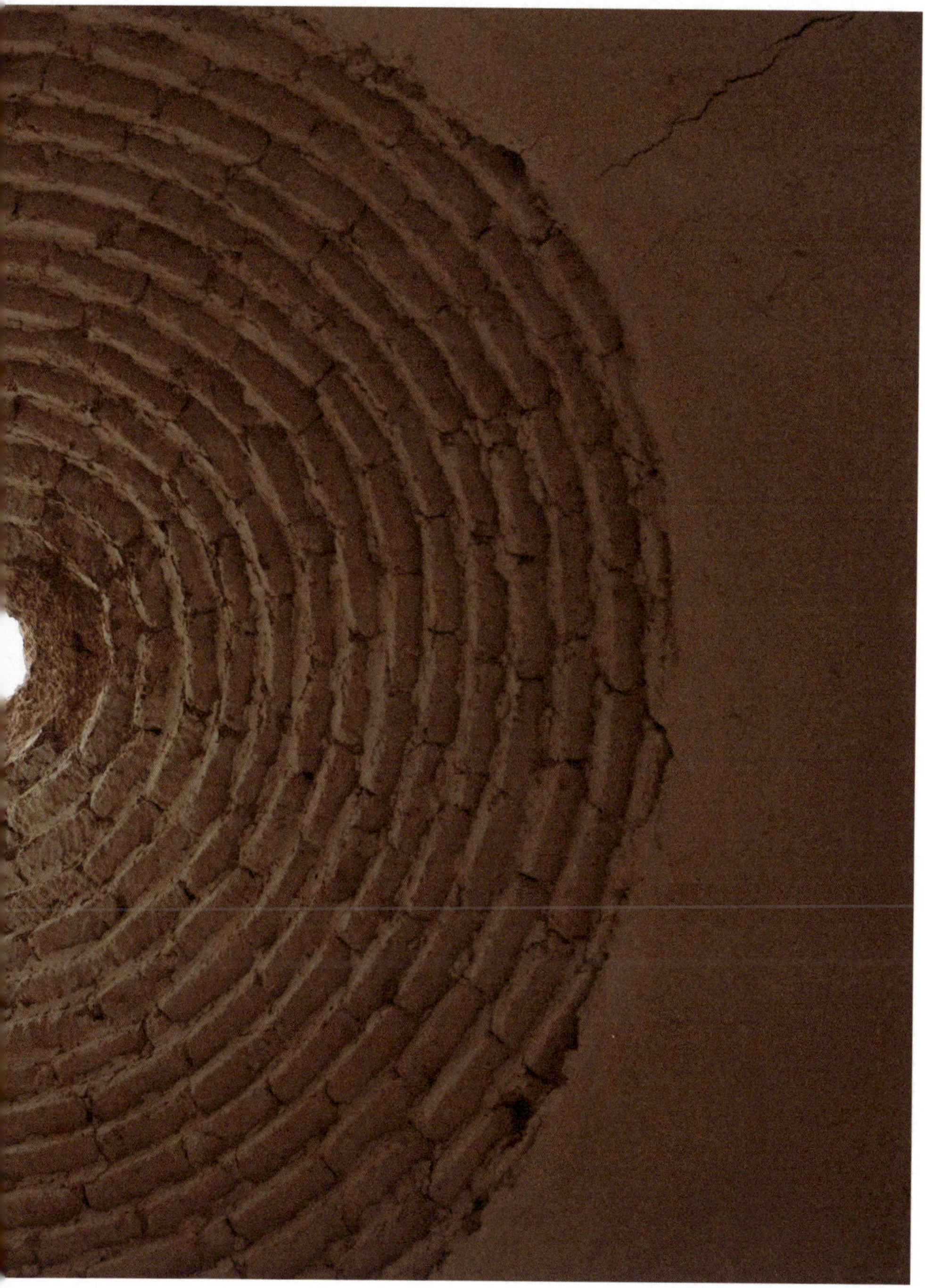

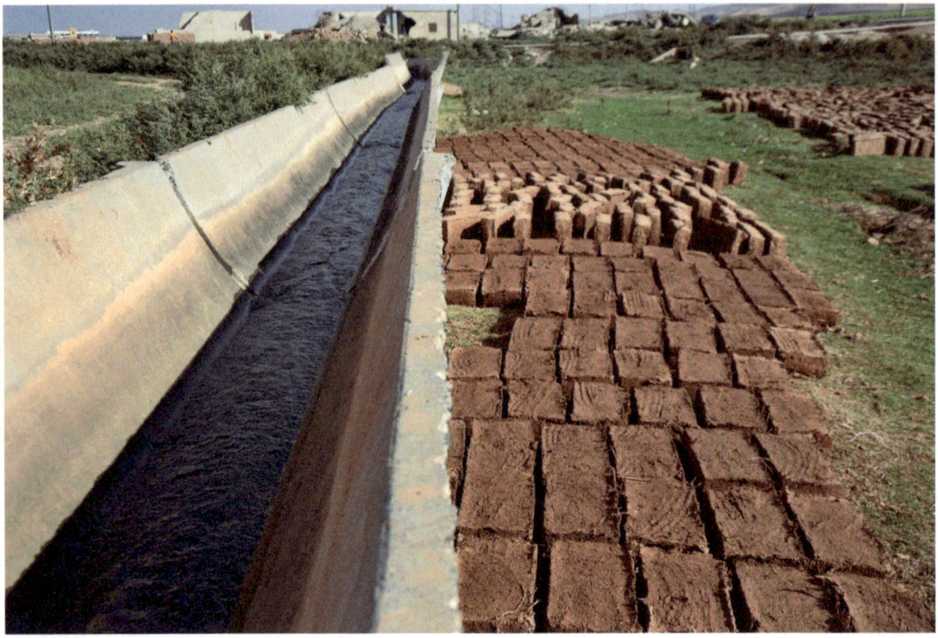

fig. (004) Mud brick making in summer 2022, near Sfiera. Photo by author.

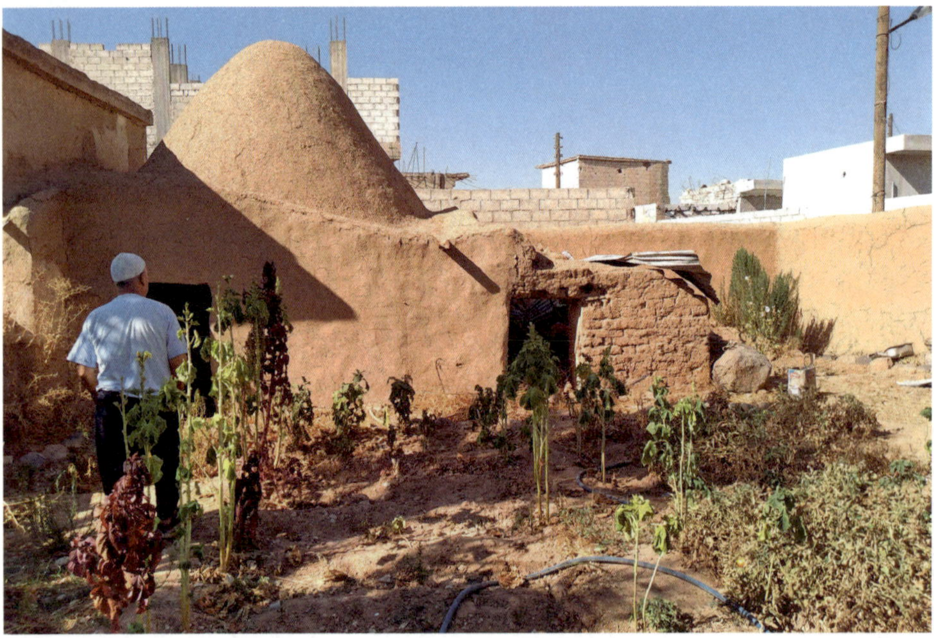

fig. (005) Al Hajj Ali's house in Sfeira. Photo by author.

As for the construction of the dome itself, it is subject to a generalized rule of corbelling bricks, stacked spirally in a continuous path from the beginning to the end of the dome construction. The whole process depends on ergonomics. The distance of the cantilever of bricks from the previous row is estimated using the width of fingers called *esbaa'*. For the lower parts, the cantilevering distance between the sequent rows is two or three fingers, and it becomes four in the upper part of the dome. In the upper part of the dome, the construction process becomes more laborious and relatively slow. In the case of domes resting on walls like those of Al Hajj Ali, the builder stands at the top of the wall, called the *tyakh*, to cover the dome. In other cases, the builder arranges stones or wood protruding onto the dome's body during construction. These elements, called *dawasat* or pedals, will become the ladder designated for building on the one hand and for future maintenance on the other. In the absence of these stones, the builder digs holes in the dome to use it as a ladder. Thus, the worker's body and limbs become the most comprehensive determinant for the construction of the dome so that it takes its shape in his likeness. After completing the work for the body of the building, it is covered with a mix of mud and straw. This clad shell becomes the skin that the building changes every two or three years, and the shield that resists weather factors as long as it is changed and maintained. Finally, the construction uses *hawwar* stone, a fragile limestone, to clad parts of the building by dissolving it in water.

Heading south, on the path to Basra, Al Kalafa Abu Rihana still uses gypsum to build barrel vaults for ceilings in Baghdad and Basra. He does not fasten halves of the vault on the ground anymore but stands on a scaffold bridging the space between two beams with a sequence of very shallow arches. The technique, locally called *akada*, is still in practice today. Because it relies on the fast-setting gypsum or plaster of Paris, the work of Abu Rihan offers a fast and formwork-free process for ceiling construction compared to reinforced concrete. He works with his two hands, one hand adding the gypsum mortar while the other catches a flying mud brick, thrown to him by his apprentice, and places it in the arch. The 1.2-meter span shallow vaults on beams became common in Iraq after the 1920s; today they are mainly used in informal settings. The vaults-on-beams system is a variant of the very sophisticated brick vaulting culture in Iraq and Mesopotamia, where pitched brick squinch or crossed vaults cover the full area of the room without the use of beams. This formwork-free construction is called *akada hasiriyah*, referring to *hasirya* (woven carpet), which resembles the herringbone coursing of the brick structure. For such a craft to continue, it had to move from the large sail vaults to a more industrialized system of vaults-on-beams.

Moving further south down the Arabian Peninsula to Al Bidya in Fujairah, is another structure that astonished Portuguese and Dutch travelers in the seventeenth century for its earth-domed ceiling. Al Bidya Mosque in today's UAE still stands as a singular and rare example of earthen-domed buildings in a region where mosques are usually roofed with flat wooden ceilings.† [17] The mosque, located in Al Bidya near Khor Fakkan, was mentioned as early as 1645 by the Portuguese as an "old strange structure." The region's "mountainous" coast, as Pietro Della Valle described it in 1625 while passing through the Gulf on his way to Basra, offered basalt stone, earth, and lime for the construction of the mosque.† [18] The mosque contains four domes that spring from a square plan, intersecting in the middle to rest on one central column thought to be made with a single piece of timber and many layers of plaster.† [19] The domes, built without any temporary support or shuttering, are not very different from other mosques in nearby regions, such as Al Hammouda Mosque in Jaalan which contains 52 domes. While archeological investigation shows that the mosque was built around 1446, the origin and style of its construction are thought to be a fusion of different building cultures: from earthen buildings in Iraq and Iran to the domed mausoleum in Yemen. Al Bidya Mosque is an example of how local building techniques can be exchanged when approached through its contextual conditions. Building with earth, or without wood, is associated with aridity. This aridity becomes a vehicle of exchange, where local building techniques can also be global. A dome in Aleppo or a vault in Basra are, in fact, the same manifestation of building strategies rooted in local resources, found in Al Bidya Mosque.

17

Didier Willems, "Les Mosquées Anciennes Dans l'Emirat de Fujaïrah: Un Maillon Entre Les Côtes Méridionales Du Golfe Arabo-Persique et Le Sultanat d'Oman ?," (*Archéologie Islamique* 10, 2000) 169–94.

18

Della Valle, *The Travels of Sig. Pietro Della Valle, a Noble Roman, into East-India and Arabia Deserta in Which, the Several Countries, Together with the Customs, Manners, Traffique, and Rites Both Religious and Civil, of Those Oriental Princes and Nations, Are Faithfully Described.*

19

Nasser Hussein Al Aboodi, *Al Bidya Mosque, One of the UAE's Old Mosques: A Historical Archeological Study* (Sharjah: Ittihad Kutaba' wa Udaba' Al Imarat, 2009).

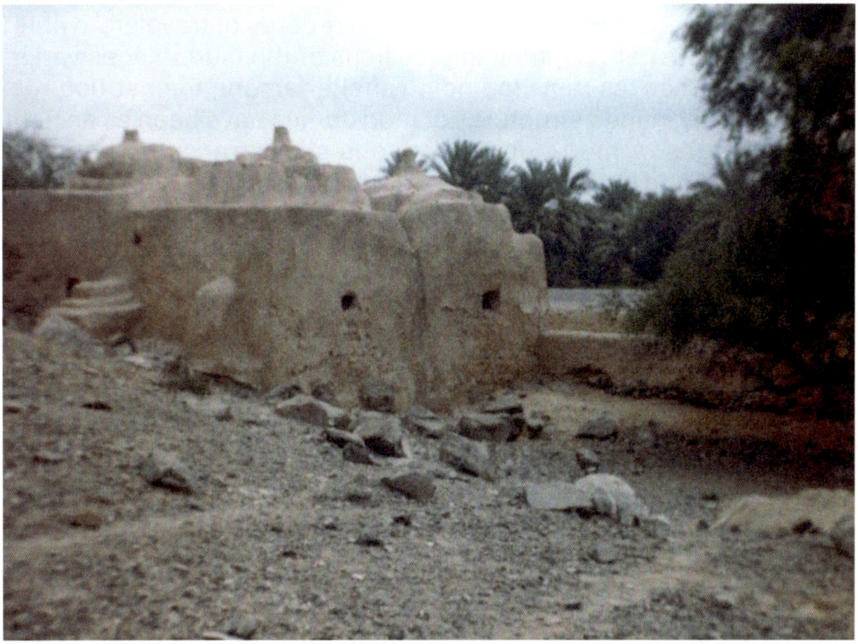

fig. (006) Al Badiyah Mosque in Fujairah built in 1446 © UAE National Library and Archives.

Never Out of Repair: Desolation and Return

"The dome does not fall," Al Hajj Ali says with great enthusiasm. He repeats the sentence in anticipation of the usual comments he hears again and again from engineers and architects questioning the durability of earth. He pauses after the statement and adds a condition, "as long as I am alive." For him, clay certainly crumbles and falls in the lab under increasing humidity, but the mud in his house is not at all similar to the mud of a laboratory, as it is alive as long as the family is alive. At the beginning of every winter, Al Hajj Ali climbs the *tyakh* at the edge of his house around the dome to check its condition; he removes the nests of birds or the holes from mice and closes them with a bit of mud. Every five years, he changes the upper part of the dome cladding. The work needs a day or two and is simple, periodic, and direct to help the giant keep standing.

In architectural history, a domical circular dwelling has always been considered a transitional dwelling – from nomadic to settled living, from ephemerality to permanence. However, a domical house in today's mud architecture is not an ancient state of transition stuck in time and culture, or a glitch in the evolution process. It is a dynamic expression of this transitionality, evolving with materials from mud to concrete. It is with this transitionality that the mud-domed house survived. Since the earliest known records of travelers' writing in the sixteenth century, their impressions of the mud villages varied from seeing them as ruins to finding shelter among their structures. Put differently, ruined structures of mud domes have been as ancient as the villages. A mud-domed house is still a transition between ephemerality and permanence. It is both a tent and a home. Therefore, a domed mud house's permanency does not stem from the strength of its building material but from the ease and accessibility of its construction, destruction, and reconstruction. With this notion, the mud villages themselves become mobile, following resources in the plains of Aleppo. Through this scope, domed houses are found in southern Anatolia through West Mesopotamia made throughout the centuries by builders from Abraham to Al Hajj Ali.

Today, many of these villages, cupulas, and prefabricated vaults are in ruin, as they were centuries ago. Relearning techniques is very different from rebuilding monuments. The resulting structures of these techniques do not matter as much as the continuation of the knowledge of how to make them. "The house stands as long as we stand." Al Hajj Ali affirms while looking up at the bricks of his dome. Also, one could add; the house is ruined as long as we are displaced. It is a tent, if we like, or a castle. The house is made from stone if we climb the mountain, straw if we follow the river, or mud if we descend into the swamps. The house stands if inhabited with care, and it melts back into soil if abandoned.

Kevin Mitchell

Privileging the Pragmatic

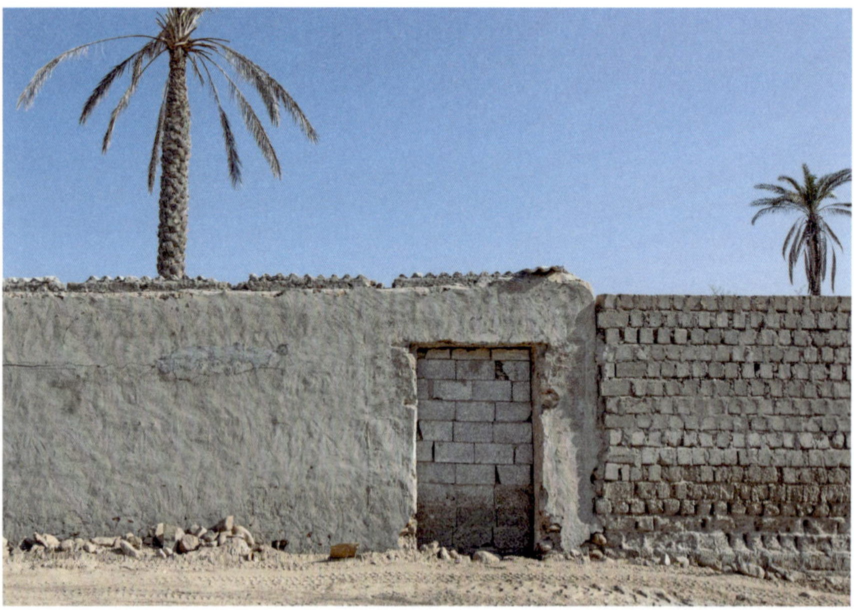

All photos by author.

The large-scale infrastructural interventions and small-scale provisional modifications to the landscape encountered along E88, E89, and Khorfakkan Road when traveling from the city of Sharjah to Khor Fakkan reveal differences in how time is made visible. As one winds through Al Hajar Mountain range, erosion and the removal of earth to accommodate the highways and tunnels connecting the east and west coasts of the United Arab Emirates (UAE) expose approximately 30 million years of natural history through remarkable geological formations. Conversely, photographs from small farms along the route illustrate the temporary and transient nature of the adaptations to the landscape that enables the production of agriculture.

01

Rasā'il Ikhwān al-Ṣafā', Volume 1, *Risāla* 8 as quoted in Mohammed Hamdouni Alami, *The Origins of Visual Culture in the Islamic World: Aesthetics, Art and Architecture in Early Islam*, (London: I.B. Tauris & Company, Ltd., 2015) 43.

02

Rasā'il Ikhwān al-Ṣafā', Volume 1, *Risāla* 2 as quoted in Alami, *Islamic World*, 63.

Cultivation in a water-scarce environment requires ingenuity and labor-intensive work to make the most of the minimal. The use and re-use of materials arranged in particular relationships in the service of agricultural production result in visually and texturally rich combinations, although the reasons for selecting materials and employing construction techniques were likely more pragmatic than poetic. The *Rasā'il Ikhwān al-Ṣafā'*, a treatise believed to have been written around the tenth century that addresses mathematics, epistemology, and metaphysical cosmology, defines agriculture – along with building and weaving – as crafts based on primary needs:

> [...] the primary purpose of some of these crafts is imposed by need, while other crafts follow and serve the first ones. Other crafts complement and complete them. And among the crafts some are meant for beauty and adornment. There are three crafts of the first kind [imposed by need]: agriculture, weaving, and building. All other
> [01] crafts follow, serve, and complete those three [...]†

The *Rasā'il Ikhwān al-Ṣafā'* also emphasizes the importance of the consideration of arithmetic, geometry, and proportions in the process of "estimation" prior to beginning work:

> [...] because every craftsman who builds and combines volumes needs to estimate beforehand the place where to make the work, when to make it and when to start. He must consider if he can do it, and reckon with which tools he might make it. He also needs to imagine how to combine its parts and make them match each other. This is the Sensory al-Handasa that is used in most crafts which is the
> [02] matching of diverse volumes with each other.†

Whereas agriculture, weaving, and building are considered crafts of the same order in the *Rasā'il Ikhwān al-Ṣafā',* – and therefore all should be subject to planning prior to initiating work – the contemporary activities on the farms support and challenge the premise set forth in the treatise as there is evidence of work that both relies on and eschews arithmetic, geometry, and proportions in the process of "estimation." The seasonal organization of crops into precise rows and the ordered positioning of irrigation systems have clearly been planned and laid out in a systematic fashion to maximize land use. In terms of building, the gates that allow access to fields are, in many instances, adorned with geometrically constructed and well-proportioned patterns by skilled metalworkers. However, site-built elements such as boundary walls reveal processes of assembly characterized by improvisation and resourcefulness.

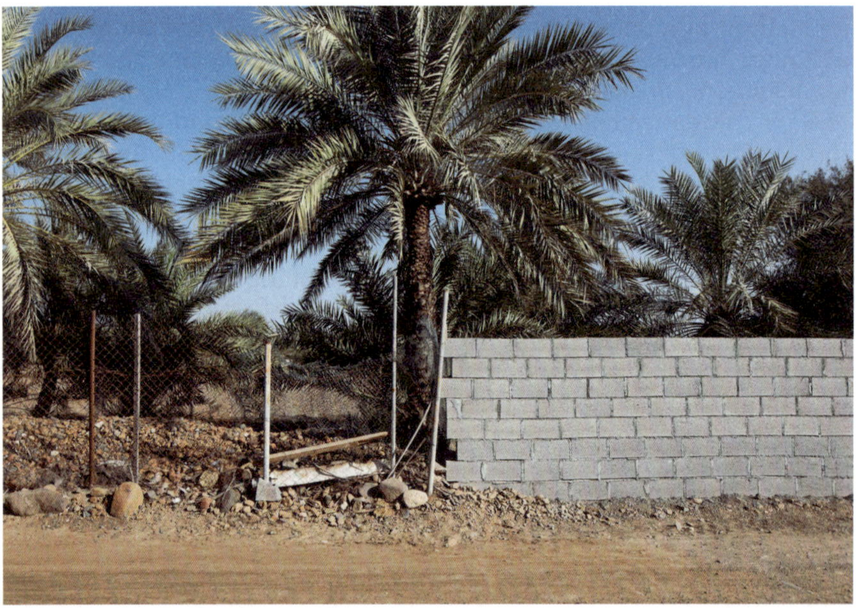

Walls separating arid from cultivated areas, define property limits and protect yields. Although the walls play an important role, they are often composed in a makeshift manner without consideration of arithmetic, geometry, and proportion. Even in cases where materials such as concrete masonry units provide a proportional system based on standardized modules, variety results from unexpected changes in bond patterns, the reuse of material to renovate and repair, and additions to extend existing wall planes with dissimilar materials. Transitions from one material to another along a wall surface are rarely treated in ways that enable integration, yet the juxtaposition of texture, color, and varying degrees of transparency at the junctures are engaging because of the visual contrast that ranges from subtle to strong.

Material used for walls also includes woven shade cloth intended for reducing the impact of solar radiation on plants. As the cloth is not self-supporting, it is often stretched and attached to chain-link fencing. Exposure to wind and temperature fluctuations reduces its tautness which, over time, results in draping that enhances the interplay of light and shadow across the billowing surface. The cloth is also activated by the silhouette of vertical supports and delicate diagonal lines of the chain-link fencing that are cast on the material.

In contrast to the geologic time encountered when traveling across Al Hajar Mountains to reach the farms, the plants, shade cloth enclosures, and walls constructed of concrete masonry units also reveal the passage of time – albeit in far shorter intervals that may be measured in growing seasons. The rows of crops that are barely visible after sowing become more evident when the plants emerge from the ground before disappearing after harvesting. Walls and enclosures, although more long-lasting, appear transitory: the interplay between intense sunlight in the UAE and the textures of surfaces causes change throughout the day; and the transformation precipitated by weathering, repairs, and renovations results in irregularities that render the passage of time discernible.

The classification of agriculture, weaving, and building as crafts imposed by need in the *Rasā'il Ikhwān al-Ṣafā'* acknowledges the importance of these activities for providing food, clothing, and shelter. Even though the treatise is a reflection of the period in which it was written, it importantly affirms the value of craft and recognizes the investment of labor in activities necessary to feed, clothe, and house us.

The photographs of fragments from farms along E88, E89, and Khorfakkan Road frame particular aspects of built work created to support the craft of agriculture. In addition to depicting informal approaches to building that do not rely on arithmetic, geometry, and proportions, the images indicate that privileging the pragmatic can, nevertheless, result in picturesque moments that transcend the intended purpose.

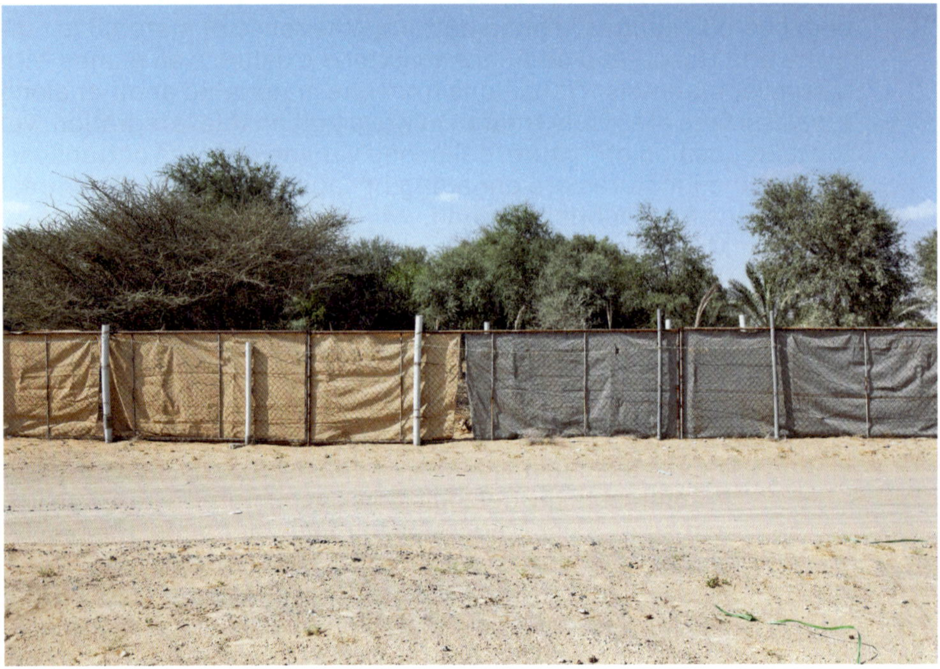

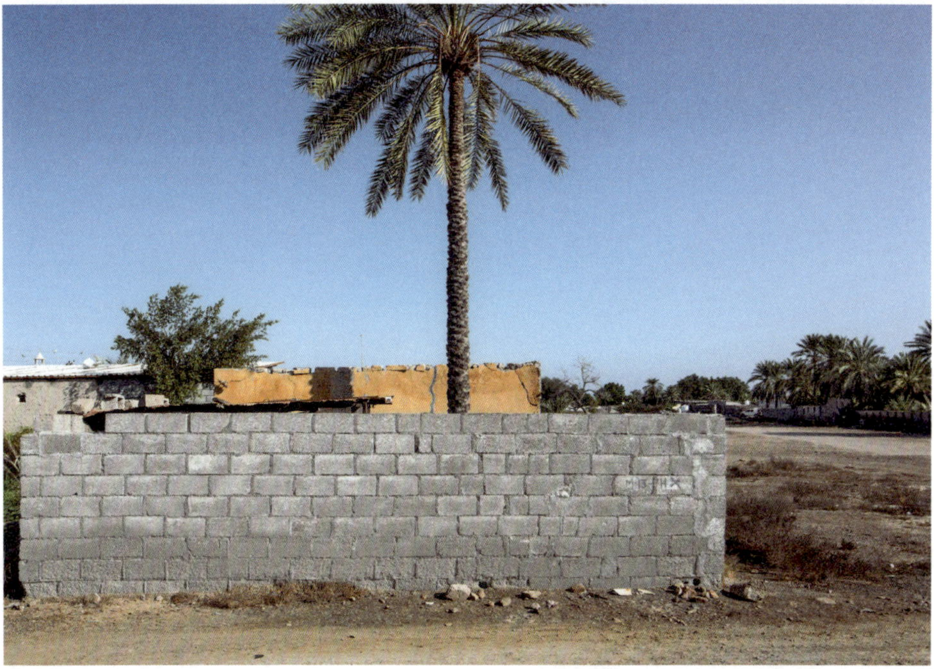

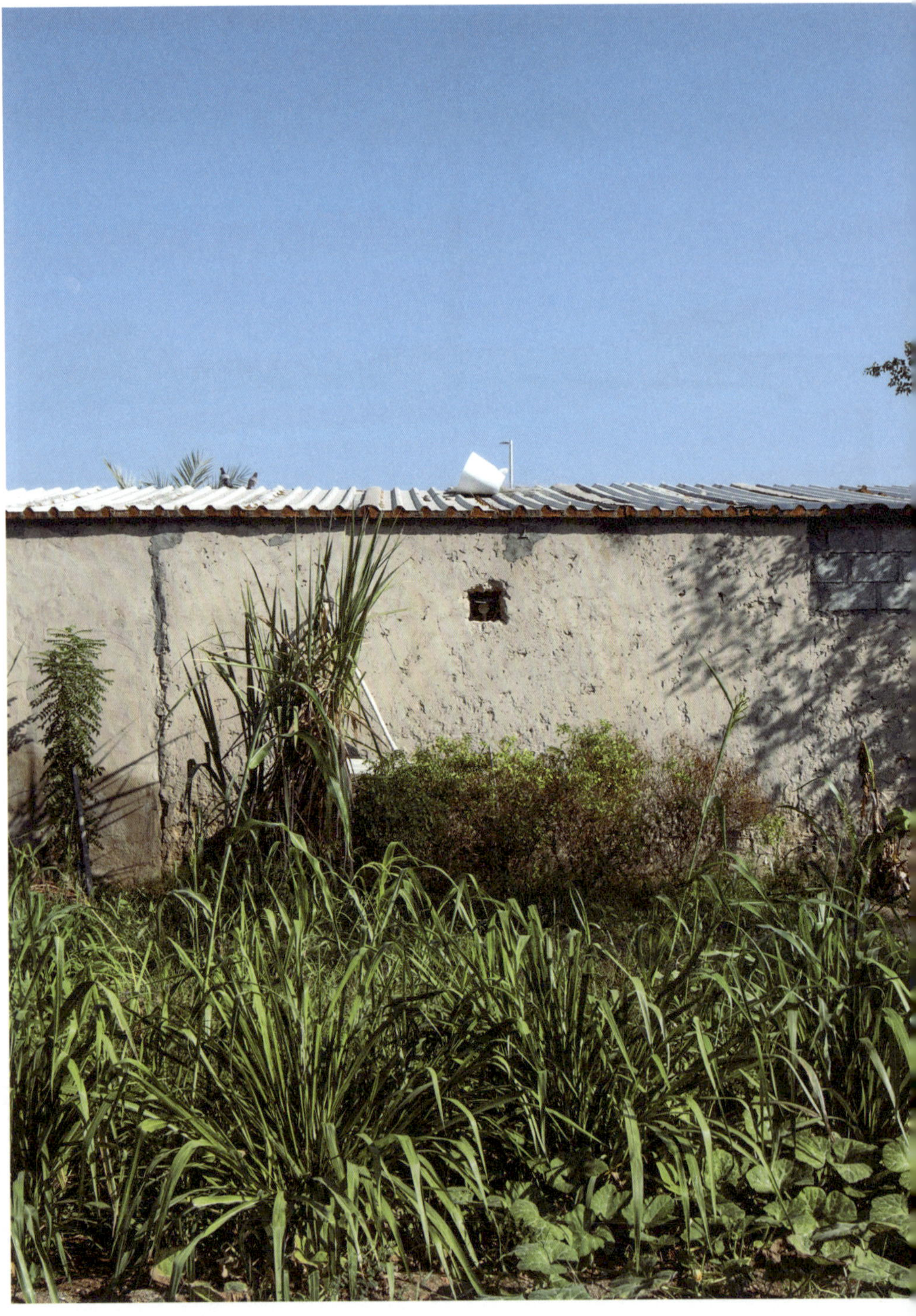

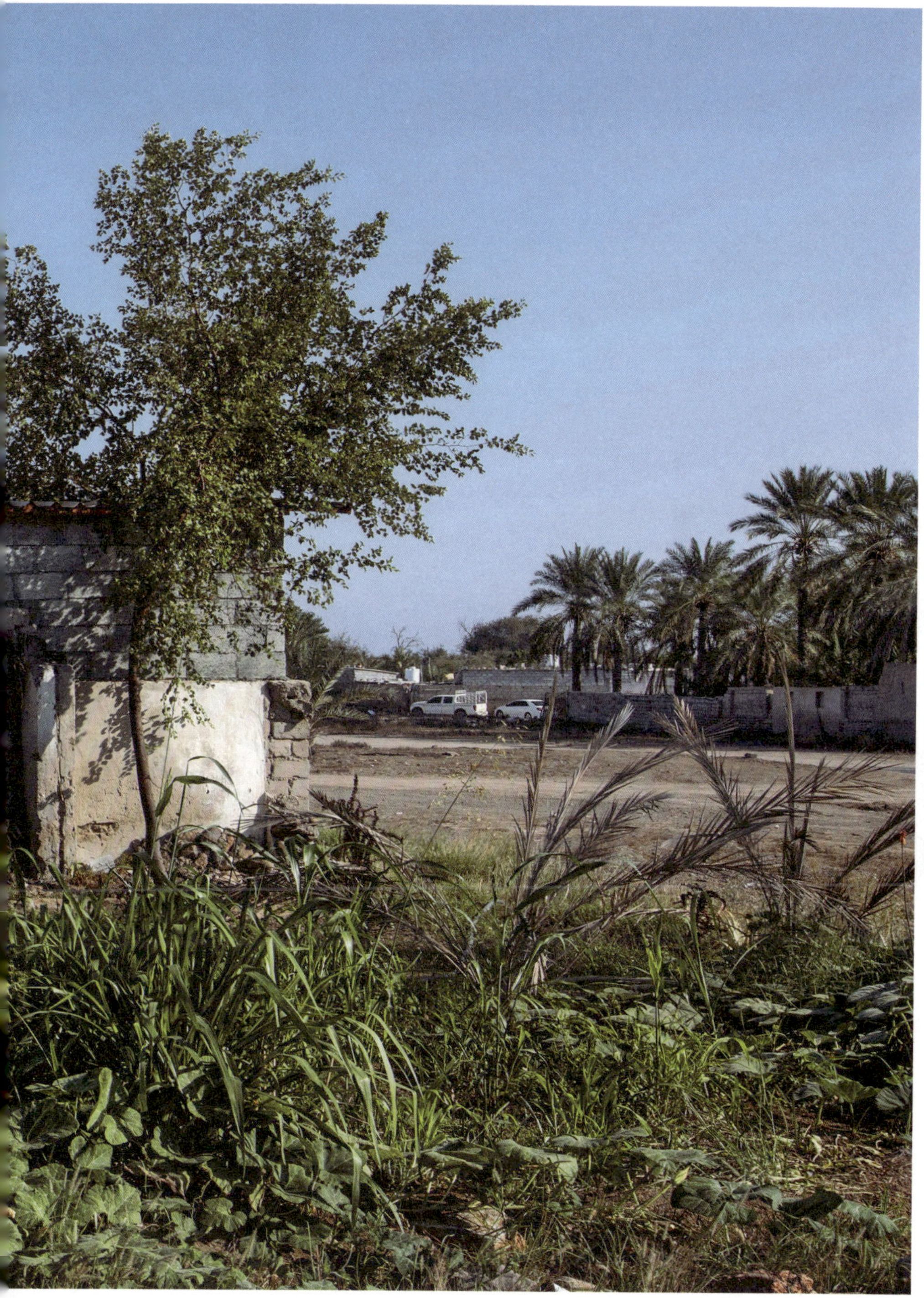

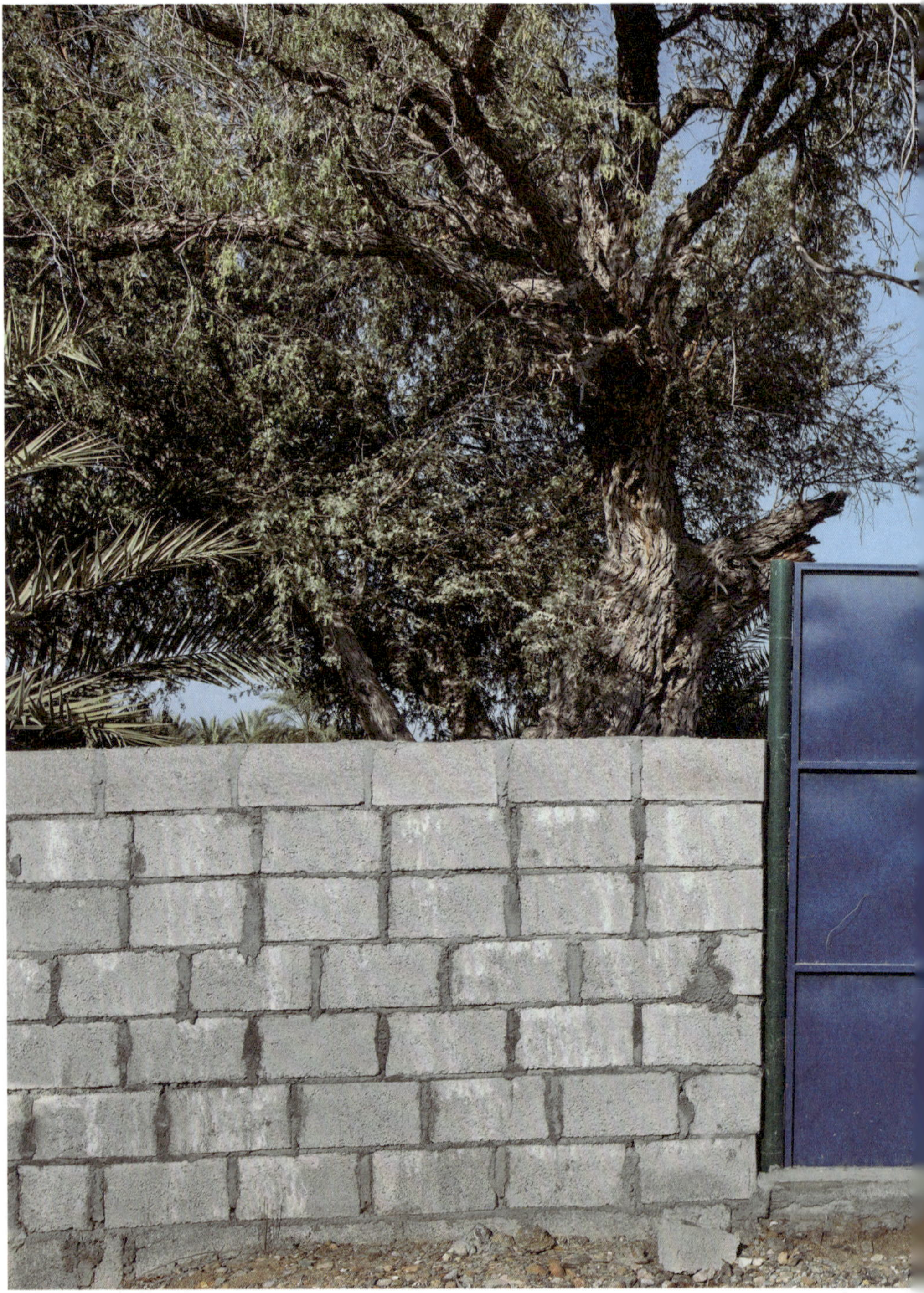

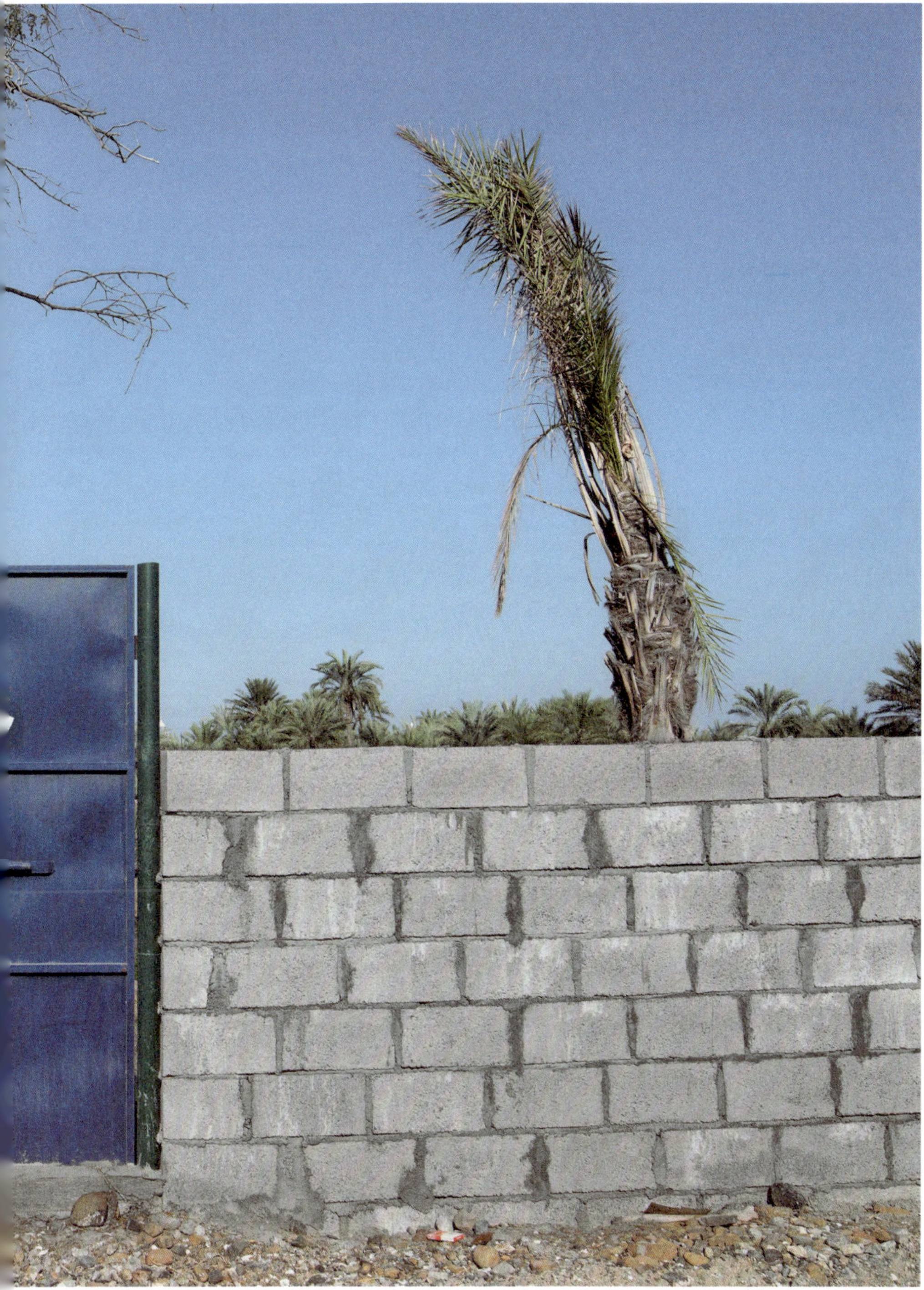

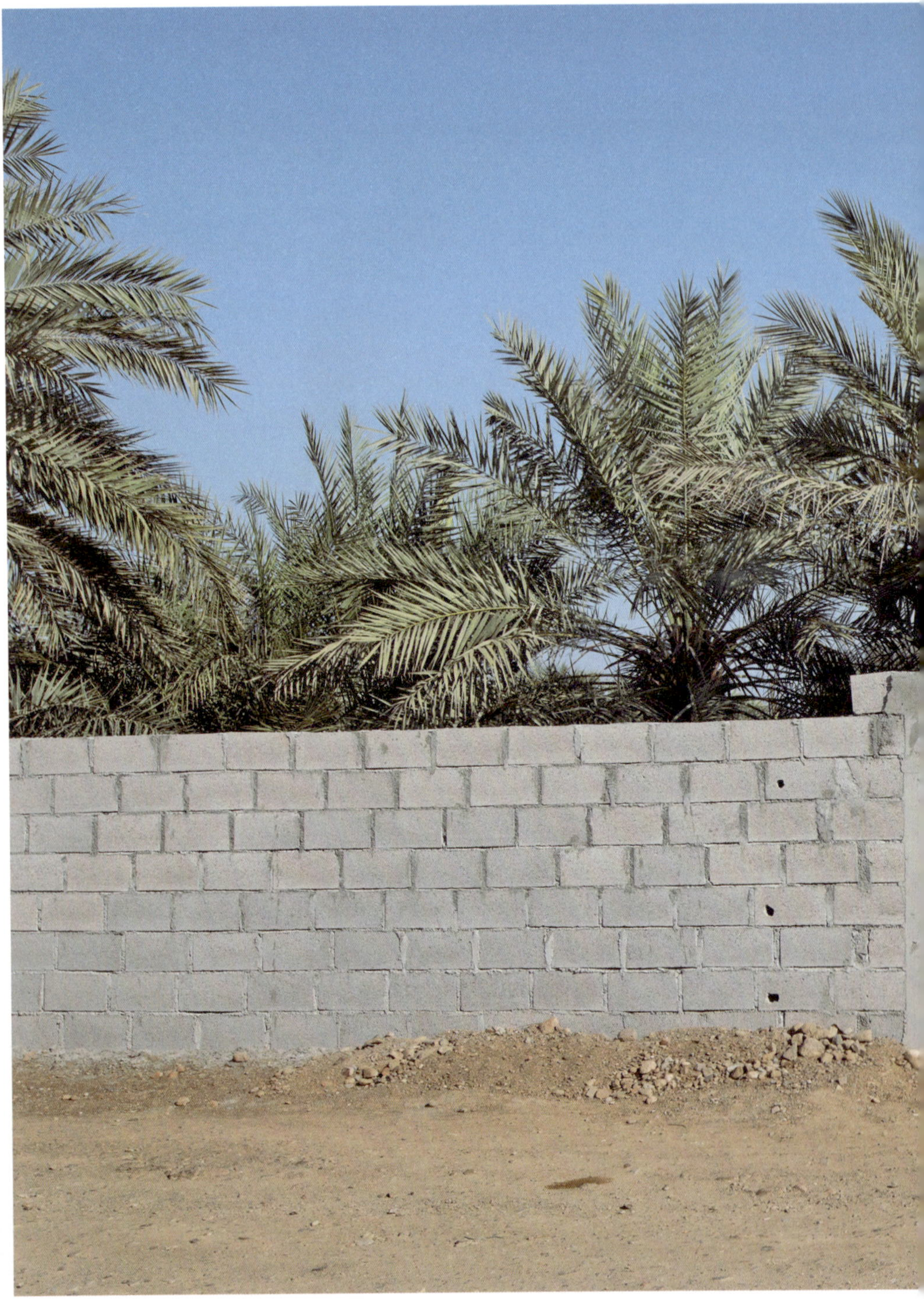

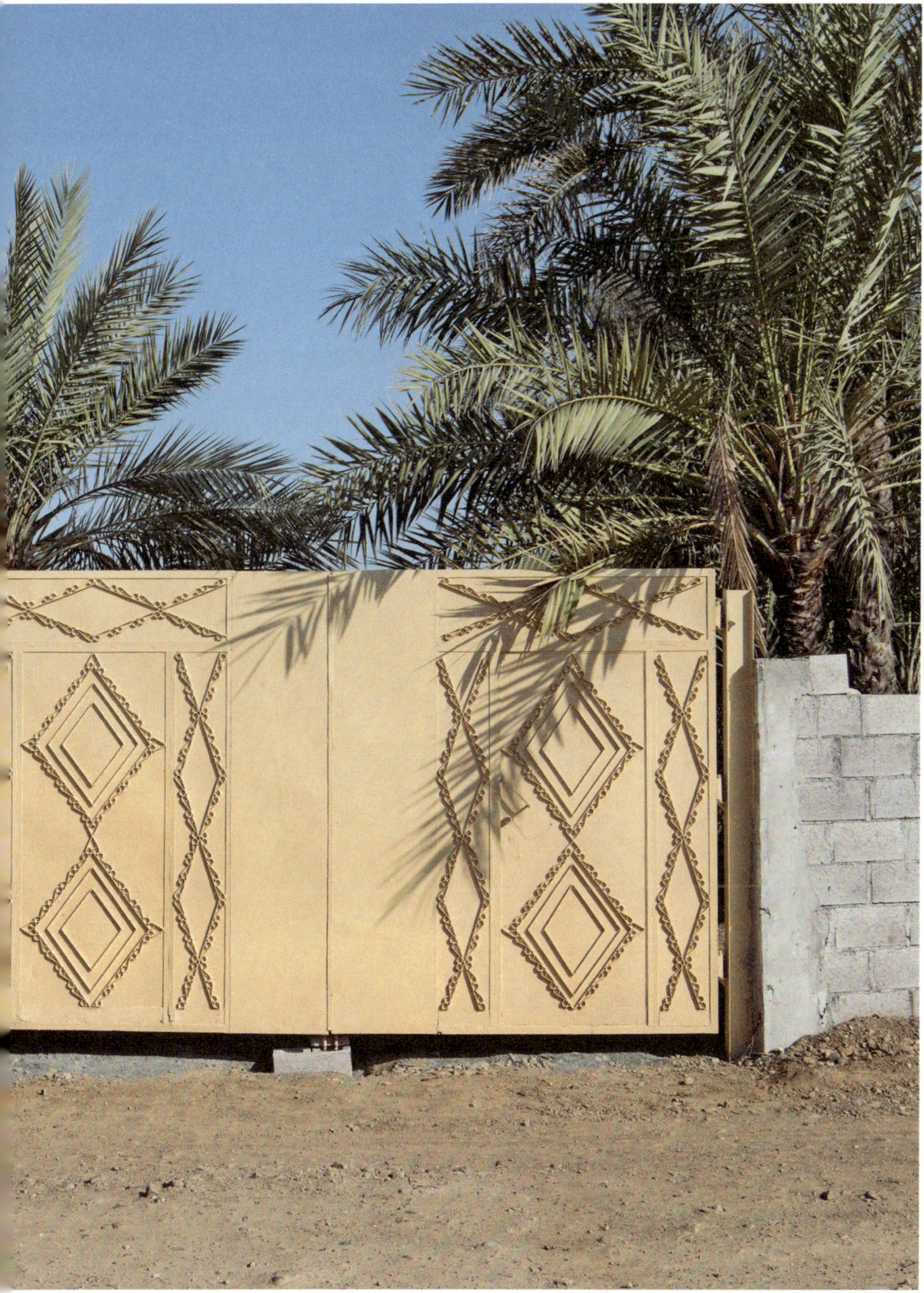

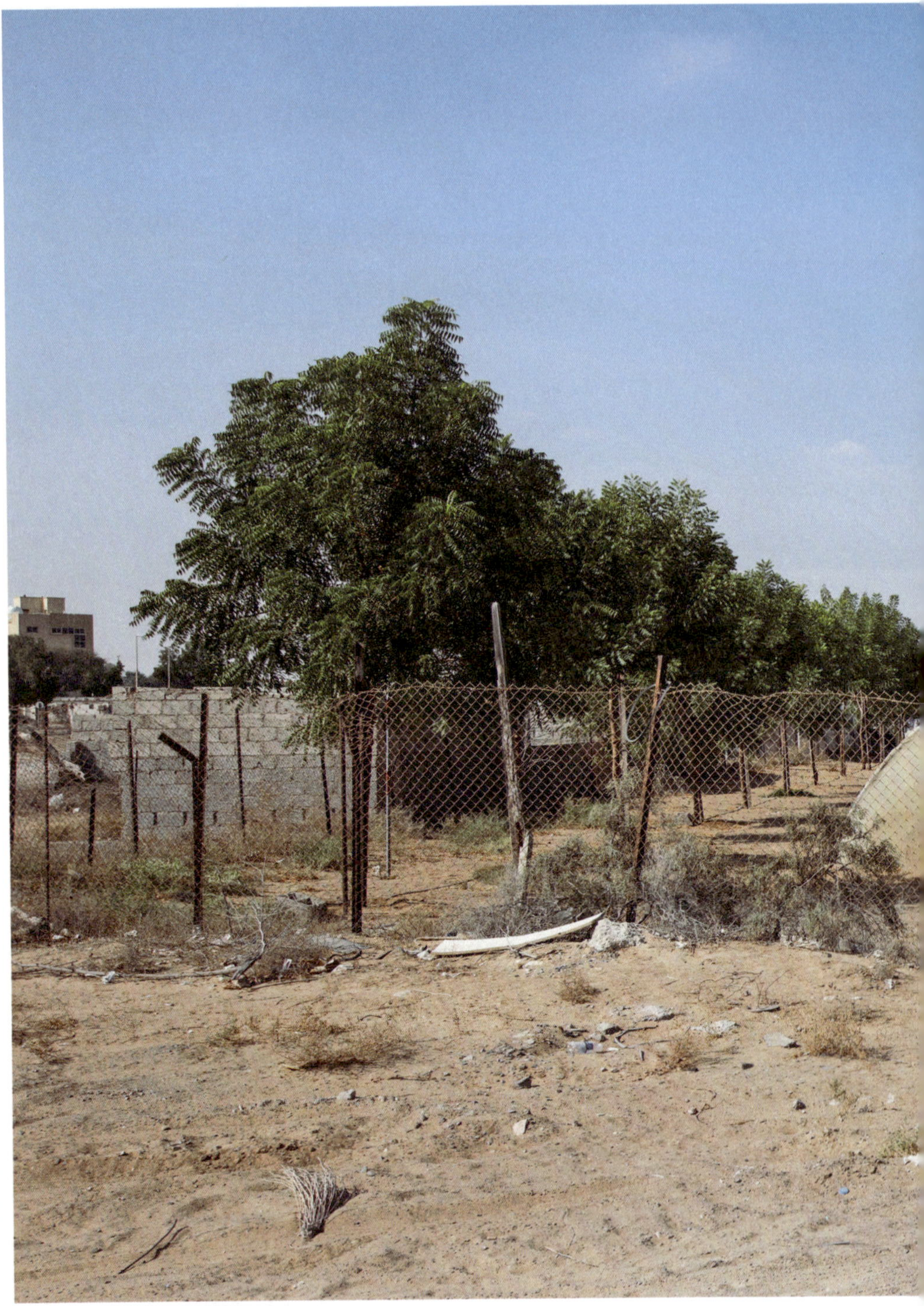

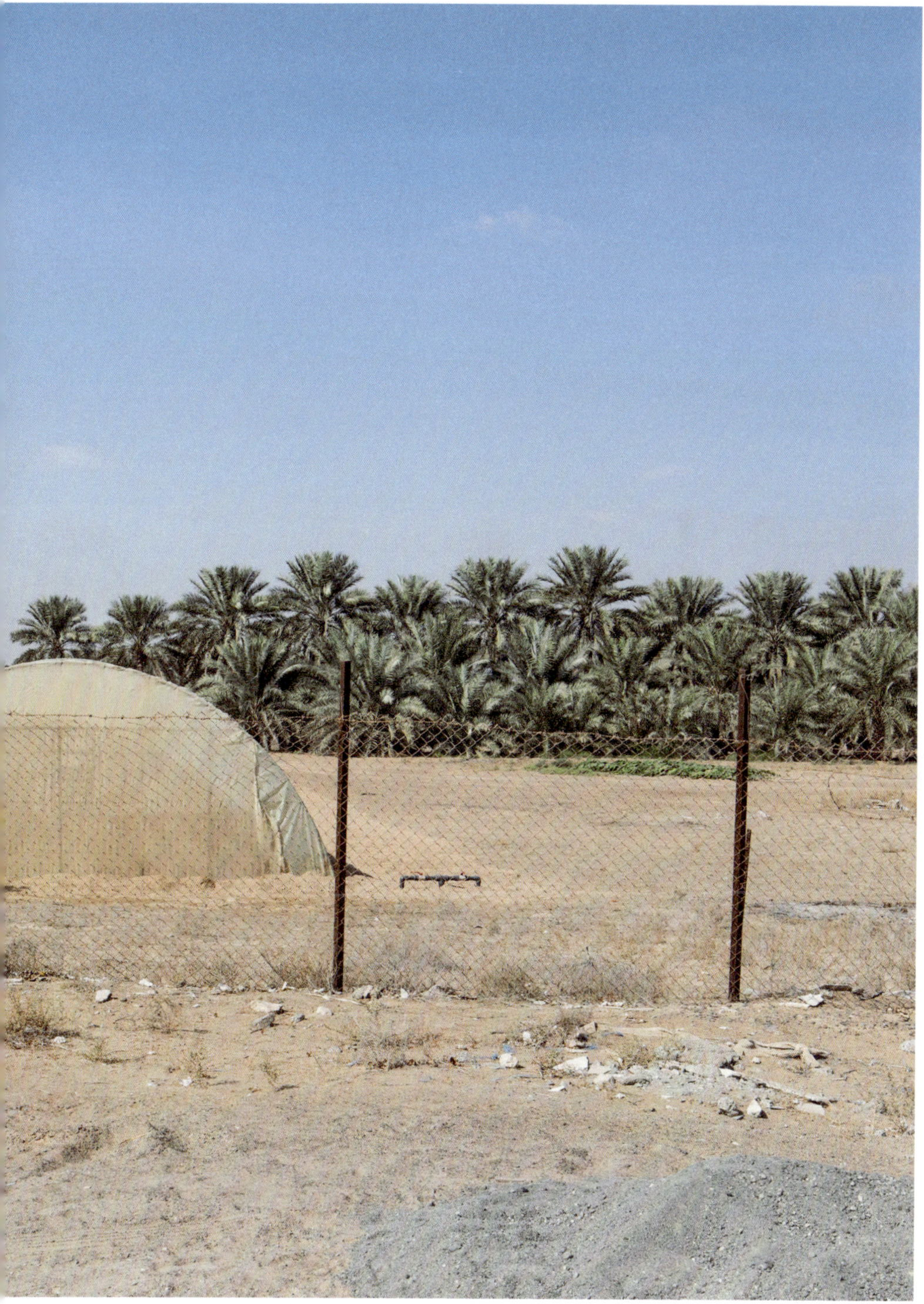

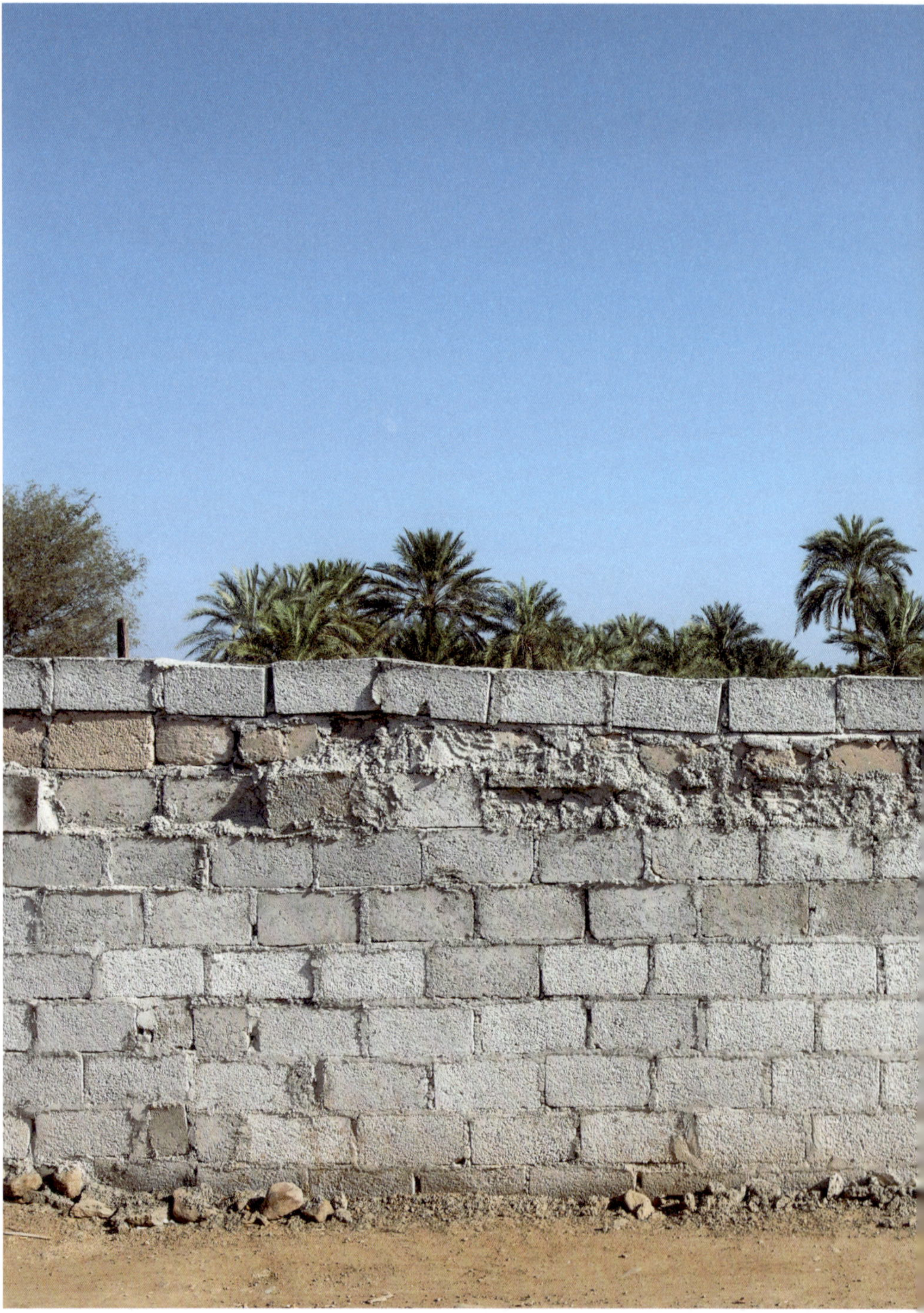

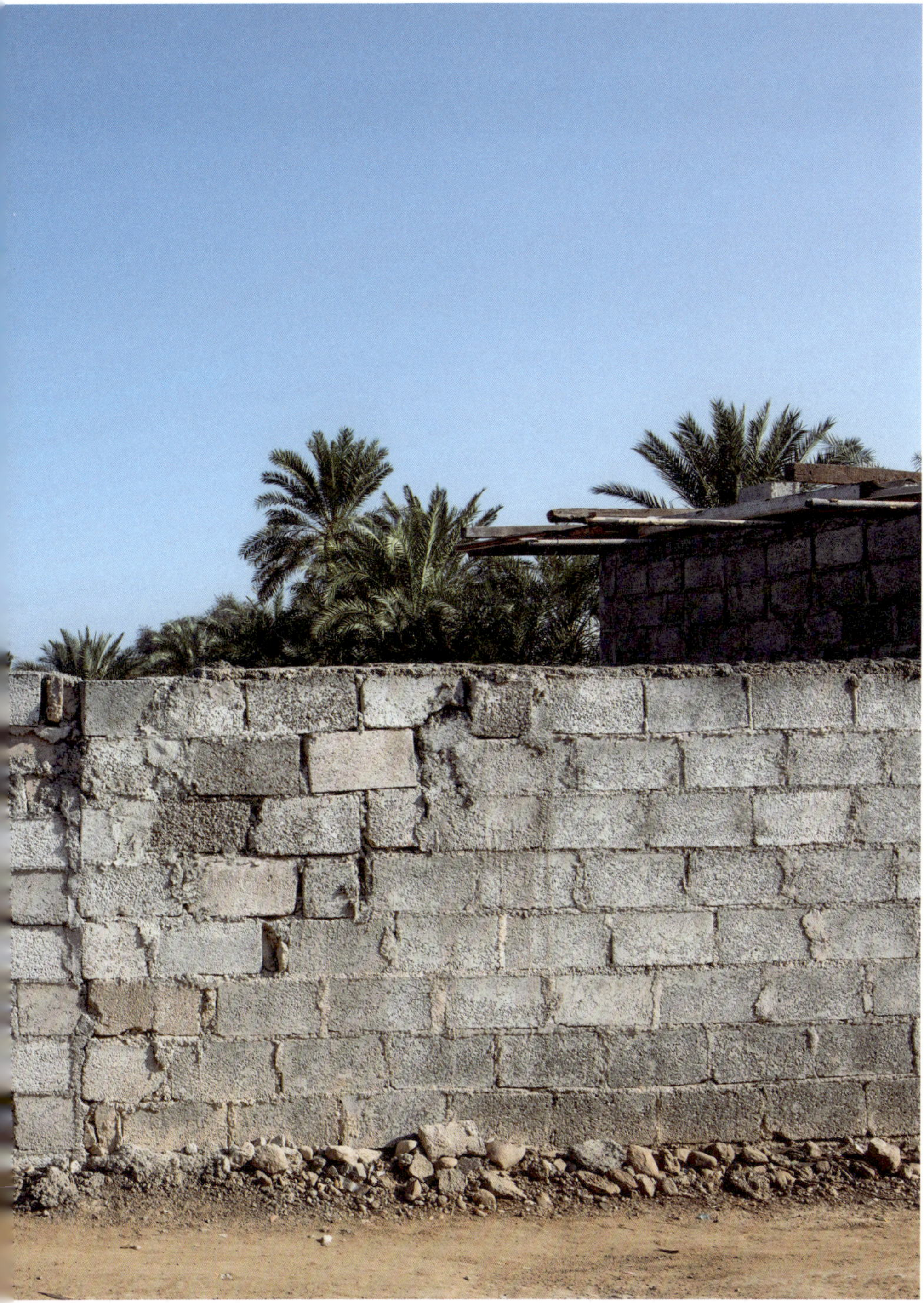

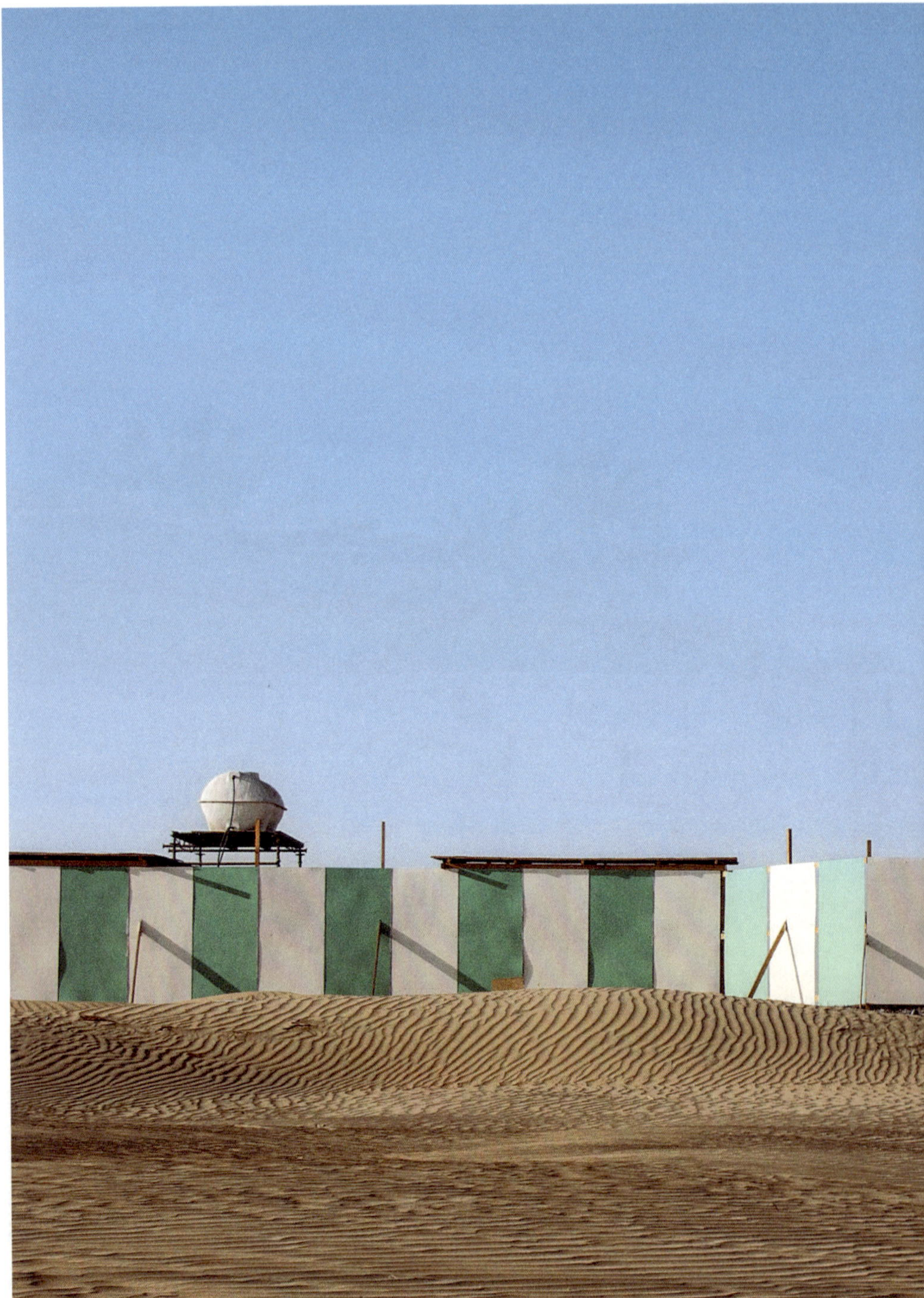

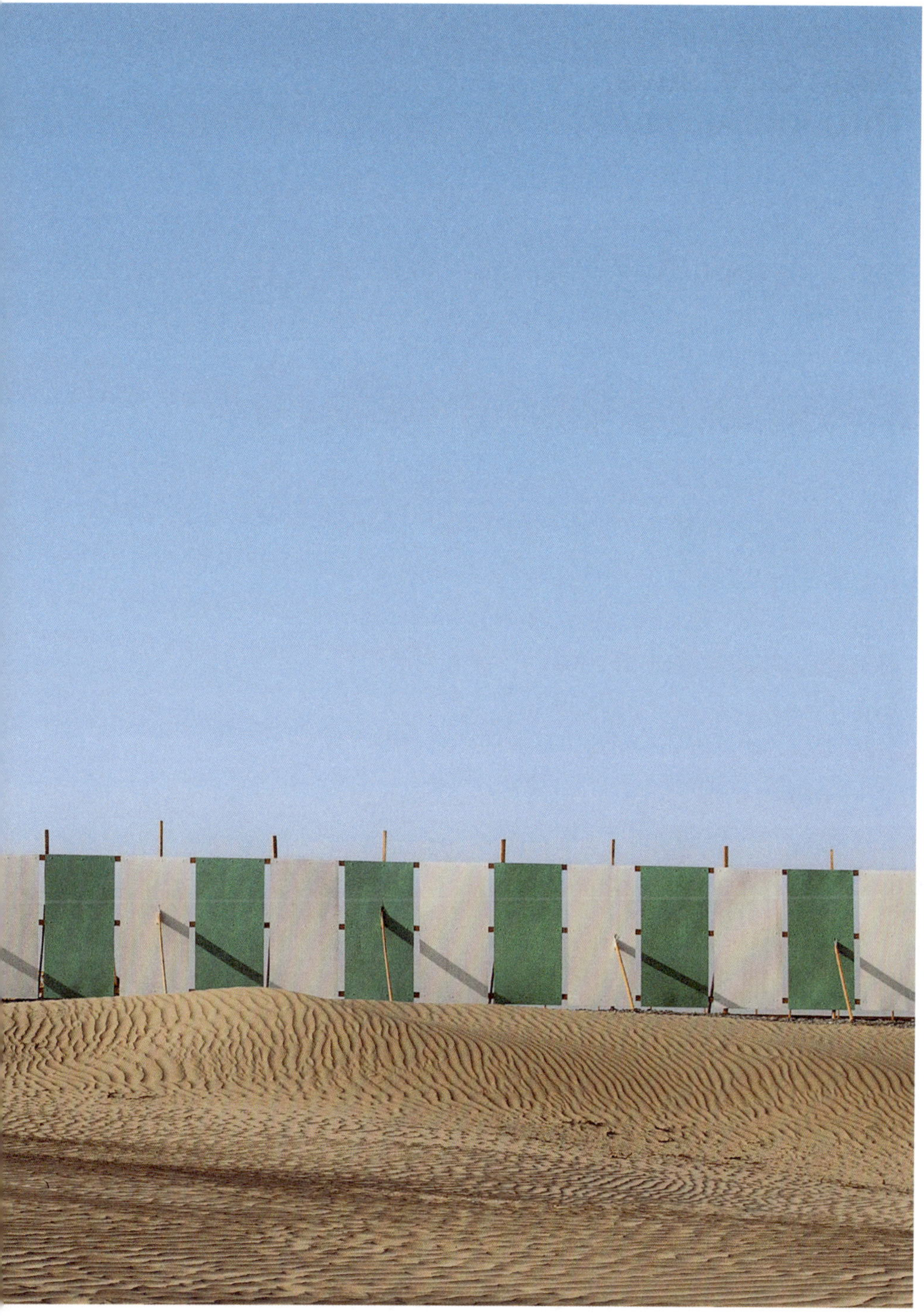

Samar Halloum

Avian Odysseys Through Aridity

Take out a map of the Northern Hemisphere and place your index finger to the west of Alaska. Now drag your finger westward across the Bering Strait to arrive in Siberia; move it southwest to Kazakhstan, through Mongolia, across Iran and the Gulf into the United Arab Emirates (UAE). After a brief pause, resume moving your finger west along the Arabian Peninsula and across the Red Sea to finally land it in Northern Sub-Saharan Africa, somewhere in Sudan, Uganda, or Kenya. This is the vast expanse through which the northern wheatear (*oenanthe oenanthe*) travels, wingbeat by wingbeat, to reach the distant climes that it
[01] inhabits during its non-breeding season.† The seemingly fragile songbird, around 15 centimeters long and weighing a feathery 25 grams, takes a journey of roughly 15,000 kilo-
[02] meters in each direction.† The travels of the wheatears are part of the millions of journeys undertaken twice a year that form a massive semi-permanent redistribution of the global bird population.

Birdwatchers in the UAE repeatedly spot and record the appearances of the wheatear, with its white rump and darker wings, and other species during their foraging and resting stops in dispersed grounds across and around Al Hajar Mountains. Among these recordings, wheatears were spotted in Huwaylat – a road crossing through
[03] Al Hajar connecting Hatta to Khor Kalba† –
[04] and Al Ain.† These recordings, and others from all over the world, are uploaded into the central database eBird, an online network managed by the Cornell Lab of Ornithology that converts these sightings of passing and breeding migratory birds into a real-time visual interactive map of the ebb and flow of migration.

01

During non-breeding seasons, migratory birds travel to their "non-breeding site," a geographical area that birds occupy during parts of the year when they are neither breeding, nor migrating.

02

Franz Bairlein, et al., "Cross-Hemisphere Migration of a 25 G Songbird." *Biology Letters* 8, no. 4 (2012): 505–7. https://doi.org/10.1098sbl.2011.1223.

03

Hatta is an exclave of the Emirate of Dubai located on the western plateau of the mountains, while Khor Kalba is part of the fertile strip on the east coast of the UAE.

04

Al Ain is an inland oasis city situated within the western plateau; "Northern Wheatear: *Oenanthe oenanthe*," eBird, accessed January 4, 2023, https://ebird.org/species/norwhe/AE

The recorded sightings reveal that the birds, who could choose to travel across any region in the world, deliberately stop in Al Hajar, adapting to its particularities. By understanding the ways in which wheatears travel through and inhabit aridity, our anthropocentric attitudes towards the ecological conditions of our surrounding environments are challenged. We learn that birds evaluate environments through their potentialities and have the ability to adapt to fluctuating resources. The historical documentation and recent tracking of birds within the Arabian Peninsula is a testimony to the often overlooked resources in the region.

A History of Birding in the Arabian Peninsula

The fascination with bird migration began when their disappearances and reappearances were first noticed thousands of years ago. The first writings that reflected a curiosity and scientific documentation of bird migration across the Arabian Peninsula appeared as early as the ninth century in the writings of Abu Othman Amr bin Bahr (famously known by the nickname Al Jahidh, or the goggle-eyed). The Basra-born writer, philosopher, and naturalist recorded his acute observations on animals, reflections on pre-Islamic poetry, and his take on Aristotle's zoological texts, not without sarcasm, in his seven-part compendium *Kitab Al Hayawan (Book of Animals)*. His texts on animal behavior and habitats note the disappearance and return of birds in Basra, attributing the return to the availability of fruit and date palms. He elaborates on the distances birds could travel looking for food resources once they are no longer accessible at their familiar grounds:

هِدايةُ العُصْفورِ:

والعُصْفورُ يَتَعالى وَيَطيرُ، وَيَهْتَدي وَيَسْتَجيبُ. وَلَقَدْ بَلَغَني أَنَّهُ قَدْ رَجَعَ مِن قَريبٍ مِن فَرْسَخ. وَهِيَ
تكونُ عِنْدَنا بالبَصْرة فِي الدّور، فَإذا أَمْكَنَتِ الثِّمارَ لمْ تَجِد مِنْها إلّا اليَسِيرُ، فَتَصيرُ مِنَ القَواطِعِ إِلى
قاصي النَّخْلِ، وَذلِكَ أَنَّها إِذا مَرَّتْ بِعَصافيرِ القُرى وَقَدْ سَبَقَت إِلى ما هُوَ إِلَيْها أَقْرَب، جاوَزَتْها إِلى
ما هُوَ أَبْعَد، ثُمَّ تقرب الأَيّام الكَثيرَة إِلى ما هُوَ أَبْعَد، ثمّ تَقرَبُ الأيّام الكَثيرة المِقْدار، في المَسَافةِ إِلى
أَكْثَرَ مما ذَكَرْتُ مِنَ الفَرْسَخ أَضْعافًا.† [05]

The Bird's Guidance:

The bird transcends, flies, follows, and responds. I have been informed
that he recently flew back a parasang's distance. † When the fruits [06]
are ripe here in Basra, you will find plenty of these birds. And when
the sedentary village birds have already taken the fruits close by, the
migratory birds proceed by traveling to palm trees further away. Then,
as many more days pass, they travel even farther away, multiple times
the parasang distance.† [07]

To survive the long and perilous journey, birds instinctively prepare through distinct physiological adaptations such as increasing their fat percentage, reducing the size of their organs, and increasing the size of their feathers. The rate by which birds increase the fat within their bodies, as well as the time they choose to migrate, is intertwined with the length of their journeys and the availability of food and rest stops along the way. Using his observations, Al Jahidh illustrates practices of breeding, nesting, and incubation *fig.* (001), and documents the physical changes in birds, linking them to changes in their geographical location:

05

Amr Al Jahidh, *Kitab Al Hayawan* [The Book of Animals], (Beirut: Dar Al Kitab Al Arabi, 2015), 2:328.

06

Parasang is an ancient unit of linear length that measures approximately 5.5 kilometers.

07

Al Jahidh, *Kitab Al Hayawan*, 2:328; Quote translated by the author.

تبدّل حال الحيوان إذا أخرج من مَوْطِنه:

وقد عَلِمْنا أنّ الطائر الصَّيود مِن الجَوارِح، لو أَقام في بِلادِه مائة عام لم يَحدُثْ لمَنْسرِهِ زوائد، وعَيْرَ
العانة إذا أقام في غيرِ بلاده احتاجَ إلى الأخْذِ من حافِره، وإلى أَنْ يُخْتَلَف به إلى البَيطار، والطائر
[08] الوحشيّ من هذه المَغنِّيات والنوائح، لو أقام عندنا دهرًا طويلاً لم يُصوِّتْ إذا أخذناه وقد كُرِّز.†

Changes in an animal's condition once displaced from its homeland:

As we know it, the hunting bird is a raptor. Its sharp beak doesn't change even if it remains sedentary for over a hundred years, but even a veteran will notice that it molts (sheds) when it inhabits other grounds. Although these brutal birds of prey can chatter and cry, they
[09] **remain quiet when held and blindfolded.†**

The adaptations observed and noted by Al Jahidh almost 12 centuries ago emerged from a geographical location that exhibited the phenomenon of birds traveling out of their homeland. Geographically, the Arabian Peninsula offers an alternative route from the Sahara into the Sub-Saharan region and the south of Africa. For birds that breed in central and northern Asia, the Himalayas present a barrier. It obstructs direct migration to the south, which directs birds to a longer south-westerly route along the East Asia-East Africa Flyway. William Bourne, a

08

Al Jahidh, *Kitab Al Hayawan*, 7:100.

09

Al Jahidh, *Kitab Al Hayawan*, 7:100; Quote translated by the author.

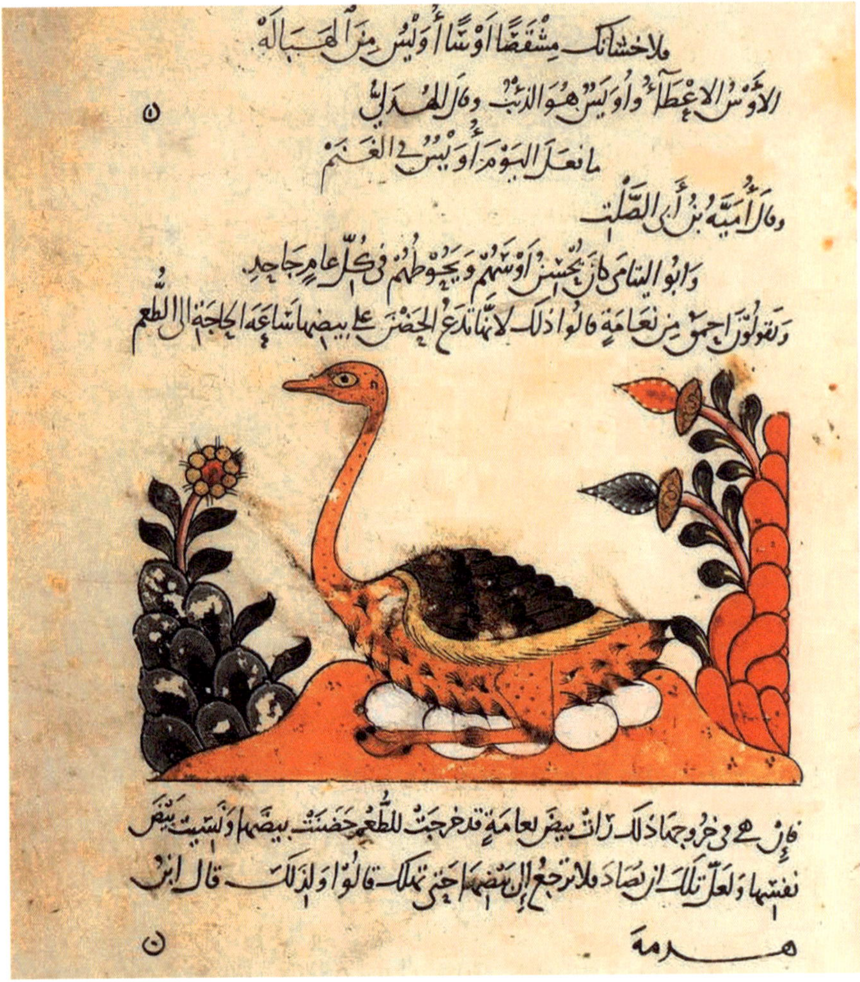

فلا تخشانك مشفقاً أوساً أويس من الهبالة

الأوس العطاء وأويس هو الذئب وقال الهذلي

ما فعل اليوم أويس في الغنم

وقال أمية بن أبي الصلت

وأبو اليتامى كان يحسن أوسهم ويحوطهم في كل عام جاحد

ويقولون أحمق من نعامة قالوا ذلك لأنها تدع الحضن على بيضها ساعة الحاجة إلى الطعم

فإن هي خرجت لذلك رأت بيض نعامة قد خرجت للطعم حضنت بيضها ونسيت بيض

نفسها ولعل تلك أن تصاد فلا ترجع إلى بيضها حتى تهلك قالوا ولذلك قال ابن

هرمة

fig. (001) An ostrich incubating eggs. Illustrated in *Kitab Al Hayawan.* Al Jahidh notes that an ostrich changes its behavior once incubating. He also notes that despite sharing attributes of wings, feathers, and eggs, an ostrich doesn't fly. © Veneranda Biblioteca Ambrosiana.

dedicated birdwatcher, used his free time while in Jordan and Iraq to write his *Notes*
[10] *on Autumn Migration in the Middle East*.† In his notes, he argues against researchers' low estimations of desert crossings during the first half of the twenty-first century:

10

Bourne helped in establishing the Cyprus Ornithological Society while working as a Royal Air Force medical officer. He is also the founder of the Seabird Group in the UK.

> The behaviour of these birds suggests that it is their normal procedure to undertake a direct flight across the Arabian desert [...] The desert crossing sounds a formidable undertaking, but several relevant points deserve consideration. All the Palaearctic migrants wintering in Africa must cross the desert zone somewhere, although the volume of passage observed anywhere in this region, and especially along the "routes" across the desert postulated by some authorities, is quite inadequate to account for the transfer of populations which is known to occur. Conditions are rather different in different segments of the desert zone [...]. Thus it appears that Arabia is in fact one of the easier approaches to Africa; not only is the width of the desert less here than further west, while it has at least many oases, but there is
> [11] good cover in the hills on its borders.†

Today, ornithologists track and map general migration routes using observation records and data collected through bird banding. Bourne's notes are confirmed by the recent tracking records of The National Center of Wildlife in Saudi Arabia, reporting more than 500 million
[12] migratory birds crossing its landscape in 2020.† These immense numbers reflect a rich biodiversity of flora and fauna. The mapped routes reveal that the Arabian Peninsula's location is at the intersection of three out of eight major flyways – the East Asia-East Africa Flyway, the Central Asia Flyway, and the Mediterranean and Black
[13] Sea Flyway.† While flyways are often drawn as hard lines on tidy maps, the term flyway is used to describe the whole area covered by species of migratory birds during the cyclical movements between breeding and non-breeding grounds. When crossing the Arabian Peninsula, for example, the migrating birds could enter it through a route extending north as far as northern Iraq or south into Oman.

11

W. R. P. Bourne, "Notes on Autumn Migration in the Middle East." *Ibis* (London, England, 1957) 101 (2): 170-176.

12

Tareq Al Thaqafi, "500 million birds migrate through Saudi Arabia every year," *Arab News*, September 4, 2020, https://arab.news/japxn

13

Andy Symes, et al., "*The Conservation Status and Distribution of the Breeding Birds of the Arabian Peninsula*." (Sharjah: Protected Areas Authority, Government of Sharjah, 2015).

14

"Discover Our Biodiversity - Birds." Environment Agency - Abu Dhabi. Accessed December 12, 2022. http`s://www.ead.gov.ae/en/discover-our-biodiversity.

15

A circumpolar range is one that occurs only at high latitudes, surrounding the North Pole in this case, yet extends across a wide range of longitudes.

The UAE, located at the eastern borders of the Arabian Peninsula, is populated with sparsely vegetated areas and its oases are scattered within the region making it a route of survival for many of its migratory species. In 2021, the monitoring and conservation program by the Environment Agency Abu Dhabi (EAD) recorded more than two million migratory avians, many of which were seen surrounding the long sinuous range of Al Hajar.† These geographies offer food and [14]
rest for the birds to recover before continuing their journeys crossing vast landscapes with a physical tenacity that humans struggle to fathom. The routes taken by these avian travelers stitch together the scattered and beleaguered productive sites within Al Hajar into destinations for noble odysseys.

Transitory Resources

The long and perilous journeys that predominantly follow a north-south axis illustrate food and resource cycles. In habitats occurring above roughly 60 degrees north latitude, food availability is cyclical, with alternating seasons of abundance and shortages. Similar cycles occur within Al Hajar, but when shortages occur elsewhere on the route, Al Hajar abounds aplenty. Thus, the phenomenon of migration enables its travelers to inhabit various environments at different times of the year, whether to benefit from seasonal flushes of resources or avoid seasonal shortages.

Wheatears, with their circumpolar† nesting range that [15]
expands west of Alaska eastward towards the Canadian Arctic, exhibit a fascinating side of their migration journeys in their itineraries. Their journey could start from opposing sides of North America, depending on the location of their nesting ground. Wesley Hochachka, assistant director of bird population studies at the Cornell Lab of Ornithology, explains that while some of the wheatears embark on a migration route from Alaska to Sub-Saharan Africa, passing through the Arabian Peninsula, their fellows nesting in the east will take a different route across the vast stretch of the Atlantic Ocean reaching Europe before turning south towards various grounds west of Africa.† [16]

Wheatears crossing the ocean east towards Europe prepare by doubling their percentage of fat to endure the 7,500 kilometers journey (almost half the length of the journey west) on

a route that offers few possible stops due to its geographical nature. At the same time, travelers of the same species starting their trip from Alaska take a less risky, albeit longer, route passing through the UAE and other surrounding landscapes in a journey that critically depends on fueling and resting stops. These elaborate seasonal journeys take roughly five and a half months, compared to the three months the wheatears spend
[17] around nesting grounds.† The radically opposing routes require their travelers to take varying physiological preparations before their journey. The discrepancy in the preparations confirms the significance of stops made en route for the travelers to survive the journey from Alaska to Sub-Saharan Africa.

16

Wesley Hochachka, "Migrating Northern Wheatears Go the Distance-and Pack Accordingly," *All About Birds*, May 11, 2015. https://www.allaboutbirds.org/news/for-migration-northern-wheatears-go-the-distance-and-pack-accordingly/.

17

Bairlein,"Cross-Hemisphere Migration of a 25 G Songbird.", 505–7.

18

Ian Newton, "Fueling the Flights," in *The Migration Ecology of Birds*, (Amsterdam: Elsevier, 2008), 95–137.

Refueling Along the Way

Throughout the migration journey, most species spend their time alternating between actively migrating and resting. The former is when the fat added in preparation for the journey is consumed, while the latter is when birds stop en route to feed, recover, and wait for preferable weather conditions. Ornithologists refer to environments where birds rest as stopover habitats. In theory, migratory birds tend to adaptively break down their flights into shorter segments
[18] when flying over landscapes suitable for rest and foraging.† Since wheatears stop in various areas within the UAE, their stops must indicate the availability of shelter and resource abundance. Accordingly, the sections of unfavorable seascapes and landscapes encourage longer flight durations, and subsequently, are followed by lengthy refueling stopovers.

The stopover habitats, also referred to as migration traps, are not necessarily successively inhabited by migratory birds. Depending on habitat conditions, certain areas can be used for months at a time, but only at intervals through seasons and years. The result is unpredictable migrating populations that concentrate in dispersed locations. The reality that one realizes while examining research findings, tracking maps, and compiled records of sightings is that spatiotemporal variations and complexities are a recurring theme. These variations are, partially, a reaction to forces imposed by climate change, or anthropogenic environmental interventions.

Broadly identified, agricultural fields, peninsulas, coasts, and shorelines are habitats that constitute potentially rich grounds for migrating birds.†[19] In most cases, human interventions largely impact the conditions of these habitats. Certain farming practices in agricultural fields are more often associated with their use as stopover habitats than others. Habitats that have non-cultivated plant diversity, heterogeneous plant species, and decreased use of pesticides are classified as attractive stopover habitats.†[20] Areas of uncultivated native trees and shrubs, known as edge habitats, are also associated with abundance and diversified food resources. Thus, one can argue that, within Al Hajar, traditional farming practices that display a reluctance in eliminating non-cultivating plants and avoid the full utilization of land cover for intense farming, consequently, offer attractive habitats.

19

Melissa Mayntz, "Are We There Yet?" in *Migration: Exploring the Remarkable Journeys of Birds*. (London: Quadrille, an imprint of Hardie Grant Publishing, 2020), 74-80.

20

J. David Blount, et al., "Avian Use of Agricultural Areas as Migration Stopover Sites: A Review of Crop Management Practices and Ecological Correlates," in *Frontiers in Ecology and Evolution*, 9 (2021). https://doi.org/10.3389/fevo.2021.650641.

Nurturing Resources

While the wheatear passes through the Arabian Peninsula to reach its non-breeding ground in Africa, other species use the UAE as their breeding ground. Navigating through migration routes with stopover locations aren't the only practices that exhibit responses to changing environments across far-flung landscapes. Birds' ecological niches and terrestrial habitats display construction behavior that reveals impressive consistency in adapting to, and depending upon, their selected nesting grounds.

As winter approaches in the UAE, one starts to encounter bird nests populating trees across different habitats. Variable sizes, forms, and materials make up the intricate nests to rear new generations of feathered avians. Michael Hansell, senior lecturer in the Institute of Biomedical and Life Sciences at the University of Glasgow, explains how avian nest building follows the repetitious steps of selecting, gathering, and assembling (or sculpting).†[21] Most bird species are specialists when it comes to material selection.†[22] This means that their intuition when selecting materials results in microhabitats with species-specific characteristics that achieve intricate requirements of size, weight, accessibility, protection, ventilation, and pest control. However, the selection process that favors specialization over generalization leaves plenty of room for adaptability to what's available in their surroundings.

The process by which a nest is constructed broadly reflects an underlying adaptive behavior; birds make use of materials surrounding them, of a size and weight they can carry, which, once assembled, meet their requirements of sheltering and nurturing their young. This translates into a versatile use of a wide selection of potential materials. While searching for these materials, birds seek ones that, when a construction tactic is applied, behave as intended. Through the versatility of material selection and the ingenuity in their utilization, the birds' attitude facilitates the adequacy and sufficiency of materials within a certain ground. Adapting to the environment, birds can efficiently find suitable materials despite choosing different nesting grounds in consecutive breeding seasons. After the nestlings fledge and the seasonal nurturing period is concluded, the avian nests fall into disuse. Their structures disintegrate and the materials are left, making them available for future nest building.

Potential materials used in nest building include organic material (e.g., grass, twigs, weeds, lichens, rootlets, fine grass) and minerals (e.g., stone and mud). The two categories fall under collected materials that can be assembled
[23] intact or after modification. † For example, when a bird chooses a stick, it might be applied to the nest construction without modification or may be cut or shaped to make it more suitable for its purpose. In other cases, collected materials are combined with self-secreted ones, a product of the bird's own metabolism, like saliva, which is used in gluing nest materials together.

21

Michael H. Hansell, *Bird Nests and Construction Behaviour*. (Cambridge: Cambridge University Press, 2005), 14–20.

22

Michael H. Hansell, *Bird Nests and Construction Behaviour*. (Cambridge: Cambridge University Press, 2005), 153.

23

Michael H. Hansell, *Bird Nests and Construction Behaviour*. (Cambridge: Cambridge University Press, 2005), 39-59.

24
Michael H. Hansell, *Bird Nests and Construction Behaviour.* (Cambridge: Cambridge University Press, 2005), 129-151.

Material, time, and energy are interconnected resources that guide birds to make decisions during the nest construction process. The amount of resources a bird uses in building a nest makes up its cost of construction, therefore, keeping the cost low largely dictates the process. While the three resources are intertwined, energy and time are most affected by the length and frequency of trips taken to gather the selected material, hence building near the material source is a favored decision.† [24]

To a large degree, the process of assembly imposes equal demands upon the attitude and actions of their builders as it does on the materials' properties. In taking nest construction to its most basic level, Hansell identifies sculpting and assembling as the primary nest construction techniques. While the former describes the production of a desired form by the removal of material, assembling embraces a more extensive range of techniques that include piling up, sticking together, interlocking, sewing, and weaving.

The techniques can be employed with an array of materials at varying scales. Interlocking, for example, is a simple term that indicates diverse tactics. Their commonality lies in the inter-reliance of the materials, ensnaring them together by virtue of their geometrical assembly without an adhesive. Weaving, on the other hand, enables the use of vegetal strands in a deliberate effort that involves looping, knotting, and hitching.

A Bird's-Eye View

Birds tell us about our environment. Understanding the utterly extraordinary itineraries of migratory birds' seasonal journeys, the tireless leaps across a world map, and the intricate repertoire of behaviors continues to give us evidence that there is still abundance in distant climes. Guided by scents of lands, slants of sunlight, and inherited predilections, the birds reveal that environments thousands of kilometers apart are tightly and inextricably bound by their very resourceful odyssey, perhaps challenging our fragmented understanding of the ever-changing ecological conditions of our world. These moments of epiphany upend our perception of environments that are fraught with challenges, yet filled with promise.

Ibrahim Nehme

The Open Road

1. The plane touched down in Dubai as the closing credits for *Nomadland* began rolling up the tiny screen on the seat in front of me. The movie stars Frances McDormand as Fern who, after losing her job and husband, decides to leave her life behind and travel around the United States in a van. Armed with a few belongings and an inner calling for freedom, she takes to the open road, meeting on her way fellow nomads who have learned to rely on self-sufficiency and treat the land and each other with kindness. Out there, there are very few rules, but a very big promise: When you let go of the safety of your tried and tested path, you let the vastness of infinite possibility carry you to where you have never been. The film is a compelling, yet at times painful, meditation on that promise. I felt a strange sense of synchronicity after watching it just before landing, since the adventure I was about to embark on seemed charged with a very similar premise.

2. Before coming here, I enlisted some friends to help me navigate the sweeping terrains of the United Arab Emirates (UAE). My brief to them was rather loose: I have one week, a rental car, and an open mind. It wasn't long before the voice notes began to ding. The suggestions varied from the things you would read in your average travel guide to more heartfelt suggestions of histories to navigate, ideas to contemplate, borders to cross, people to meet, and foods to try. I made an initial list of everything, then circled the ones that sparked my intuition and made another list of my own. My list looked like a map, with arrows growing from Dubai to destinations in many directions.

3. My friend Haya's six-minute voice note became the key that unlocked a curious chain of events. "Obviously, you experience the UAE differently depending on the people you get the recommendations from or the ones you experience it with," she started. "But the thing that comes to mind is the concept of abundance; of how the energy of this land is so spacious, so expansive, so infinite." She added that I must let the land touch me, and then swerved to tell me about the Cosmic Healing Center in Karama, in the old part of Dubai, which has been an entry point for her to access multiple layers of her being. She described the experience as an uncovering of abundance, and advised me to go see Sreeja.

4. The astrology app on my phone sent its daily notification, this time it read: "Right now, your travel guide is [your] inspiration."

5. I called the Cosmic Healing Center and the only appointment I could find with Sreeja was on the last day of my trip. "I'll be there," I told the receptionist, who asked to spell my name. "Like Abraham," I said, "but replace the first and last A's with strident I's."

6. In contemplating abundance, I planned to steer away from the usual suspects on the west coast (namely, the cities of Dubai, Abu Dhabi, and Sharjah, which have been blessed by so much of it) and head east towards the coastal plain, where I'd never been, and where the lure of unearthing the possibilities of novel territory became too good to ignore. I decided to focus on three areas along the eastern coast: Dibba in the north, which promised the best natural beaches in the UAE, amazing seafood, and a time-traveling trip to the 1980s; Khor Fakkan in the center, known for its Shark Island and well-kept secrets, as well as the stunning road that extends from Sharjah into its old town, apparently the most scenic in all the UAE; and Kalba in the south, which has become a prime ecotourism site in the country and from where I decided to start this trip and slowly make my way up north.

7. The guy from the rental company who brought the car to my hotel in Dubai made sure I checked all the black spots on the white car. As he showed me around the car, my mind was already in the east. I thanked him and grabbed the keys, then called Haya and my friend Marc, who happened to be visiting Dubai, and invited them to join me on the open road. "But I don't really have a solid plan," I cautioned. "Let's see where the road takes us." They agreed. I jumped in excitement.

8. There were times in the past when my life hung on a bag of dates and a bottle of water. I've learned to always keep them in my pack. As I prepared for this trip, I found an anomaly in how much this land has been blessed by dates but much less by water. I couldn't help but see this as a balancing act, like the roots of a palm, which have to reach wide and deep underneath the soil to fetch water, so that the tree could rise and keep rising. I also discovered that the ground where the palm roots nest and grow is like a sacred site that cannot be spoiled. That was humbling to learn, as well as to be reminded that everything circles back to the roots. It's only from deep down there that a palm or plant, a place or person, can emerge from the infinite to become the infinite.

9. The road to Kalba gently transfuses into your soul as it transitions from desert to highlands until it finally unites with the sea. There is a peaceful silence that resides on top of these rocks and vibrates throughout the sandy landscapes. It is in stark contrast to the cacophony of urban noise we have left behind, which disappears in the rearview mirror as we make our way through the vastness of land. Inside the car, the conversation takes an intimate turn as we start disclosing ghosts from our past. Talking about the ways through which we came to understand, accept, and transform our relationships with these ghosts, it ended with the idea that eventually daunting fears could be liberated by the skin of new awareness. As we approached Kalba, Haya mentioned how a lot of people start their healing journeys in the UAE, but her thought was interrupted when she saw a conservation center and proposed that we stop and take a look.

10. At the Hefaiyah Conservation Center, I learned that the Arabian Tahr has been registered as endangered on the Red List of Threatened Species. It has rectangular pupils, which allow them a 340-degree range of vision. Imagine being able to see virtually everything around you without lifting an eyebrow!

11. The telescopes installed at the different corners of the conservation center are a portal into another reality. You fix your eyes, adjust your gaze, and the world suddenly becomes a small maze of impeccable beauty. As I peered through, examining twigs, rocks, and particles of dust, looking for the tiny rock hyrax, which is bizarrely the closest living relative to the elephant, I had a transcendental experience. It was purely fascinating to witness the world in its minutest carrying so much marvel on its shoulders. It also reminded me of how nature is an intricate and intimate ecosystem, where every unit depends on another in a boundless cycle of production and consumption, of giving and receiving, of loving and loving back. And it made me think of how abundance cannot exist in isolation, because, after all, we all depend on one another to bring life forward.

12. Every tree tells a tale, and the ghaf's story is one of defiance in the heart of the desert. This miracle of a tree is also a testament to the fact that way deep underneath the lifeless sands, there is water, the source of all abundance.

13. By the time we reached Kalba's seaside front, we were ready for a break and a cup of coffee. We drove around the corniche a number of times trying to find a cafe with some charm and character, but we eventually, and rather shamefully, gave in to Starbucks. Marc laid down on a couch and took a nap, while Haya and I sat facing the blue waters and the soothing mangroves. We started sharing with each other some of the lessons that were taught to us by scarcity. I told her that, in the beginning, I used to think that resources were scarce and asking for them felt scary, because the logic went that if I take something, then there will be less of it for you. "But that's not true!" I protested. "There is enough for me and for you and for everyone else, if we really start believing this way. And because everyone somehow depends on everyone else, then my abundance is also somehow your abundance, and equally so." Then, a pigeon relieved itself on my shorts. Haya chuckled and joked that the bird agrees with me.

14. On our way out of Kalba, Marc saw a sign that says *monajem* (astrologer in Arabic) and asked me to pull over. He thought that we could stop and have our fortunes read. I drove back, but we quickly found out that the name reads Monajem Decor. The realization that the place sells furniture and not the future was a little disappointing, but also very hilarious, and the laughs took us all the way to Addis Ababa, an Ethiopian food joint on the outskirts of Fujairah, which people recommended to us with these words: "The food is good, but it's a little shady." The place sits in front of a huge parking lot that was devoid of cars, and Al Hajar Mountains in all their majesty are right there in front of you. The shade of the place was actually comforting, but the food wasn't good, and in the end, a lot of it went to waste. I thought of all the incredibly complex networks that had coalesced to bring this food to our table, and I felt a little ungrateful for throwing it away. It's not a big deal, some might say, but if we zoom out to see the much larger picture, I couldn't help but think of abundance that is sometimes taken for granted and goes unchecked, and the kinds of abundant futures we really want to magnetize and manifest.

15. Al Hajar stretches westward along the UAE's eastern plain and extends 3,000 meters above sea level. The mountains are home to a delicate ecosystem of flora and fauna, which thrive on a variety of vegetation, permanent water sources, cooler temperatures, and extensive shelters within rocks and caves. They are dry, dark, and very gorgeous, and they have a non-foreboding energy, like an emperor who sits on his throne and exudes the gentlest of powers. And imagine that all of this darkness holds so much life!

16. In the Hisn Khor Fakkan Museum, I learned about the many ancient settlements that found their home in this region since the Stone Age. I saw rock fragments with beautiful inscriptions, drawings of figures, and abstract geometries. I learned about the trade networks that flourished, the copper mining histories that existed, and the stone tombs that were recently found of people who were buried with their belongings. I also discovered Ahmad Bin Majid, whose books of prose and poetry on the topic of navigation became indispensable guides for the seafarers crossing the Indian Ocean. This rich history stood in contrast to all the newness that I've experienced on the west coast, and made me realize how this land has, in fact, been touched and blessed by many ancestors who came before and paved the way, who lived, loved, and left their marks, so that eventually others could come and leave theirs.

17. It turned out that Khor Fakkan's best-kept beaches are indeed a well-kept secret, because we could find none of them. Instead, we had to compromise and pay 25 dirhams to take a 15-minute boat ride to visit the highly touristic Shark Island. We arrived just before sunset and the views were breathtaking, but the smell of gasoline from the boats, which zap between the island and coast, bringing tourists to take pictures, made me nauseous. And witnessing all that oil from the boats littering the surface of the Indian Ocean was really painful. Oh, if the water could speak! Oh, if our ancestors could come back and say something!

18. Sandy Beach Hotel in Dibba, with its delightful 1980s aesthetic and laid-back resort experience, was precisely what we needed as we neared the end of the road. We arrived there at the same time Qatar was lighting the opening fire of its World Cup and revealing the games' mascot, La'eeb, whose figure reminded me of Casper, the ghost. Social media was on fire. Then, I saw a post by a friend quoting Adrienne Maree Brown when she said in a recent interview: "Freedom is not a destination." I found myself at an incredible junction in my history thinking of the straight ways and sly shortcuts that have led me to this point. I thought that the journeys that really mattered were, in the end, the ones that were not overridden by the drive to arrive, but by the joy of discovery and the intention to be expansive at every step along the way. Facing our hotel room was Snoopy Island, which looked, in the darkness of the night, like a ghost. I couldn't help but see it as another Casper from our collective past, the one that stands as an antithesis to abundance, embodying old ways of living and being that we have dragged on with us for way too long, and which we now must surrender to the waters and move on.

19. On my first day in Dubai, I came across the concept of vision quests, which are retreats in the desert that were described on one website as a "time-out, where the outer, everyday life is temporarily left behind, where one fasts from food and words, and the subtle becomes loud and evident." These quests are like a reset button that pushes one towards the most expansive version of oneself. But what really stuck with me after reading the brochure of an upcoming quest is how the organizers believe that the expansion of oneself is not only a commitment to the self, but also to nature, because "we are a part of nature, not above it." On our last day in Dibba, Marc pulls out a chapter from Carl Jung's *Modern Man in Search of a Soul* and reads a passage that talks about how the evolution of man into a rational and scientific being has led him to believe that he could dominate nature. "Great minds have wrestled with the question whether it is the glorious sun that illuminates the worlds, or whether it is the human eye by virtue of its relation to the sun." Modern man believes it to be the eye, but after a week on the road observing how there is so much more to life than our partial human experience, and how much more we still have to witness, discover, and become, I found myself siding with the sun.

20. I went to see Sreeja on the day the first rains came and flooded the streets of Dubai, which made me a little late for my appointment. When I finally reached the center, Sreeja greeted me with a big smile and invited me into her space. She asked me about the reason I came to see her. I told her that I have spent one week dwelling on abundance and would like to see what might come up for me in this regard. She asked me to sit down on a lounge chair and gave me two crystal balls to hold in each hand, and then dimmed the lights and told me to close my eyes. I did, and then she did her thing, which I deciphered in the darkness to involve soft humming, instrument banging, and incense burning. When she was done, she turned up the lights and recited her verdict. "You are a very good giver, but not a very good receiver. But the key to unlocking abundance is to allow yourself to receive it," said Sreeja, whose name in Sanskrit means the one who is born in prosperity. I left the building with her last sentence ringing in my two ears, and I thought that she could not have scripted a more appropriate ending for my trip.

21. On the flight back home, I opened the list of award-winning movies and pressed play on *Driveways*. What followed was the tender story of Del, an old man, who forms a bond with Cody, a young boy who has just moved next door with his mother. The movie is soft on all its brilliant edges, and slowly burns its way towards the end, when, in the very last scene, Del tells Cody that if he were to go back in time, he would go on another road trip with his now deceased wife, but this time, they would "drive a little slower, take our time, take a good look at stuff, really see the country." I sighed, looked out of the plane's window into the endless skies, and smiled, assuring myself that this was just what I have spent a whole week doing.

Rand Abdul Jabbar

Eons Unfolded: Revelations at Wadi Wurayah

Preface

My contribution to this publication was prompted by an instigation to challenge the representation of arid landscapes within historical travel journals and present a response through a text that describes a personal journey through a landscape.

As I reflected on my own ongoing
[01] engagement with the Gertrude Bell Archive,†
I was reminded of a passage I once read in a letter she wrote to her father in 1922, in which she describes looking out at the desert landscape around Hatra in Iraq and witnessing "a scene in which past and present were so bewilderingly mingled that you might have looked down upon
[02] its (sic) like any evening for 20 centuries."† I was
struck by this depiction of a seemingly static, desolate place which, over millennia, remained undisrupted by the forces of time. One might think of aridity and imagine sparsity, but within the arid landscape of Al Hajar Mountains lies a series of wadis, valleys of abundance with rich ecosystems that have sustained life and provided favorable conditions for human settlement for over 200,000 years.

I became particularly drawn to Wadi Wurayah in the Emirate of Fujairah due to its unique perennial freshwater habitats and extensive network of hydrological features. The Wadi Wurayah National Park, the country's first protected mountain area and national park, has been closed to the public since 2009 while it undergoes rehabilitation and a management plan is put into place for its reopening. After being granted an access permit by the Fujairah Environment Authority (FEA), I embarked on a journey through Wadi Wurayah accompanied by Nasser Obeidat, Principal Environmental Researcher at FEA, and Kenta Sayama, a DPhil candidate at the Oxford Resilient Buildings and Landscapes Lab who is currently conducting research in Fujairah. As we set out to trace and explore the hydrological features of the site, I discovered through observations and conversations a landscape dotted with time's vestiges, visible across a variety of scales that span a few hours or days, to hundreds of thousands of years. I also witnessed how the fluctuating presence and flow of water had been a persistent factor of change throughout these varied timescales. The text below, composed as a collection of short poems, aims to describe how the relationship between land and water could be read through the layers of time embedded within the landscape of Wadi Wurayah, from its geologic formation all the way to the light drizzle we experienced on the morning of our walk.

01

The Gertrude Bell Archive at Newcastle University holds the photographs, letters, diaries and personal memorabilia of the British explorer, writer, archeologist, and colonial diplomat Gertrude Bell (1868 –1926).

02

Gertrude Bell, "Letter from Gertrude Bell to her father Hugh Bell" Gertrude Bell Archive, November 1922.

I. Ophiolites

On a journey through the rugged terrain
Here, I came to know

That along these wadis, from the rarest of processes
The mantle of the Earth lay exposed

Twenty million revolutions stood witness to
A nascent plate boundary, embarked on a collision course

Swirling in heat towards its continental edge
Folding, scraping, rising oceanic crust

A tale of obduction
Al Hajar Mountains live to tell

II. Erosion

Perennial streams of abundance
Graze the surface of the earth

Over millions of revolutions more
Wind and water wear away
The land at their tender touch

Channels swell, channels recede
Cascading through their force

Creases and crevices transformed
Into valleys and canyons, behold

III. Sedimentation

Deep and shallow striations reveal
The fluctuating sea

The base, a gush of powerful force
A mass of minerals, boulders, and cobbles

Preceding slow and steady flows
Where pebbles and stones within granules are held

Mapping a trajectory across epochs of time
Evidence and consequence along its course

IV. Aquifers

Abundant aquifers in porous ground
Replenished by bouts of rain and floods

An active refuge amidst cycles of aridity

The source from within the cracks and clefts
Gushing rush, descending flood

The pooling body
An even quivering, oscillating rhythm

The remnants of a recent deluge
Rippling and swaying
Fluttering across the rocks

The soothing ponds, steady and poised
Where the Warrah of Wurayah dwell

V. Floods

Foreign vestiges and shifting ground
Topography in persistent reformulation

Torrential deluge polishing away
Any trace of a precise edge, smoothed

Displaced residuals by the stream
Bathed in warm and glistening light

Reverberations at every step
Encroach with care and caution

VI. Raindrops

Rumblings from the sky above
Rejuvenate, renew

Embracing skin and surface alike
Soft trickle, a welcome respite

Salinity precipitates
Saturation and release

Outlets at the surface spring
The enduring valley of the reeds

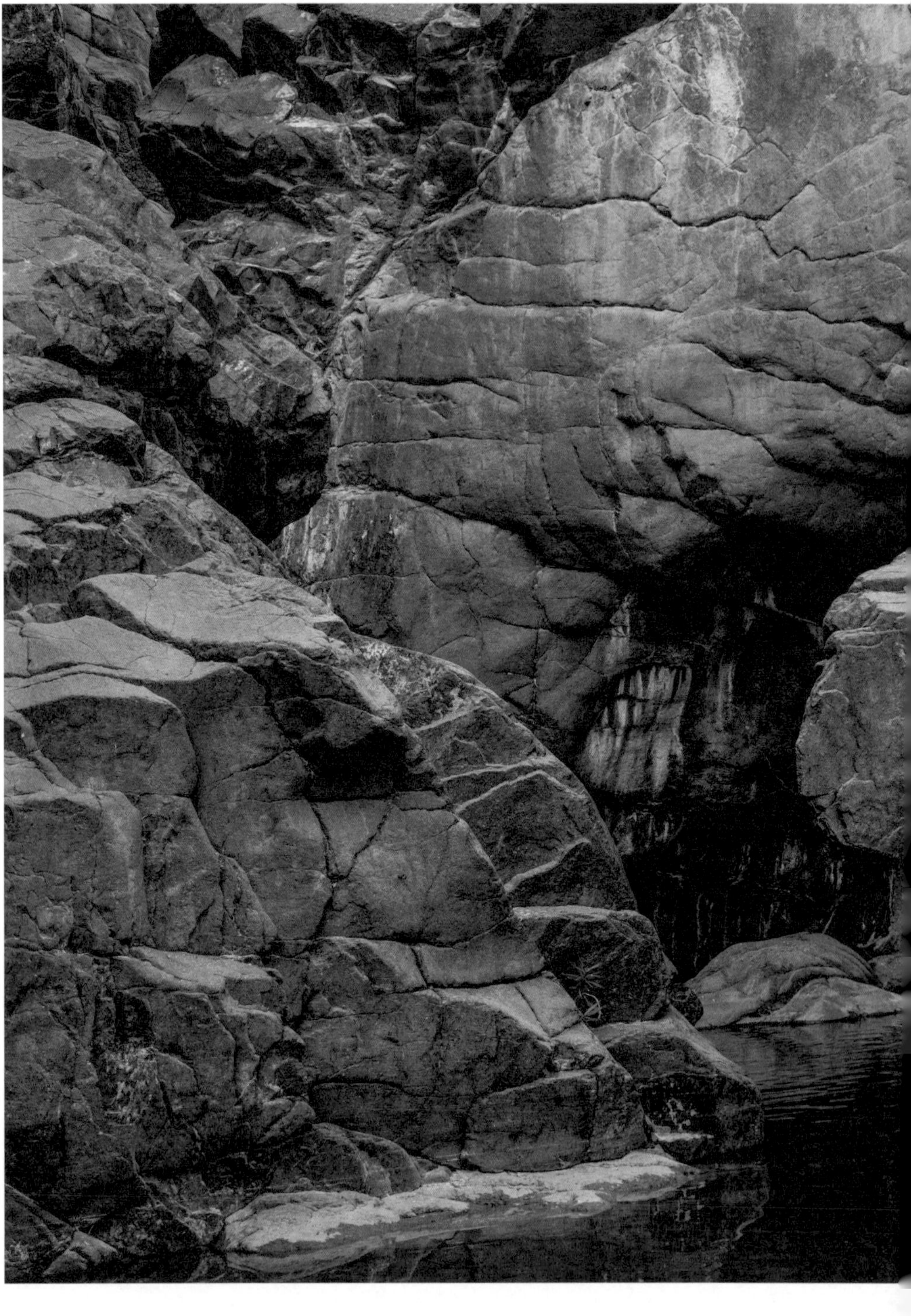

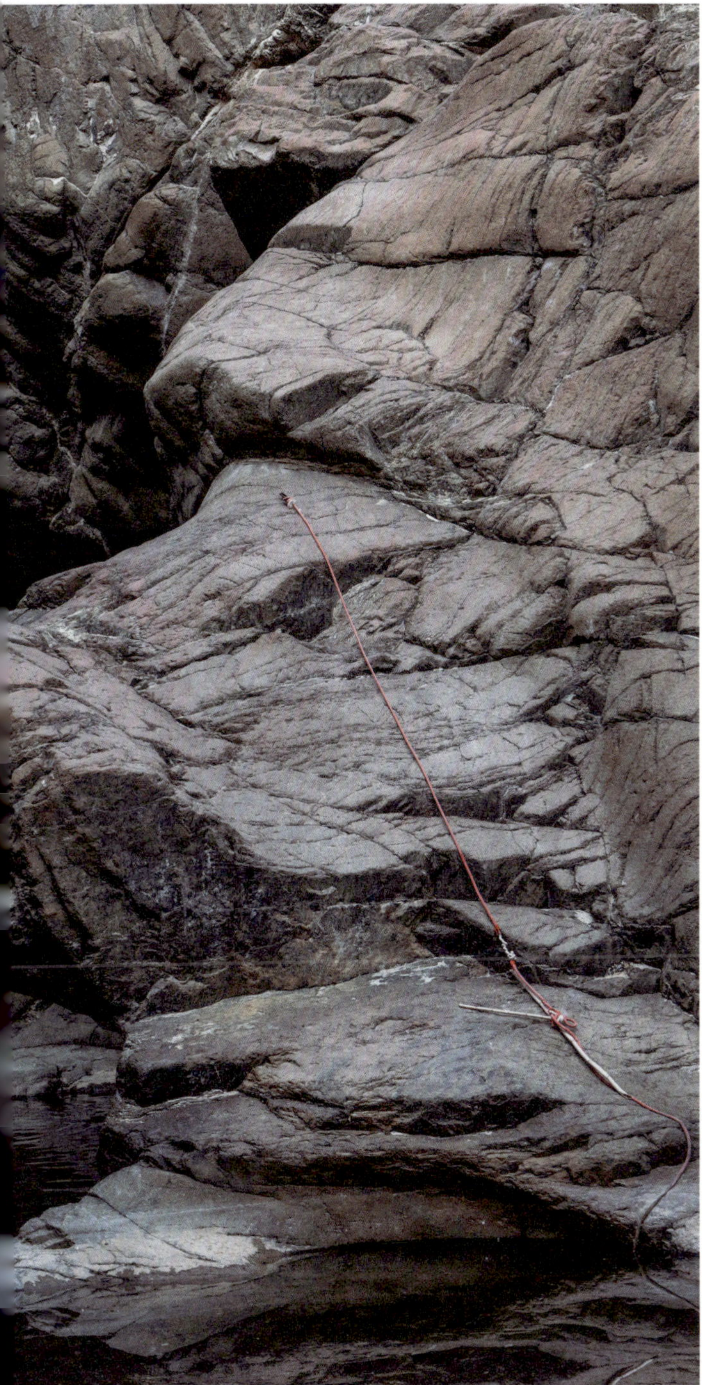

fig. (001) Waterfall at Wadi Wurayah. Photo by Reem Falaknaz.

Acknowledgments

My sincerest thanks to the Fujairah Environment Authority and Wadi Wurayah National Park for welcoming me into the majestic landscape of Wadi Wurayah, and to Nasser Obeidat and Kenta Sayama for their company and generous insights.

Deepak ഉണ്ണികൃഷ്ണൻ

My Grandmother and the Giants

..حَتَّى نَشْعُرَ بِالْعَطَشِ مَرَّةً أُخْرَى وَنَنْظُرُ نَحْوَ ٱلسَّمَاءِ.

...until we are thirsty again and look towards the sky

The elders keep the kids indoors when it rains.

That's when the giants prowl. They bring the rain.

It doesn't rain often. Four, maybe five times a year.

If the rain is good, there will be enough to sustain the tribe.

To celebrate, an animal will be slaughtered. There will be food, there will be mirth. There will be life. The seeds will sprout, the roots will live.

And relief, until we are thirsty again and look towards the sky.

Our mountains are rock and dust, the color of smoke.

Our animals don't need color either.

Our goats look like they are crafted from the cliffs.

Even the sheep look like brutes. They get that way by licking salt from the stones. That's how tough they are. The same with the snakes and the scorpions with their claws. And the birds they hide from.

Everything that has managed to live here, my elders say, has figured out how to survive. That's why we remember the names of our ancestors, because they earned the right to have their names and the names of their fathers and their mothers and those who came before them, and before them, repeated. Because they survived, they are remembered.

My grandmother was the first one to ask me if I knew where rain came from.

I was eight.

I said yes and pointed to the sky. But she persisted and asked if I knew why it rained and I said no, I couldn't say. "Take me to the mountains in the morning and I'll show you." We'll have to go slow, she cautioned, patting her knee.

My grandmother was the sixth of eleven kids. Her parents called her wild because she liked to run up the mountain to look for honey and edible flora. She was always covered in mountain dust. Every evening, she waited patiently for the animals to return from their graze, even though children weren't permitted outdoors past dusk.

But my grandmother took off whenever she pleased, even at night, because she was curious. It got so bad her mother tied cattle bells and a blade to her ankle. But most nights, my grandmother found a way, to sneak out into the darkness. And she could bear the cold, she said, because she'd run out barefoot. "Over time, your heels get hard and tough, better than shoes."

One winter, she spotted two kid goats missing from the family's herd, and without checking with her elders, went to look for them. "And I suppose," she said, "I shouldn't have kept going, but I kept going, towards the top." To wander at night, when the thieves are out, and when the spirits roam, is something nobody does.

That's when she spotted them, she said, "a family of large-limbed beasts, man-like yet not man-like and tall and proud, with roots for legs."

"They were four or five of them," she said, and they had started a fire. "There was a child among them, stacking rocks bigger than me on top of each other, the same game I played with my siblings."

"That's when I found out why my tribe counted the kids at night," she said. "Because this child-thing spotted me, then grabbed me before I could go anywhere, and kept me like a pet. I played along by keeping quiet and not fighting much. What was I going to do? And I figured out quickly I didn't understand them, and they didn't understand me, but those in charge of the child-thing found me harmless, and I suppose permitted it to keep me for a bit, before figuring out what to do with me, or how to eat me, because I noticed after a week or so that the other child-things didn't keep pets. Or anyone who looked like me."

The way my grandmother puts it, the day of her escape was an accident. Because the child-thing had ventured out with its family to the sea, which appeared calm. It was nighttime and they were joined by others like them. Then, they waded into the water. The child-thing gripped my grandmother, as they began to churn the ocean with their arms, making the waves grow bigger and wilder. Until they began scooping the water and throwing it up into the air, making sport of it, flinging liquid farther out, higher up, over the mountains we came down, watching the water run, making it rain. And as they did this, they roared and swung, and caused a wind that forced the birds to perch and wait the chaos out, because it was too windy to fly. And then when they were done, my grandmother said, "they walked away from the sea, and returned to the mountains, where they walked to the top, and watched the dark sky part to reveal clouds with gray-blue accents, inviting the sun to take over once again, so they could see the damage their waters had done."

"What damage?" I asked.

"Water," my love, my grandmother said. "Water from that height, coming at you with speed, takes things with it, the animals, the trees, the people." As the man-like things and child that took my grandmother made their way down the mountain, they would pick the things they fancied most, a toppled tree, a drowned goat, pieces of homes, a child's toy. And occasionally, a human, which my grandmother noticed "they only picked up if it was still alive, because they'd check first." During that forage, they found a boy my grandmother's age, a child she recognized, whose name she refused to share, but who hadn't seen her, because "he was out cold, waiting to die, because no one survives the floods and the mud." Suddenly, the child-thing put my grandmother down and picked up her muddied friend, and walked away.

The gesture didn't feel like a mistake to me, but my grandmother was convinced she got lucky, as she made her way downhill, to the relief of her family. In her hurry to get away, my grandmother tripped. The injury, my grandmother said, tapping her knee for effect, "never healed completely." And she never went up the mountain again.

"So," she said, "whether you believe me or not, if you are my granddaughter, and you are asked, who makes rain and why does it rain, what will you say?"

I am a mountain girl. We trust our own. I said to my grandmother, may her spirit know peace.

Now, what I say to those who ask, especially the children, is that the giants make the rain, and they make rain to nab playthings for their children. So, if you go up there, and you hear the wind and smell the sea in the distance, if you look up and see the clouds darken, go home, stay home, and watch for the water coming from the top. When the water leaves, step outside and look at the mud and see if anything has been taken. Though, the first thing you need to do is count the kids, and pray they followed the rules.

Reem Falaknaz

Epilogue

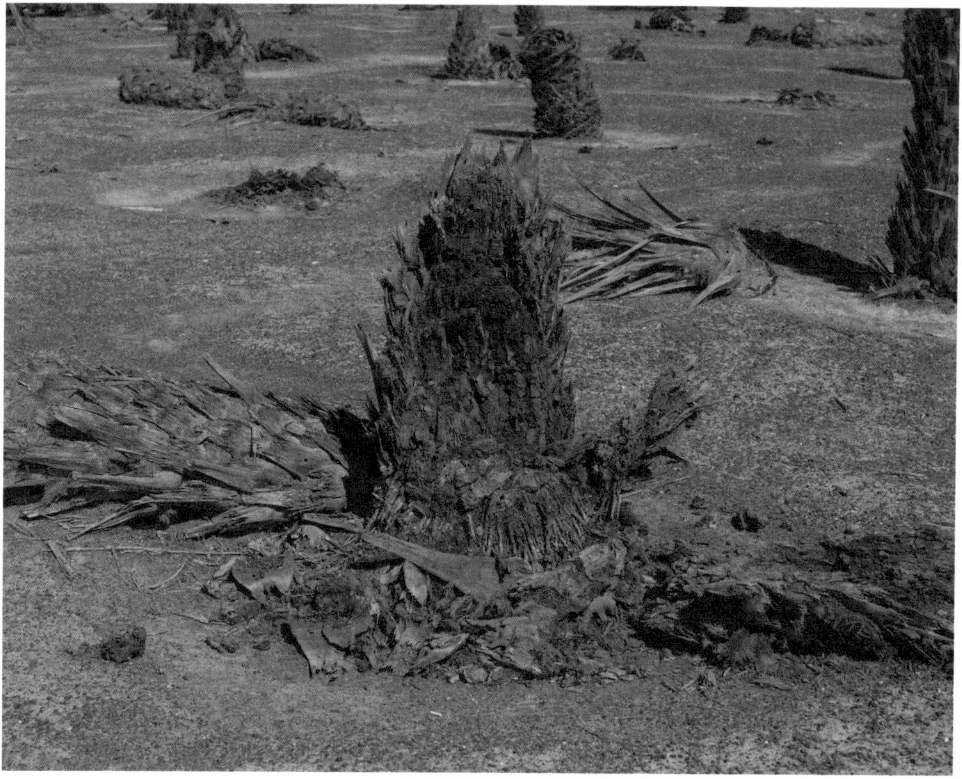

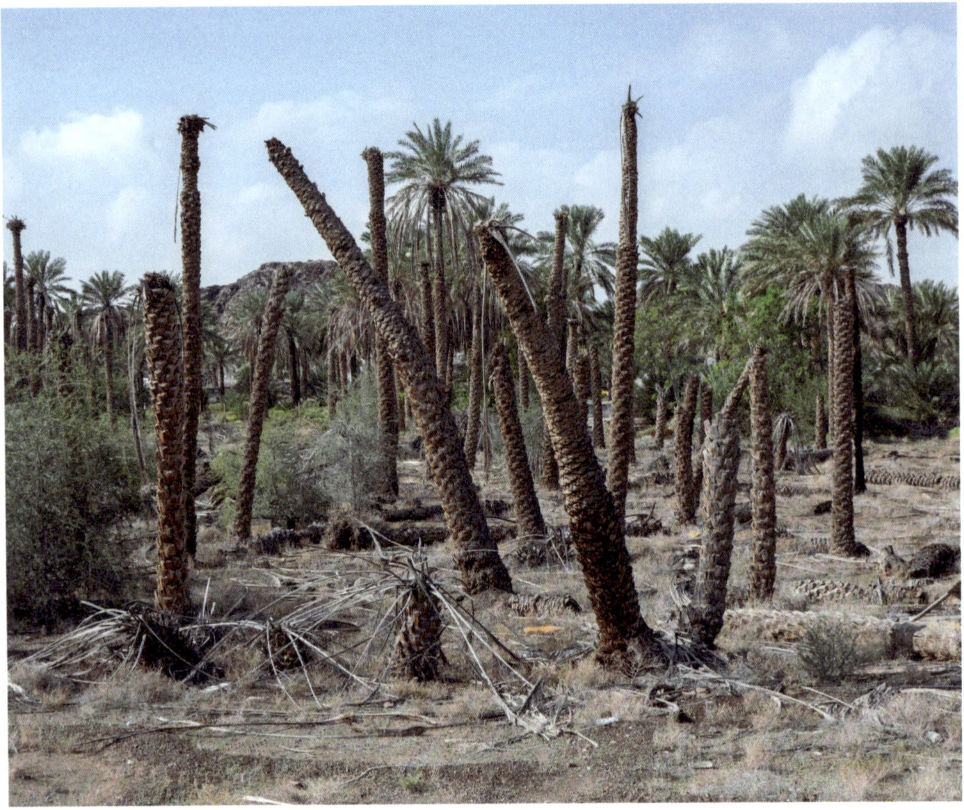

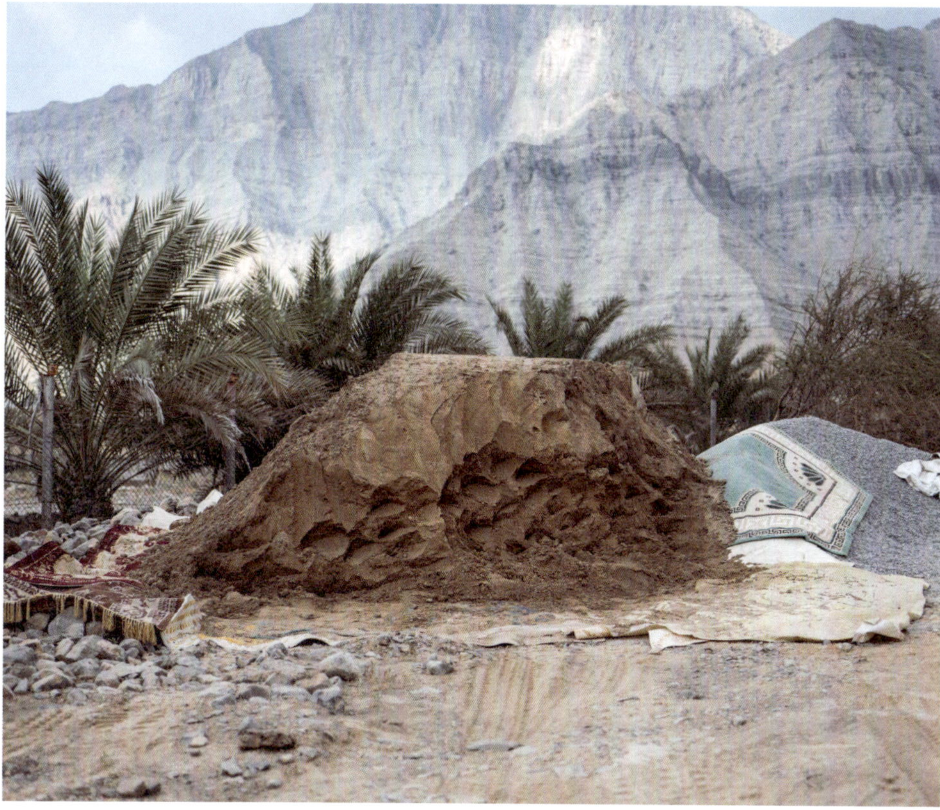

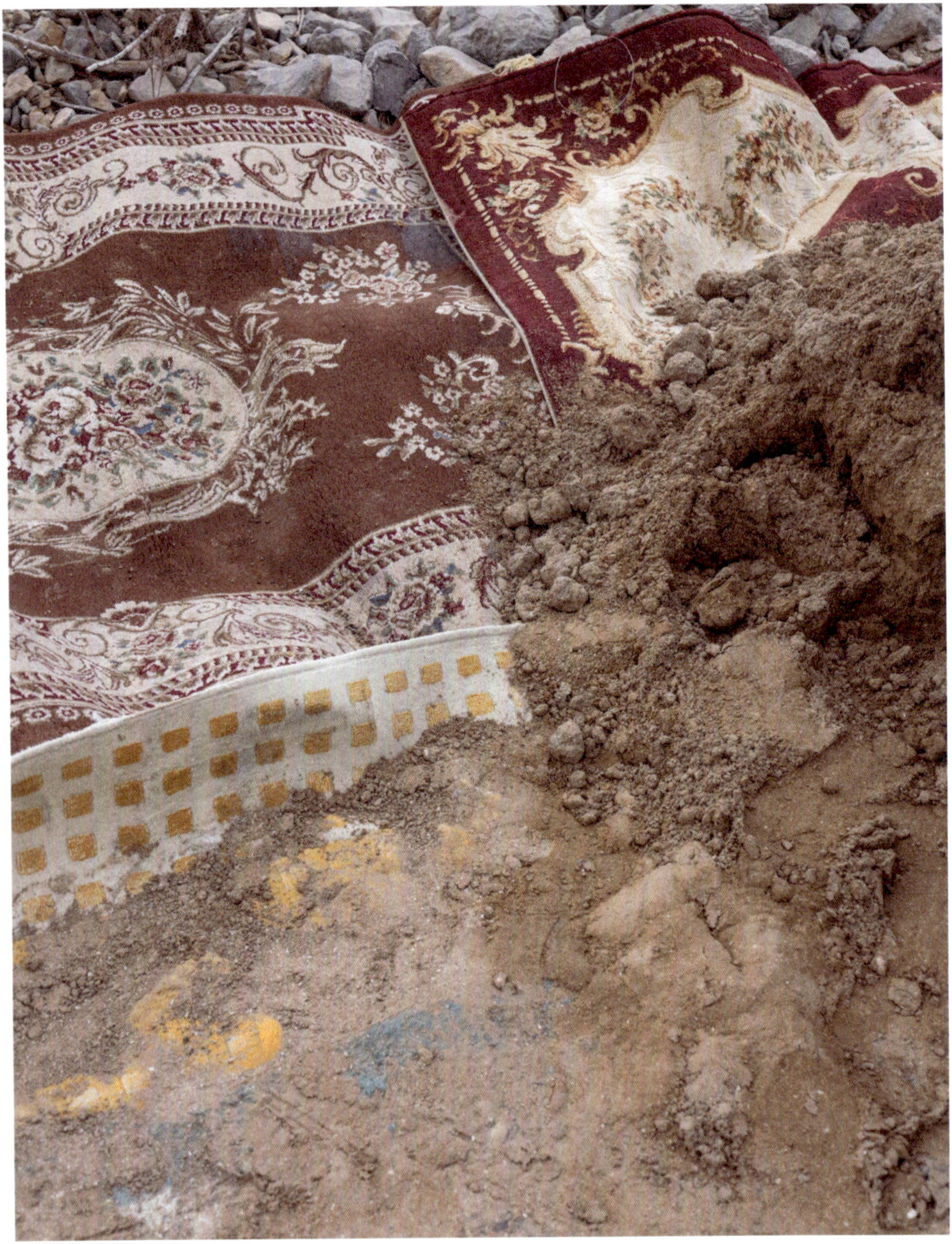

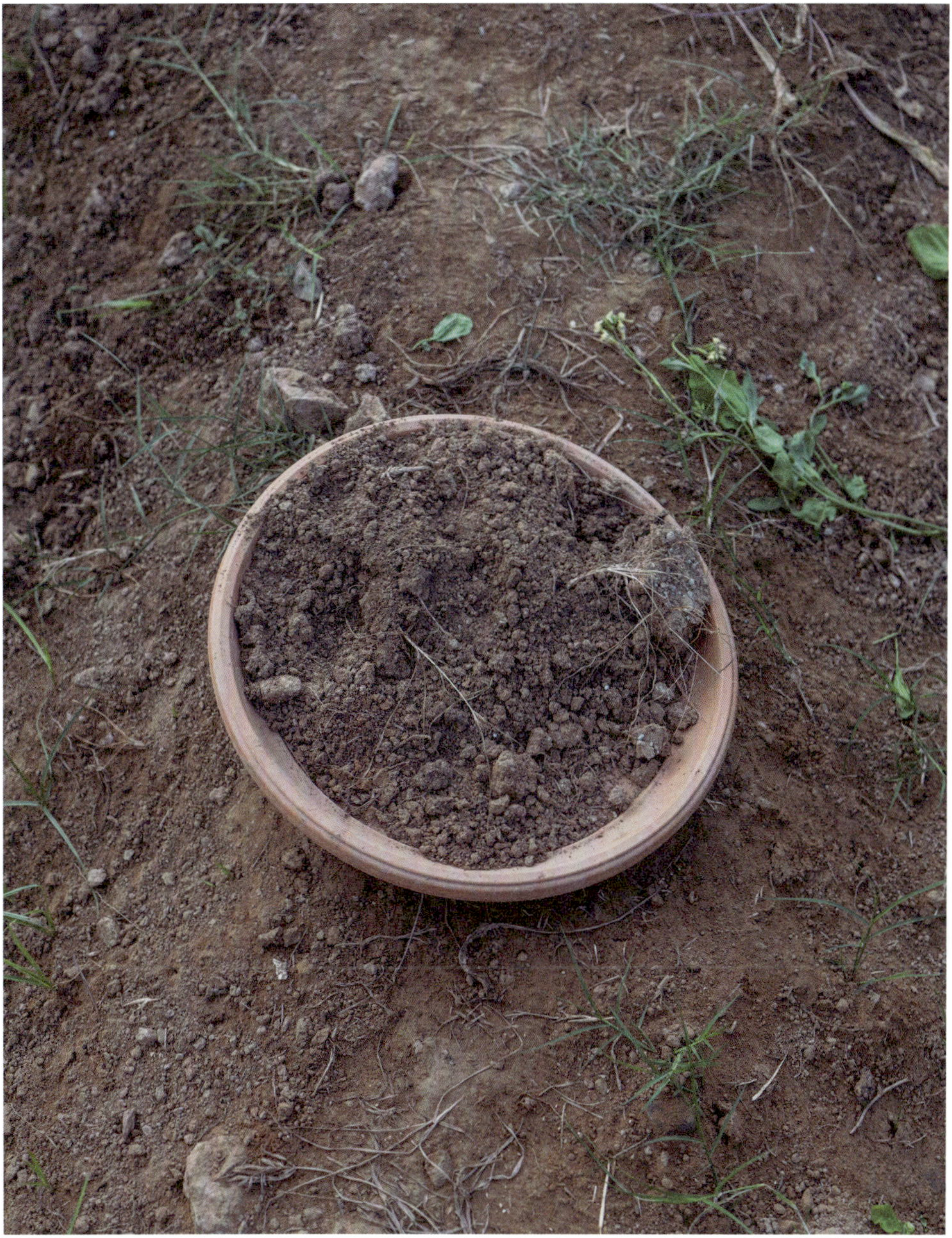

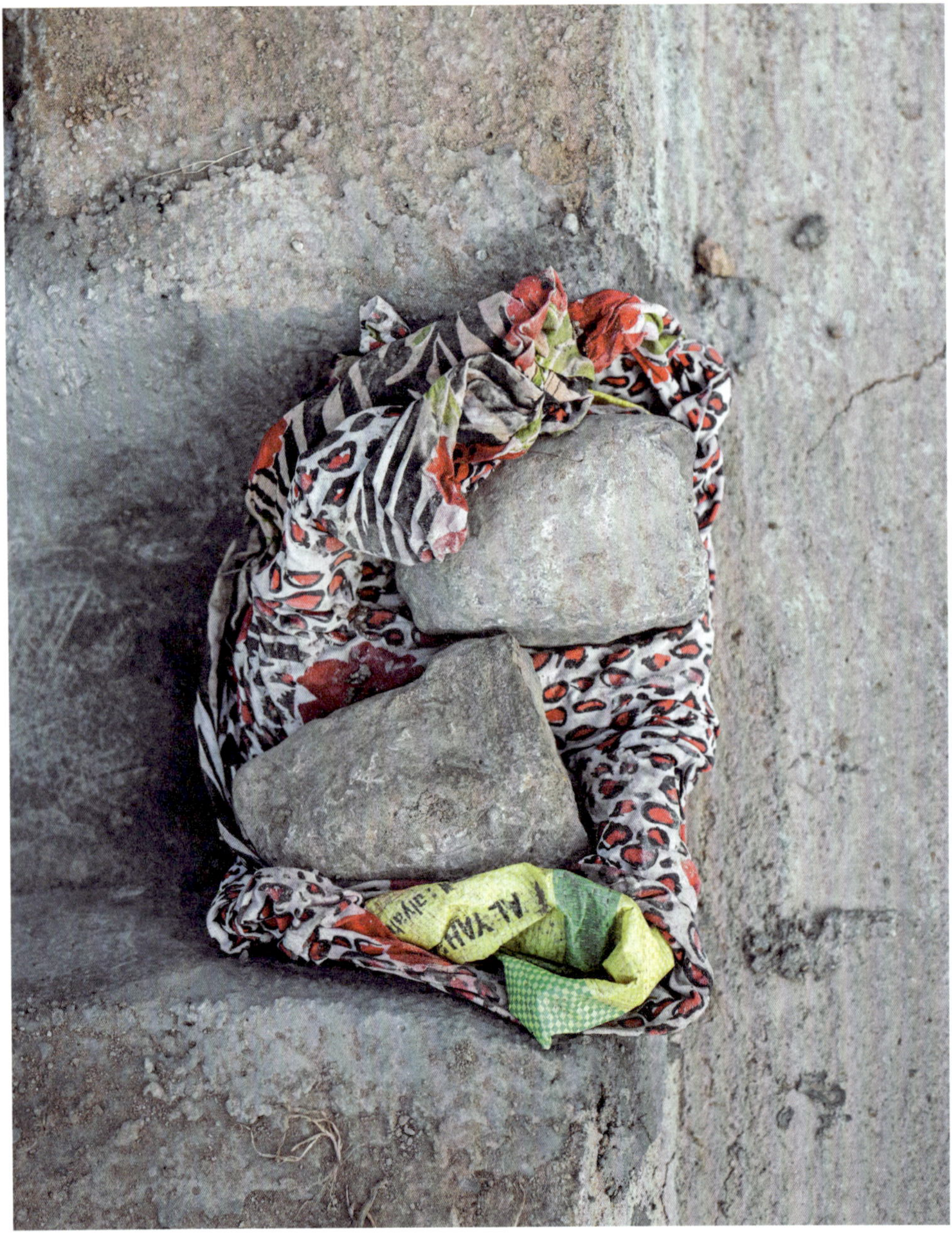

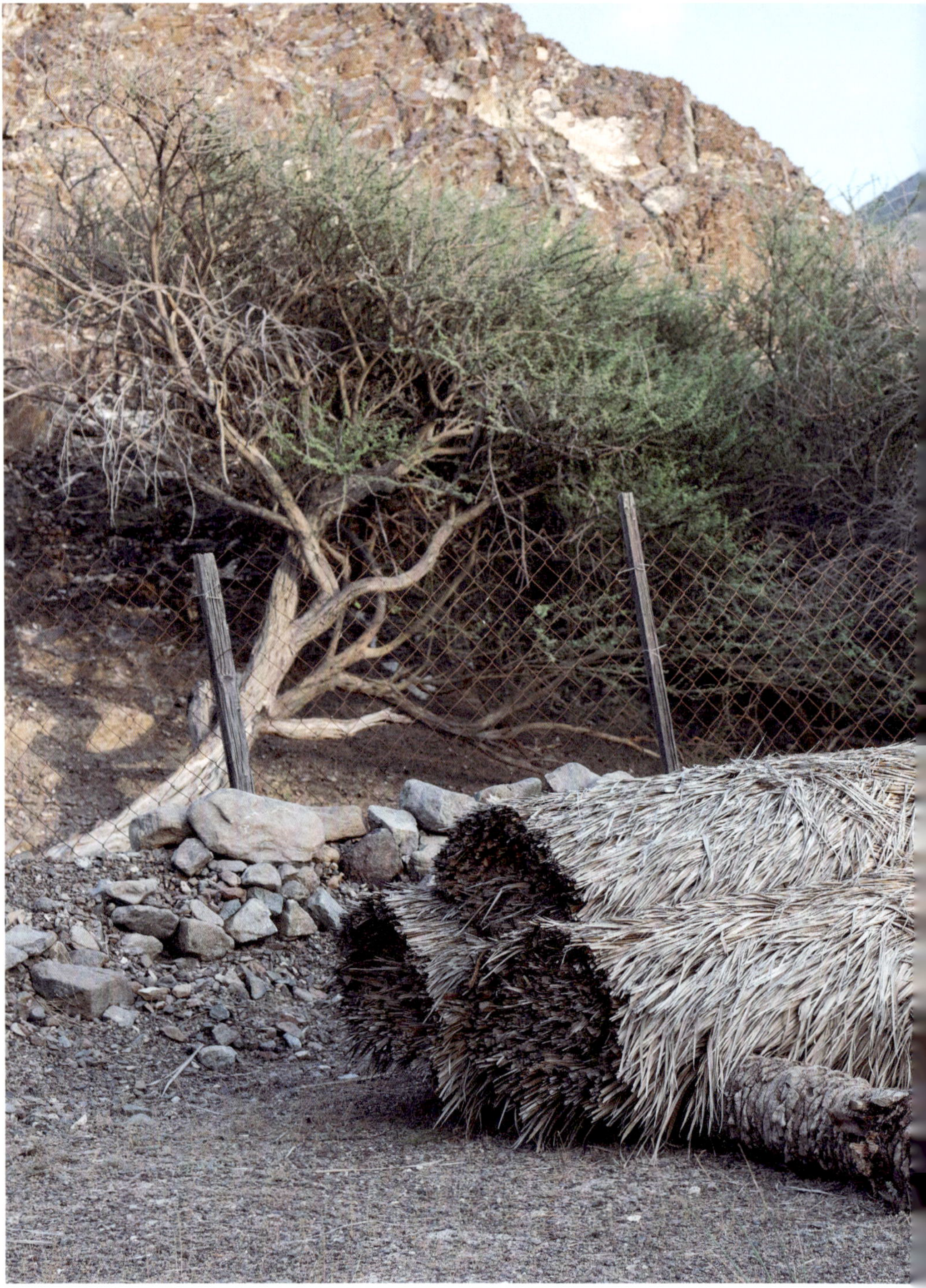

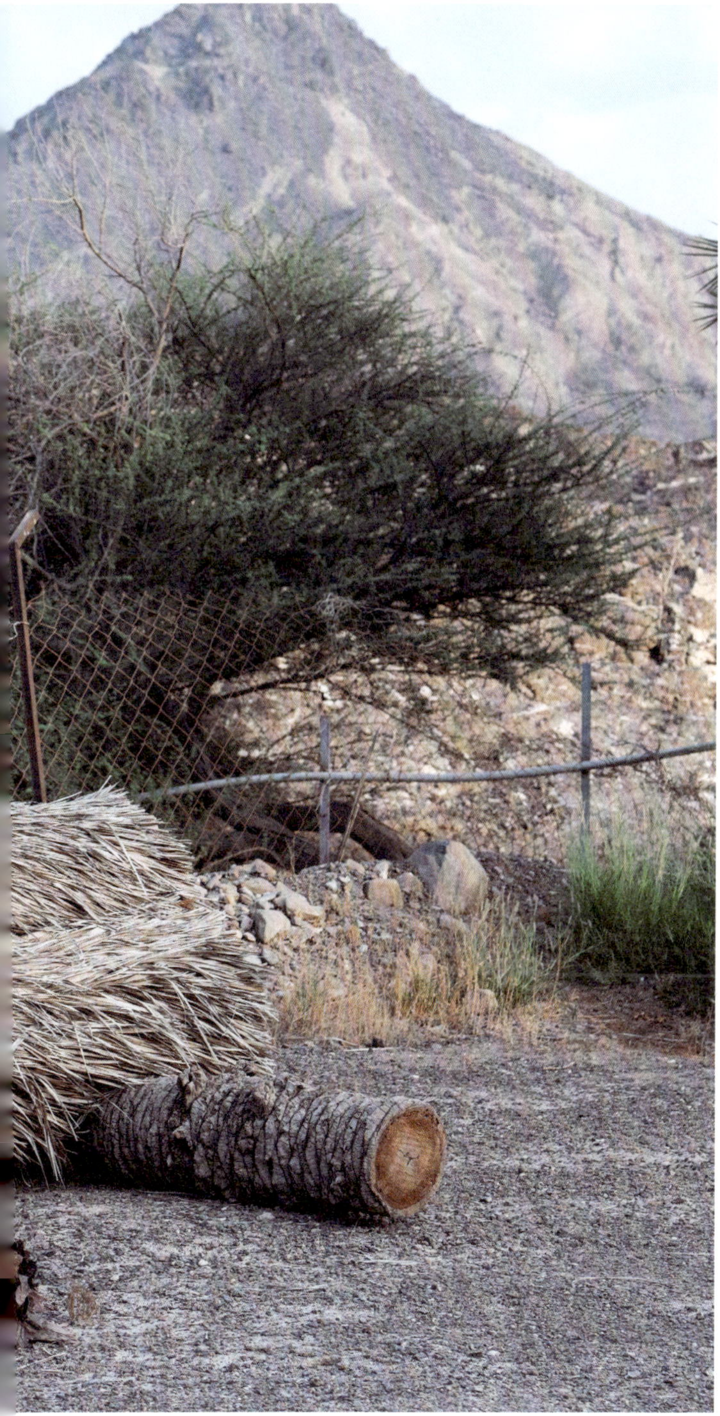

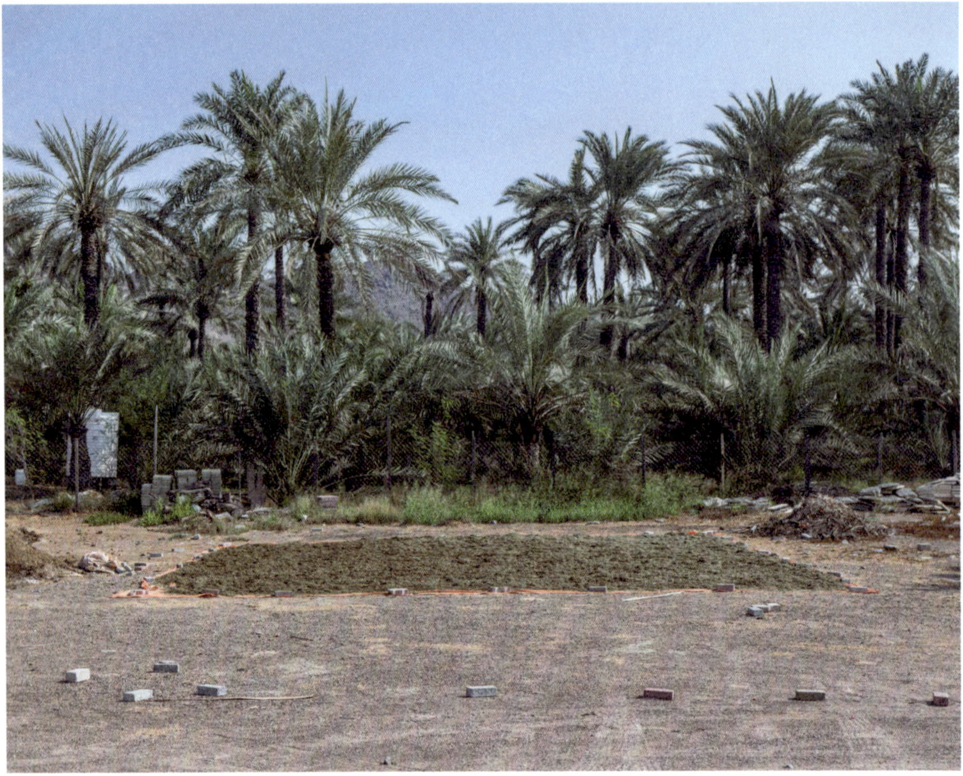

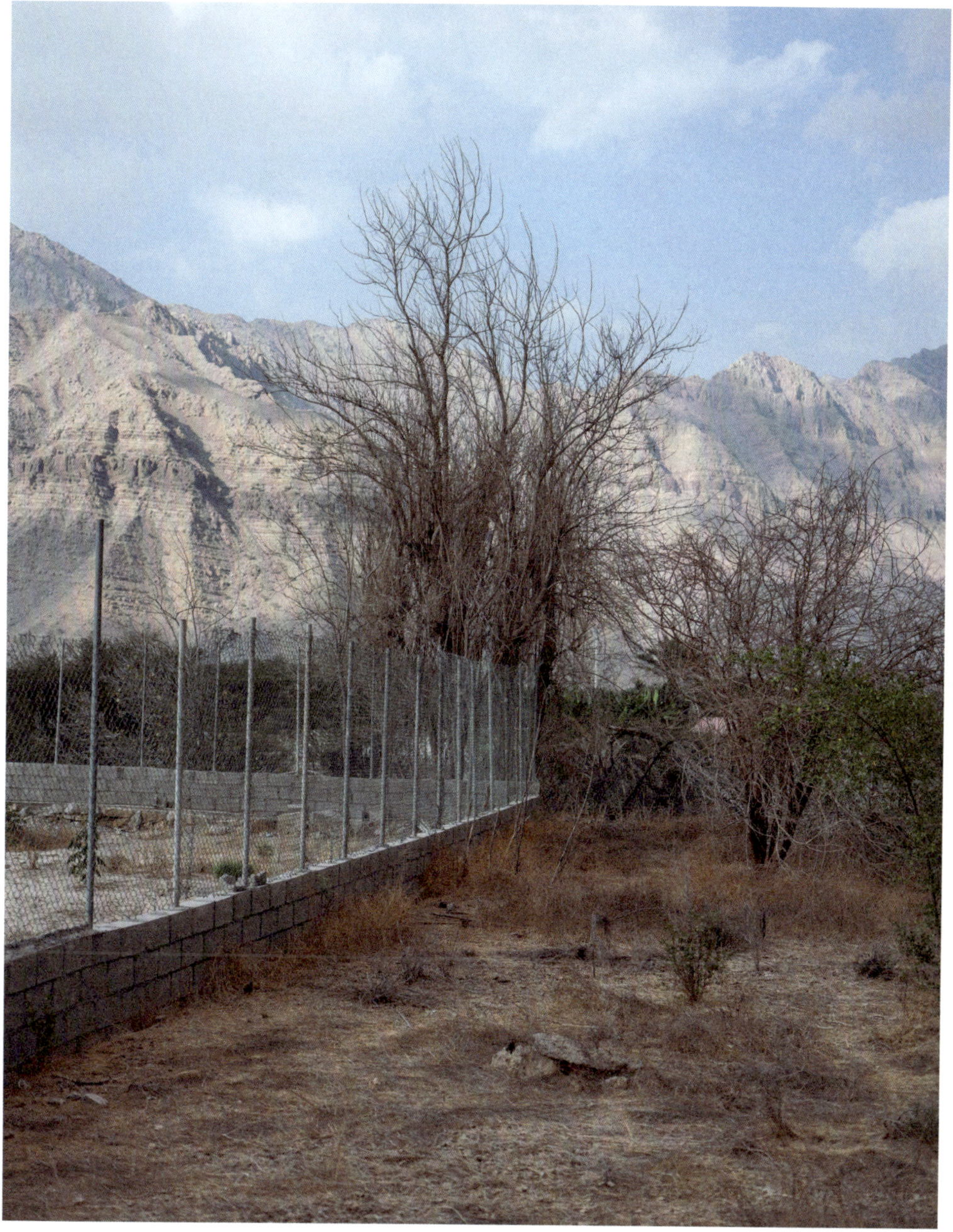

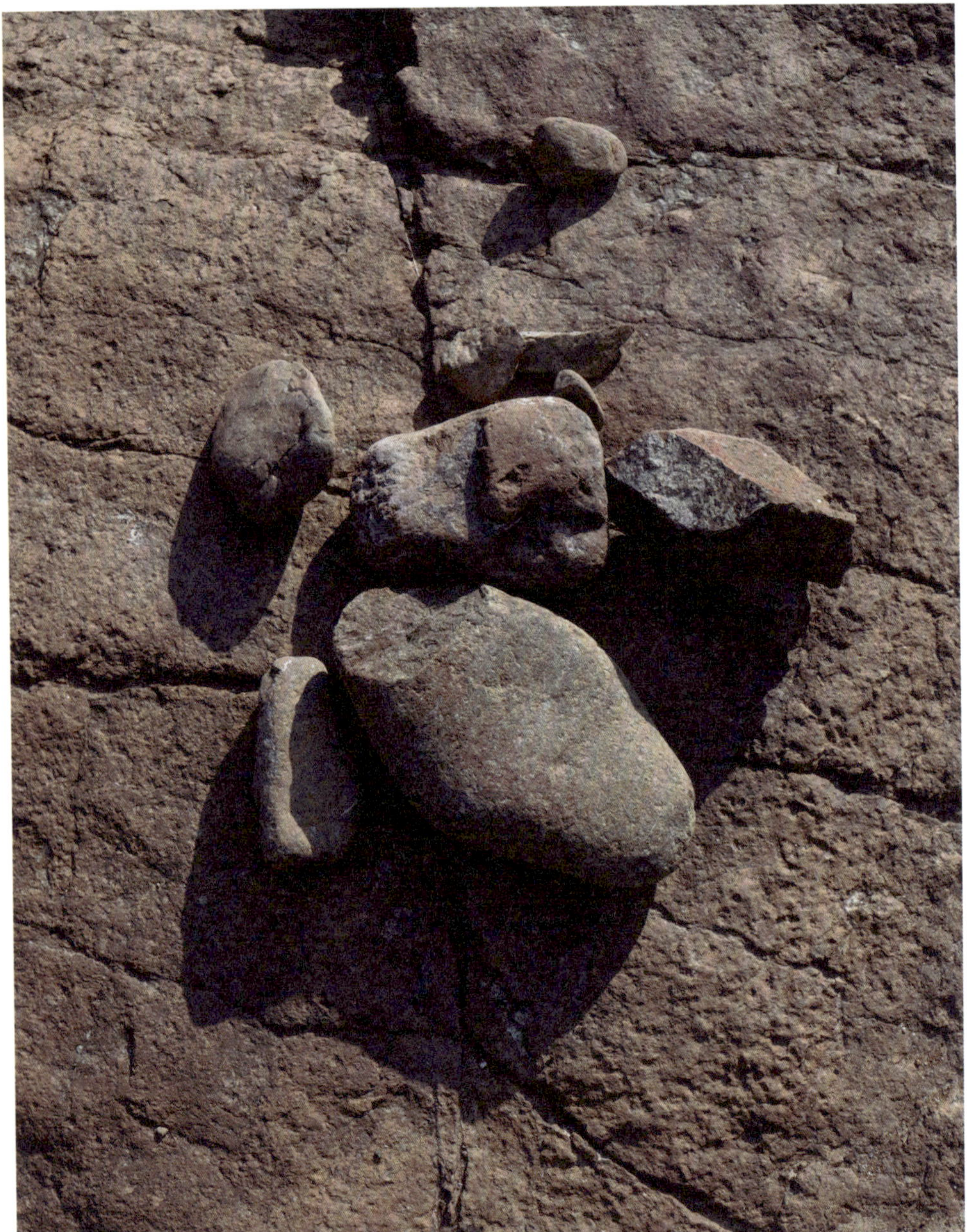

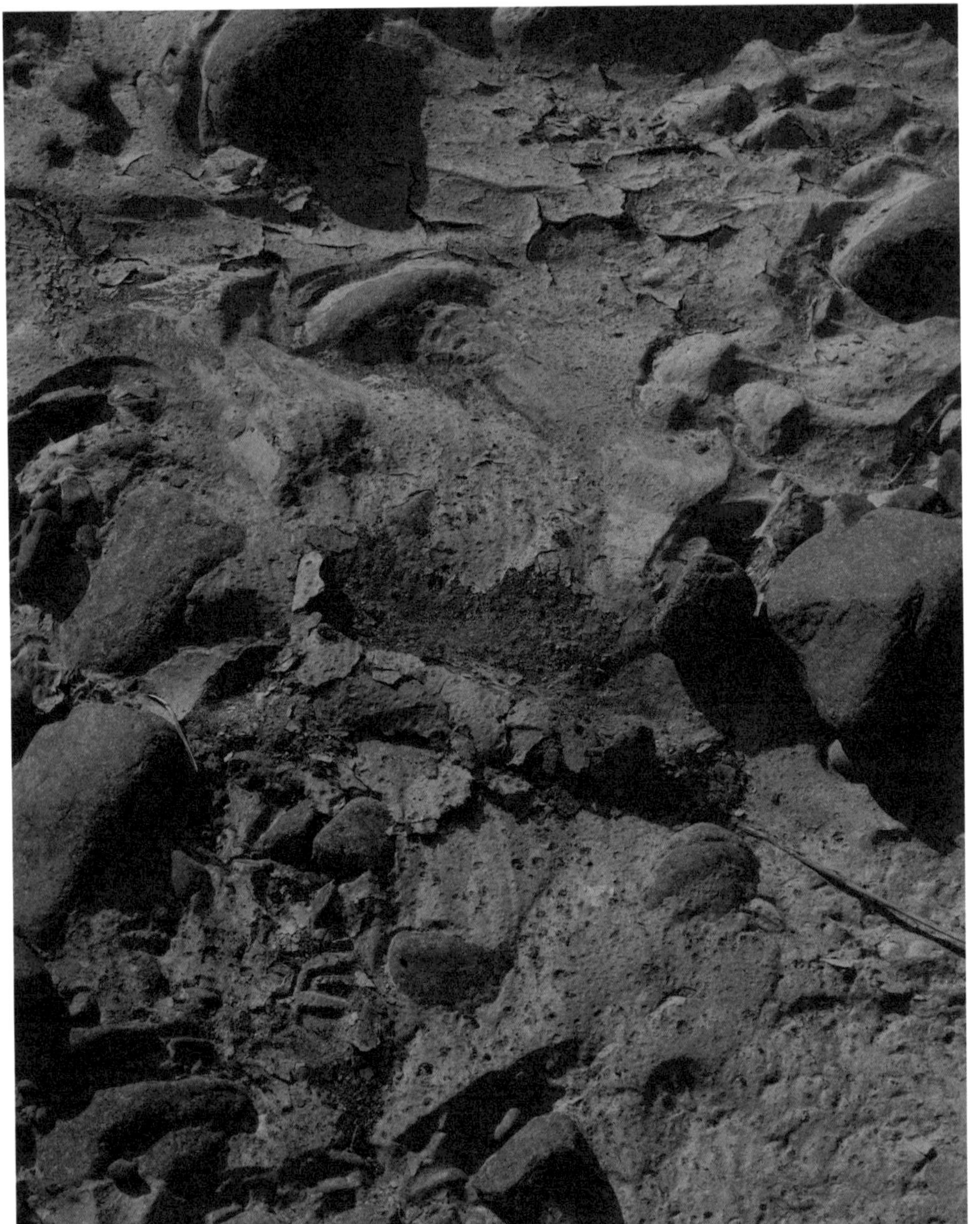

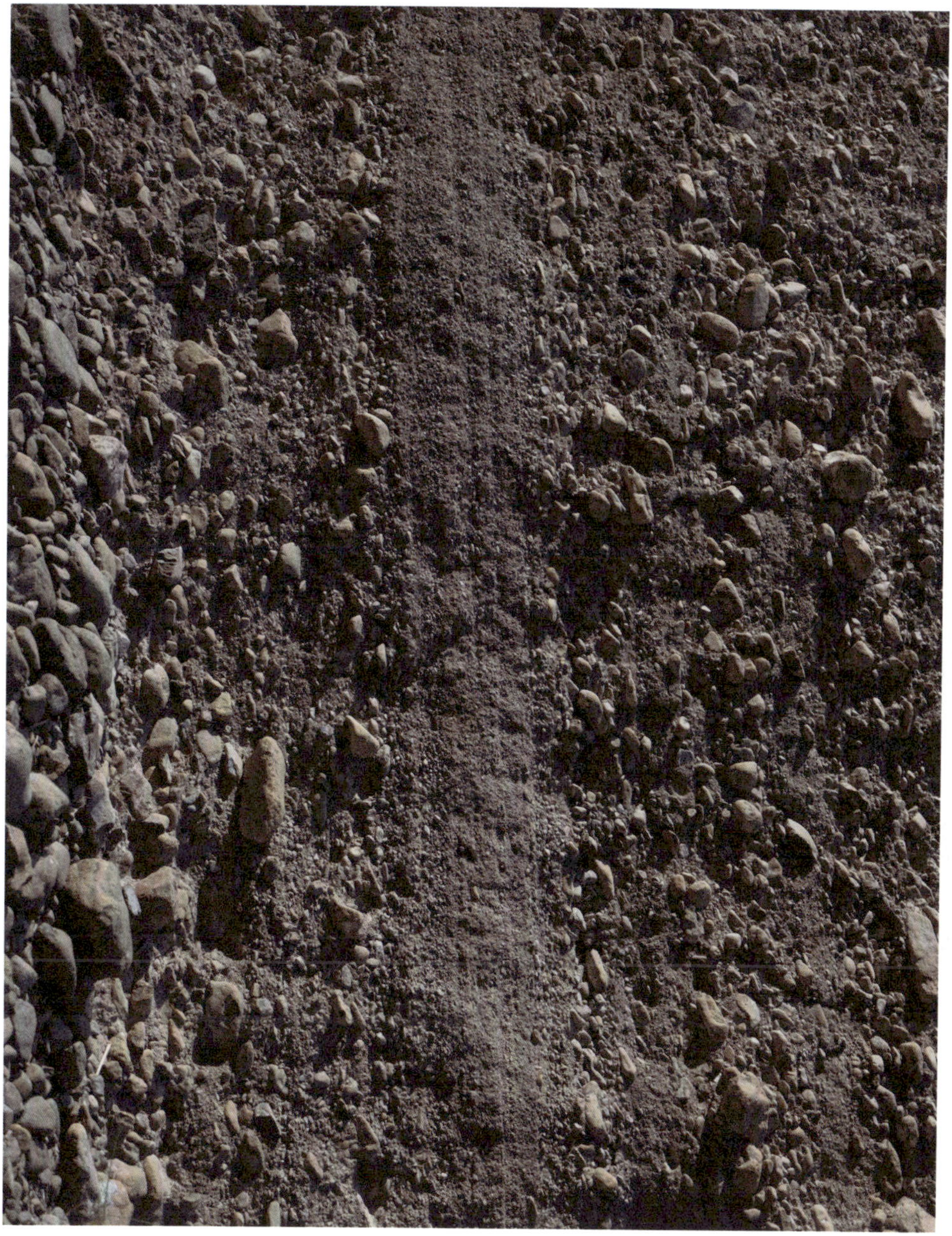

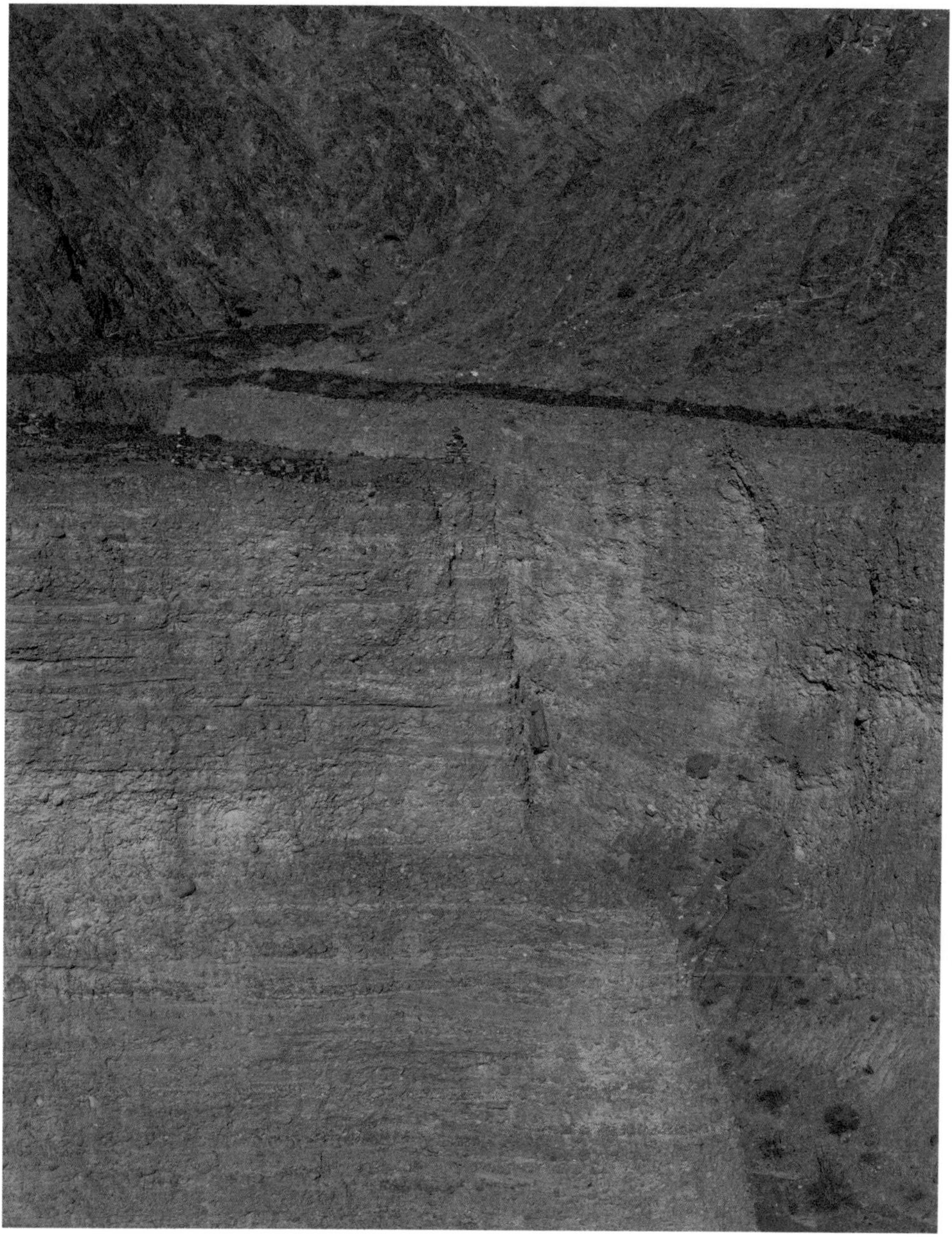

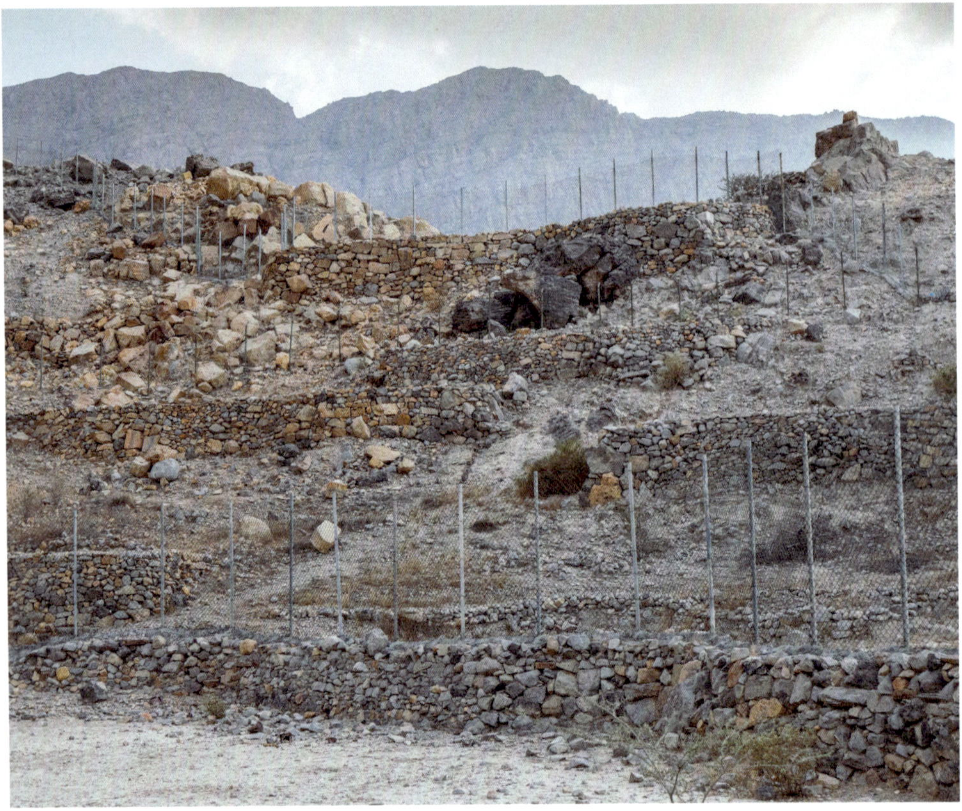

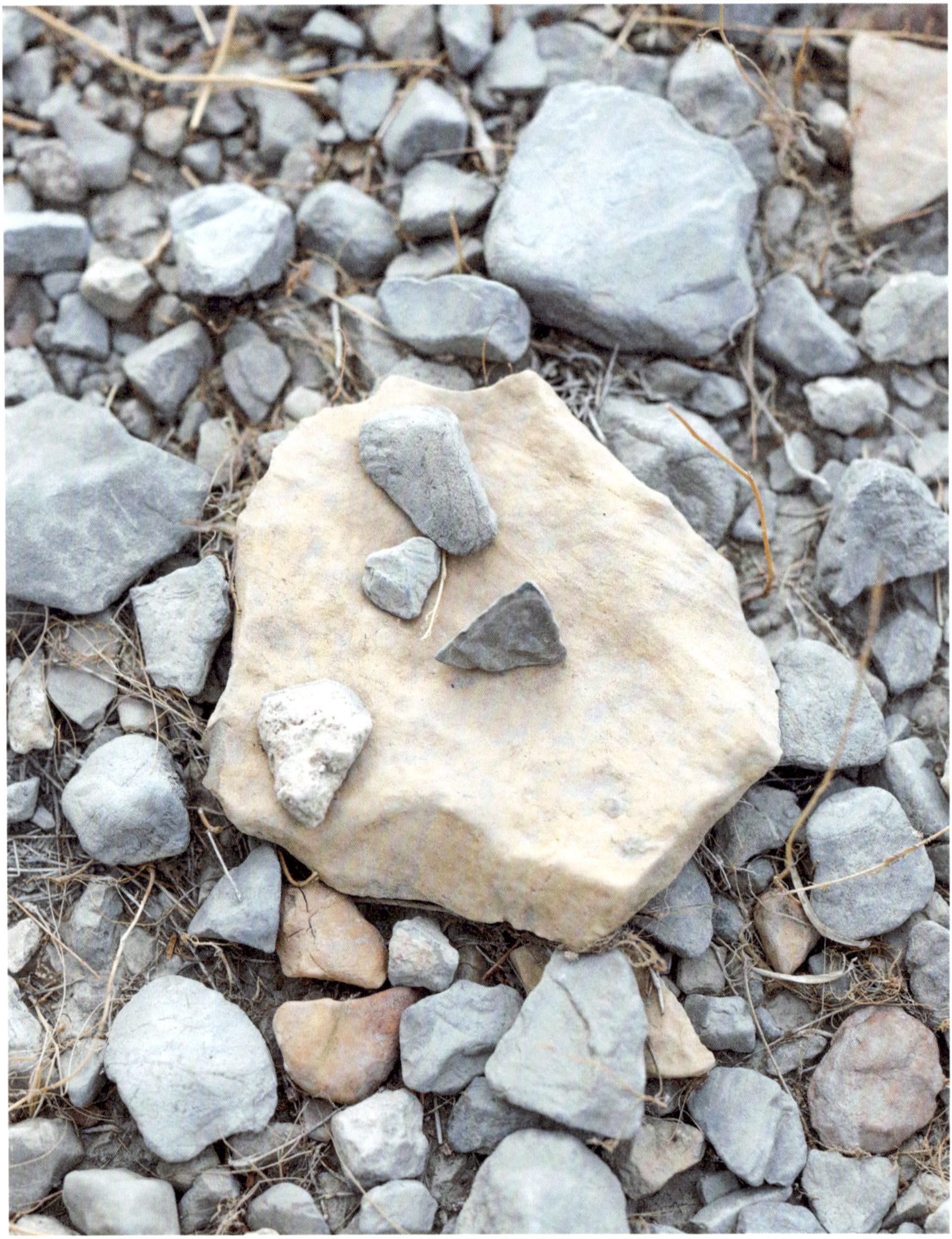

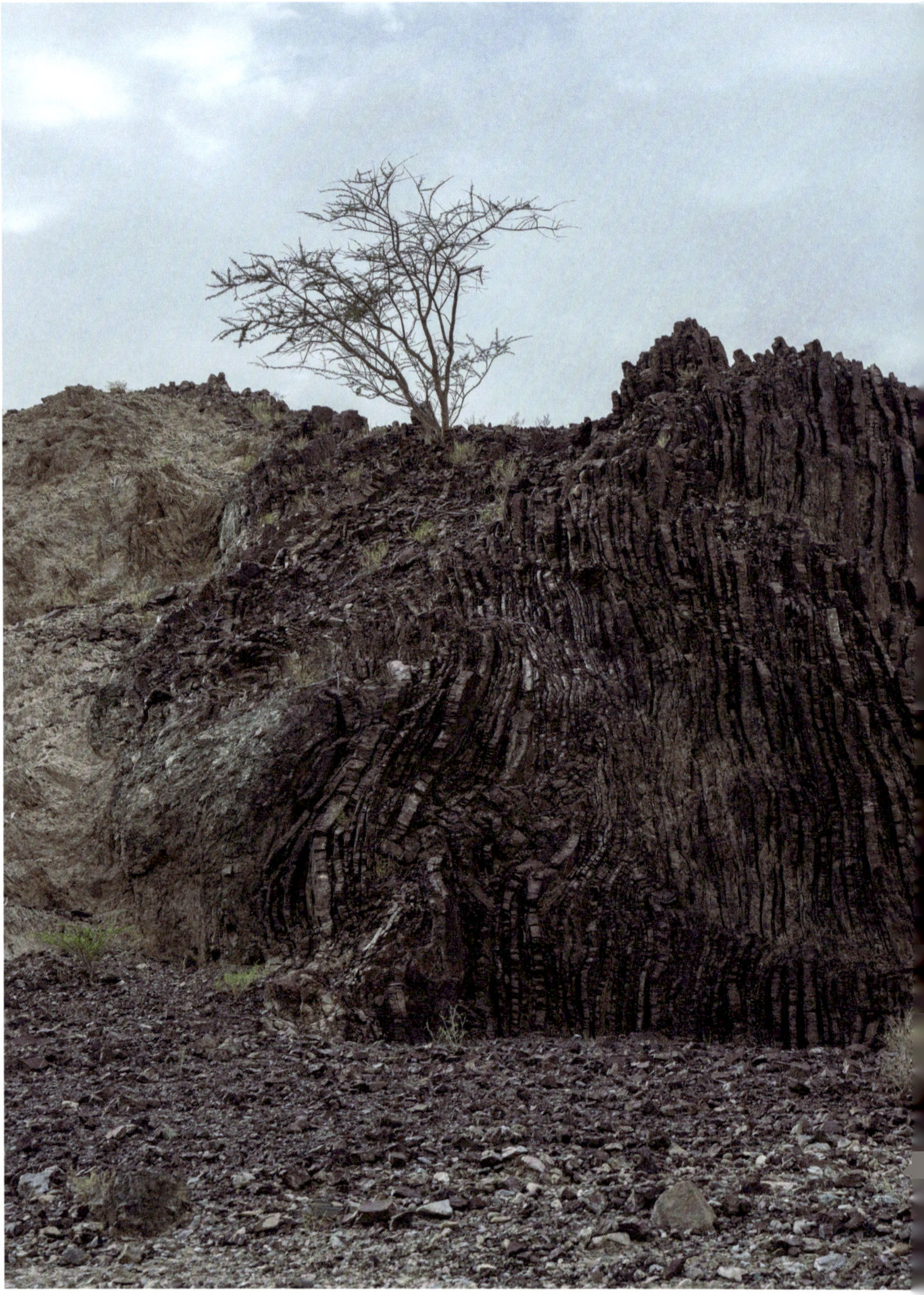

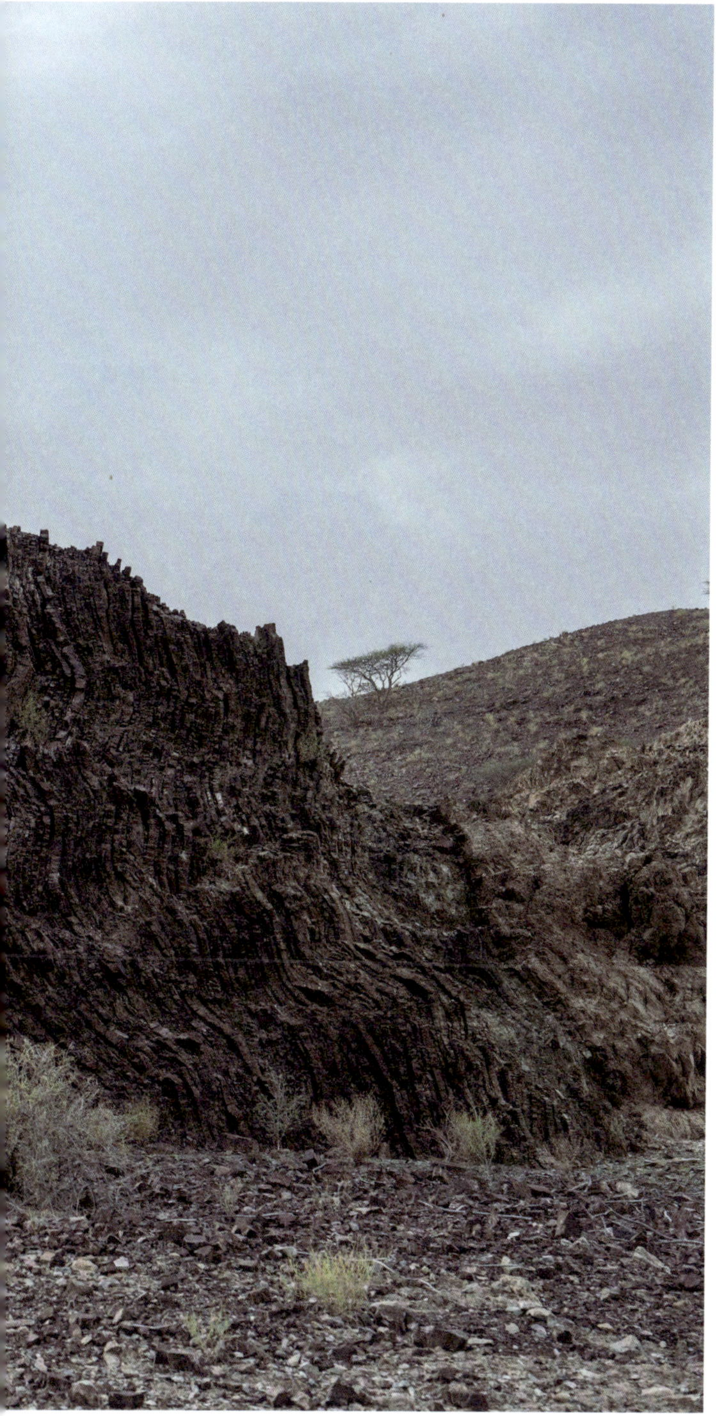

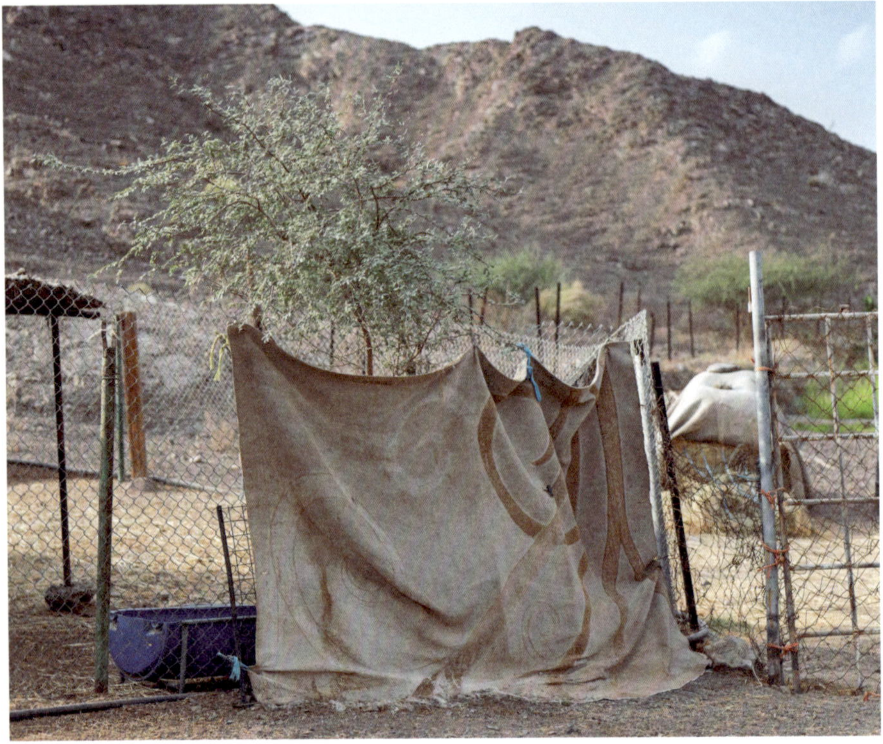

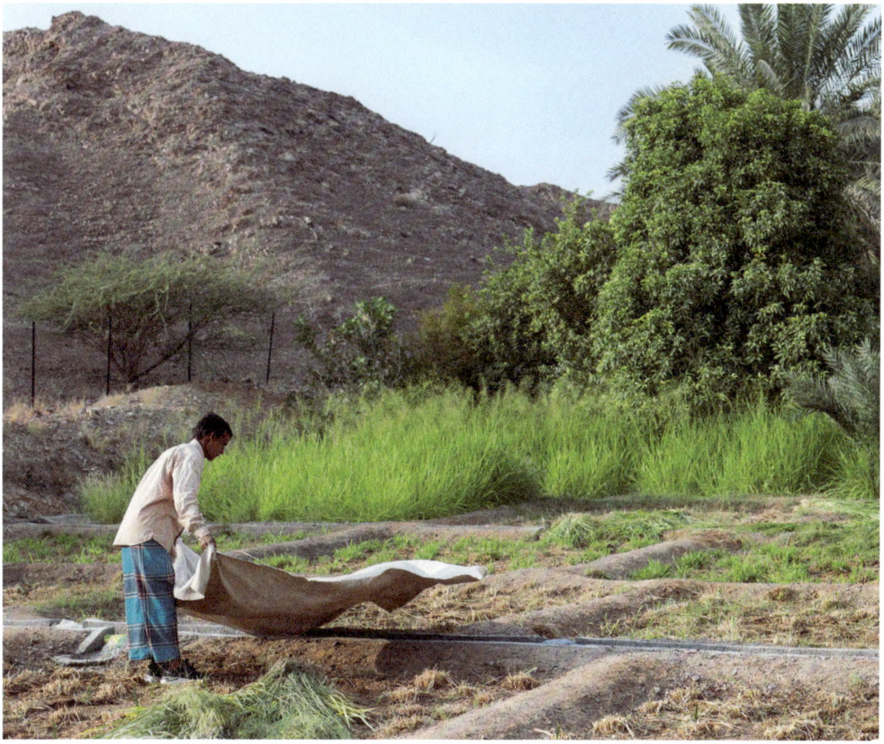

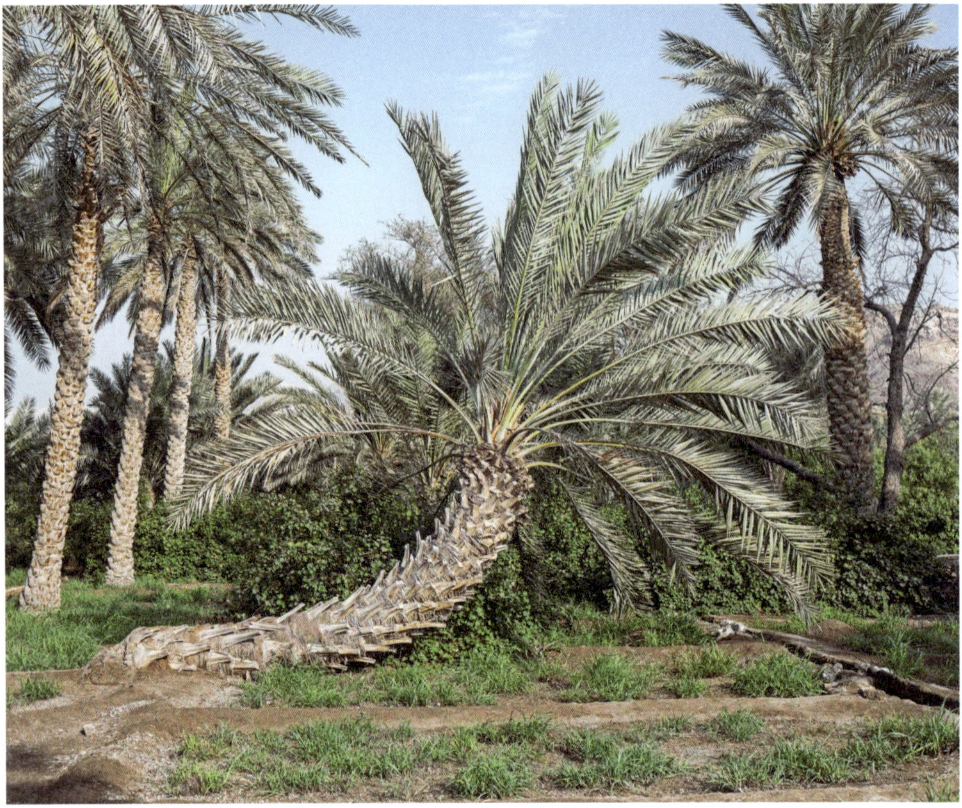

Bibliography An Archive of Travel

Abd Al Razeq, Mohammed Mahmoud. *Dawr Al RahAla Al Gharbiyoon fee Tawtheeq Tareekh Al Kuwait [The Role of Western Travellers in Documenting the History of Kuwait]*. Kuwait: Dar Suad Al Sobah, 2018.

Al Azem, Nazih Moayed. *Rehla fee Al Belad Al Arabia Al Saeeda min Masr ila Sana'a [A Journey to the Happy Arab Countries from Egypt to Sana'a]*. Beirut: Manshoorat Al Madina, 1985.

Al BAlady, Ateq bin Ghaith. *Al Rehla Al Najdiya [A Trip to Najd]*. Mecca: Dar Mecca, 1982.

Al Baqer, Zein Al Abideen bin Hassan. *Al Rehla Al Shaboriya: mn Arabistan ela Abu Dhabi fee Arjoza RehAliya 1936 [The Shaburiyan Journey: From Arabistan to Abu Dhabi in a Travel Poem 1936]*. Beirut: Arab Institute for Research & Publishing, 2021.

Al Batnoni, Mohammed Labeeb. *Al Rihla Al Hijaziya: Le Waley Al Neam Al Hajj Abbas Helmi Basha Al Thani [The Hijazi Journey: by Hajj Abbas Helmi Basha the Second]*. Cairo: Cultural Library, 2017.

Al Jaser, Hamad. *Molakhas Rehlati: Ibn Abd Al Salam Al Dore'e Al Maghriby [My Travel's Summary: Ibn Abd Al Salam Al Dore'e Al Maghriby]*. Riyadh: Dar Al Rifai, 1982.

Al Nazuri, Fatima. *Wain Al Taroosh? Badiyat Abu Dhabi during the 30's and 60's of the 20th century. [Where is the Courier? The Abu Dhabi Desert During the 1930's to the 1940's]*. Abu Dhabi: Department of Culture and Tourism, 2007.

Al Noamani, Shebli. *Rahala Hindi fee Belad Al Sharq Al Arabi [An Indian Traveller in Eastern Arabia]*. Egypt: National Center for Translation, 2009.

Al-Idrisi, Muhammad. Kitab Nuzhat Al-Mushtaq fee Ikhtiraq Al-Afaq [*The Excursion of the One Who Yearns to Penetrate the Horizons*]. 1100.

Al-Maqdisi, Muhammed. *Ahsan Al-taqasim fee ma'rifat Al-aqAlim [The Best Divisions for Knowledge of the Regions]*. Reading: Garnet Publishing, 2001.

Alphonse de Lamartine. *A Pilgrimage To The Holy Land: Comprising Recollections, Sketches, And Reflections, Made During A Tour In The East.* South Carolina: Nabu Press, 2011.

Barbosa, Duarte. *The Book of Duarte Barbosa Vol. 1.* London: Bedford Press, 1918.

Bent, Theodore, ed. *Early Voyages and Travels in the Levant: I.- the Diary of Master Thomas Dallam, 1599-1600. II.- Extracts from the Diaries of Dr John Covel, 1670-1679. With Some Account of the Levant Company of Turkey merchants.* Abingdon: Routledge, 2010.

Bernard, Marius. *Turquie d'Europe et d'Asie [Turkey from Europe and Asia]*. Paris: Librarie Renouard, 1899.

Bey, Ali. *Travels of Ali Bey: In Morocco, Tripoli, Cyprus, Egypt, Arabia, Syria, and Turkey, 1803-1807.* Philadelphia: James Maxwell, Printer, 1816.

Browne, John Ross. *Yusef: Or, The journey of the Fungi (I.E Frangi): A Crusade in the East.* South Carolina: Nabu Press, 2010.

Burckhardt, Johann Ludwig. *Travels in Arabia*. London: Henry Colburn, 1829.

Carruthers. Douglas, ed. *The Desert Route to India: Being the Journals of Four travellers by the Great Desert Caravan Route Between Aleppo and Basra.* New Delhi: Asian Educational Services 1996.

Champney, Elizabeth W. *Three Vassar Girls in the Holy Land.* London: Forgotten Books, 2018.

Cowper, H. Swainson. *Through Turkish Arabia: A Journey from The Mediterranean To Bombay By The Euphrates And Tigris Valleys and Persian Gulf.* London: Forgotten Books, 2018.

Cursetjee, C. M. *The Land of the Date: A Recent Voyage from Bombay to Basra and Back, 1916-1917.* Reading: Ithaca Press, 1996.

Curzon, Robert. *Visits to Monasteries in the Levant*. London: John Murray, 1849.

Damer, Miss Dawson. *Diary of A Tour in Greece, Turkey, Egypt, and The Holy Land (1841).* Whitefish: Kessinger Publishing, 2008.

Dankoff, Robert and Sooyong Kim, ed. *An Ottoman Traveler, Selections from the Book of Travels of Evliya Çelebi.* London: Eland, 2011.

Della Valle, Pietro. *The travels of Sig. Pietro della Valle, a Noble Roman, into East-India and Arabia Deserta.* London: J Macock, 1655.

Dostal, Walter. *The Traditional Architecture of Ras al-Khaimah (North).* Wiesbaden: Dr. Ludwig Reichert Verlag, 1983.

Doughty, Charles M. *Travels in Arabia Deserta.* Cambridge: Cambridge University Press, 1888.

Eames, Jane Anthony. *Another Budget: Or, Things Which I Saw in the East.* Boston: Ticknor and Fields, 1855.

Eddy, D. C. *Eddy's Travels in Asia and Africa.* Australia: Wentworth Press, 2016.

Feetz, Amelia. Chow-Chow: *Being Selections from a Journal Kept in India, Egypt, and Syria.* London: Hurst and Blackett, 1857.

Foster, Donald S. *Landscape with Arabs: Travels in Aden and South Arabia.* Brighton: Clifton Books, 1969.

Fromentin, Eugene. *Un Eté dans le Sahara (A Summer in the Sahara).* Paris: Librairie Plon, 1856.

Green, Lenamay. *A Girl's Journey through Europe, Egypt, and the Holy Land.* Nashville: M. E. Church, 1889.

Groome, P. L. *Rambles of a Southerner in Three Continents.* Greensboro: Thomas Brothers 1891.

Guarmani, Carlo. *Northern Najd: A Journey from Jerusalem to Anaiza in Qasim.* London: The Argonaut Press, 1938.

Hahn-Hahn, Ida. *Letters of a German Countess.* London: Henry Colburn, 1845.

Hamza, Effat Wesal. *Emra'a fee Al Sahraa Al Arabiya [A Woman in the Arabian Desert].*Cairo: Dar Al Fikr Al Arabi, 1990

Hansen, Thorkild. *The Danish Expedition 1761-1767.* New York: NYRB, 2017.

Hassan, Zaki Mohammed. *Al Rahla Al Muslimoon fee Al Osoor Al Wosta [Arab Travellers in the Middle Ages].* Beirut: Dar Al Raed Al Arabi,1981

Hatta, Mohammed Kamel. *Fee Ard Al Mojezat [In the Land of Miracles].* Cairo: Dar Al Kitab Al Masri, 1957.

Helfritz, Hans. *The Yemen: A Secret Journey.* Abingdon: Routledge, 2016.

Heude, William. *A Voyage of the Persian Gulf and a Journey Overland from India to England in 1817.* London: Longman, Hurst, Rees, Orme, and Brown, 1819.

Heyerdahl, Thor. *The Tigris Expedition: In Search of Our Beginnings.* New York: Doubelday, 1984.

Hillyard, Susan. *Before the Oil: A Personal Memoir of Abu Dhabi 1954-1958.* London: Country Books, 2002.

Holmboe, Knud. *Desert Encounter.* London: The Quilliam Press, 1994.

Howell, Georgina. *Gertrude Bell: Queen of the Desert, Shaper of Nations.* New York: Sarah Crichton Books 2007.

Ibn Hawqal, Muhammad. *Surat Al-Ard [The face of the Earth].* Cairo: Sharikat Nawabigh Al Fikr, 2009.

Ibn Jubair. *Rihlat Ibn Jubair [The travels of Ibn Jubair].* Riyadh: Markaz Al Turath Lilbarmajiat, 2013.

Ibrahim, Abd Al Aziz Abd Al Ghani. *Rewayat Gharbiyah an Rehlat fee Shebh Al Jazeera Al Arabia [Western Accounts of Travels in the Arabian Peninsula].* Beirut: Dar Al Saqi, 2013.

Ingrams, Harold. *Arabia and the Isles.* Abingdon: Routledge, 2010.

Jacob, Robert Urie. *A Trip to the Orient: The Story of a Mediterranean Cruise.* Philadelphia: The John C. Winston Co., 1907.

Jones, George. *Excursions to Cairo, Jerusalem, Damascus, and Balbec From the United States Ship Delaware, During Her Recent Cruise.* New York: Van Nostrand and Dwight, 1836.

Kendall, William E. *Letters from Europe and the East.* New York: G. A. Whitehorne, Book, and Job Printer, 1860.

Kinglake, Alexander William. *Eothen: Traces of Travel Brought Home from the East.* London: John Ollivier, 1845.

Kirk, Martha. *Green Sands: My Five Years in the Saudi Desert.* Lubbock: Texas Tech University Press, 1994.

Knox, Thomas Wallace. *The Story Teller of the Desert: Backsheesh! or, Life and adventures in the Orient.* Hartford: A. D. Worthington & Co., Publishers, 1885.

Lancaster, Fidelity and William Lancaster. *Honour in Contentment: Life Before Oil in Ras Al-Khaimah (UAE) and Some Neighbouring Regions.* Gottingen: De Gruyter, Inc., 2011.

Lawrence, Thomas Edward. *The Diary Kept by T. E. Lawrence While Travelling in Arabia During 1911*. Reading: Garnet Publishing, 1993.

Lewis, Agnes Smith. *Eastern Pilgrims: The Travels of Three Ladies.* London: Hurst & Blackett, 1870.

Bell, Gertrude. *Amurath to Amurath*. New Jersey: Gorgias Press, 2001.

Mackintosh-Smith, Tim, ed. *The Travels of Ibn Battutah*. London: Picador, 2003.

Mandeville, John. The Voyages of Sir John Mandevile. London: Macmillan and Co. Limited, 1900.

Martineau, Harriet. *Eastern Life, Present and Past*. London: E. Moxon, Son, and Co., 1875.

Maxwell, Gavin. *A Reed Shaken by the Wind.* London: Eland, 1994.

Miller, D. L. *Letters to the Young from the Old World: Notes of Travel.* Mount Morris: The Brethren's Publishing Company, 1896.

Monroe, Elizabeth. *Philby of Arabia*. Reading: Ithaca Press, 1996.

Montefeeore, Judith Cohen. *Notes From a Private Journal of a Visit to Egypt and Palestine, By Way of Italy and the Mediterranean*. London: Joseph Rickerby, 1844.

Morris, Jan. *A Writer's World: Travels 1950 - 2000*. London: Faber and Faber, 2003.

Myres, William, and William Polk. *Passing Brave.* New York: Alfred A. Knopf, 1973.

Najila Hassan. *Thekrayati fee Dar el Oroba [Memories in the Land of Arabia]*. Beirut: Dar Maktabat Al Haya, 1965.

Nakano, Eijiro. *Al Rehla Al Yabaniya ila Al Jazeera Al Arabiya [The Japanese trip to the Arabian Peninsula].* Riyadh: Isdarat Darat Al Malik 'Abd Al Aziz, 1999.

Niebuhr, Carsten. *Travels Through Arabia and Other Countries in the East.* Edinburgh: R. Morison and Son, 1792.

Nippa, Annegret, Peter Herbstreuth and Hermann Burchardt. *Along The Gulf: From Basra to Muscat*. Dar Al Kutub Al Wataniya, 2013.

Norwich, John Julius. *A Taste for Travel: An Anthology*. New York: Alfred a Knopf, 1987.

Owen, Roderic. *The Golden Bubble: Arabian Gulf Documentary*. London: Collins, 1957.

Paine, Albert Bigelow. *The Ship-Dwellers: A Story of a Happy Cruise*. New York: Harper & Brothers, 1910.

Palgrave, William Gifford. *Narrative of a Year's Journey Through Central and Eastern Arabia*. London: Macmillan and Co., 1873.

Parsons, Abraham. *Travels In Asia And Africa.* London: Longman, Hurst, Rees, Orme, and Brown, 1808.

Pelly, Lewis. *Report on A Journey to Riyadh in Central Arabia*. Cambridge: The Oleander Press, 2013.

Pfeiffer, Ida. Visit to the Holy Land, Egypt, and Italy. London: Ingram, Cooke, and Co., 1852.

Pliny the Elder. *The Natural History of Pliny*. London: H. G. Bohn, 1855.

Plumley, Matilda. *Days and Nights in the East*. London: The British Library, 2010.

Raban, Jonathan. Arabia*: Through the Looking Glass*. London: Eland, 2018.

Ricketts, Clemuel Green. *Notes of travel, in Europe, Egypt, and the Holy Land, including a visit to the city of Constantinople.* London: Forgotten Books, 2018.

Rihani, Ameen. *Around The Coasts of Arabia*. London: Constable, 1930.

Ross, Henry James. *Letters from the East*. London: J.M. Dent & Co., 1902.

Ruthven, Malise. *Freya Stark in Iraq & Kuwait*. Reading: Garnet Publishing, 1994.

Sadleir, G. Forster. *Diary of a Journey Across Arabia*. Cambridge: The Oleander Press: 2013.

Samuel, Jacob. *Journal of a Missionary Tour Through the Desert of Arabia to Baghdad*. Edinburgh: Maclachlan Stewart and Co., 1844.

Sanger, Richard H. *The Arabian Peninsula*. Ithaca: Cornell University Press, 1954.

Smith, William Alexander. *From Occident to Orient*. London: Forgotten Books: 2018.

Stanhope, Hester. *Travels of Lady Hester Stanhope; Forming the Completion of Her Memoirs*. London: Henry Colburn, 1846.

Stark, Freya. *Beyond Euphrates*. London: John Murray, 1951.

Stern, Henry Aaron. *Dawnings of Light in the East*. London: Charles H. Purday, 1854.

Stine, Milton H. *A Winter Jaunt Through Historic Lands*. Philadelphia: Lutheran Publication Society, 1890.

Strangford, Emily Anne. *Egyptian Sepulchres and Syrian Shrines, Including a Visit to Palmyra*. London: Macmillan and Co., 1874.

Taylor, Bayard. *The Lands of the Saracen*. New York: G. P. Putnam's Sons, 1892.

Thesiger, Wilfred. *Arabian Sands*. London: Penguin, 2011.

Toy, Barbara. *The Highway of the Three Kings*. London: John Murray, 1968.

Twain, Mark. *The Innocents Abroad*. Hartford: American Publishing Company, 1869.

Tweedie, Alec. *Mainly East* (in Prose, Perhaps Prosey). Australia: Wentworth Press, 2016.

Tweedie, William. Turkish Arabia: Being an Account of an Official Tour in Babylonia, Assyria, and Mesopotamia. Calcutta: The Superintendent of Government Printing, 1888.

van der Meulen, Daniel. *Aden to the Hadhramaut, a Journey in South Arabia*. London: John Murray 1947.

Wansleben, Johann. *Johann Michael Wanslen's Travels in the Levant, 1671-1674*. Leiden: Brill, 2018.

Wellsted, J. R. *Travels to the City of Caliphs Along the Shores of the Persian Gulf and the Mediterranean*. London: Henry Colburn, 1840.

Whaley, Buck. *Buck Whaley's Memoirs*. London: Forgotten Books, 2018.

Whittle, Walter Andrew. *A Baptist abroad; or Travels and adventures in Europe and All Bible lands*. South Carolina: Nabu Press, 2010.

Wilkinson, John Craven. *Water and Tribal Settlement in South-East Arabia: A Study of the Aflaj of Oman*. Oxford: Oxford University Press, 1977.

Wise, Daniel. *Boy Travelers in Arabia: Or, From Boston to Bagdad: Including Pictures, Sketches, and Anecdotes of the Wandering Arabs, and of the City of Good Haroun Alraschid*. Australia: Wentworth Press, 2016.

Zurbonsen, Anthony. *Rambles through Europe, the Holy Land and Egypt*. Australia: Wentworth Press, 2016.

Zwemer, S. M. "Three Journeys in Northern Oman," *The Geographical Journal* Vol. 19 No. 1 (January 1902).

Editors

Faysal Tabbarah

is an Associate Dean and Associate Professor of Architecture at the College of Architecture, Art and Design at the American University of Sharjah (AUS), and co-founder of the experimental architecture and design studio, Architecture + Other Things (A+OT), which is based in Sharjah. Tabbarah's work, across teaching, research, and practice, explores the relationships between regional environmental and architectural imaginaries, or how people bring their natural surroundings to bear on how they understand and shape their world, to develop alternative building practices that are rooted in their surrounding material and cultural environments. To achieve this, Tabbarah's work moves between computational tools, emergent technologies, materials research, and historical archives.

Meitha Almazrooei

is a current PhD student in History, Theory, and Criticism of Architecture at the Massachusetts Institute of Technology. She received her MS in Critical, Curatorial & Conceptual Practices in Architecture from Columbia University's Graduate School of Architecture Planning and Preservation. Her curatorial and editorial work encompassed; public programming for Guggenheim Abu Dhabi, publications for The National Pavilion of the United Arab Emirates in Venice, and establishing WTD Magazine, an architecture and design publication in 2012 as a platform to collect urban narratives from the Arabian Gulf, Eastern Mediterranean and North Africa.

Ahmad Makia is a geographer and editor from the United Arab Emirates. He writes and makes books under his hyperpublishing alias HOUSE. His articles and essays have been published in *Identities: Journal for Politics, Gender and Culture* (forthcoming), *The Funambulist*, *Ibraaz*, *The Outpost*, *The Hypocrite Reader*, *The Avery Review*, *Future Anterior: Journal of Historic Preservation, History, Theory, and Criticism* and *Chapati Mystery.* Makia was also founding editor of the Dubai-based publishing projects THE STATE, ZIGG and Dubailand.

Alia Al-Sabi is a writer and PhD candidate currently based in Brooklyn, New York. Her research is focused on carceral networks and technologies and the various practices of subversion and modes of knowledge production that are possible within logics of confinement. Her dissertation studies a prisoners' archive located in various parts of the West Bank and records the writing and annotative practices of the Palestinian Prisoners' Movement in the 1970s and 1980s.

Aziza Chaouni is an Associate Professor of Architecture at the University of Toronto, John H. Daniels Faculty of Architecture, Landscape, and Design and the founding principal of the design practice Aziza Chaouni Projects (ACP) with offices in Fez, Morocco and Toronto, Canada. She is also the director of the Designing Ecological Tourism Research platform at the Daniels Faculty. Chaouni's practice, research and teaching focuses on sustainable design and construction in the developing world. She is also interested in the integration of architecture and landscape, particularly through the implementation of sustainable technologies in arid climates. She is the author/ editor of three books: *Desert Tourism, Tracing the Fragile Edges of Development* (with Virginie Lefebvre), *Out of Water, Design Solutions for Arid Regions* (with Liat Margolis), *Ecotourism, Nature Conservation and Development, Reimagining Jordan's Shobak Arid Region*, and *Sidi Harazem, Une Oasis Moderne* (with Lucy Haufbauer).

Dalal Musaed Alsayer is an Assistant Professor of Architecture at Kuwait University. Her research lies at the intersection of architecture, environment, and development in the context of Arabia during the twentieth century. She holds a Bachelor of Architecture from Kuwait University; postgraduate degrees from Columbia and Harvard; and a PhD in Architecture from the University of Pennsylvania. She is an academic visitor at St Antony's College, University of Oxford for the academic year 2022-2023.

Deepak ഉണ്ണികൃഷ്ണൻ is the author of *Temporary People*, winner of the Restless Books Prize for New Immigrant writing, the Hindu Prize and the Moore Prize.

Ibrahim Nehme is a writer and multimedia creator living and working in Lebanon. His work is a cross-pollination between journalism, activism and creative expression, and could be understood as a series of attempts to shift the collective consciousness. Through his work, he is interested in activating transnational, cross-border forms of thinking that could give birth to new forms of politics and economics.

Kevin Mitchell is Profesor of Architecture at the American University of Sharjah (AUS), where he has taught courses in architecture, interior design and the Foundations Year since 1999. His teaching contributions have been recognized with awards from AUS the American Institute of Architects. He has served in a number of administrative positions at AUS, including Director of the Foundations Year, Associate Dean of the College of Architecture, Art and Design, Vice Provost for Undergraduate Affairs and Instruction, and Interim Provost. He led the university as Chancellor from 2019 until 2021. In addition to ongoing work as a designer, Mitchell continues to write on issues related to education, design, and architecture and urbanism in the Gulf region. In 2022, the AUS Board of Trustees appointed Mitchell as the university's first Trustees Professor.

Mohamed M. Elnagar is an Egyptian architect and writer, born and raised in Alexandria. Currently based in UAE since 2007, he has published two short story books in Egypt in 2013 and 2018.

Omar Abdel-Ghaffar is a JD-PhD candidate at Harvard University. His research interests revolve around questions of medieval Islamic legal practice, archival habits, and court systems. Raised between California and Alexandria, he lived in New York before moving to Cambridge, Massachusetts, where he is currently based.

Rand Abdul Jabbar is an artist, writer, and researcher whose work borrows from and reconstructs the ephemera of place, history, and memory. Engaging with institutional archives and examining historic, cultural, and archeological narratives, she interrogates the fragility of natural and built environments while simultaneously exploring and contesting with individual and collective memory. Her work has been exhibited at Shubbak Festival (UK), SAVVY Contemporary (Germany), Rabat Biennale (Morocco), Biennale d'Architecture d'Orléans (France), Jameel Arts Centre, Louvre Abu Dhabi, and Warehouse 421 (UAE). She has contributed texts to *Monumental Shadows* (Art Jameel, forthcoming), *Architecture of the Territory: Constructing National Narratives in the Arab World* (Kaph Books), the Kuwait Pavilion at the Venice Biennale and *WTD Magazine*. Abdul Jabbar received a Master of Architecture from Columbia University in 2014.

Reem Falaknaz's work documents the social and physical landscape of the UAE and its inhabitants. In 2014, she took part in the Arab Documentary Photography Program that is funded by the Arab Fund for Art and Culture, the Prince Claus Fund, and Magnum Foundation. Her commissions include UAE's National Pavilion at the 2016 Venice Architecture Biennale, Lahore Biennale 2020, and Expo 2020.

Samar Halloum is a Palestinian-Jordanian architect and researcher who recently received her Master of Architecture degree from Yale University. Upon graduation, Halloum was awarded the William Wirt Winchester Travel Fellowship, the Yale School of Architecture's most prestigious award, for her independent research project "Negotiations within Refugee Camps." Halloum's work and research emphasizes individual and collective ad-hoc practices that are rooted in their environmental and cultural contexts to challenge and shape their built environments. She received her Bachelor of Architecture from the American University of Sharjah and worked on design and research projects in the UAE, Qatar, Saudi Arabia, Denmark, and USA.

Wesam Al Asali is an architect, educator, researcher, and enthusiast for combining digital and manual fabrication technologies with local building crafts and natural materials. He is an Assistant Professor at IE School of Architecture and Design. His work spans construction history, building technology, and craft studies to explore the role of culture and society in rethinking architectural practice in the context of climate challenges. Al Asali received his PhD in 2021 from the University of Cambridge and was the 2021-2022 Global Fung fellow at Princeton University. His research received the RIBA President's Awards for Research in Architecture (2021) and the Salje Medal for Best Doctoral Research in Arts and Humanities at Clare Hall, Cambridge University (2022). As a practicing architect, Al Asali is a design and innovation lead at his co-founded architectural practice (IWlab) and founder of the social enterprise (CERCAA), a center for learning and innovation in building crafts and natural materials in Spain-Valencia.

National Pavilion United Arab Emirates 2023

In Plain Sight: Scenes from Aridly Abundant Landscapes

This book is published on the occasion of the National Pavilion United Arab Emirates' exhibition, *Aridly Abundant*, at the 18th International Architecture Exhibition– La Biennale di Venezia, titled *The Laboratory of the Future*, from May 20 to November 26, 2023.

Commissioner:
Salama bint Hamdan Al Nahyan Foundation
Supporter:
UAE Ministry of Culture and Youth
Curator:
Faysal Tabbarah

Editors:
Faysal Tabbarah and Meitha Almazrooei
Arabic Editors:
Faysal Tabbarah and Meitha Almazrooei
Lead Editorial Researcher:
Samar Halloum
Publication Researcher:
Sara Alchaar
English Copy Editor:
Zeina Assaf
Arabic Translators:
Ban Kattan and Manal Khader
Arabic Copy Editor:
Mohamad Hamdan

Designer:
40MUSTAQEL, Cairo

Publisher:
National Pavilion UAE
La Biennale di Venezia
Co-Publisher:
Kaph Books

Exhibition Research and Design
Research and Design Lead:
Samar Halloum
Researcher and Designer:
Dina Hirzallah
Researcher and Designer:
Basil Al Taher
Researcher and Designer:
Rana Salah
Researcher and Designer:
Sara Alchaar
Computational Consultant:
Aya Shaker

Commissioned Artist (Photography and Audio/Visual):
Reem Falaknaz

Exhibition Production
Exhibition Design:
Architecture + Other Things
Graphic Design:
40MUSTAQEL, Cairo
Lighting:
iGuzzini illuminazione, Recanati
Exhibition Construction and Audio/Visual:
Tosetto Allestimenti, Venice

National Pavilion UAE
Director:
Laila Binbrek
Communications Manager:
Dana Al Sadek
Exhibitions Manager:
Farah El-Rafei
Programs Manager:
Rawan Al Ramahi
Internship Coordinator:
Anita Buscaino
Office Coordinator:
Jay Yambao
Venice Coordinator:
Emanuela Semiani

Special Thanks
College of Architecture, Arts and Design, American University of Sharjah (AUS)
International Center for Biosaline Agriculture (ICBA)
Irthi Contemporary Crafts Council
In5 FZ LLC, Research Space
TransGulf Enterprises

Distribution in Europe:
Les Presses du Réel
35 rue Colson
21000 Dijon
France
www.lespressesdureel.com

Idea Books
Nieuwe Hemweg 6R
1013 BG Amsterdam
The Netherlands
www.ideabooks.nl

Distribution in the Middle-East:
CIEL Book Distribution
3rd Interchange, Al Quoz Industrial I
P.O.Box 282005
Dubai, UAE
www.ciel.me

Distribution in the Americas, Asia and Australia:
ARTBOOK | D.A.P.75
Broad Street,
Suite 630
New York, NY 10004
www.artbook.com

National Pavilion UAE
La Biennale di Venezia
P.O. Box 769307, Abu Dhabi, UAE
nationalpavilionuae.org

Printed in Belgium

ISBN9786148035586

9 786148 035586